Foundations of Counseling Psychology

AF838007

Foundations of Counseling Psychology is the first textbook written and designed for undergraduate students, offering a comprehensive introduction to the field of counseling psychology in a reader-friendly, practical, and dynamic tone.

With the goal of sparking excitement about the wide range of work that counseling psychologists do, each chapter highlights at least one counseling psychologist and describes their work and setting. Each chapter also lays out self-reflection prompts for students to consider and offers a "what would you do?" question that focuses on compelling ethical issues and other dilemmas.

This textbook is essential to undergraduate students aspiring to be counseling psychologists. It will be useful to educators, students, and scholars specializing in counseling psychology worldwide.

Julie M. Koch, PhD, is a Professor in the Counseling Psychology program at the University of Iowa.

Douglas Knutson, PhD, is an Associate Professor in the Counseling Psychology program at Oklahoma State University.

"To my knowledge, this is the first book that provides a comprehensive introduction to counseling psychology for undergraduate students. It covers history, theories, and skills, and how counseling psychology is unique with its focus on human strength, wellness, career development, cultural diversity, and social justice. Readers will gain exposure to the diverse careers and work settings with a counseling psychology degree. I love how the book uses real life examples and self-reflection exercises."

Y. Barry Chung, *PhD, Dean of the College of Education, San Diego State University*

"Koch and Knutson's *Foundations of Counseling Psychology: An Introduction to the Field* fills an important gap in in the field by providing a resource that introduces undergraduate students to the field of Counseling Psychology. This is a much needed text to expose undergraduate students to a specialty area that many students do not know about but can be a good fit for many students exploring careers in applied psychology. The text is grounded in Counseling Psychology's values and helps students to understand career opportunities available to them through training in Counseling Psychology. I am excited to use this book in my undergraduate courses!"

Lisa Flores, *PhD, Frederick A. Middlebush Chair of Social Sciences and Professor of Psychological Sciences at the University of Missouri, Columbia*

"Koch and Knutson bring counseling psychology to life as they speak directly to students with an authenticity that is rare in academic writing. With a perfect blend of scholarship, practical examples, and personal voice, this book will motivate students to see themselves as future professionals who can make meaningful contributions to the field."

Martin Kivlighan, *PhD, Professor of Counseling Psychology and Department Executive Officer, Psychological & Quantitative Foundations, University of Iowa*

Foundations of Counseling Psychology

An Introduction to the Field

Julie M. Koch and Douglas Knutson

Routledge
Taylor & Francis Group
NEW YORK AND LONDON

Designed cover image: diane555 © Getty Images

First published 2026
by Routledge
605 Third Avenue, New York, NY 10158

and by Routledge
4 Park Square, Milton Park, Abingdon, Oxon, OX14 4RN

Routledge is an imprint of the Taylor & Francis Group, an informa business

© 2026 Julie M. Koch and Douglas Knutson

The right of Julie M. Koch and Douglas Knutson to be identified as authors of this work has been asserted in accordance with sections 77 and 78 of the Copyright, Designs and Patents Act 1988.

All rights reserved. No part of this book may be reprinted or reproduced or utilised in any form or by any electronic, mechanical, or other means, now known or hereafter invented, including photocopying and recording, or in any information storage or retrieval system, without permission in writing from the publishers.

For Product Safety Concerns and Information please contact our EU representative GPSR@taylorandfrancis.com. Taylor & Francis Verlag GmbH, Kaufingerstraße 24, 80331 München, Germany.

Trademark notice: Product or corporate names may be trademarks or registered trademarks, and are used only for identification and explanation without intent to infringe.

ISBN: 978-1-032-56804-1 (hbk)
ISBN: 978-1-032-56803-4 (pbk)
ISBN: 978-1-003-43989-9 (ebk)

DOI: 10.4324/9781003439899

Typeset in Times New Roman
by codeMantra

Access the Support Material: https://www.routledge.com/9781032568034

Dedication

For our students, whose curiosity, passion, and desire to help others inspire us every day.

Author Note

Julie M. Koch, University of Iowa
Douglas Knutson, Oklahoma State University
We have no known conflicts of interest to disclose.
Correspondence concerning this book should be addressed to Julie M. Koch, Psychological and Quantitative Foundations, University of Iowa, 361 Lindquist Center, Iowa City, IA 52242.

Contents

Foreword

by Dr. John Westefeld

As an undergraduate student at The University of North Carolina at Chapel Hill, during the years 1968–1972, when I was not obsessing about UNC Tarheel basketball, I was thinking about what I wanted to do with my life. Because I had lost a close friend to suicide growing up, I knew I wanted to work in mental health. What was unclear to me were the specifics of how to make that happen. Graduate school? Masters? Doctorate? In what field specifically? Perhaps some of you have these same questions concerning your vocational goals. Over a 52-year journey, thankfully I achieved my goal of working in mental health. However, I think if a book like this one had existed in 1968 that decision, the details, and the journey itself would have been far easier and more meaningful. That to me is the gift of this text to you. You will not only learn about Counseling Psychology, but you will also read about the joys of the profession, the contributions the field makes to society, and how you can potentially become a Counseling Psychologist.

Fast forward 42 years from 1968. I was sitting in a counseling psychology faculty meeting at the University of Iowa in 2010, and we began a conversation about the possibility of offering an undergraduate course in counseling psychology. Iowa had offered a PhD degree in counseling psychology since about 1980, with all the requisite graduate courses, but never an undergraduate course. At that time, almost no colleges or universities offered such a course. Nationwide, there were multiple graduate courses focusing on many aspects of counseling psychology, these offerings often being components of doctoral programs in counseling psychology. However, an undergraduate course at that time anywhere in the country was a rarity. I also do not think there was a dedicated textbook focusing on counseling psychology for undergraduates. In the view of our faculty, these were two missing links in our profession.

The Iowa faculty continued to discuss the issue of an undergraduate course over almost two years, exploring such issues as what it should include, who among us would teach the course, scheduling, how to deal with the lack of a textbook, and what was the overarching goal for the course offering. The biggest question however was the fundamental question of whether to even offer the course. We carefully examined the pros and cons of that question.

From the very beginning of our discussions, I supported offering such a course, and I was very interested in teaching it. I had taught undergraduates throughout my career (but not a course like this) and enjoyed teaching undergraduates. I also believed that such a course was very important to the profession, not only in terms of educating students about counseling psychology but also as a potential mechanism for encouraging undergraduates to consider entering the profession, and perhaps explore graduate programs in counseling psychology. So, I volunteered to teach the course, and I offered it for the first time in 2012. That first offering had approximately 30 students from a multiplicity of undergraduate majors. It was a wonderful experience for me – and I hope the students – and I came away from that convinced we had made the correct decision to offer the course.

Looking back, I think this experience was transformative for our faculty specifically and doctoral program in counseling psychology more generally. It caused us to explore in more creative ways other potential courses, as well as many aspects of our entire doctoral program.

As I prepared for that first offering, I became acutely aware of the lack of a counseling psychology textbook written for undergraduates. Because I could not identify what I thought would be an appropriate text, I constructed the course utilizing multiple readings from a wide variety of sources. Many of the readings were from *The Counseling Psychologist* and the *Journal of Counseling Psychology*. I also delivered lectures about a wide range of counseling psychology topics. We had a series of guest speakers to augment the course. These were primarily counseling psychologists who worked in a variety of settings. I was trying to provide role-modeling for the students and illustrate the possibilities for a career that counseling psychology offered. For example, I had someone from private practice, a university counseling center, a community mental health center, the military, and a hospital. I also had a panel of current doctoral students from our counseling psychology program present about graduate education in counseling psychology and the many aspects of applying to graduate school. I felt good about the course, and enjoyed teaching it, but realized once again the need for a comprehensive counseling psychology textbook focusing on undergraduates.

The course has been taught continuously since that initial offering in 2012. There is currently one section offered each semester, taught by Dr. Julie Koch, senior author of this textbook. There are approximately 150 students from numerous undergraduate majors who take the course each semester. Though I have not taught the course since 2015, I continue to present a guest lecture in the course on suicide, my career-long area of focus, and I have had the honor and privilege of delivering this lecture every semester after I retired from the university in 2016. Thus, my involvement with the course spans about 13 years. It has been one of the joys of my career.

Thanks to Dr. Julie Koch and Dr. Douglas Knutson, we now have an outstanding textbook for the Iowa undergraduate course and for colleges and universities across the country, *Foundations of Counseling Psychology*. The essentials of the profession of counseling psychology are discussed extensively, and with great skill and care. The authors do an excellent job of explicating what counseling psychology is, its many important contributions, and how it differs from other human service professions. A significant core component of the field has always been focusing on human strengths, and this concept emerges strongly throughout the work. Multiculturalism has also been a building block of the profession, and concepts related to human diversity and cultural competence are woven skillfully throughout the text. One of the earliest foci of counseling psychology was vocational/work issues, and the chapter devoted to this topic explicates work issues specifically, as well as examining the relationship of work to emotional health and well-being. Other key aspects of counseling psychology are discussed in depth in this volume, including the many different approaches to conducting psychotherapy (there are many!), what is effective in psychotherapy, and assessment. I found the chapters examining research, ethics, and the use of the self in therapy to be very additive, and these are all germane to counseling psychology as well as to the entire human services field. The final three chapters discuss the roles of counseling psychologists in leadership and advocacy, specific settings in which counseling psychologists may work, and how to pursue a career in counseling psychology. Each of these topics provides invaluable tutelage about the profession.

When all the chapters of this book are explored, they are outstanding as stand-alone chapters. However, when this book as a whole is read and digested as an entity, the contributions of this volume emerge as especially remarkable. Stated another way…the whole of this book is greater than the sum of its parts. In my view, this is the signal contribution of *Foundations of Counseling Psychology.*

I hope readers will appreciate the significance of this work. It fills a void that has existed for decades. Readers will learn about the profession, psychological principles, and why the profession matters. But it will also inspire readers to consider a career in counseling psychology. And for that I am especially grateful to the authors for writing this book and to all of you for reading and experiencing it.

We currently have a significant need for mental health professionals nationwide and worldwide, with a concurrent high demand for services. I hope you will consider responding to this need as you explore your own career choices. You can enter the mental health profession through Social Work, Psychology, Psychiatry, Counseling, the Clergy, and other avenues. Obviously, the avenue of counseling psychology is the emphasis of this text. But there are multiple ways to get there.

It was one of the best decisions of my life to become a counseling psychologist. Not only did I meet great people, have a lot of fun, and work on exciting issues, but I believe that I – and counseling psychologists generally – have also made a difference in the world. And that is what made counseling psychology special for me.

So enjoy this wonderful textbook. And consider the magical profession of counseling psychology!

John S. Westefeld, MPH, PhD
Professor Emeritus of Counseling Psychology, University of Iowa
Board-Certified in Counseling Psychology
Iowa City, Iowa
John S. Westefeld

John S. Westefeld was born and grew up in Princeton, New Jersey. From a young age he wanted to work in mental health. His challenge was how to get to the endpoint of being a mental health worker. Psychiatry? Psychology? Social Work? Something else? Once he decided on Psychology, the issue became Clinical Psychology or Counseling Psychology. John eventually decided on counseling psychology because of its focus on client strengths, its multicultural emphasis, and the fact that at that time – in the 1970s – there was a heavy emphasis in the profession on working with college students. John completed undergraduate and graduate school at the University of North Carolina at Chapel Hill. He completed his psychology internship in Atlanta at the Georgia State University Counseling Center which at that time also included a brief hospital rotation. His career then took him to the Iowa State University Student Counseling Center in Ames, Iowa; the Hood College Psychology Department in Frederick, Maryland; the counseling psychology doctoral program at Auburn University, where he served as director of the program for eight years; and finally in 1991 to the counseling psychology program at the University of Iowa where he served as program director for ten years and as a faculty member for 25 years. John's career has been a lifelong synthesis of providing psychotherapy – primarily in college/university counseling centers and private practice – as well as teaching/training/research. His primary professional focus throughout his career has been suicide and suicide prevention. He is the recipient of numerous awards and honors. He served as the President of the Society of Counseling Psychology in 2010. He lives in Iowa City with his wife of 45 years, Dr. Debora Liddell, and remains active in the profession. He has two children and three grandchildren, all of whom bring him great joy.

Preface

Dear Reader:

Hello, and welcome! We are so glad you're taking an interest in counseling psychology and are excited to take you on this journey to learn more about our field.

When Julie first started teaching an undergraduate Introduction to Counseling Psychology course, she realized there is not a great textbook out there for undergraduate students who just want to learn a little about counseling psychology. There are great texts for graduate students, but her students found them difficult to digest and unrelatable for their current studies. She was inspired to create a text that was designed especially for you, the undergraduate student, to help spark passion about counseling psychology and helping professions. She knew that Douglas shared her excitement about counseling psychology and how to communicate about it in a practical way that "real" people can understand. And so, we wrote this book for you! We hope you enjoy it!

We encourage you to try to engage with the material in this book and think about how it reflects your life experiences, thoughts, and ideas. Think about what do you find relevant? How could points within each chapter be applied to real life and your future career?

We know that college is hard. And you may be struggling with stuff in your own life even as you are trying to take classes and learn about counseling psychology. You should know that, as this book is an introduction to the field of counseling psychology, we talk about topics related to mental health such as suicide and mental illness, as well as topics such as poverty and health disparities. We understand, and expect, that these topics are sometimes difficult to hear and think about. However, as a field and community that serves human beings, we must strive to listen to, learn about, and advocate with people with respect and dignity. These topics are not avoidable in our field, and we encourage you to engage with bravery, a stance of humility, and a commitment to self-care.

If something seems particularly upsetting to you, or makes you uncomfortable, consider why you are having those reactions. We encourage you to reach out to your instructor, teaching assistant, advisor, university counseling service, diversity office, or other resources if you have them on your campus. If you are reading this book and you are not affiliated with a campus or institution, we encourage you to discuss your reactions with a trusted friend, mentor, family member, or seek counseling services in your area.

Welcome to the world of counseling psychology. We are excited that you are joining us in discovering more about this field!

Warmly,
Julie and Douglas

About the Authors

Dr. Julie Koch. Photograph by Mei-Ling Shaw.

Julie M. Koch (pronounced "cook," she/they), PhD, is a Professor of Counseling Psychology at the University of Iowa. She is a Licensed Health Service Psychologist. As a child, she would climb a tree with her stuffed animals and teach them math from leftover worksheets from school. She never imagined that someday she would have the joy and privilege of being an educator and counseling psychologist and touching college students' lives. Julie is passionate about getting undergraduate students excited about pursuing careers in the helping fields. Her favorite day is any day a student comes to office hours. Growing up she learned that having empathy and being in touch with her emotions was a strength as a helping professional, and she enjoys helping others tap into those strengths as well. Julie is a mother of three humans and three cats and enjoys spending time in nature and adding native plants to her yard when she's not at work.

Douglas Knutson (pronounced "nut-son," he/him), PhD, ABPP, is an Associate Professor and Director of Training for the Counseling Psychology Doctoral Program at Oklahoma State University. He is a Licensed Health Service Psychologist and is Board Certified in Counseling Psychology. When he was about six years old, his mom gave him a journal and on one of the first pages he wrote, "I want to get a phd in science," something he knew he would need in order to teach at a university. Much of his early education was in theology, ministry, and English Literature (he went to seminary at Boston University) and his goal was always to train and mentor people who would go on to change the world. There is a rainbow sign in his office that reads, "FOR A BETTER WORLD." That mantra is the driving force behind his work with students, his dedication to the profession of counseling psychology, and his investment in his family. On most weekends, you can find him and his partner helping out on their families' farms in rural and remote parts of Oklahoma. Douglas and his partner share their home with an adorable Australian Shepherd and four chickens.

Dr. Douglas Knutson. Photograph by author.

Chapter 1

What Is Counseling Psychology?

What is counseling psychology? Take a second to reflect on what you think counseling psychology is, or looks like, or means. Some concepts that might come up for you could include *therapy*, using *theories* to approach therapy, or *helping people* with their problems. Often, when people imagine a counseling psychologist, they might picture a professional in a chair (often with a clipboard) and a client sitting across from them or maybe even lying on a couch. It is true that counseling psychologists practice therapy, but what most people do not know is that they also do research, assessment, prevention and health promotion, community engagement, psychoeducation, and all kinds of other things! In this book, we hope to help you understand the wide range of things that counseling psychologists do.

In this introductory chapter, you will discover how counseling psychology is different from, and similar to, other helping professions and fields. We introduce the main core values of counseling psychology, provide a history of counseling psychology as a field, and establish the field of counseling psychology as crucial to promoting the well-being of diverse people across the lifespan. This chapter also serves as an introduction to the rest of the text, with a brief overview of the structure of the book, introduction to settings in which counseling psychologists work, and what readers can expect from each chapter. Here, we will begin to answer the questions: What is counseling psychology? How is counseling psychology different from other fields? What do counseling psychologists do? Where do counseling psychologists work? What is the future of counseling psychology? We will also discuss job projections in the future.

You may also be wondering what the difference is between counseling psychology and *clinical* psychology, *counseling*, *psychiatry*, *social work*, and other similar fields. You may wonder, for example, if you should pursue a career path toward being a school counselor or a counseling psychologist who works with children. Or whether you want to be a clinical psychologist who works in a hospital or a counseling psychologist who works in a hospital. Or whether you want to be a marriage and family therapist or a counseling psychologist who specializes in work with families. All of these career paths fall under the *helping professions* umbrella, in which professionals work with humans to promote mental health and wellness. In some settings, the work that a clinical psychologist and a counseling psychologist do could look identical. Or the work that a counseling psychologist and a counselor do could be quite similar. Often, the main difference is the underlying *philosophy* that the work is built upon, but there are also differences in training programs, credentials, and licensing. In practice, a counseling psychologist, a clinical psychologist, and a social worker might be working with a client and doing very similar things, but their underlying philosophy and how they approach the work might be different. Later in this chapter, we will dive more into some of these different fields and will flesh out for you what some of these differences are.

DOI: 10.4324/9781003439899-1

What Are the Values and Philosophies of Counseling Psychologists?

The mission of the Society of Counseling Psychology (SCP) states:

> We cultivate a 'home' for all counseling psychology professionals and affiliates to connect, to collaborate, and to coordinate efforts toward creating a more just and equitable world where ALL people and communities can thrive. Our members share a commitment to a holistic psychological perspective that is strengths-based, person- and community-centered, systems-oriented, contextually aware, multiculturally inclusive, socially just, and integrative of vocational and lifespan issues. We promote this perspective within the field of psychology and in the public sector through practice, research, education and training, advocacy, consultation, and leadership.
>
> (Society of Counseling Psychology, 2025b, para. 1)

The key terms in this mission statement are (a) strengths-based; (b) contextually aware, multiculturally inclusive, socially just; and (c) vocational and lifespan issues. These concepts have been counseling psychology's guiding lights over time and contribute to how counseling psychology is unique from other areas of applied psychology.

According to Gelso and Williams (2021), the five defining values of counseling psychology traditionally have been: strengths and optimal functioning; lifespan development; vocational growth; social justice and multicultural awareness; brief, educational, and preventive interventions; and the scientist-practitioner model. You will find that in this textbook, we have chapters that specifically focus on some of these areas. For example, in Chapter 2, How Counseling Psychologists Promote Human Strengths and Flourishing, we introduce the counseling psychology focus on strengths, prevention, and positive psychology. This is a primary value of counseling psychology; we focus on an individual's strengths and their health rather than on pathology. This is an optimistic approach that focuses on individuals' assets that they can utilize to solve issues in their own lives. Some of the first questions a counseling psychologist might ask a client could be "What do you see as your strengths?" or "What are your hopes for therapy?" or "What is your vision or dream for your future?" As we discuss in Chapter 4, A Counseling Psychology Approach to Wellness across the Lifespan, counseling psychologists understand the role that human development plays in mental health. For example, if a man seeks therapy for anxiety, his concerns will be very different if he is 18 and about to leave home for the first time to attend college versus if he is 54 and his son has just been deployed in the US military. This value also shows the emphasis counseling psychologists have on considering the whole person and their stage of development. Another unique focus of counseling psychologists is on the role of work, career, or vocation in people's lives. We talk about this in Chapter 5, The Role of Work in People's Lives. "Work" could be going to school (the "work" of an eight-year-old), establishing a career, or *avocation* (you probably have not heard of this word before; it means hobbies and recreation or volunteer work). Another strong value shared by counseling psychologists over time is understanding the cultural context of clients. We introduce this concept in Chapter 3, Cultural Context in Counseling Psychology Practice, and talk about counseling psychologists as advocates and leaders for change in Chapter 13, Counseling Psychologists as Leaders and Advocates. Focus on cultural context allows the counseling psychologist to consider the whole individual within their unique sociocultural context and take into account their intersecting identities. Here, if we go back to the 54-year-old man whose son is being deployed, rather than just focusing on anxiety symptoms, a counseling psychologist might consider how his identity as a Native American rancher in rural New Mexico contributes to his stress as well. The final value, the scientist-practitioner model, refers to counseling psychologists using research to inform practice and practice to inform research. We explore this further in Chapter 10, Common Research Methods that Counseling Psychologists Use.

What Do Counseling Psychologists Actually Do? Where Do They Work?

Counseling psychologists have so much variety in their work – the possibilities are really endless! One of our favorite parts of this textbook is the Counseling Psychology Spotlights in each chapter. Through the Spotlights, you will get to know real-life counseling psychologists who are practitioners, researchers, consultants, parents, spouses, runners, and readers. One theme you will see across the Spotlights is the fact that with the same degree, counseling psychologists have a lot of flexibility in their work. It is like being in a candy shop! You can choose salt water taffy AND jelly beans AND chocolates. Or you can just become a super expert on licorice. Likewise, counseling psychologists can teach AND practice AND do research. Or they might be a super expert on children of first responders, for example. It is important to note that most of us do not have beards and clipboards and do not have our clients lie down on couches. A lot of our work takes place outside the therapy space.

We have a bunch of chapters highlighting the variety of what counseling psychologists actually do in their work. In Chapter 6, we introduce you to Theories and Approaches in Counseling Psychology, so you'll learn how a *psychodynamic* therapist approaches their work with clients differently than someone who is a *Gestalt* therapist. And you'll learn about how individual therapy is different from work with couples, families, or groups (spoiler alert: all of these approaches are beneficial). In Chapter 7, you will learn about some of the Key Skills that Counseling Psychologists Use. Did you know that a key skill is just saying "yeah?" Or just giving a client time and space to talk out loud? In Chapter 8, we discuss Counseling Psychology Processes and Outcomes so you can learn more about what actually works in therapy – in other words, what we know about how clients get better (it's probably not what you think!). Chapter 9 reviews Assessment in Counseling Psychology, so you will learn how and why counseling psychologists select certain tools to assess what is going on for their clients. In Chapter 11, we discuss Ethics in Counseling Psychology. This chapter is called "Shades of Gray" because generally there is not a "right" or "wrong" answer to ethical dilemmas – usually, we find ourselves in the gray areas. In this chapter, we will talk about the American Psychological Association (APA) Ethics Code, laws that guide counseling psychologists, and how to problem-solve ethical dilemmas that might arise. Chapter 12, Person as a Therapist: Use of Self in Counseling Psychology, introduces you to the most important tool a counseling psychologist has: themselves. We also talk about how being a human and helping professional can contribute to burnout and ways that counseling psychologists can engage in self-care.

We really want you to get a feel for the wide range of settings in which counseling psychologists work and the populations with whom they work. In addition to the Counseling Psychologist Spotlights, we have a whole chapter dedicated to this. Chapter 14 is Counseling Psychology Applied to Special Settings. In this chapter, you will learn about the work that counseling psychologists do in hospitals, in corrections facilities, and in community-based agencies, among others. And our final chapter, Chapter 15, So, You Want to Be a Counseling Psychologist? is all about applying to graduate programs. Even if you are not planning on pursuing a graduate degree, or perhaps you will pursue a graduate degree in another field like engineering or business, we hope this chapter is helpful to you with some tips from faculty members' perspectives. We hope you are as excited about learning all this stuff as we are about sharing it with you!

What Is a Counseling Psychologist?

If you decide to apply for a counseling psychology graduate program and you are invited for an interview, you will probably be asked the question, "Why counseling psychology?" Interviewers often want to know why you picked counseling psychology instead of some other field like clinical psychology, school psychology, or even social work or mental health counseling. As directors of counseling psychology programs, we hear a lot of answers to that question. In our experience, applicants usually pick counseling psychology programs because of their focus on multicultural training and their holistic approach to psychotherapy. In other words, counseling psychology tends to have a reputation for a strengths-based model that is flexible and considers the context of clients to improve their well-being.

You may be wondering what the difference is between counseling psychology and other fields that also provide counseling or clinical-type services to people. First, we will talk about the differences in doctoral *health service psychology* programs, then we will address other related helping professions. In the United States, most counseling psychology programs are doctoral programs – either PhD or PsyD programs. The APA Commission on Accreditation accredits these programs to provide education and training in "health service psychology," which they define as "the integration of psychological science and practice in order to facilitate human development and functioning" (APA Commission on Accreditation, 2015, p. 2). Two health service psychology specialties that are closely related to counseling psychology are clinical psychology and school psychology.

One of the biggest differences is the historically underlying philosophies of each of the specialties. For example, the counseling psychologist might refer to their *client*, whereas a clinical psychologist might refer to their *patient*. Although this may seem on the surface like a minor difference, it actually demonstrates a clear difference in philosophy. In counseling psychology, clients are viewed as autonomous human beings who are on an equal level as the therapist; therapists are not "experts" but work with clients collaboratively and tap into their strengths to help them solve their problems. On the other hand, clinical psychologists have traditionally worked from a more medical model, in which a problem or diagnosis is to be treated by an expert using evidence-based practices. School psychologists usually work with students in educational systems and they focus on supporting students' academic, behavioral, and emotional well-being, usually in collaboration with school staff and families.

Let's unpack some of those differences a little more and compare them to counseling psychology (Table 1.1).

If you want to learn more about some of these differences, there is some information available to you online. We encourage you to take a look at the website of the APA. Some of you may be familiar with the APA (https://www.apa.org), the professional association for psychologists. There are over 50 divisions of APA representing member interests. For example, Division 2 is the Society for the Teaching of Psychology, whose members are interested in how students learn and the best ways to teach psychology in high schools, colleges, graduate programs, and postdoctoral programs. As another example, Division 34 is the Society for Environmental, Population, and Conservation Psychology, bringing together members with a shared interest in ecopsychology. Some divisions are focused on specific cultural groups, such as Division 35: Society for the Psychology of Women; Division 44: Society for the Psychology of Sexual Orientation and Gender Diversity; and Division 45: Society for the Psychological Study of Culture, Ethnicity, and Race. Division 17 is the Society of Counseling Psychology, whose members identify as counseling psychologists and students. Often, psychologists will

Table 1.1 Counseling, clinical, and school psychology

Specialty	*Counseling Psychology*	*Clinical Psychology*	*School Psychology*
Special knowledge	Evidence-based Health and strengths of clients Environment and context of clients Career and work Advocacy for equity and social justice	Evidence-based Psychopathology Assess cognitive, behavioral, emotional, interpersonal functioning Biosociocultural context & developmental stage	Children's development Cognitive, behavioral, social, and emotional problems Federal laws and regulations for schools Historical influences of educational, community, federal dynamics
Problems addressed	Focus on normative development Issues across lifespan Systemic challenges Strengths-based	Adjustment issues, traumatic stress Emotional and psychological problems Interpersonal and social problems Behavioral problems Intellectual, neurological conditions	Educational and developmental problems Social or interpersonal problems and disabilities that affect learning and behavior Averse social conditions that threaten health
Population	Individual, group, workplace, organizational, community All ages and cultural backgrounds	Individuals, couples, families Groups and communities All cultural backgrounds	Birth to young adulthood with learning or behavior problems Children and teens with specific disabilities, chronic, or acute conditions Families who request services Organizations and agencies, teachers, and school staff
Skills and procedures	Individual, family, group counseling Crisis intervention, trauma management Assessment Prevention and psychoeducation Consultation Program evaluation Test construction Research	Assessment and interviewing Administration and interpretation of psychological tests Evidence-based interventions Consultation	Assessment and evaluation Prevention and intervention to promote developmental, educational, and psychological well-being Crisis intervention Consultation with teachers, parents, administrators

*Adapted from APA (2023)

be members of several different divisions that represent their interests. For example, Douglas Knutson is a member of Divisions 17 (Counseling Psychology), 31 (State, Provincial, and Territorial Psychology Association Affairs), 35 (Psychology of Women), and 44 (Sexual Orientation and Gender Diversity); Julie Koch is a member of Divisions 2 (Teaching), 17 (Counseling Psychology), and 52 (International Psychology) (But she secretly wants to be a member of a bunch of other divisions too).

These divisions are then often divided into smaller sections to focus on shared interests. For example, in the Society of Counseling Psychology, there are sections on Health Psychology, International Counseling Psychology, and University Counseling Centers. There are groups for students, such as the Student Affiliates of Seventeen (SAS), and groups for Early Career Practitioners.

You may also wonder about the difference between *counseling* and *counseling psychology*. Counselors (often you will hear the term mental health counselors) and counseling psychologists share the same focus on strengths-based, holistic counseling that considers cultural context across the lifespan. There are some differences, though. Typically, mental health counselors have a terminal, two-year master's degree and are licensed as professional counselors. Counseling psychologists, as we mentioned earlier, have a doctoral degree (which usually takes around five to six years to complete) and are licensed as health service psychologists. Generally, master's level counselors do not have the same emphasis on the scientist-practitioner model that counseling psychologists do. Some master's programs may require students to complete a research thesis, but most do not. Doctoral counseling psychology programs have a pretty heavy emphasis on research – students must become competent, independent researchers and consumers of research.

Another big difference is the ability to do certain psychological assessments. There are always exceptions, but generally speaking, master's level counselors do not have the same level of training to do assessments, such as intellectual assessment and some personality assessments, and this is not usually a part of their work. At the master's level, counseling is an umbrella term that refers to mental health counseling, rehabilitation counseling, and school counseling. Counselors may also work toward a doctorate in counselor education and supervision (with greater emphasis on research), but licensure is always at the master's level. Finally, a big difference is that while counselors usually affiliate with the American Counseling Association, most counseling psychologists affiliate with the APA. However, there are a lot of people who see benefits to membership in both, and there is a lot of crossover activity.

We believe that all of these fields in the helping professions – counseling, social work, or counseling psychology – have much in common, and they can all make important contributions to people's well-being. Often, the differences are subtle or nuanced. The work that counseling psychologists do may be referred to as therapy, counseling, psychotherapy, or clinical practice. Likewise, clinical psychologists or school psychologists may engage in counseling. Often, differences are found in the historical foundations of the field and the philosophical approach, attitude, or *way of being* (Rogers, 1980) through which the practitioner approaches work with a client. Our counseling psychology values are what set us apart.

Gelso and Williams (2021) said that counseling psychologists traditionally have had three roles: remedial, preventative, and developmental. We agree that historically this has been true and yet based on new developments in the field of counseling psychology and modern trends, we conceptualize these roles differently. Roles of counseling psychologists might include therapist, supervisor, researcher/educator, teacher, manager, consultant, advocate, leader, assessor, prevention specialist, community member, crisis intervention specialist, and vocational psychologist. As Gelso and Williams (2021) noted, often in real life, these roles overlap.

How Did Counseling Psychology Emerge as a Field?

Did you know that often, counseling psychology doctoral programs are housed in colleges of education rather than in traditional psychology departments? A lot of people are surprised at this and wonder why. Like many things in history, there was not one single event, but rather a convergence of different events or things that happened over time that evolved into the field of counseling psychology. In his book on the history of counseling psychology, *The Evolution of Counseling Psychology*, Donald Blocher (2000) wrote about how it is important to see counseling psychology as a field that evolved over time within a unique sociopolitical context. He wrote:

> The history of counseling psychology is, after all, much more than a mere chronology of meetings and publications, organizations and committee reports. It is rather a history of ideas, and the story of the men and women who generated, articulated, and applied those ideas on behalf of the values, causes, and ideals to which they were personally committed.
>
> (pp. 3–4)

We are going to start our story of counseling psychology in the late 1800s to the early 1900s. You may remember from history courses that the Industrial Revolution was happening in the United States at this time. This time was characterized by more workers moving from rural areas to cities; women and children entering the labor force in high numbers; and an influx of immigrants who also entered the workforce. Work conditions were often poor and unsafe, and workers were not paid well for their labor. As a result, there was a social reform movement that included a movement to counsel and advise people, called *the guidance movement*. People started to notice the poverty and difficult conditions and began to speak out and advocate for change. Around this time, the field of social work began to emerge. Social work specifically sought to improve education and opportunities for people, especially children, in poverty. At this time, many efforts were through charity and relief, but social workers also raised awareness about child labor and sought reform of laws to restrict children from working in unsafe conditions.

In the early 1900s, people started talking about, and developing, vocational (career) education and vocational guidance programs across the United States. Centers designed to offer vocational guidance, such as the Vocation Bureau in Boston, popped up in schools and in communities. Around this time, Frank Parsons (1909) published a book, *Choosing a Vocation*, that offered a general framework for vocational guidance that was well-received and likely earned him the title of "Father of Vocational Guidance." The book became a sort of manual for people who did vocational guidance and education. It offered tips on interviewing skills and ways for a guidance counselor to gain information about someone's interests and aptitudes, as well as vocational information and descriptions of jobs and skills or abilities that people would need for those jobs. He spoke about the importance of offering vocational guidance to children, women, and immigrants. As these centers grew, and more people did vocational guidance work, they began to form professional organizations and conferences to discuss their work. Over time, vocational education and vocational guidance began to be more and more integrated into school systems, and academic preparation began to be intertwined with vocational preparation. As this happened, vocational guidance became less a "social reform" issue and more a normal, expected part of the educational system to be provided by professionals knowledgeable in vocational guidance.

Something else that heavily influenced the development of counseling psychology was the emergence of testing – psychological testing for vocational purposes – in the military, colleges, and schools. Testing programs in colleges tried to assess students' abilities and vocational interests.

Testing initially conducted in college settings by psychologists and guidance counselors eventually shifted into middle and high schools: guidance counselors in schools worked to identify skills, aptitudes, and interests of students to help them determine career paths. The testing movement also developed through the military in World War I and World War II, when the military realized, for example, that if they could pinpoint the skills, aptitudes, and interests of soldiers, they could match them to jobs they would be good at.

Also, in the late 1800s, applied psychology, or clinical psychology, was developing as a field in Europe, and gradually made its way to the US Psychologists became interested in clinical diagnoses and treatment as well as things like measuring intelligence. At this point, the vocational guidance counseling movement and the development of psychology were quite separate. In the 1930s–1940s; however, a group of psychologists put forward a set of professional competencies and skills needed by professionals – psychologists – who did "clinical counseling" (Blocher, 2000, p. 71). These psychologists argued that clinical counseling should be developmental and should include not only vocational counseling but also personal and educational problems (Blocher, 2000). This was the first time that a counselor was "defined as an expert, highly qualified, and specially prepared psychologist" (Blocher, 2000, p. 71). In 1946, the Society of Counseling Psychology was founded as a part of the APA "to promote personal, educational, vocational, and group adjustment in a variety of settings" (Society of Counseling Psychology, 2025a, para. 1). (Side note: Just before this, in 1945, the "Division of Clinical and Abnormal Psychology," which is now the Division of Clinical Psychology, was founded. Note the focus on abnormal psychology, which is very different from the focus of counseling psychology on normal human development.)

Table 1.2 History of counseling psychology

Late 1800s: Industrial Revolution
Late 1800s: Social Reform Movement, Guidance Movement emerged
Late 1800s: Sigmund Freud developed psychoanalysis
1892: American Psychological Association was founded
Early 1900s: Social Reform Movement, Guidance Movement continued
1908: Vocation Bureau
1909: Choosing a Vocation (Frank Parsons) was published about "talent matching"
1939: The US Government established the US Employment Service and started the Dictionary of Occupational Titles
1942: Carl Rogers published the Theory of Personhood
1940s: Psychologists helped train the military, did vocational placement
1946: Society of Counseling Psychology was founded
1950s: Albert Ellis developed Rational-Emotive Behavior Therapy
1950s: Erik Erikson Theory of Human Development
1950s: American Personnel and Guidance Association established
1950s: Super's Vocational Development Theory
1950s–1960s: Gilbert Wrenn helped shift counseling psychology from a strict focus on vocation toward a more holistic approach
1950s: States began psychology licensure
1960s–1970s: Aaron Beck developed Cognitive Therapy, Cognitive-Behavioral Therapy
1960s–1970s: Civil Rights Movement, Title IX, anti-discrimination laws, counselors needed to be better prepared
1980s: Multicultural counseling emphasized
1990s: Constructivist theories, integrative approaches emerging
2000s-present: Emphasis on social justice advocacy and leadership

In the mid-1900s, psychology was exploding. All kinds of theorists and researchers were putting forward new ideas about how humans learn, develop, grow, and behave. In Chapter 6 on Theories and Approaches in Counseling Psychology, we review some of the most important counseling psychology theories, and we have some of these developments listed in Table 1.2. We think it is important for you to know about Gilbert Wrenn, who started his career as a high school guidance counselor and then went back to school to get a Ph.D. in personnel psychology (Parker, 2002). He was a professor for many years and studied and wrote about vocational counseling, personal counseling, and personnel counseling. He paused his faculty job during World War II and was a Personnel Officer in the U.S. Navy. He was awarded the Bronze Star Medal for his service. We point him out to you because he was one of the first people to say that counseling psychologists should not just focus on vocation but be a holistic approach (Parker, 2002). Gilbert Wrenn (1962) also wrote about multicultural issues and cultural context, warning counseling psychologists about "cultural encapsulation," or the dangers of living in your own bubble and not exposing yourself to people with other backgrounds and beliefs.

This emphasis on the role of culture in counseling psychology continued through the 1980s to the present. These discussions are still happening in the field of counseling psychology. In the 2000s, there was a gradual shift from focus on multicultural counseling competence (See Chapter 3) to social justice advocacy and action. Currently, however, there is some uncertainty about what training can look like. Although the Society of Counseling Psychology and the APA emphasize the need to train socially just counseling psychologists, the reality is that state and federal legislation have restricted colleges' ability. For example, some training programs are disallowed from using terms like "social justice" or "gender identity." So, some counseling psychologists are feeling a little in limbo right now: Do they teach from their values or from legal mandates? It will be interesting to see how the field of counseling psychology is affected by these recent developments and pushback on diversity, equity, and inclusivity initiatives across the United States.

What Is the Future of Counseling Psychology?

The demand for counseling psychologists and other mental health care workers is expected to increase in the future. According to a CNN report (2024), job growth in mental health is expected to be three times that of all other jobs in the United States from 2023 to 2033. The Bureau of Labor Statistics (2025) projected growth for clinical and counseling psychologists from 2022 to 2032 to be 11%, which is considered much faster than average growth speed, and the APA (2018) estimated growth to be 13% from 2015 to 2030. So, the outlook is good for employment in the field of counseling psychology and mental health professionals overall. There are likely many reasons for this increasing demand, but two of the main reasons are that people in the United States increasingly report stress and distress in their lives, and stigma around mental health treatment has begun to decrease (CNN, 2024). There are other factors as well, such as an increase in retirement numbers of current mental health professionals (Bureau of Labor Statistics, 2025). Over the last 40 years or so, master's-level clinical mental health programs have mostly been accredited by a group called the Council for Accreditation of Counseling and Related Educational Programs (CACREP), but a couple of years ago, the APA Commission on Accreditation began accrediting health service psychology (including clinical, counseling, school, or a combination of these) programs at the master's level, based on the demand for more mental health providers (APA, 2025). These programs are very new and so we do not yet have a sense of how this will affect the field. There is also uncertainty about how technology, such as artificial intelligence, will play a role in the future work of counseling psychologists.

Summary

At the beginning of this chapter, we asked you to consider what you think counseling psychology is, or looks like, or means. What, if anything, has changed in your initial perspective as a result of reading this chapter? Hopefully, you have a better sense of how counseling psychology as a field is different from other helping professions, especially based on its unique values and viewpoints. In this chapter, we started to answer some questions you might have had, like what counseling psychologists do and where they work. We also reviewed how counseling psychology developed

Kriti Jain. Photograph by Neeraja Janardhanan.

as a field over time and where it is going in the future. Now, we are going to dive into all of these things a lot more in the chapters that follow. We are excited about you joining us as you read the rest of the chapters in this textbook and see how counseling psychology has the power to change people's lives.

What Would You Do?

Throughout the book, in each chapter, we will pose some situations for you to think about and consider how you might respond. Here is the first one: you are an undergraduate student and are excited about a new course you're taking, Foundations of Counseling Psychology. In this class, you are learning about different counseling theories and approaches, the importance of context in considering people's mental health, and you are especially excited to practice some of the skills you'll learn toward the end of the semester! About midway through the semester, you have a dentist appointment – a routine appointment for a cleaning – and as you sit down, your dental hygienist asks about what classes you're taking. You tell her how excited you are about your counseling psych class. She then proceeds, as she is cleaning your teeth, to tell you all about her sister, who she says "is bipolar," and over the 30 minutes you are there, recounts numerous stories of recent issues within the family related to her sister's behavior. She expresses concerns about her nieces. She then asks you, "Do you think she's probably bipolar? Do you think her girls are okay?" She expresses low confidence in her sister's therapist and asks you for a recommendation for a better one, asks about whether she should intervene in any way related to the care of her nieces, and asks if they should all be going to family therapy.

- What would you do in this situation?
- How would you handle the questions and request for information?
- What might you consider as you decide how to answer her questions?
- The next time someone asks you what classes you're taking, how will you answer?

Counseling Psychologist Spotlight: Doctoral Student

Kriti Jain

Kriti Jain (any pronouns) is a third-year doctoral student in the counseling psychology program at the University of Tennessee, Knoxville (UTK). They were first introduced to the field of counseling psychology in the third year of college, when a new professor joined the psychology faculty at their university in India. The professor had recently graduated with a PhD in Counseling Psychology from the University of Maryland and Kriti was fascinated when they learned that, in addition to teaching and conducting research, the professor also worked as a therapist on the side. This was something Kriti could see themself doing, and so they decided to apply to counseling psychology programs in the United States. Applying as an international student came with its own set of challenges and it took Kriti three attempts to get accepted into a program. Although facing rejection multiple times was disheartening, it challenged Kriti to reflect on what they wanted to get out of the degree. It led them to first get a master's degree, which allowed them to gain more research experience and hone their research interests. Kriti says this experience definitely allowed them to feel more prepared as they entered the doctoral program at UTK.

As a PhD student, they are constantly juggling multiple responsibilities. This includes completing coursework, conducting research, providing psychotherapy, and teaching. As part of their research responsibilities, they also have regular meetings with their advisor, write papers for publication, and get to travel for conferences, which they say is always fun! Kriti says that while managing all of this can feel overwhelming, getting to wear so many hats offers flexibility and excitement, which they really appreciate. Kriti loves knowing that their work has a positive impact on people's lives. Their research and clinical interests focus on supporting the well-being of individuals from marginalized communities, including those that they are a part of, and so the work feels personally meaningful and inspiring. Kriti says it is especially powerful when they hear clients share how they have grown in therapy or when they see actual data showing improvements in mental health among research participants. They also love having such a strong bond with their cohort. (*Note: A cohort is a small group of students who enter a doctoral program together. They often take classes together across the years of their doctoral program. We talk more about the experiences of students in Chapter 15.) Kriti and their cohort have gotten very close over the past few years, having navigated the successes and challenges of graduate school together. They know that the friendships they have made at UTK will last a lifetime.

Kriti says they strongly align with the values of counseling psychology, particularly its emphasis on attending to the whole person. They believe that each individual, regardless of their background or mental health status, has inherent value and strengths that make them who they are. As a counseling psychologist-in-training, Kriti wants to help individuals see their inherent worth and maximize their potential. They really appreciate being able to receive training from counseling psychologists who share similar values.

Kriti says the most rewarding experience of their PhD journey so far has been the wellness program that they have been developing along with their advisor. It started with an interest of theirs in developing a wellness intervention for the LGBTQ+ community, particularly racial/ethnic minority members, that centered on the strengths of the community. They say they were lucky enough to have a supportive advisor who was enthusiastic about this project and they eventually got a grant from the university to test the intervention. Kriti finds it very rewarding to see participants' response to the wellness program. Participants have shared how the program improved their relationship with their identities, helped them feel more connected to their communities, and allowed them to learn more about themselves.

Kriti shared that recently, they and a group of students within the counseling psychology program at UTK organized a student-led conference, called Connecting across Disciplines, aimed at addressing mental health needs within the East Tennessee region. They invited various local community organizations as well as speakers from across multiple mental health-allied disciplines, including psychology, social work, and counselor education. The conference was attended by around 200 individuals and was a huge success! Kriti says it was wonderful to see community members, academics, and students all come together to address real-world concerns, and they hope to continue to help create more spaces like this.

Through all of the hardships of the PhD journey, these moments remind Kriti of why they chose this path! Kriti thinks the hardest part about being a PhD student is having limited time. They say the work truly never ends and so they try to be intentional about recognizing what their capacity is and taking time to take care of their own well-being. For Kriti, that looks like cooking, spending time with friends, and carving out time when they can switch their brain off. In their free time, they love to travel. They enjoy walking around and exploring new cities and cultures. They also enjoy going to drag shows and being a part of local queer spaces and events.

Kriti serves on the Board of the Society of Counseling Psychology (APA Division 17) student group called SAS. The role is called a Tri-Chair, meaning there are three people who share leadership responsibilities. In this role, they get the opportunity to advocate for the interests and needs of counseling psychology graduate students from across the country. They say it has also been a great way to connect with leaders in the field and get an insider perspective on how the Society of Counseling Psychology works.

Kriti has a BA in Psychology from Ashoka University in India, an MA in Clinical Psychology from Columbia University, Teachers College, and an MA in Counseling Psychology from the University of Tennessee, Knoxville. They also hold a certificate as a Certified Wellness and Health Coach.

References

American Psychological Association. (2018). *APA fact sheet series on psychologist supply and demand projections 2015–2030: Supply scenarios for the psychologist workforce*. https://www.apa.org/workforce/publications/supply-demand/supply-scenarios.pdf

American Psychological Association. (2023). *Recognized specialties, subspecialties, and proficiencies in professional psychology*. https://www.apa.org/ed/graduate/specialize/recognized

American Psychological Association. (2025). *Master's level accreditation*. https://accreditation.apa.org/about-coa/masters-accreditation

American Psychological Association Commission on Accreditation. (2015). *Standards of accreditation for programs in health service psychology*. https://www.apa.org/ed/accreditation/standards-of-accreditation.pdf

Bureau of Labor Statistics, U.S. Department of Labor. (2025). Strong growth projected in mental health-related employment. *The Economics Daily*. https://www.bls.gov/opub/ted/2024/strong-growth-projected-in-mental-health-related-employment.htm

Blocher, D. H. (2000). *The evolution of counseling psychology*. Springer Publishing Company, Inc.

Gelso, C. J., & Williams, E. (2021). *Counseling psychology* (4th ed.). American Psychological Association.

Parker, C. (2002). *Charles Gilbert-Wrenn* (1902–2001). *American Psychologist 57*(9), 721–722. https://doi.org/10.1037/0003-066X.57.9.721

Parsons, F. (1909). *Choosing a vocation*. Houghton Mifflin.

Rogers, C. R. (1980). *A way of being*. Houghton Mifflin.

Society of Counseling Psychology. (2025a). *About SCP*. https://www.div17.org/about-scp

Society of Counseling Psychology. (2025b). *SCP mission and values*. https://www.div17.org/mission-values

Wrenn, C. G. (1962). The culturally encapsulated counselor. *Harvard Educational Review, 32*(4), 444–449.

Chapter 2

How Counseling Psychologists Promote Human Strengths and Flourishing

What Do You Believe about Human Nature?

Before we get started, take a moment to reflect on what you believe about human beings. It is true that people do a lot of messed-up things, but why do you think people do things that hurt themselves and others? What if a person has lots of love, tons of support, and the ability to do whatever they want? Will that person decide to do healthy things or unhealthy things? Is there such a thing as "good" people and "bad" people? Do people behave the way they do because of their upbringing or because of their innate character?

If you noticed yourself thinking, "People do hurtful things because they have been hurt and when people are supported and free they will make healthy decisions" you might be a counseling psychologist. In other words, counseling psychologists tend to take a strengths-based, wellness-oriented, positive psychological approach to behavioral health. As we mentioned in Chapter 1, counseling psychologists tend to see people as a work in process rather than as disordered or sick. They generally believe that clients are filled with potential and, given optimal conditions, will make health-fostering decisions (Rogers, 1946). In other words, people want to be healthy and they will behave in healthy ways if they are given the chance to do so.

In this chapter, we will dive into one of the core concepts of counseling psychology, which is to focus on diverse people's strengths. This chapter discusses how a focus on strengths sets counseling psychology apart. We describe how positive psychology is tied to the concept of prevention and will introduce readers to the APA Prevention Guidelines. Prevention is defined in relation to other concepts like psychoeducation and outreach. Counseling psychologists utilize positive psychology in therapeutic interventions as well as non-therapeutic interventions. We describe some examples, such as promotion of well-being, anti-racist interventions, sexual assault prevention, and alcohol and tobacco education. This chapter ties positive psychology and prevention to public health and uses a case example to illustrate interventions in practice in real life.

Background

In Chapter 1, we talked a little about the differences between counseling psychology and clinical psychology. Traditionally, clinical psychology as a field has approached people through a focus on symptoms and pathology. Pathology is basically a focus on problems or diseases. So clinical psychology might be interested in the study of obsessive-compulsive disorder: how it develops, how it is maintained, and how it can be improved. A counseling psychologist, on the other hand, might be interested in a *person* with obsessive-compulsive disorder as well as the development, maintenance,

DOI: 10.4324/9781003439899-2

and improvement of the disorder. First and foremost, they are interested in the human being who is experiencing obsessive-compulsive disorder. This interest drives questions like:

- What is their physical health like?
- What is their environment like?
- What are their relationships like?
- What kinds of things has the person done so far to cope with the problem?
- What has worked for them so far? What helps and what makes it worse?

Now, we are not saying that clinical psychologists do not ever ask these questions. There are always exceptions and nuances and things have changed over time. We are simply trying to point out that historically and traditionally, in clinical psychology, the study of the mental health disorder came first. In counseling psychology, the wellness of the human being comes first. As we discussed in Chapter 1, counseling psychology emerged from work with humans on vocational, educational, and psychological needs, so even when someone does have psychological problems or concerns, the approach that counseling psychologists take is based on the person's strengths and positive factors.

Human Potential

There are a lot of ways of framing this positive approach to therapy and humans more broadly. A belief in human potential and a focus on growth is a core part of many humanistic theoretical approaches, which you will read more about in Chapter 6, such as person-centered therapy, narrative therapy, and solution-focused therapy. But this belief in human potential underlies all of the work that counseling psychologists do, regardless of their theoretical orientation. Counseling psychologists frequently are attuned to, and use, concepts like optimal functioning, fostering potential, well-being, strengths-based self-actualization, self-compassion, human agency, and positive words like promote, foster, flourish, positive, and health. A lot of this work emerged from Maslow and Rogers in the mid-1900s. We briefly introduced you to their work in Chapter 1 when we discussed the history of counseling psychology, but we will go into more depth here because they had such a big influence.

For example, Rogers said that people have something called *the actualizing tendency*, or a natural drive toward growth and self-improvement (1963). Rogers suggested that this actualizing tendency was what motivated people to behave. It was not an end goal, but rather what drove people in a certain direction. Maslow also talked about how people could realize their full potential, and he called it the process of *self-actualization* (1943), but he saw this as an end goal toward which people moved across their lives. Another person who has written a lot about human potential is Seligman (2011). His focus is on human flourishing and how optimism, motivation, and character help people get the most out of life. He developed a model called PERMA, which includes Positive Emotion (happiness), Engagement, Relationships, Meaning, and Accomplishment (Seligman, 2011).

There have been critiques about this heavy focus on strengths and self-actualization. People have argued that strengths-based and actualization-focused approaches are overly individualistic and ignore the needs of communal societies or communities. For example, you have probably heard a lot about Maslow's (1943) Hierarchy of Needs and seen a pyramid showing that, according to Maslow, an individual needs:

1) Their physiological needs met
2) Then their safety needs

3) Then belongingness and love needs
4) Then esteem needs
5) And only then can they achieve their full potential, or self-actualization

Maslow has been accused of borrowing heavily from the Siksika (Blackfoot) people and their philosophy as he developed this theory (Ravilochan, 2021). People have also made comparisons between Maslow's work and other non-Western philosophies. For example, Das (1989) found similarities between the notion of self-actualization and the Eastern concept of self-realization, and Afrasibi and Fattahi (2017) compared self-actualization to Islamic principles. However, there are mixed opinions about how Maslow's philosophy emerged. For example, Maslow did not actually frame his ideas as existing in a pyramid. The pyramid you have probably seen associated with Maslow's hierarchy is something other people put together, based on his work (Ravilochan, 2021). Other people have criticized Maslow for being too focused on individuals, but he later wrote a critique of his earlier work, arguing that community and relationships with other people were needed (Maslow, 1991).

The Development of Positive Psychology

The positive thread in humanistic theories and efforts among leading psychologists to move beyond the historical, problem-focused models of psychology gave rise to a more optimistic form of behavioral health theory referred to as *positive psychology* (Magyar-Moe et al., 2015). Positive psychology is defined as:

> A field of psychological theory and research that focuses on the psychological states (e.g., contentment, joy), individual traits or character strengths (e.g., intimacy, integrity, altruism, wisdom), and social institutions that enhance subjective well-being and make life most worth living.
>
> (American Psychological Association [APA], 2018, para. 1)

It is important to note that positive psychology is a specific theoretical orientation or structured set of principles and testable constructs or ideas (Magyar-Moe et al., 2015). Sometimes, people say they practice positive psychology or call themselves positive psychologists, but they are using those terms in a more general sense. You will notice that we did not title this chapter "Positive Psychology" because we wanted it to be broader and more inclusive of positive principles in counseling psychology such as human strengths and flourishing. This chapter includes a lot of information about positive psychology, but not all counseling psychologists identify as positive psychologists, and the values that counseling psychologists hold reach well beyond standard positive psychology theory and research.

Over the years, there have been a lot of debates about whether counseling psychology by definition is strengths-focused, and therefore calling it positive psychology is redundant, or whether positive psychology as a field is completely separate, or whether positive psychology is a subset of counseling psychology as well as its own field. It all becomes very confusing. Waterman (2013) described exchanges between humanistic psychologists and positive psychologists as "marked by tension and ambivalence" (p. 124). Schneider asked, "Why can't we just get along?" (2011, p. 32). Honestly, these arguments seem a little silly and dramatic to us. We feel that any approach that is positive and affirmative and helps humans along in their self-exploration and discovery and growth is bound to be a good idea. We are just pointing this out so you know there are different opinions on the matter.

Table 2.1 Positive psychology, counseling applications, and cultural considerations

Theme	*Definition/Key Components*	*Application*	*Cultural Implications*
Well-being	Resources, skills	Gratitude letter/ journal Acts of kindness Goal-setting	Impacted by socioeconomic status, global location, and social networks
Meaning	Purpose and significance	Building growth-oriented narratives Meaning-making activities	Impacted by global location and social networks
Hope	Flexible thinking and motivation	Skills training Group therapy	Impacted by risk factors and exposure to oppression
Strengths	Self-improvement and managing limitations	Character strength assessments Skill building exercises	Shaped by context, socialization, and other cultural variables
Broaden and build	Adaptive emotions expand possibilities	Exposure Skill building Fostering resilience	Target emotions and emotional stages may differ
Positive empathy	Identification of hidden desires	Paraphrasing Reflecting feelings	Requires rapport and awareness of cultural variables
Diagnosis	Labels are powerful	Person-first language Collaboration Psychoeducation	Involves awareness of social implications and respect for client agency

Note. Table contents were adapted from Magyar-Moe et al. (2015).

Positive psychology is so favored by counseling psychologists that several members of the Society of Counseling Psychology (SCP) got together and formed a sub-group or section on positive psychology (Section on Positive Psychology, n.d.). Still, counseling psychologists, like positive psychologists, tend to hold a set of common beliefs about human beings and the healing power of psychology. For example, counseling and positive psychologists tend to emphasize strengths, well-being, mindfulness, meaning, purpose, resilience, and thriving (Magyar-Moe et al., 2015). As we have mentioned elsewhere in this text, theory informs practice and shapes the way counseling psychologists approach their practice.

Take a look at Table 2.1 and reflect on the points of connection between the perspectives counseling psychologists take and the ways they practice using a positive psychology lens. For example, read over the key themes and ask yourself, "Which of these ideas is most important to me in my own life?" Read over the application column and see if you can pick out activities you have already tried without reading about positive psychology in depth. Maybe you already journal or think deeply about the meaning of your life. You may notice that some parts of positive psychology come naturally to you. In other words, positive psychology is about helping you reach your full potential, but you already have the tools necessary and the innate ability to thrive.

Positive Psychology in Practice

So far, we have been focusing on the aspirational and theoretical parts of positive psychological practice. However, there are a lot of ways that positive psychology shapes the way that counseling psychologists practice behavioral health care. Let's use a made-up case example to explore how counseling psychologists may differ from other behavioral health providers. Imagine you received a referral for Kari, a client who is 25 years old, and identifies as a Korean, lesbian, cisgender woman, who is currently single, able-bodied, neurodivergent, and unemployed. On Kari's intake paperwork, you can see that she is reportedly experiencing insomnia, agitation, elevated heart rate, and restlessness. She reports playing several recreational sports including soccer, softball, and tennis. She states that she rarely talks to her parents and has few close friends. She also shares that she was assaulted in a grocery store by an angry man who called her names about two years ago. Kari shares that she is looking forward to counseling. She says she has a strong sense of hope that things will get better, and she is committed to treating others like she would like to be treated instead of letting anger "get the best of her."

As you read over the sample case, what stood out to you? Did you notice yourself diagnosing Kari with a specific disorder? Did you tend to focus on her difficulties or her strengths? Without looking back at the case, take a moment to write down or list in your head what you remember about Kari and her situation. Were your memories mostly positive, negative, or neutral?

First, let's analyze the case using a medical model approach. We talk more about the medical model in Chapter 13, but basically it is a model that starts with defining the problem and then applying evidence-based solutions to that problem. If our primary focus is on the problem, or the *psychopathology* (which is a fancy way of saying psychological problems), we might emphasize the fact that Kari seems to have an anxiety disorder diagnosis. We might think about the event in the grocery store as a possible traumatic experience, and we might explore ways that Kari's neurodivergence might interact with her symptoms in a negative way. We could conduct a psychological assessment to give her a diagnosis, identify an evidence-based technique with demonstrated effectiveness at reducing anxiety, and explore possible medications that could be used to address Kari's anxiety-related symptoms.

Of course, a counseling psychologist with a strengths-based outlook would notice many of the same factors and possibilities, but their focus would probably be very different. They might notice that Kari has a number of strengths, such as a strong sense of hope, motivation, and kindness, that can be tied into treatment to help Kari counteract the symptoms she is experiencing. The counseling psychologist might highlight her connections to others that are maintained through participation in recreational sports and celebrate the resilience that Kari exhibits as a person with multiple marginalized identities. As you look at the case from this perspective, your mind is probably filling up with ideas about how these social relationships, characteristics, and resilience strategies could be used to help the client regulate her emotions and reestablish key relationships. Of course, it is still important to consider assessment, diagnosis, and the best course of treatment for Kari. It is just that the focus or underlying philosophy driving the counseling work is different.

There are a lot of ways a counseling psychologist could use strengths-based, wellness-oriented, and positive psychology-supported behavioral health interventions to support Kari. In future chapters, we will talk about ways to integrate different theories, strategies, and clinical interventions to meet clients' needs in a way that is tailored to their unique contexts and identities. As we have

Table 2.2 Sample positive psychology interventions

Strengths-Based Counseling	*Well-Being Therapy**	*Quality of Life Therapy**	*Strengths-Centered Therapy**	*Hope Therapy*
Therapeutic alliance	Environmental mastery	Objective circumstances	Explicitizing	Hope finding
Strengths identification	Personal growth	Subjective attitudes	Envisioning	Hope bonding
Presenting problem assessment	Purpose in life	Fulfillment standards	Empowering	Hope enhancing
Encouraging/ instilling hope	Autonomy	Importance for well-being	Evolving	Hope reminding
Framing solutions	Self-acceptance	Overall life satisfaction		
Building strength/ competence	Positive relations with others			
Empowering				
Changing				
Building resilience				
Evaluating and terminating				

Note. *Components may not be addressed in the order they are listed and/or may be repeated during treatment. Strengths-Based Counseling (Smith, 2006). Strengths-Centered Therapy (Wong, 2006). Quality of Life Therapy (Frisch, 2006). Well-Being Therapy (Ruini & Fava, 2004). Hope Therapy (Lopez et al., 2000).

already pointed out, there are many theories that intersect with or relate to positive psychology such as person-centered, existential, and narrative therapies. You can even reference Table 2.1 to identify specific theory-based interventions that could be used with Kari.

Counseling psychologists who identify as positive psychologists have a lot of intervention strategies that build on positive psychology theory more directly and specifically. There are benefits to using a specific theoretical approach or theory-based intervention such as the fact that theory-based interventions offer a consistent, clear, and coherent way to provide care. Table 2.2 offers a summary of some positive psychology interventions. Look at the different components (rows one to ten) and identify one that stands out to you the most. Then look at the positive psychology intervention that uses that intervention. Could you imagine yourself working as a hope therapist? Do you think well-being therapy would be a good fit for you? As you answer these questions, you are doing the work of finding a theory that fits for you.

Now take a step back and compare the content in Tables 2.1 and 2.2. What are the common themes you notice? You should be able to trace the ways that key themes in positive psychology show up in counseling psychology interventions and strategies that are based on those themes. You will notice that there is not a bold dividing line between positive psychologists and counseling psychologists who work from other perspectives, but the approach a counseling psychologist takes matters. It shapes the way care is provided, what gets emphasized, and how care is delivered. We talk a lot more about this in Chapter 6. Another great thing about positive psychology is that it isn't just useful when people are in crisis or when things get bad enough for them to need psychological care. Positive psychology is also closely tied to prevention science. In other words, counseling psychologists work to intervene before things get bad and they advocate for positive change in society.

Prevention Science

It may not surprise you that there is also a subgroup of counseling psychologists in the Society of Counseling Psychology that focuses on prevention science, called the Prevention Section. The definition of prevention involves two primary approaches to psychological care: (a) stopping, reducing, or delaying the onset of a problem behavior, and (b) promoting wellness-fostering activities and policies that reduce the likelihood that problem behaviors will develop (APA, 2014). Another definition has five components: (a) stopping a problem behavior from ever occurring; (b) delaying the onset of a problem behavior; (c) reducing the impact of a problem behavior; (d) strengthening knowledge, attitudes, and behaviors that promote emotional and physical well-being; and (e) promoting institutional, community, and government policies that further physical, social, and emotional well-being (Romano & Hage, 2000). A lot of people think prevention is just about *preventing* bad things from happening, but that is not the case: it is also about *promoting* the good things through education and outreach. The mission of the Prevention Section is to advance theory, research, training, practice, advocacy, and policy initiatives in prevention among counseling psychologists (Prevention Section, 2025). There is a great deal of overlap between positive psychology and prevention in the field of counseling psychology, given that they share a focus on strengths, wellness, and the potential for positive change (Romano et al., 2012).

A further indication of the fact that prevention is an important part of a counseling psychologist's job, the APA published prevention guidelines for psychologists (APA, 2014). The guidelines address several key areas of prevention practice by encouraging the use of:

- Theory- and evidence-based prevention practices
- Culturally appropriate prevention interventions
- Risk reduction and strengths-based approaches
- Assessment, research, and evaluation tools
- Ethically grounded and informed procedures
- Educational materials and continuing education
- Strategies to improve institutional systems and public policy

Take a moment to read back over the bulleted list and make note of the guidelines that seem directly related to or compatible with some concepts of positive psychology we discussed earlier. If you have a paper copy or an interactive electronic copy of this book, you can even highlight the specific points of overlap. Did you notice how intertwined the goals of prevention and positive psychology are? As you can see, counseling psychologists not only address problems after they have developed, but they also work to prevent those problems before they happen.

For example, imagine providing therapy for Sam (she/her), a 12-year-old client. The client's parents send Sam to you because she is experiencing high anxiety and panic attacks. When you talk to Sam, she shares that her parents are very anxious and share with her all of their fears, concerns, and frustrations. They regularly tell her they are afraid they will not be able to "put food on the table" or "keep the power on" at home. She overhears them talking about not being able to make the rent payment this month. You work hard to teach Sam anxiety reduction skills, and she usually manages her stress well when she is working with you, but at the end of each session, you send her back to an environment at home that ramps up her anxiety all over again.

Counseling psychologists realize that there is a lot that can be done to reduce mental health concerns for clients, but if we keep sending clients back into harmful environments, they will keep getting hurt and needing help. In Sam's case, a great way to prevent future panic attacks is to improve her parents' coping skills and perhaps refer them to a financial counselor, but you probably noticed that there are even bigger ways prevention efforts might help. For example, changes to local and national policies such as an increase in minimum wage, caps on rent increases, lower prices on essential resources, or access to job training and education would go a long way toward preventing the stress levels and pressures that Sam's parents pass on to her. In big and small ways, prevention efforts can create sustainable change by reducing barriers and expanding access to key resources that support human success and thriving. Just like positive psychology is based on the principle that removing limitations frees people to reach their full potential, prevention efforts allow people to thrive as well.

Prevention and Public Health

As we mentioned in Chapter 1 and earlier in this chapter, there are a variety of different behavioral health providers and health service workers who are similar to counseling psychologists in some of the job titles they hold and services they offer. Any of these behavioral health providers (counselors, social workers, school psychologists) can use a positive psychology approach to supporting clients. One of the things that differentiates counseling psychologists from other providers is the values they hold and the ways they work to tailor their interventions to unique individual and community-based needs.

One area in which there is a great deal of overlap between counseling psychology and other disciplines is in prevention. In particular, public health officials share counseling psychologists' emphasis on community-level intervention and prevention of behavioral health concerns. According to the American Public Health Association (APHA), public health promotes and protects the health of all people and their communities (APHA, n.d.). APHA further states that public health is responsible for things like:

- Administering vaccines to prevent the spread of diseases
- Setting work safety standards
- Increasing access to healthy food for kids
- Identifying racism as a public health crisis

As you read over the list above, you are likely to notice a wide range of prevention initiatives you could imagine counseling psychologists joining and even participating in. As a possible future counseling psychologist, you may feel inspired by the focus of public health workers on safety, nutrition, and social justice. So what sets public health workers apart from counseling psychologists? What might be outside the scope of practice for a counseling psychologist?

You might have noticed that many of the activities in the list involved administering medications (vaccines), setting public policy standards (work protections), and direct intervention in nutritional programs (increasing access to food). It is true that some counseling psychologists contribute key research to and strongly advocate for better treatment standards and the reduction of health access barriers. However, the way they accomplish these tasks is different. Most counseling psychology interventions are delivered through talk therapy and communication with groups and organizations aimed at individual and group-level psychological health and behavior change. As we discussed earlier, counseling psychologists generally operate outside of the medical model and counseling psychology training does not include, for example, a focus on administering shots (this is a relief to us).

The considerable overlap between counseling psychology and other behavioral and health service providers shows up in a lot of the prevention activities that counseling psychologists research and become involved in. For example, counseling psychologists might be more focused on issues related to mental health, such as promotion of psychological health and well-being, sexual assault prevention, substance use disorder prevention and intervention, and anti-racist efforts. We will briefly discuss the unique role of counseling psychologists in each of these areas. As you read the following sections, please reflect on what makes the work of counseling psychologists different from other professions. Keep in mind that prevention can be both promotion of good things and prevention of things that perhaps aren't as healthy.

Promotion of Well-Being

Earlier, we talked about Seligman's (2011) emphasis on human flourishing. His research indicates that children can be taught positive psychology principles, and these have a long-lasting effect on the children's emotional well-being as well as academic success (Chamberlin, 2011). Seligman has also developed trainings to build resilience and teach positive psychology to enlisted soldiers in the US Army and found that these trainings resulted in better coping skills and less catastrophic thinking (Chamberlin, 2011). Seligman has called for more positive psychology trainings in educational settings, corporate settings, and government organizations globally.

Anti-Racist Efforts: Liberation, Joy, Pride, and Resilience

Counseling psychologists have worked hard to research ways to prevent racism and to buffer the harmful effects of racism. For example, Singh (2020) and Comas-Díaz (2020) have promoted a counseling psychology of liberation, or freedom from oppression. Liberation counseling psychology is not just for marginalized people but rather for all of society because dominant restrictions on human growth hurt everyone, including those in power (Singh, 2020). Some counseling psychologists focus on liberation and affirmative practice for specific populations such as American Indian and Indigenous populations (Gone, 2021), transgender and non-binary people (Singh et al., 2023), and Black and African American populations (Pieterse et al., 2023).

Counseling psychologists have also focused on other affirming practices such as focusing on pride, joy, resilience, and healing (for example, Neville, 2024). They have recommended, for example, systemic changes at the university level (Knutson et al., 2021) aimed at enhancing the educational environment for graduate psychology students. They have called for de-emphasizing deficit models that only focus on problems or issues that groups might have and emphasizing resilience models that understand and highlight the strengths that groups have. We talk about these themes in more depth in Chapters 2 and 13, but they are core to preventive efforts and are important to discuss in the context of positive psychology and prevention. Why? Because sustainable prevention efforts are dependent on changing the system or systems that caused the problem in the first place.

Sexual Assault Prevention

In Chapter 14, we will more thoroughly discuss the different settings and specialized services provided by counseling psychologists. For example, we will note that many counseling psychologists work at college and university counseling centers. Given the troublingly high rates of sexual assault on college and university campuses (Steele et al., 2024), counseling psychology practitioners on those campuses are ideally positioned to engage in sexual assault prevention activities. College and university counseling centers usually provide consultation services, participate in student support committees, and offer outreach services across the campuses where they work. For example, counseling psychologists in these settings might offer an educational training about sexual consent to incoming first-year and transfer students. The psychoeducational and inclusive prevention programming and advocacy they provide is an essential part of reducing the prevalence of sexual assault on campuses.

Substance Use Disorder Prevention

There are a lot of ways that counseling psychologists contribute to the prevention of substance use disorders. One simple way is by foregrounding person-centered values that challenge marginalizing language. For example, most people in your life probably refer to people with substance disorders using condescending and marginalizing language like druggie, addict, or junkie. The more you learn about positive psychology, the more you will probably notice problems with that approach. You may even be thinking, "Wait, where is the humanity in that sort of language?" If so, you are thinking like a counseling psychologist. Counseling psychologists honor human dignity by using person-first language when possible. This means we might say "person with a substance use disorder" rather than something like "drug abuser" (Martin et al., 2016). Another way counseling psychologists are working to prevent and reduce risk for substance use disorders is by developing innovative ways to involve parents in those efforts (Florsheim & Burrow-Sánchez, 2023) and by helping marginalized communities connect with cultural values and strengths (Burrow-Sánchez & Hops, 2019). As we discussed in Chapter 1, core counseling psychology values like cultural competence, human dignity, and human thriving overlap and inform the ways counseling psychologists approach a broad range of tasks and issues.

Focusing on Strengths

Imagine that someone asks you: What are your strengths and weaknesses? You may be able to quickly identify your weaknesses. But what about your strengths? See if you can come up with a list of five areas of growth and five strengths. For most people, it is incredibly difficult to name their strengths. This is partially due to societal expectations that we not come across as bragging or egotistical and may be partially due to self-doubt or being blind to our own strengths. Counseling psychologists often can help people identify and name their strengths, which can contribute to self-confidence, hope, and motivation. Scheel et al. (2012) found five ways that counseling psychologists use positive processes with clients: (a) amplifying strengths; (b) keeping in mind cultural context; (c) using strength-oriented processes; (d) working toward strength-oriented outcomes; and (e) helping clients find positive meaning-making.

We think one of the most important things for clients, especially young people, to do is to identify their strengths. One way is to look at a list of character strengths and have a conversation with a client about what they think might fit for them. Another way is to have a client complete an assessment of strengths like the Values in Action Inventory (VIA) (Peterson & Seligman, 2004), which is based on 24 strengths like curiosity, gratitude, kindness, love of learning, perseverance, spirituality, and one of our personal favorites, "zest" (vital, enthusiastic, full of energy). We have found that understanding strengths can be particularly useful for adolescents and young adults who are learning more about themselves. For example, a client may be able to say she is a good friend to others, but if she takes the VIA and learns that one of her greatest strengths is *teamwork*, this is perhaps something that she can highlight in a resume, job application, or interview. Similarly, a client may see himself as curious, but through the assessment, is able to define himself as a lifelong learner; this may help him with a decision to pursue a graduate degree.

Challenges to Positive Psychology

Over time, there have been world events that have challenged counseling psychologists' beliefs about human freedom and the drive to be healthy and whole. For example, World War II and the Holocaust were reminders of the fact that humans have great potential to improve the world and themselves, but they also have great capacity to cause destruction. As you read this book, you may be living in a time or place that challenges your own beliefs about what humans are capable of and how they function. Counseling psychologists recognize the terrible things that people are capable of and they commit themselves to improving the world by focusing on and expanding the potential humans have to change the world for the better.

As you consider a possible future as a counseling psychologist or another career, it may be important for you to identify your "why?" Why might you want to be a (insert career here)? How do you think you can make the most positive impact on the world? Answering these questions will help you explore whether counseling psychology is right for you. For example, a corrections officer might try to change the world by enforcing rules. A lawmaker might try to make the world better by passing laws and setting standards. A counseling psychologist's job is quite different from that. From a positive psychology perspective, counseling psychologists set up the optimal conditions for people to grow, offer them the freedom to make choices, and believe that focusing on growth helps people to heal.

As you can see, counseling psychology takes a lot of trust, care for others, and belief in human potential. Counseling psychologists learn to be present with clients, encourage the psychological healing process, and support them as they find answers to their own problems in a non-judgmental, unconditional way. Counseling psychologists open up space for clients to be more authentic and fully themselves. People have also pointed out ways that a focus on positive psychology can minimize important human struggles and systemic challenges such as discrimination and oppression. For example, we were careful in Table 2.1 to refer to emotions as *adaptive* rather than positive emotions. When a counseling psychologist singles out a specific range of emotions such as joy and contentment as "positive," they run the risk of implying that "negative" emotions like anger or discontentment are bad or to be avoided. The truth is that anger, discontentment, and other emotions may be unpleasant, but they can also make total sense and be healthy to experience and express. For example, it might be unhealthy to feel joy while you are being yelled at by someone else.

Likewise, counseling psychologists who are attuned to cultural context note that it is important not to ignore or try to escape from the troubling and powerful implications of discrimination, oppression, and marginalization. For example, counseling psychologists have been at the forefront of researching the harmful experiences of microaggressions, or everyday prejudice, bias, and discrimination (Sue & Spanierman, 2020). They have also been exploring microaffirmations or subtle, indirect ways of encouraging others that are sometimes hard to notice (Koch et al., 2020, 2025; Wong et al., 2025). In their work, those researchers acknowledge that a focus on microaffirmations is not intended to distract from or replace research on microaggressions or discriminatory behaviors (Koch et al., 2020, 2025; Wong et al., 2025). As we discussed in our case examples earlier in this chapter, counseling psychologists do not ignore clients' issues or concerns, even while they focus on the client's strengths and potential to develop more healthy behaviors.

Summary

At the beginning of this chapter, we asked you to consider what you believe about human beings and human nature. We wanted you to reflect on your own core beliefs about whether humans are innately good or bad. What do you think now, after reading this chapter? Are humans capable of change? Are all people capable of change? In this chapter, we talked about how counseling psychologists believe in human potential and take a strengths-based approach to promote human flourishing. We reviewed the role of positive psychology and described what positive psychology interventions might look like. We also introduced you to the notion of prevention, which includes preventing harmful things as well as promoting beneficial things. We hope this overview of the counseling psychology focus on human strengths and flourishing helped you gain a better sense of one of the main core values of counseling psychologists. In the next chapter, we will dive into another core value, considering humans within their unique cultural contexts.

What Would You Do?

You walk into a new class at the beginning of the fall semester and notice a student, Xander, sitting in the back of the classroom all alone. You always feel drawn to people who are treated like outsiders, so you decide to sit next to Xander. Right away, you notice how unhappy Xander seems. You ask how their day is, and they grumble, "Good, I guess." After class, a few of your friends tell you, "We would sit with you, but Xander is just so negative. They are hard to be around." Over the next few class periods, you find yourself agreeing. It seems like everything Xander says to you is critical or grumpy. They share with you that they do not like the professor, the temperature in the classroom, the harsh lighting, and the homework assignments. They also share that they were forced to attend your university, and they are miserable. You notice that Xander is very studious, engaged, and capable as a student. They are always on time for class, they take notes, and they always get the highest grades on assignments. Still, no matter how well things seem to go for Xander, they do not seem to find joy or inspiration. By the end of the third week of classes, you find yourself thinking about moving to a different spot in the classroom, far away from Xander. Before you give up entirely, you decide to reflect on your value for a strengths-based outlook and what it might tell you about your current situation.

- First, take a step back and focus on your own values and goals. What strengths and positive qualities have you been showing as you have been trying to connect with Xander?
- Second, try to see past all of the negativity. What strengths and advantages do you notice Xander exhibiting? For now, resist any pressure you feel to diagnose Xander or explain their grumpiness.
- Next, make space for a sense of awe about what Xander has accomplished. Reflect on the ways that, despite their hopelessness and dissatisfaction, they have managed to make high grades and succeed at a university they did not want to attend. What do you notice about Xander's level of resilience and adaptability?

- Then, explore how Xander could build on their strengths (e.g., commitment, dedication, determination) to better manage and decrease their growth areas (e.g., social isolation or hopelessness).
- Consider how you could advocate for systemic change for students like Xander. What could you do to advocate for support for students like Xander to increase their well-being and expand support for them?
- Reflect on how your support of Xander might tie into broader prevention efforts. Given how unhappy Xander reports being, it is possible they could decide to use alcohol, drugs, or other unhelpful strategies to regulate their mood. How does supporting Xander prevent future problems they might face?
- How might you actually talk to Xander about their attitude and what makes them act this way? What wording might you use?

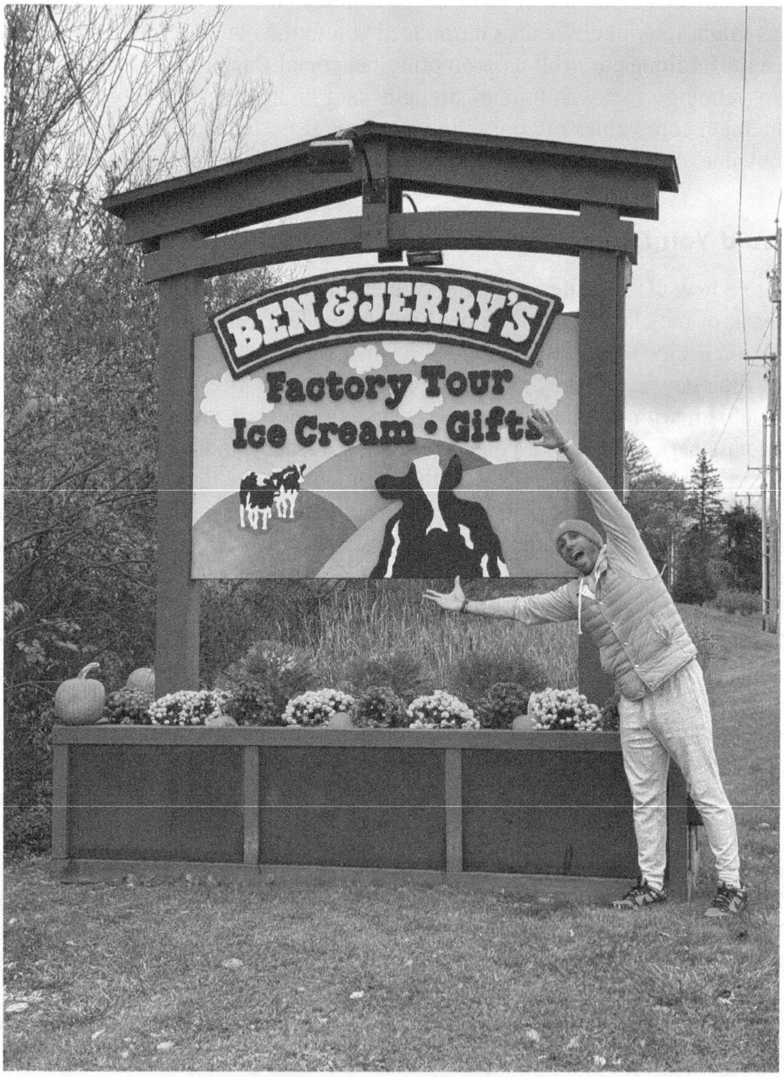

Dr. Milo Dodson at Ben & Jerry's. Photograph by author.

Counseling Psychologist Spotlight: Corporate Setting

Dr. Milo Dodson

Dr. Milo Dodson is the Senior Manager of Diversity and Inclusion and Community Outreach for Belkin International, Inc. (Yes, the Belkin you have heard of – the global tech accessories company). Milo says that working at Belkin is honestly a dream come true. When he was a kid, he vividly remembers spending hours walking through Best Buy with his grandpa and getting lost in all of the tech (so effectively that staff called him out on the loudspeaker to tell him to meet his grandpa at the front of the store). Other times during childhood, he would ALWAYS ask his mom "why?" about everything – from "why is the sky blue?" to "why does the toilet flush that way?" right before he would run outside and play with his friends. At the core of this insatiable curiosity was a desire to learn more and help people. He says that having the opportunity to work at Belkin as a counseling psychologist offers something exciting and meaningful every day. What he loves the most is leveraging psychological science and highlighting relevant data to build community, offer psychoeducational workshops, improve wellness, and empower collaborative innovation! Not only with colleagues in the United States, but also around the world.

One of Milo's favorite experiences from his job was in May of 2023 when he traveled to Athens, Greece, to present two workshops for colleagues. They covered everything from adopting a growth mindset to creating psychological safety to enhancing active listening. He says that traveling to Greece had been a lifelong dream and considers being able to do so for work – working as a counseling psychologist at a tech accessories company – as a blessing.

The Society of Counseling Psychology has been Milo's professional "home" since his first days of grad school. He says:

> The breadth and depth of training we receive (as counseling psychologists) is remarkable and second to none. My curiosity was initially pulled in by leaders in the field and my heart is still centered there because of SCP's Mission and Values: 'Our members share a commitment to a holistic psychological perspective that is strengths-based, person- and community-centered, systems-oriented, contextually aware, multiculturally inclusive, socially just, and integrative of vocational and lifespan issues.'

Milo lives out this mission through advocacy work. Since 2018, he has volunteered with Colin Kaepernick and Nessa Diab's Know Your Rights Camp. In various cities across the country, he has led workshops with hundreds of youths about destigmatizing mental health in Black and Brown communities and the importance of finding joy. Milo previously co-hosted a podcast with nationally acclaimed radio personality Yesi Ortiz called Mental Health is R.E.A.L. (Reflecting Empathy And Love) to discuss wellness, mental health, and social justice.

Outside of his job, Milo loves to travel with his wife around the world. He says he tries to "Peacefully place my feet in the grass to feel grounded but uplifted at the same time." He practices mindful photography. He highly recommends "ice cream, ice cream, ice cream" to everyone and gives a shoutout to his friends Ben & Jerry for helping empower him to finish his dissertation (see his photo as evidence of his devotion to ice cream!).

Milo serves SCP as a representative to the American Psychological Association Council of Representatives. He is also a member of Alpha Phi Alpha Fraternity, Inc. Before he joined Belkin, he worked as a staff psychologist at UC-Irvine's Counseling Center. Milo earned his PhD in counseling psychology from the University of Illinois Urbana-Champaign (UIUC). He also holds an MS in counseling psychology from UIUC and a BA in psychology with a minor in Africana

Studies from the University of Notre Dame. He is a licensed psychologist in California and holds a Mindfulness Certification.

Milo's message to you, the reader, is his motto in life: "Love and BE loved."

References

Afrasibi, S., & Fattahi, Z. (2017). A comparative study of self-actualization perspective in psychology and Islam. *World Family Medicine, 15*(9), 104–111. https://doi.org/10.5742/MEWFM.2017.93104

American Psychological Association. (2014). Guidelines for prevention in psychology. *American Psychologist, 69*(3), 285–296. https://doi.org/10.1037/a0034569

American Psychological Association. (2018). Positive psychology. *APA Dictionary of Psychology*. https://dictionary.apa.org/positive-psychology

American Public Health Association. (n.d.). *What is public health?* https://www.apha.org/what-is-public-health

Burrow-Sánchez, J. J., & Hops, H. (2019). A randomized trial of culturally accommodated versus standard group treatment for Latina/o adolescents with substance use disorders: Posttreatment through 12-month outcomes. *Cultural Diversity and Ethnic Minority Psychology, 25*(3), 311–322. https://doi.org/10.1037/cdp0000249

Chamberlin, J. (2011, October). Flourish 2051. Martin E. P. Seligman's new initiative calls for a global boost in well-being by 2051. *Monitor on Psychology, 42*(9), 56. https://www.apa.org/monitor/2011/10/seligman

Comas-Díaz, L. (2020). Liberation psychotherapy. In L. Comas-Díaz & E. Torres Rivera (Eds.), *Liberation psychology: Theory, method, practice, and social justice* (pp. 169–185). American Psychological Association. https://doi.org/10.1037/0000198-010

Das, A. K. (1989). Beyond self-actualization. *International Journal for the Advancement of Counselling, 12*, 13–27.

Florsheim, P., & Burrow-Sánchez, J. J. (2023). Preparing for parenthood: Validating a mixed method approach to assessing the coparenting capacity of young expectant fathers and mothers. *Family Process, 63*(3), 1336–1355. https://doi.org/10.1111/famp.12904

Frisch, M. B. (2006). *Quality of life therapy: Applying a life satisfaction approach to positive psychology and cognitive therapy.* John Wiley & Sons Ltd.

Gone, J. P. (2021). Decolonization as methodological innovation in counseling psychology: Method, power, and process in reclaiming American Indian therapeutic traditions. *Journal of Counseling Psychology, 68*(3), 259–270. https://doi.org/10.1037/cou0000500

Knutson, D., Matsuno, E., Goldbach, C., Hashtpari, H., & Smith, N. G. (2021). Advocating for transgender and nonbinary affirmative spaces in graduate education. *Higher Education, 83*(2), 461–479. https://doi.org/10.1007/s10734-020-00673-5

Koch, J. M., Knutson, D., Lee, H. S., Robitschek, C., Wang, K., Burdine, K., & Shin, J. (2025). Microaffirmations as positive social actions: Boosting protective factors and support for marginalized populations. *Journal of Prevention and Health Promotion, 6*(4), 1–28. https://doi.org/10.1177/26320770241309101

Koch, J. M., Knutson, D., Loche, L., Loche, R. W., Lee, H. S., & Federici, D. J. (2020). A qualitative inquiry of microaffirmative experiences among culturally diverse graduate students. *Current Psychology, 41*(5), 2883–2895. https://doi.org/10.1007/s12144-020-00811-3

Lopez, S. J., Floyd, R. K., Ulven, J. C., & Snyder, C. R. (2000). Hope therapy: Helping clients build a house of hope. In C. R. Snyder (Ed.), *Handbook of hope: Theory, measures, and applications* (pp. 123–150). Academic Press. https://doi.org/10.1016/B978-012654050-5/50009-9

Magyar-Moe, J. L., Owens, R. L., & Conoley, C. W. (2015). Positive psychological interventions in counseling: What every counseling psychologist should know. *The Counseling Psychologist, 43*(4), 508–557. https://doi.org/10.1177/0011000015573776

Martin, J. L., Burrow-Sánchez, J. J., Iwamoto, D. K., Glidden-Tracey, C. E., & Vaughan, E. L. (2016). Counseling psychology and substance use: Implications for training, practice, and research. *The Counseling Psychologist, 44*(8), 1106–1131. https://doi.org/10.1177/0011000016667536

Maslow, A. H. (1991). Critique of self-actualization theory. *The Journal of Humanistic Education and Development, 29*(3), 103–108. https://doi.org/10.1002/j.2164-4683.1991.tb00010.x (Unpublished paper, 1966).

Maslow, A. H. (1943). A theory of human motivation. *Psychological Review, 50*(4), 370–396.

Neville, H. A. (2024). Justice & joy: Transforming healing praxis in counseling psychology and beyond. *The Counseling Psychologist, 52*(8), 1372–1396. https://doi.org/10.1177/00110000241298715

Peterson, C., & Seligman, M. E. P. (2004). *Character strengths and virtues: A handbook and classification.* Oxford University Press; American Psychological Association.

Pieterse, A. L., Lewis, J. A., & Miller, M. J. (2023). Dismantling and eradicating anti-Blackness and systemic racism. *Journal of Counseling Psychology, 70*(3), 235–243. https://doi.org/10.1037/cou0000660

Prevention Section, Society of Counseling Psychology. (2025). *Prevention section.* https://www.div17.org/prevention

Ravilochan, T. (2021, June 14). What I got wrong: Revisions to my post about the Blackfoot and Maslow. *GatherFor.* https://gatherfor.medium.com/i-got-it-wrong-7d9b314fadff

Rogers, C. R. (1946). Significant aspects of client-centered therapy. *American Psychologist, 1*(10), 415–422.

Rogers, C. R. (1963). The actualizing tendency in relation to "motives" and to consciousness. In M. R. Jones (Ed.), *Nebraska symposium on motivation* (pp. 1–24). University of Nebraska Press.

Romano, J. L., & Hage, S. M. (2000). Prevention: A call to action. *The Counseling Psychologist, 28*(6), 854–856. https://doi.org/10.1177/0011000000286007

Romano, J. L., Koch, J. M., & Wong, Y. J. (2012). Prevention in counseling psychology: Promoting education, health, and well-being across the life cycle. In N. A. Fouad, J. A. Carter & L. M. Subich (Eds.), *APA handbook of counseling psychology, Vol. 1.* Theories, research, and methods (pp. 345–367). American Psychological Association. https://doi.org/10.1037/13754-013

Ruini, C., & Fava, G. A. (2004). Clinical applications of well-being therapy. In P. A. Linsley & S. Joseph (Eds.), *Positive psychology in practice* (pp. 371–387). John Wiley & Sons, Inc. https://doi.org/10.1002/9780470939338.ch23

Scheel, M. J., Klentz Davis, C., & Henderson, J. D. (2012). Therapist use of client strengths: A qualitative study of positive processes. *The Counseling Psychologist, 41*(3), 392–427. https://doi.org/10.1177/0011000012439427

Schneider, K. J. (2011). Toward a humanistic positive psychology: Why can't we just get along? *Existential Analysis, 22*(1), 32–38.

Section on Positive Psychology. (n.d.) *APA Division 17 Positive Psychology.* http://www.div17pospsych.com

Seligman, M. E. P. (2011). *Flourish: A visionary new understanding of happiness and well-being.* Free Press.

Singh, A. A. (2020). Building a counseling psychology of liberation: The path behind us, under us, and before us. *The Counseling Psychologist, 48*(8), 1109–1130. https://doi.org/10.1177/0011000020959007

Singh, A. A., Finan, R., & Estevez, R. (2023). Queer and trans resilience: Moving from affirmation to liberation in our collective healing. In J. M. Koch, E. E. Townsend-Bell & R. Hubach (Eds.), *Identity as resilience in minoritized communities* (pp. 1–22). Springer Nature Switzerland AG. https://psycnet.apa.org/doi/10.1007/978-3-031-38977-1_1

Smith, E. J. (2006). Strengths-based counseling. *The Counseling Psychologist, 34*(1), 13–79. https://doi.org/10.1177/0011000005277018

Steele, B., Martin, M., Sciarra, A., Melendez-Torres, G. J., Esposti, M. D., & Humphreys, D. K. (2024). The prevalence of sexual assault among higher education students: A systematic review with meta-analyses. *Trauma, Violence, & Abuse, 25*(3), 1885–1898. https://doi.org/10.1177/15248380231196119

Sue, D. W., & Spanierman, L. B. (2020). *Microaggressions in everyday life* (2nd ed.). John Wiley & Sons, Inc.

Waterman, A. S. (2013). The humanistic psychology-positive psychology divide: Contrasts in philosophical foundations. *American Psychologist, 68*(3), 124–133. https://doi.org/10.1037/a0032168

Wong, Y. J. (2006). Strengths-centered therapy: A social constructionist, virtues-based psychotherapy. *Psychotherapy: Theory, Research, Practice, Training, 43*(2), 133–146. https://doi.org/10.1037/0033-3204.43.2.133

Wong, Y. J., Cheng, H. L., Pérez-Rojas, A., Kang, J., & Koch, J. M. (2025). Cross-racial microaffirmations: Concepts and practical applications. *The Counseling Psychologist, 53*(7), 927–957. https://doi.org/10.1177/00110000251352573

Chapter 3

Cultural Context in Counseling Psychology Practice

What Does It Mean to Be You?

Around the world, people and societies are constantly faced with the question, "What does it mean to be us?" In other words, what does it mean to be American, South Korean, or German? What does it mean to be African American or Asian American? What does it mean to be Muslim, Jewish, or Catholic? What does it mean to be neurodivergent or disabled? What does it mean to be poor, working class, or middle class? Think about the parts of what make up "you." You may have all kinds of different identities that contribute to who you are. We think that the abundant differences (and similarities) of human beings are beautiful and are what make our world so rich and full of potential.

Unfortunately, these differences can also contribute to a lot of conflict and misunderstanding. People's beliefs about culture and who "belongs" can motivate political elections, show up in laws and policies, and inspire entire social movements. For example, when a country accepts and resettles a large number of refugees, there can be a social backlash driven by fears that the country's identity, traditions, and cultures will be compromised. When there is social unrest, vulnerable populations can become the target of laws, policies, and political and legal backlash. Another example in the United States is the large number of recent laws and policies limiting the rights of transgender people. The access of transgender people to bathrooms has been used as a tool to drive election turnout and motivate support for specific social and economic policies (Knutson et al., 2021b).

Supporting marginalized people like transgender populations and immigrant communities can be risky business. Discussions about inclusion, diversity, and equity can cause strong reactions and be viewed as counter-cultural by people in power. Terminology like *diversity, equity, and inclusion* (DEI) have been taken up in political discussions and used to justify laws, mobilize voters, and reshape education systems. Across the United States and globally, political and educational leaders seem to be at odds about what diversity means and how it should be taught, if taught at all. Multicultural awareness itself has even become a political issue. In some places, if you are culturally attuned, you are assumed to have a progressive or liberal belief system. Our perspective is that counseling psychologists can have a wide range of beliefs and backgrounds. But regardless of those beliefs and backgrounds, counseling psychologists do not get to select who they serve as clients. All people have varying cultural backgrounds, so all counseling psychologists need to be prepared to care for all human beings with their varying pains, backgrounds, experiences, and beliefs. This is not a political issue; it is a human being issue.

We want to be up-front and honest with you: These discussions and conflicts are affecting the world of counseling psychology. Counseling psychologists have long been at the forefront of movements to include people through multicultural counseling and social justice advocacy.

DOI: 10.4324/9781003439899-3

However, the reality that counseling psychologists face is that we live in a world that is not always ready for these movements. In this chapter, we attempt to bring you an approach that respects the long tradition of counseling psychology considering the cultural context in which people live. Later, in Chapter 13, we discuss advocacy efforts to promote social change. We want to start by saying that we believe multicultural issues are vitally important for everyone inside and outside of the profession of counseling psychology and we will expand on this throughout the chapter and the book. If you love and value people and want the best for them, this chapter is for you.

Toward that end, in this chapter, you will discover how considering cultural context, or seeing a person with unique identities in their unique systems, is another defining feature of counseling psychology. We introduce you to the concepts of diversity, multicultural counseling, and social justice, from a counseling psychology lens. We describe the interactions of mental health with factors such as poverty, social class, nation of origin, religion, race, ethnicity, gender, sexual orientation, disability, languages spoken, location, and age. You will learn about microaggressions, intersectionality, and minority stress, as well as the importance of celebrating cultural backgrounds and identities with joy and pride.

Cultural Trends in Focus

It is easy to get distracted by cultural trends in any country, society, or culture. The passage of marriage equality laws or legal restrictions on reproductive health can cause tears of joy and tears of disappointment. The important thing to remember is that the goal of counseling psychologists is to create optimal conditions for any client to be the best version of themselves they can possibly be, not to encourage clients to have certain beliefs or behaviors. In other words, counseling psychologists are aware of the current sociopolitical context, but when they provide therapy for a client, they must be fully and empathically present with the person across from them as who they are and recognize that their identities, beliefs, and cultural backgrounds shape them. You will remember from the chapter on human flourishing that counseling psychologists believe, given optimal conditions to thrive, people will heal and become the healthiest version of themselves (Rogers, 1957).

Case Example

With the frame for this chapter set, we want to start by introducing you to a client. Let's imagine Yukiko, who comes to counseling for worries and anxiety that she describes as all-consuming and getting in the way of doing her work. If we focus on her concerns and diagnosis of Generalized Anxiety Disorder, we might give her a series of tests to determine the level of anxiety, we might work specifically on ways to get the anxiety down (perhaps using cognitive-behavioral therapy), and we might encourage her to see a psychiatrist or physician about medication to ease her feelings of anxiety. However, if we think about her concerns more holistically and focus on who she is as a human being, we might learn that Yukiko is Japanese-American and her family has been in the United States since the 1800s. Her grandparents were forced to give up their home and business during World War II to go to internment camps.

Yukiko lives in Texas, and her son attends a large state university a few hours away. In following the news, she has learned about high anti-Asian sentiment and recent physical attacks targeting Asian-American people on his campus. She also reports that she is an engineer in a largely male work environment. Her company went through a reorganization and she was put on a new team. On this team, her new coworkers seem to expect her to do menial tasks like answering the phone, making coffee, fixing the copier, and so on, and her manager told her she wasn't being a team player when she talked to him about it.

With all of this in mind, it makes a lot of sense that Yukiko is worried – about her son's safety and about her productivity at work – but rather than thinking "Yukiko is an anxious person," we might think "Wow, Yukiko's mental health is being affected by some situations related to her cultural context – as a mom, as a woman, as a Japanese-American person, as a Texan, as an engineer." This could possibly shift the approach we take with Yukiko in addressing her anxiety. For example, rather than just teaching coping mechanisms, the counseling psychologist might also work with Yukiko on role-playing how to advocate for herself in her workplace.

Cultural Context as a Foundation

The field of counseling psychology has a long history of valuing work with human beings within their context. As mentioned in the previous chapter, counseling psychologists consider humans holistically. Consideration of culture and context has historically been a large part of the mission and values of the Society of Counseling Psychology and counseling psychologists (Vera & Speight, 2003). The mission of the Society of Counseling Psychology states that counseling psychologists have a perspective that is contextually aware, multiculturally inclusive, and socially just (Society of Counseling Psychology [SCP], n.d.). Issues of culture are explicitly recognized through their Value 3: "Considering context, systems, and intersecting social identities in conceptualizing individuals, communities, problems, and interventions" (SCP, n.d., para. 1). The focus on culture is also integrated into values around research, practice, training, policies, advocacy, and leadership. Therefore, throughout this text, issues related to cultural context are integrated into each chapter.

Some people consider multicultural counseling to be counseling psychology's *fourth wave* or *fourth force*, after psychodynamic theory, humanistic/existential theory, and cognitive-behavioral theory (we talk about all of these other theories in Chapter 6) (Pedersen, 1991). But rather than thinking of it as a separate or fourth group of theories, we think multicultural issues should always be considered as part of the foundation of counseling psychology practice. Counseling psychologists have been at the forefront of the development of inclusive psychological theories such as liberation psychology, social justice training, anti-racist efforts, and advocacy in psychology (Gone, 2021; Goodman et al., 2004; Singh, 2016; Vera & Speight, 2003). As we discuss in other chapters, counseling psychology has a strong reputation for focusing on strengths and multicultural competence in training and practice.

What Do We Mean by Culture?

Before we get too much further, we should probably consider this question: What do we mean by *culture*? What do you think of when you hear the word culture? What are the aspects that make up someone's culture? You might think about food, art, customs, and so on that make up a group's or nation's culture. As counseling psychologists, we think about those factors, but we are mostly focused on how they relate to the cultural background of the clients or people whom we serve. One model to consider different aspects of individuals' culture is the "RESPECTFUL" model (D'Andrea & Daniels, 2001). As the acronym indicates, this model includes a special recognition of or emphasis on:

- Religious or spiritual identity
- Economic class background

- Sexual identity and gender identity
- Psychological maturity
- Ethnic or racial identity
- Chronological or developmental challenges (lifespan development)
- Trauma and threats to well-being
- Family background and history
- Unique physical characteristics (including disabilities)
- Location of residence and language differences

This model is a little dated, but it gives you an idea of the different things that can contribute to someone's cultural background and identities. We would argue that there are other aspects of culture and context that might not be included here, such as enlisted military or veteran status, rural or urban location, political affiliation, neurodivergence and other invisible disabilities such as long COVID, generation group such as Baby Boomers or Generation Z, and educational background (Armstrong, 2015; Atuel & Castro, 2018; Iyengar et al., 2012; Nalbandian et al., 2021; Smalley et al., 2012; Twenge et al., 2010). Can you think of any others that perhaps are not captured by this model? As our sociopolitical climate shifts and changes, it is likely that other cultural factors will emerge in the future. It is important for counseling psychologists to understand and be comfortable with different aspects of people's identities. Counseling psychologists also need to understand their own identities and biases they may hold.

Everyone has different aspects of their culture that come together to make them a unique person. Some people think that *multicultural counseling* is only for clients who have some kind of marginalized or oppressed identity, but we believe that all people have different cultural backgrounds and identities that may play a role in their mental health and reasons for seeking counseling. Further, we believe everyone is harmed by racism, sexism, discrimination, and oppression. Some have described multicultural counseling as attending to the factors that are different between a counselor and client – but in fact, there will never be a true cultural match between a counselor and client, so all counseling should be considered multicultural counseling. Multicultural counseling, therefore, is hugely important to a counseling psychologist's work with clients. All counseling psychologists should approach each client or interaction with the understanding that there will be cultural similarities, and differences, some of which will be visible, such as skin tone, and some of which will be invisible, such as some disabilities.

Words Matter

It is important to acknowledge that words matter. We want to note that worries about what words, terms, or language to use can be super anxiety-provoking for many people. And just when you think one term might be okay to use, you might learn someone else takes offense or a new term becomes in fashion. On the other hand, you may feel that one particular term is the only one that is "correct" and may shut other people down for having a different understanding. This makes many people avoid talking about issues related to culture out of fear. We encourage you to give yourself and others grace and flexibility as we are all learning. The American Psychological Association (APA) has guidance on language for counseling psychologists. They wrote the APA Publication Manual with a chapter on bias-free language, and they have *Journal Article Reporting Standards* for publications (APA, 2020).

These guides are meant to support psychologists in the language they use. For example, they recommend that when working with specific racial or ethnic populations, it is best to define them as specifically as possible: "Hmong people living in Minnesota" is more descriptive than "Asian American people in the Midwest." The guides also suggest using person-first language, such as "person who has bipolar disorder" rather than "a bipolar person," but there is flexibility because some groups want to be defined by their identity, such as some autistic people (APA, 2020). We strongly recommend that readers of this text take a moment to review these APA publications

Table 3.1 Terms commonly used interchangeably

Terms Used Interchangeably	*Key Issues*	*What To Do Instead*
Race **Ethnicity** **Nationality** **Culture**	Race relates more to the socially constructed categories used to classify people in society, often based on visible physical characteristics, whereas ethnicity refers to ancestry and traditions. Sometimes people use "culture" as a euphemism for race or ethnicity.	Be specific. For example: Race: Asian American Ethnicity: Hmong Culture: This could mean all kinds of things that could include race, ethnicity, and nationality but could also include religion, socio-economic status (SES), disability, and other things. Try not to use it as a substitute when what you really mean is something like race or ethnicity.
Sex **Sexuality** **Sexual orientation** **Gender** **Gender expression** **Gender identity**	People often use broad acronyms to group people such as LGBTQ+ or queer, but there are important differences in sex, gender, and relationships. For example, gender identity is a person's core sense of who they are whereas gender expression is how a person interacts with the world around them (e.g., dresses, accessorizes, behaves).	It's a great idea to look for resources online to help you understand all these differences. We recommend that you use the language that other people use to describe themselves or their communities. For example, if a woman describes herself as a lesbian, you might not want to refer to her as gay. And a lot of transgender people don't identify as queer or part of the queer community. Please don't assume anything about anyone based on their appearance.
Social class **Social status** **Socioeconomic status (SES)**	These terms differ from someone's actual financial income and include things like perceived standing in society. People generally use SES to collapse various aspects of social resource access under one label. Social class isn't just defined by income but also by culture, education, and occupation and may not change much over generations. SES might be more related to wealth or financial resources and may change across someone's life. Social status is more like someone's perceived prestige.	Again, it's great to understand the differences between these terms and to be specific whenever possible.

for further guidance related to appropriate language use (APA, 2020). We will not rehash those documents here, but we want to draw attention to some ways people use groups of terms interchangeably that are not directly related, as we demonstrate in Table 3.1. We also want to note that language is constantly changing and evolving, and it can be hard to keep up, so just do your best.

As you read over the opening pages of this chapter, you may have started noticing another set of terms people tend to use interchangeably: diversity, equity, inclusion, multiculturalism, social justice, and so on. Just like the terms we discussed in Table 3.1, it's a good idea to understand key terms and approaches to inclusive psychological practice. Before we move forward with this chapter, it is important for us to define terms and clarify our approach to the topic. This is good practice in counseling psychology work. For example, there are a ton of acronyms to describe different LGBTQ+ communities: lesbian, gay, bisexual (LGB), GLBT, TN/B, LGTBTQIA++, and more. In their writing and publications, counseling psychologists who work with LGBTQ+ populations will identify the acronym they plan to use, define it, and explain why they are using that acronym in place of other options. In this text, we use LGBTQ+ to include people who identify as lesbian, gay, bisexual, transgender, and queer, and the + includes related identities such as non-binary or questioning.

- *Multicultural therapy* considers clients' diversity in race, ethnicity, spirituality, sexual orientation, ability and disability, and social class and socioeconomic status (SES). It also takes into account the potential bias of the counseling psychologist and the history of oppressed and marginalized groups (APA, 2018).
- *Diversity* is a broad umbrella term that refers to the collection of identities that vary such as age, race, ethnicity, gender identity, sexual orientation, religion, and disability(APA, 2023b).
- *Equity* refers to providing resources needed to support flourishing in populations that face disadvantages and barriers to resources that impact well-being (APA, 2021).
- *Inclusion* refers to "an environment that offers affirmation, celebration, and appreciation of different approaches, styles, perspectives, and experiences, thus allowing all individuals to bring in their whole selves (and all their identities) and to demonstrate their strengths and capacity" (APA, 2023c).
- *Social justice* refers to efforts to reduce inequities and promote changes that reduce human suffering and increase human thriving (Vasquez, 2012).
- *Cultural humility* is an internal process by which an individual engages in critical self-exploration and commits to remaining open to learning from people who are different from them (Hook et al., 2013).
- *Cultural competence* involves an ability to effectively engage with clients and others across cultural differences and diverse identities (APA, 2023a).
- *Intersectionality* is a theory that attempts to explain or identify how various diverse identities interact or overlap to generate contextually specific experiences of social inequity, privilege, discrimination, and so on (Crenshaw, 1991).
- *Identity* refers to an individual's sense of self, defined by physical, psychological, and interpersonal characteristics that are not wholly shared with any other person (APA, 2018).
- We also use the terms *marginalized* and *minoritized* (instead of minority) in this text. Both of these terms refer to a group of people being placed in an unimportant or depowered place in society (APA, 2023d). You may wonder why we use this. It's because *minority* is a misnomer. For example, Latinx people in some places in the United States outnumber White people, so they are not actually the minority of the population. Also, terms like these point out that people are marginalized by others (or systems) and there is nothing inherently problematic about being in the minority or at the margins.

Take a moment to reflect on the differences between these terms and how they interact with each other. In this chapter, we use the broad term *multicultural* to refer to efforts by counseling psychologists to make psychological practice effective for the broadest range of individuals possible. However, as you continue to read through this chapter, please keep in mind how the terms we use interact and inform each other. Multicultural topics are complex, and you will get the most out of this chapter if you reflect on the deeper, nuanced meaning of the content we present here.

Origins of Multicultural Counseling

The emphasis on multicultural counseling arose from the need to consider the history, experiences, and worldviews of diverse populations in understanding mental health and treatment (Sue et al., 2022). There has been a lot of discussion in the field of counseling psychology about the need for *multiculturally competent* counseling psychologists (Arredondo et al., 1996). As we mentioned in Chapter 1, all the way back in 1962, Gilbert Wrenn, a notable counseling psychologist, wrote about the problems of *cultural encapsulation*, what we might describe today as basically living in your own cultural capsule or bubble (Wrenn, 1962). Since that time, in the United States, we have seen civil rights movements, women's rights movements and calls for counseling psychologists to be better prepared to offer culturally sensitive, responsive, and appropriate approaches with clients (Sue et al., 2022). Historically, counseling psychology theories and approaches have been based on Western (Europe/United States) ideas (Pedersen, 1991). Unfortunately, this means they have not been inclusive of many populations of human beings that we as counseling psychologists serve. So multicultural counseling emerged as an answer to that lack of inclusivity.

Common Theories, Models, and Approaches

Counseling psychologists have proposed several models to help psychologists provide better multicultural services (Arredondo et al., 1996; Sue et al., 2022). Some current models are highly theoretical, and others have spawned a long line of research studies, projects, and clinical tools (Ridley et al., 2021a). There are also ongoing debates over the strengths and limitations of multicultural approaches and frameworks (Ridley et al., 2021a). We review some of the most common approaches below, but you should be aware that the field of multicultural counseling psychology is constantly expanding. Self-awareness and cultural humility are a process of lifelong learning and multicultural counseling psychologists work hard to keep up with emerging developments in the field (Hook et al., 2013).

Multicultural Counseling Competence

One leading approach, the *multicultural counseling competence* model, was proposed by Derald Wing Sue and colleagues (1992) and further developed over the years by teams of scholars (Sue et al., 2022). This approach to education and training in multicultural counseling includes three main components: knowledge, awareness, and skills. Over time, Sue and colleagues added a further emphasis on action or social justice advocacy (Sue et al., 2022).

- *Knowledge* refers to the actual content knowledge that a counseling psychologist might have about a certain cultural group (Sue et al., 1992).

  For example, a counseling psychologist might study and engage with the history of Asian immigration to the West Coast of the United States.

- *Awareness* refers to the awareness a counseling psychologist has of themself such as their biases, groups they feel comfortable with, or groups they might hold stereotypes about (Sue et al., 1992).

  For example, a counseling psychologist might realize they hold an inaccurate belief that Asian American people are naturally gifted and smart, so they educate themselves about the harms of perpetuating the Model Minority Myth (Rajagopal & Durkee, 2024).

- *Skills* refer to a counselor's ability to provide effective, quality care for diverse clients (Sue et al., 1992).

  For example, a counseling psychologist might use more collectivist, mindfulness-based approaches when working with South Korean clients.

- *Action* refers to the need to be more directly involved in broader social systems and power imbalances (Sue et al., 2022).

  For example, a counseling psychologist might provide trainings at a university counseling center to raise awareness of the impact of discrimination on Asian-American students.

Over the years, other scholars have added or proposed other factors that could contribute to multicultural counseling competence. For example, one newer version of the model emphasizes the counseling relationship and incorporates elements of intersectionality theory (Ratts et al., 2016). Ridley and colleagues recently introduced the process model of multicultural counseling competence (2021b), which offers practical guidance about how to implement awareness, skills, and knowledge across different phases of counseling, with a deep-structure incorporation of culture. The key tenets of multicultural counseling competence have been adopted and incorporated into many behavioral health training programs and accrediting standards. It is important for you to be familiar with key concepts that have shaped the history of multicultural competence in counseling psychology.

Multicultural Orientation

Another newer model that counseling psychologists have put forward to consider working with diverse populations is called the *multicultural orientation* framework (Davis et al., 2018). The framework was developed to complement multicultural counseling competence and place a greater emphasis on a counseling psychologist's *way of being* with clients (Davis et al., 2018). In other words, some people consider multicultural counseling as a way of *doing* things or how well therapists implement knowledge, awareness, skills, and action, whereas multicultural orientation might be considered more as a way of *being* with the client. Multicultural orientation also includes three main components: cultural humility, cultural comfort, and cultural opportunities (Davis et al., 2018). Counseling psychologists may use one, two, or all three of these components at any time in their work with clients.

- *Cultural humility* refers to a counseling psychologist's ability to accurately identify their own limitations and to focus on the needs and experiences of others (Davis et al., 2018).

  For example, a counseling psychologist might acknowledge ways they were socialized to hold bias against Northeast Asian people while helping a South Korean client to process experiences of discrimination and oppression enacted by people from a similar racial and ethnic background as the therapist.

- *Cultural opportunities* refer to whether counseling psychologists are motivated to engage with a client's salient cultural identities (Davis et al., 2018).

  For example, a counseling psychologist might make space for a South Korean client to share what it has been like to transition from one culture to another or to recount specific experiences of marginalization or oppression.

- *Cultural comfort* refers to things like how comfortable the counseling psychologist is talking about cultural differences and similarities, or how comfortable they are in interacting with people different from (and similar to) themselves (Davis et al., 2018).

  For example, as a counseling psychologist practices cultural humility and takes cultural opportunities, they may notice themselves relaxing into the conversation, trusting themselves to use accurate terms, and holding fewer biases and discriminatory views.

A great thing about the multicultural orientation framework is that there is emerging research that this approach is linked to psychotherapy effectiveness. Research shows that therapist's use of multicultural orientation, and particularly the aspect of cultural humility, is linked to perceived improvement and better alliance between the therapist and the client (Davis et al., 2018; Owen, 2013).

Stressors

Minority Stress

As we mentioned at the beginning of this chapter, one of the reasons we consider cultural context is that culture can play a role in both psychological distress and resilience for people. Here, we will elaborate on some of the factors that contribute to people's mental health. One of those factors is called *minority stress*. Minority stress is a theory that originally attempted to explain the impact of discrimination and marginalization on LGB people (Brooks, 1981; Meyer, 2003). Meyer (2003) hypothesized that LGB people experience a different kind of stress than the rest of the population because of their stigmatized social status, which puts them at higher risk for negative health outcomes.

Since then, scholars have expanded the notion of minority stress to include other marginalized groups and identities such as low socioeconomic status and People of Color (for example, Balsam et al., 2011; Shangani et al., 2020). The minority stress model is an important tool for counseling psychologists because it brings awareness to the deep and impactful role discrimination and marginalization can play in mental health (Frost & Meyer, 2023). It basically says that people don't have mental health issues because they're gay, for example. Rather, they have mental health issues because of how society treats them because they're gay.

Microaggressions

Another key dynamic that is important to understand is the role of microaggressions in mental health. Microaggressions are seemingly small, indirect, and hard to identify markers of rejection or discrimination (Sue et al., 2007; Pierce, 1970; Wong et al., 2024). Because microaggressions are so subtle, they can be hard to identify. Here are some examples for you to reflect on:

- At her intake session, Jennifer tells her therapist that she grew up in a rural area and the therapist quickly asks Jennifer if she finished high school.
- A White therapist appears fascinated by her Black woman client's hair.

- A therapist asks their client, Tom, for an emergency contact and then briefly widens their eyes when Tom says his emergency contact is his husband, Chad.
- A therapist tells a client who was born in India that their English "is so good."

Take a moment to reflect on this short list of examples. Do you think that all of the examples qualify as microaggressions? How would you feel if your therapist assumed you were uneducated or acted like your relationships were strange? Have you ever exhibited behaviors similar to the ones in these examples? One of the things about microaggressions is that they are so subtle that other people may invalidate these experiences with statements like "You're imagining it" or "I'm sure they didn't mean it that way." This can actually perpetuate the harm of microaggressions. As you reflect on these questions, explore ways you could use your awareness to increase your multicultural competence.

Resilience

There is often a strong focus on problems and stressors for people with different cultural identities. However, focusing on only these things can create something called a *deficit model*, or the notion that people only have deficits. It is also important to recognize that underrepresented populations have incredible resilience and potential (Koch et al., 2023). In fact, often, people's cultural identities can serve as a source of strength and resilience as they offer "joy, celebration, and solidarity" (Koch et al., 2023, p. ix). For example, Neville emphasized the importance of Black joy as a way to counter some of the negative narratives around Black American identity in the United States (2024). She suggested that joy can be a "powerful force for healing" (Neville, 2024, p. 1372).

Likewise, Singh (2016, 2020), Comas-Díaz and Rivera (2020), and others have spoken about *liberation psychology*, in which people are free from discrimination and oppression, which allows them to truly heal and experience affirmation and well-being. We encourage you to keep in mind that culture can be a source of strength and resilience. For example, LGBTQ+ people may experience pride, support, and acceptance within their communities, and this can be a source of resilience (Meyer, 2015). Has this been true for you at all? Think about your own identities and cultural factors (remember the RESPECTFUL model). Have you found support and strength from your religious community? From people who share a similar heritage to you? From others who speak the same language? Has a disability been a source of strength? Or perhaps you have experienced the joy in community from attending an LGBTQ+ pride celebration.

Microaffirmations

One way to leverage connections and positive interactions inside and outside of therapeutic spaces is through microaffirmations. Like microaggressions, microaffirmations are subtle, indirect and can be hard to put your finger on (Koch et al., 2020, 2025). However, microaffirmations are a byproduct of inclusive behaviors, cultural humility, and openness. In other words, counseling psychologists who have engaged in the processes and used the strategies to build multicultural competence that we have discussed so far are most likely to microaffirm clients. Just as we did with microaggressions, we offer some examples of microaffirmations for you to reflect on, but you can find other, more detailed examples in research on this topic (Koch et al., 2020, 2025):

- At his intake session, a client shares that he was "a jock" in high school and when they get to questions about educational history, the therapist asks if the client went to graduate school.

- A client tells her therapist that she started gender affirming hormone therapy, and the therapist asks with care about how the client is feeling.
- A client who describes themselves as fat breathes a sigh of relief when they enter their therapist's office and notice that the office chairs are roomy and do not have arm rests.
- Take time to reflect again. What makes these examples affirming? How would you feel if your therapist considered who you are when they designed their office or if they assumed you had achieved great things despite the stereotypes that surround your identities? As you explore these questions, reflect on ways you could become more microaffirming in your everyday life.

It is important to note that we did not use the same examples for our discussion of microaffirmations as we did for our discussion of microaggressions. That is because microaffirmations are not the exact opposite of microaffirmations and they are not intended to replace or disqualify the damage done by microaggressions (Koch et al., 2025). Rather, they fit into the overall importance of multicultural counseling competence and further support efforts to increase cultural humility in therapeutic practice. At the same time, the most important part of microaffirmations is the relationship between people – microaffirmations can be perceived as microaggressions, depending on the context.

Multicultural Counseling Limitations

So far, we have focused on the benefits and advantages offered by multicultural counseling models, but we should also acknowledge that, as with any emerging science or structured approach to client care, there are some critiques that have been applied to these models. First, multicultural counseling models and concepts can be difficult to measure (Ridley et al., 2021a). Think back to the examples of microaggressions and microaffirmations. When you were asked to identify what made a behavior microaggressive or microaffirming, was it hard? Did you notice that sometimes the difference depends on how the recipient experiences either behavior? If so, you were noticing that some aspects of multicultural competence can be highly contextual, dependent on hard-to-detect factors, and personalized. It is hard to look inside a person's heart and determine if they truly care and really mean what they say. Even a person with the best intentions can mess up. Interpretations of one statement can differ based on context, relationship, and other factors.

Other scholars point out that these models can come across as highly aspirational and hard to practice. Scholars are continually working to apply and understand affirming and multiculturally competent approaches (e.g., Knutson et al., 2021a). In particular, researchers and scholars have criticized the idea of competence because it can imply that once someone is competent, they have achieved a certain level of skill and therefore, they are "done." In other words, it implies that no further growth is needed, although this is not what the original theorists intended when they used this term. Earlier in this chapter and in other chapters, we note that becoming a counseling psychologist is a lifelong journey and nobody ever really reaches a point of perfection. We would argue that it is okay to have aspirational goals because counseling psychologists should continually strive to be better therapists, researchers, advocates, and human beings. For example, imagine you are a mechanic who has always worked on gas-powered cars. After a while, you think you have seen it all. There is not a gas-powered car in the world you could not work on. Then one day, a customer brings in a battery-powered car and asks you to fix some issues with the car's acceleration. Would you be an incompetent mechanic if you did not know how to fix the car right away? Definitely not, but you would have some room to grow.

Another concern is that those models focus on work with individuals or small groups and do not actually do anything to change society or the environments where people live and work. This is why counseling psychologists have also focused on *social justice* action over the last 20–25 years. We expand on this in Chapter 13 but want to briefly introduce you to this idea here. Social justice has had lots of definitions over the years, and in psychology, social justice practice has been defined as "scholarship and professional action designed to change societal values, structures, policies, and practices, such that disadvantaged or marginalized groups gain increased access to these tools of self-determination" (Goodman et al., 2004, p. 795). Social justice work includes action, activism, and advocacy on a larger scale than individual counseling. The goal of social justice action is to decrease human suffering because what happens outside of therapy also matters.

For example, imagine you are working with a client named Max, a 25-year-old trans man who lives in a very transphobic setting in which he is regularly exposed to insults and hate speech that cause him anxiety and sadness. Every week, you work with Max on skills to reduce anxiety and sadness, but at the end of every session, Max goes back to the toxic environment that is the cause of Max's presenting concerns. If the environment does not change, how likely is Max to be successful in therapy? A counseling psychologist who is committed to social justice might advocate for changes in social and legal policy to make life better for Max as a way to help him heal.

Counseling psychologists also recognize that equity and justice are good for everyone. Imagine what it might be like for high school kids in Max's community. The same gender-based beliefs about Max might show up in insults exchanged between students in the hallway. For example, some young people in the community might be ostracized for not being manly enough or girls might be excluded because they are considered tomboys. That sort of exclusion increases anxiety, sadness, and suicide risk for more people in the community than just Max. A counseling psychologist working with Max would know that policies that benefit Max also help people in society who are hurt by stereotypes and discrimination.

The idea is that if we can work toward social justice, then inequities will be reduced, resulting in better mental health for all people. Counseling psychologists keep issues of diversity in mind while taking a multicultural counseling approach with clients and taking action or engaging in advocacy toward social justice in their workplace, community, or larger society. As we stated at the opening of this chapter, justice and inclusion are for everyone. We all win when we work toward a more connected, caring, and affirming society.

Summary

At the beginning of this chapter, we asked you to reflect on all of the unique components of what makes you "you." We introduced you to the RESPECTFUL model, which is just one way of helping to keep in mind all of the different kinds of cultural factors that contribute to people's identities. We emphasized that cultural context is a foundational aspect of counseling psychology, that all counseling is multicultural counseling, and that multicultural issues affect and include everyone. We discussed the importance of language and introduced some guidance from APA that can be helpful. We briefly talked about the history of multicultural counseling and introduced a couple of major theories, multicultural counseling competence, and the multicultural orientation framework. We also mentioned some limitations of these theories. We described how cultural factors can play a role in both stress and resilience for people. There are entire books that have been written on this subject, so we weren't able to address everything related to multicultural counseling, but we hope this overview gave you a better sense of the role of cultural context for counseling psychologists. In the next chapter, we go on to introduce you to another foundational aspect of counseling psychology, the emphasis on lifespan development. Cultural context also plays a role in lifespan development, as well as every topic we discuss in this textbook.

What Would You Do?

You are working as a resident assistant in a dormitory and one of your residents is Anisa (she/her), an international student from Malaysia. From the very first week of the fall semester, you notice that Anisa seems isolated and unhappy. She usually stays in her room, and she does not attend any of the semester kickoff events. One day, she stops by your room and shares that she feels overwhelmed. She talks about her fears of failing her classes and disappointing her parents. She also talks about feeling out of place and unwanted at the university. She shares that she has been mocked by other students for wearing a hijab and that most of her interactions with professors just center around her English proficiency and how her English is "so good." She has tried to attend the university's Asian International Student Association, but none of the other group members identify as Muslim and most members are from China and South Korea. Although she is proud of her accomplishments and her identities, she says she is finding it harder and harder to deal with the rejection she feels.

- What are the key cultural identities that Anisa holds and values?
- What knowledge do you hold about people with Anisa's identities, values, and experiences?
- What is your level of awareness about any biases, supportive attitudes, or similar experiences you hold as you think about Anisa?
- What skills do you have that you could use to help Anisa navigate the concerns she brought to you?
- What action could you take to change the university environment to make it a healthier place for Anisa and other students?
- Can you think of any resources on campus or in your community that you could offer Anisa?

Counseling Psychologist Spotlight: International Psychology

Dr. Gurusewak Khalsa

Dr. Gurusewak Khalsa is an Associate Professor of Practice at American University in Cairo (AUC), Egypt. At AUC, he teaches master's-level counseling students. On a daily basis, he teaches and talks to students about all kinds of things – their research projects, some aspect of their clinical training, questions about class assignments, or even just "musings on general life circumstances." Gurusewak was born in Canada, moved to the United States at a very young age, and then moved to India at age seven. He has also traveled to and lived in various parts of the world throughout his life. As such, he has always considered himself to be a member of the "global village." He found that psychology as a field presented a lot of opportunities to be actively involved in the global village in ways which he found meaning and resonant with his own experiences and identity, such as working in Afghanistan and South Sudan providing community-based mental health support. When he went back to school to get his doctorate in counseling psychology, he had hoped to work in the global mental health field as a clinician, as a researcher, and as an educator. Working in Cairo and in the Middle East and Northern Africa (MENA) region at large, he says he has been able to fulfill a lot of the career dreams and goals he had for himself as a student. In addition to teaching and his other roles at AUC, he also maintains a clinical and supervision private practice and has been involved with local Non-Governmental Organizations in Cairo that provide mental health support for refugee communities.

One of Gurusewak's favorite aspects of his job is getting to see students develop into professional counselors from their first semester in the program on to graduation and beyond. He says that counseling education is a transformative learning process for those who go through it. When the learning process is working as he hopes it will, he believes it changes people in profound ways,

Dr. Gurusewak Khalsa in front of Egyptian pyramid. Photograph by author.

both students and instructors. He says that getting to be a part of students' developmental growth, and to learn and grow himself through that experience, has been a true honor. He also finds that having students at AUC who are motivated to learn and to apply their knowledge is very rewarding. He finds the challenging parts of his work include doing administrative paperwork, case notes, or other important and necessary documentation and writing. He says,

> Counseling work can also be intense sometimes, which is an amazing part of the human experience to connect with, but it can of course be overwhelming at times, so I do my best to try to take care of myself around that as well.

Gurusewak was drawn to counseling psychology because of its holistic and contextual approach to understanding and supporting people. He feels that counseling is one of the few professions that combines applied mental health support, systemic and cultural awareness, and social justice in a way that really strives to address – in a great deal of depth – the issues people are navigating in their lives. For Gurusewak, there is a lot of meaning and purpose in working with people in that way, and he loves being a part of it.

As a psychologist, he strives to be an active member of his professional community. He serves on organizational or university boards and committees and contributes to the development of policies, resolutions, or public statements on current social issues. He has a strong sense of responsibility to advocate for and contribute to the maintenance or elevation of professional and ethical standards of the profession, which he feels supports the health of not only the counseling community but also anyone who is served by the counseling community. For example, he serves on the APA Committee for Global Psychology, whose mission is to advocate for the recognition and inclusion of global perspectives within APA. This mission is well aligned with his own professional identity and with what he believes to be an important aspect of the health of the psychology profession in general: promoting equitable connection, communication, and collaboration between psychologists from all over the world. He also stays active professionally as a member of several professional organizations, including APA (Divisions 17 [Society of Counseling Psychology], 52 [Society for Global Psychology], and 56 [Trauma Psychology]), the International Association of Applied Psychology, and the Global Psychology Alliance. He considers these organizations to be his professional community and appreciates the role they have in helping psychologists stay connected.

Outside of work, he loves to travel! He enjoys a variety of sports and outdoor activities, from table tennis to basketball. He has a love of games and puzzles that was passed on to members of his family from his grandmother and finds a challenging puzzle with family to be a lot of fun. Before he got involved in the mental health field, he aspired to be an illustrator, which he now does just for his own enjoyment.

Gurusewak earned his PhD in Counseling Psychology from the University of Northern Colorado, his master's in clinical mental health counseling with a multicultural focus from Antioch University, Seattle, and his bachelor's from the University of Washington. He is a licensed psychologist in Washington and is a licensed professional counselor in Colorado and Missouri. He is also a Registered Health Service Psychologist with the National Register of Health Service Psychologists and is an Eye Movement Desensitization and Reprocessing (EMDR) trained clinician through the EMDR International Association.

References

American Psychological Association. (2023a). Cultural competence. *APA Dictionary of Psychology*. https://dictionary.apa.org/cultural-competence

American Psychological Association. (2023b). Diversity. *APA Dictionary of Psychology*. https://dictionary.apa.org/diversity

American Psychological Association. (2023c). Inclusion. *APA Dictionary of Psychology*. https://dictionary.apa.org/inclusion

American Psychological Association. (2023d). Marginalization. *APA Dictionary of Psychology*. https://dictionary.apa.org/marginalization

American Psychological Association. (2018). Multicultural Therapy. *APA Dictionary of Psychology*. https://dictionary.apa.org/multicultural-therapy

American Psychological Association. (2020). *Publication manual of the American Psychological Association* (7th ed.). https://doi.org/10.1037/0000165-000

American Psychological Association. (2021). *Diversity, equity, and inclusion framework.* https://www.apa.org/about/apa/equity-diversity-inclusion/framework.pdf

Armstrong, T. (2015). The myth of the normal brain: Embracing neurodiversity. *AMA Journal of Ethics, 17*(4), 348–352. https://doi.org/10.1001/journalofethics.2015.17.4.msoc1-1504

Arredondo, P., Toporek, R., Brown, S., Jones, J., Locke, D. C., Sanchez, J., & Stadler, H. (1996). Operationalization of the multicultural counseling competencies. *Journal of Multicultural Counseling and Development, 24*(1), 42–78. https://doi.org/10.1002/j.2161-1912.1996.tb00288.x

Atuel, H. R., & Castro, C. A. (2018). Military cultural competence. *Clinical Social Work Journal, 46*(2), 74–82. https://doi.org/10.1007/s10615-018-0651-z

Balsam, K. F., Molina, Y., Beadnell, B., Simoni, J., & Walters, K. (2011). Measuring multiple minority stress: The LGBT People of Color Microaggressions Scale. *Cultural Diversity & Ethnic Minority Psychology, 17*(2), 163–174. https://doi.org/10.1037/a0023244

Brooks, V. R. (1981). *Minority stress and lesbian women.* Lexington Books.

Comas-Díaz, L., & Rivera, E. T. (Eds.) (2020). *Liberation psychology: Theory, method, practice, and social justice.* American Psychological Association.

Crenshaw, K. (1991). Mapping the margins: Intersectionality, identity politics, and violence against women of color. *Stanford Law Review, 43*(6), 1241–1299. https://doi.org/10.2307/1229039

D'Andrea, M., & Daniels, J. (2001). Respectful counseling: An integrative model for counselors. In D. B. Pope-Davis & H. L. K. Coleman (Eds.), *The interface of class, culture, and gender in counseling* (pp. 417–466). Sage.

Davis, D. E., DeBlaere, C., Owen, J., Hook, J. N., Rivera, D. P., Choe, E., Van Tongeren, D. R., Worthington Jr., E. L., & Placeres, V. (2018). The multicultural orientation framework: A narrative review. *Psychotherapy, 55*(1), 89–100. https://doi.org/10.1037/pst0000160

Frost, D. M., & Meyer, I. H. (2023). Minority stress theory: Application, critique, and continued relevance. *Current Opinion in Psychology, 51*, 101579. https://doi.org/10.1016/j.copsyc.2023.101579

Gone, J. P. (2021). Decolonization as methodological innovation in counseling psychology: Method, power, and process in reclaiming American Indian therapeutic traditions. *Journal of Counseling Psychology, 68*(3), 259–270. https://doi.org/10.1037/cou0000500

Goodman, L. A., Liang, B., Helms, J. E., Latta, R. E., Sparks, E., & Weintraub, S. R. (2004). Training counseling psychologists as social justice agents: Feminist and multicultural principles in action. *The Counseling Psychologist, 32*(6), 793–836. https://doi.org/10.1177/0011000004268802

Hook, J. N., Davis, D. E., Owen, J., Worthington, E. L., Jr., & Utsey, S. O. (2013). Cultural humility: Measuring openness to culturally diverse clients. *Journal of Counseling Psychology, 60*(3), 353–366. https://doi.org/10.1037/a0032595

Iyengar, S., Sood, G., & Lelkes, Y. (2012). Affect, not ideology: A social identity perspective on polarization. *Public Opinion Quarterly, 76*(3), 405–431. https://doi.org/10.1093/poq/nfs038

Knutson, D., Matsuno, E., Goldbach, C., Hashtpari, H., & Smith, N. G. (2021a). Advocating for transgender and nonbinary affirmative spaces in graduate education. *Higher Education, 83*(2), 461–479. https://doi.org/10.1007/s10734-020-00673-5

Knutson, D., Peter-Hagene, L. C., & Khera, S. (2021b). Liberal political orientation strengthens the positive relationship between religiosity and bathroom-bill support. *Sexuality Research and Social Policy, 18*, 182–191. https://doi.org/10.1007/s13178-020-00529-8

Koch, J. M., Knutson, D., Lee, H. S., Robitschek, C., Wang, K., Burdine, K., & Shin, J. (2025). Microaffirmations as positive social actions: Boosting protective factors and support for marginalized populations. *Journal of Prevention and Health Promotion, 6*(4), 1–28. https://doi.org/10.1177/26320770241309101

Koch, J. M., Knutson, D., Loche, L., Loche, R. W., Lee, H. S., & Federici, D. J. (2020). A qualitative inquiry of microaffirmative experiences among culturally diverse graduate students. *Current Psychology, 41*(5), 2883–2895. https://doi.org/10.1007/s12144-020-00811-3

Koch, J. M., Townsend-Bell, E. E., & Hubach, R. D. (Eds.). (2023). *Identity as resilience in minoritized communities: Strengths-based approaches to research and practice.* Springer Nature Switzerland AG. https://doi.org/10.1007/978-3-031-38977-1

Meyer, I. H. (2003). Prejudice, social stress, and mental health in lesbian, gay, and bisexual populations: Conceptual issues and research evidence. *Psychological Bulletin, 129*(5), 674–697. https://doi.org/10.1037/0033-2909.129.5.674

Meyer, I. H. (2015). Resilience in the study of minority stress and health of sexual and gender minorities. *Psychology of Sexual Orientation and Gender Diversity, 2*(3), 209–213. https://doi.org/10.1037/sgd0000132

Nalbandian, A., Sehgal, K., Gupta, A., et al. (2021). Post-acute COVID-19 syndrome. *Nature Medicine, 27*(4), 601–615. https://doi.org/10.1038/s41591-021-01283-z

Neville, H. A. (2024). Justice & joy: Transforming healing praxis in counseling psychology and beyond. *The Counseling Psychologist, 52*(8), 1372–1396. https://doi.org/10.1177/00110000241298715

Owen, J. (2013). Psychotherapist effects, multicultural orientation, and couple interventions. *Psychotherapy, 50*(4), 496–502. https://doi.org/10.1037/a0034617

Pedersen, P. B. (1991). Multiculturalism as a fourth force in counseling. *Journal of Counseling & Development, 70*(1), 6–12. https://doi.org/10.1002/j.1556-6676.1991.tb01574.x

Pierce, C. M. (1970). Offensive mechanisms. In F. B. Barbour (Ed.), *The black seventies* (pp. 265–282). Porter Sargent.

Rajagopal, S. K., & Durkee, M. I. (2024). Internalizing the model minority myth: Dangers for Asian American mental health and attitudes towards other minorities. *Social and Personality Psychology Compass, 18*(5), 1–13. https://doi.org/10.1111/spc3.12959

Ratts, M. J., Singh, A. A., Nassar-McMillan, S., Butler, S. K., & McCullough, J. R. (2016). Multicultural and social justice counseling competencies: Guidelines for the counseling profession. *Journal of Multicultural Counseling and Development, 44*(1), 28–48. https://doi.org/10.1002/jmcd.12035

Ridley, C. R., Mollen, D., Console, K., & Yin, C. (2021a). Multicultural counseling competence: A construct in search of operationalization. *The Counseling Psychologist, 49*(4), 504–533. https://doi.org/10.1177/0011000020988110

Ridley, C. R., Sahu, A., Console, K., Surya, S., Tran, V., Xie, S., & Yin, C. (2021b). The process model of multicultural counseling competence. *The Counseling Psychologist, 49*(4), 534–567. https://doi.org/10.1177/0011000021992339

Rogers, C. R. (1957). The necessary and sufficient conditions of therapeutic personality change. *Journal of Consulting Psychology, 21*(2), 95–103. https://doi.org/10.1037/h0045357

Shangani, S., Gamarel, K. E., Ogunbajo, A., Cai, J., & Operario, D. (2020). Intersectional minority stress disparities among sexual minority adults in the USA: The role of race/ethnicity and socioeconomic status. *Culture, Health, & Sexuality, 22*(4), 398–412. https://doi.org/10.1080/13691058.2019.1604994

Singh, A. A. (2016). Moving from affirmation to liberation in psychological practice with transgender and gender-nonconforming clients. *American Psychologist, 71*(8), 755–762. https://doi.org/10.1037/amp0000106

Singh, A. A. (2020). Building a counseling psychology of liberation: The path behind us, under us, and before us. *The Counseling Psychologist, 48*(8), 1109–1130. https://doi.org/10.1177/0011000020959007

Smalley, K. B., Warren, J. C., & Rainer, J. P. (Eds.). (2012). *Rural mental health: Issues, policies, and best practices*. Springer Publishing.

Society of Counseling Psychology. (n.d.). *Mission and values*. American Psychological Association, Division 17. https://www.div17.org/mission-values

Sue, D. W., Arredondo, P., & McDavis, R. J. (1992). Multicultural counseling competencies and standards: A call to the profession. *Journal of Counseling & Development, 70*(4), 477–486. https://doi.org/10.1002/j.1556-6676.1992.tb01642.x

Sue, D. W., Capodilupo, C. M., Torino, G. C., Bucceri, J. M., Holder, A. M. B., Nadal, K. L., & Esquilin, M. (2007). Racial microaggressions in everyday life: Implications for clinical practice. *American Psychologist, 62*(4), 271–286. https://doi.org/10.1037/0003-066X.62.4.271

Sue, D. W., Sue, D., Neville, H. A., & Smith, L. I. (2022). *Counseling the culturally diverse: Theory and practice (9th ed.)*. Wiley.

Twenge, J. M., Campbell, S. M., Hoffman, B. J., & Lance, C. E. (2010). Generational differences in work values: Leisure and extrinsic values increasing, social and intrinsic values decreasing. *Journal of Management, 36*(5), 1117–1142. https://doi.org/10.1177/0149206309352246

Vasquez, M. J. T. (2012). Psychology and social justice: Why we do what we do. *American Psychologist, 67*(5), 337–346. https://doi.org/10.1037/a0029232

Vera, E. M., & Speight, S. L. (2003). Multicultural competence, social justice, and counseling psychology: Expanding our roles. *The Counseling Psychologist, 31*(3), 253–272. https://doi.org/10.1177/0011000003031003001

Wong, J. W., Derthick, A. O., David, E. J. R., & Malaya, C. L. (2024). Twenty years of microaggression research: A systematic review and agenda for future scholarship. *Journal of Counseling Psychology, 71*(1), 1–26. https://doi.org/10.1037/cou0000721

Wrenn, C. G. (1962). The culturally encapsulated counselor. *Harvard Educational Review, 32*(4), 444–449.

Chapter 4

A Counseling Psychology Approach to Wellness across the Lifespan

What Is Development?

Take a minute to reflect on your life so far. Start with when you were a child or adolescent and try your best to answer the following questions:

- What were your hopes and dreams?
- What were your worries?
- What did it look like when you woke up?
- What was your favorite thing to do every day?
- What was your bedtime routine like?
- How has that changed over time?

Now take a lifespan perspective. Try to remember when you were five years old... then 15... and think about now. How many of your childhood friends ended up being friends for life? As you think over your lifespan, you will probably notice that a lot of things have stayed the same and even more things have changed with time. It makes sense, then, that the way counseling psychologists work with people at different points in their lives is likely to change too. Counseling psychologists try to make sure that there is a fit between their practice of psychology and the needs and challenges people are facing at specific points in their lives. The care a counseling psychologist provides for a four-year-old dreaming about getting a puppy is going to be different from the way the counseling psychologist works with a 90-year-old reflecting on the good old days. This chapter will help you explore ways that a person's *developmental stage* relates to their well-being and the strategies counseling psychologists use to increase health across the lifespan.

This chapter introduces another core aspect of counseling psychology, which is considering the development of people and the relationship of development to mental health and treatment. The approaches that counseling psychologists take will vary across the lifespan. You will learn about some different developmental models, including identity development models, with clear illustrative cases. People with unique identities such as LGBTQ+ people may have unique developmental trajectories. We discuss work with children, adolescents, and young adults, as well as with older populations. Working with these populations may require different ethical considerations, cultural considerations, and approaches. We also will introduce the readers to play therapy and pediatric psychology.

You will notice that lifespan development is not all about age. Some adults are still trying to figure out "what to do with their lives." Sadly, some young people with terminal illnesses are already looking back over their lives and reflecting on happy memories. Counseling psychologists understand that a lot of people experience things at different ages and stages, but they hold open the

DOI: 10.4324/9781003439899-4

possibility that each individual client can be different too. Still, they have to start somewhere and common developmental models provide some insights into the ways that people generally grow and change from birth to death. There are several models counseling psychologists learn about and use to understand basic things about human development.

Common Theories of Development

If you have ever taken an introduction to psychology course or a course in human development, you are were probably introduced to basic developmental models such as Piaget's Theory of Cognitive Development (Piaget, 1952), Erikson's Theory of Psychosocial Development (Erikson, 1963), Kohlberg's Theory of Moral Development (Kohlberg, 1981), and Attachment Theory (Bowlby, 1982). Attachment Theory tries to describe how infants' bond with their caregivers, which affects their relationships throughout their lives. Piaget's Cognitive Development Theory focuses on how children think, learn, and perceive the world in early childhood. Kohlberg's Moral Development Theory explains the stages that people go through as they learn about morality and how to make moral decisions. And Erikson's Psychosocial Theory proposes that there are stages that people must go through to develop ways of navigating relationships and figuring out who they are as people. Regardless of the unique approach each of these models takes to human development, they all break down the developmental process into specific, time-limited stages.

We do not have space in this chapter to provide an overview of all developmental models and theories, but it is important for us to review the basics of common developmental models so that you can situate counseling psychology and emerging developmental theories in context. You might think about development as another cultural or contextual variable that adds to the puzzle of working with clients. Remember that counseling psychologists keep an open mind to the ways that people are both the same and different. As you read over the next few pages, stay positively critical. Think about how you would not only use these models if you were a counseling psychologist but also identify ways that people "break the mold" or behave in ways that are not perfectly captured in the models and theories that we discuss in this chapter. After we talk about established theories, we will review some theories about *identity development*. Like building, you often need a solid foundation before you get to do the fun job of putting up the walls and decorating the interior.

Even when it comes to developmental models themselves, there are a lot of similarities and differences. As is so often the case in research and practice, new approaches expand, advance, and borrow from longer-standing frameworks. As you could tell from the dates in the in-text citations that followed the name of each model earlier in this chapter, the models we discuss here were published at all different times in history. That means later theories were able to build on or even contradict the ones that came before them. Table 4.1 provides an overview of common lifespan development models and their phases side by side so that you can compare how they took shape. You will notice that we refer to phases instead of stages when we compare different theories because some approaches include discrete stages, whereas others refer to ongoing developmental processes.

What did you notice about the theories as you compared them to each other? How were they similar? How were they different? As you see in Table 4.1, some developmental theories like Cognitive and Attachment Theory focus primarily on infancy and childhood. Other approaches like the Psychosocial and Moral theories of development account for development through adulthood. Some developmental processes occur quickly, and other processes play out over longer periods of time. You will also notice that the phases in Table 4.1 are associated with what is considered to be common, "normal," or ideal development. In other words, people who develop like they are expected to (based on these models) are considered healthy or well. However, as we already pointed out, not everyone grows, develops, and changes just like the textbooks say they "should."

Table 4.1 Common lifespan development models and their stages

Psychosocial (Erikson)	*Moral (Kohlberg)*	*Cognitive (Piaget)*	*Attachment (Bowlby)*
Trust vs. Mistrust: 0–18 months	Preconventional: before 9 years	Sensorimotor: 0–2 years	Pre-attachment: 0–6 weeks
Autonomy vs. Shame/doubt: 2–3 years	Preconventional: before age 9	Preoperational: 2–7 years	Attachment in the making: 6 weeks–8 months
Initiative vs. Guilt: 3–5 years	Conventional: 10–20 years	Concrete operational: 7–11 years	Clear-cut attachment: 8–24 months
Industry vs. Inferiority: 6–11 years	Conventional: 10–20 years	Formal operational: 11+ years	Goal-corrected partnership: 24+ months
Identity vs. Role Confusion: 12–18 years	Postconventional: 20+ years if achieved		
Intimacy vs. Isolation: Young adulthood			
Generativity vs. Stagnation: Middle adulthood			
Integrity vs. Despair: Late adulthood			

Note. Age ranges are rough estimates for cross-comparison purposes only and individuals may progress through stages at different rates.

It is important for counseling psychologists to have a sense, or idea, of the kinds of stages that their clients might be in, which can help them understand what some commonly understood tasks are that people go through in life. For example, if a counseling psychologist is working with an 18-year-old, they know that one of the most important aspects of this stage of life is self-exploration and understanding, as well as figuring out relationships (friendships or romantic). Likewise, if they are working with a 55-year-old woman, they should know that there are typical life things happening around this age: perhaps caring for aging parents, or children "leaving the nest," or menopause.

The Role of Context

There are lots of reasons people may develop, grow, and learn in ways that are not captured in existing models. For example, Bronfenbrenner proposed something called Ecological Systems Theory (1979), which said that human development is influenced by their environment. Bronfenbrenner (this is a fun name to try to say five times fast) proposed five *systems* (fancy way of saying environments) in which people live, work, interact, and grow. They are:

- Microsystem: This is the closest, most immediate environment that a person lives in. It includes immediate family, friends, peers at school or coworkers, and neighborhood. Let's consider a child, Ashley. Her relationship with her best friend, who lives down the street, is an example of a microsystem. Ashley's development is influenced by her family, her friends, and where she lives and goes to school. For example, Ashley's family isn't really into music, but her best friend's parents are both musicians, and whenever she visits their house, she is introduced to all kinds of music that she loves! She asks her parents if she can get a drum set.

- Mesosystem: This refers to microsystems interacting with one another. Ashley's mom is an accountant. She is also active in Ashley's school's parent-teacher organization and is their treasurer. Ashley often attends PTO meetings with her mom and reads books in the library during their meetings. Her development is influenced by seeing her mom volunteer, and by the friendly relationship, she has with the librarian who stays after school for these meetings. She asks the librarian for a book about The Grateful Dead.
- Exosystem: This layer includes systems that don't directly influence a person but have an indirect influence. It could include local laws or policies, school district lines, or parents' workplace policies. For example, Ashley's dad does cybersecurity work for a large corporation. His company allows flexibility for work hours during the day and has an excellent health benefits package. This allows him to take Ashley to her doctor's appointments and allows their family to afford good treatment for Ashley's Type I Diabetes.
- Macrosystems: This is the outermost layer, which includes broad societal norms and values, belief systems, and cultural context. Ashley and her family live in a society where there is freedom of religion. Her dad is not religious, but her grandparents are Christian. She enjoys going to church with her grandma Mimmie, singing songs, and attending Sunday School. She learns from her Grateful Dead book that Jerry Garcia was raised Catholic.
- Chronosystems: Chronosystems aren't so much an environment as they are a place in time. They consider the ways in which history or major events have an influence on someone's development. For example, during the COVID-19 pandemic, when Ashley's friends eventually went back to school, her parents continued to keep her at home for a while because of her Type I Diabetes, which is an autoimmune disorder. They feel bad about keeping her at home, so they buy her the drum set she wants. And she practices all. The. Time.

Thinking about Ashley, you can see how all these systems work independently and together to influence Ashley's development. How might her development have been different, for example, if her parents didn't have good health insurance? Or if she didn't have a friend who was interested in music? Think about your own ecological systems. A lot of us think about our parents influencing our development, but you also had your school, neighborhood, possibly religious beliefs or place of worship, norms and values about education, norms and values about sex and sexuality, societal stereotypes about different racial groups, and so on. Your development was also influenced by the time in which you were growing up. What do you think were some key factors in your own development (which is still ongoing!)? How are these systems related to cultural context, which you read about in Chapter 2?

Human Differences and Identities

Throughout this textbook, you will read about the ways that theories often focus on similarities between people and sometimes leave out the ways people are different (Sue et al., 2022). You will also learn that counseling psychologists are working to counteract this "sameness" dynamic so that more people are included in research, theory, and practice. Developmental theory is one area in which counseling psychologists are finding ways to expand existing models and approaches to include more people. When counseling psychologists and other scientists share evidence of other, unique developmental pathways and models, they are also pointing out that there are lots of ways to become and stay healthy or well, even if you are different. That is why we titled this chapter Wellness across the Lifespan. Counseling psychologists tend to focus on the positive aspects of development and look for ways all people can be supported and cared for, no matter who they are, what they have, or how others feel about them.

In this section, we will step beyond the standard models for human development you have learned about so far and will focus on ideas about how underrepresented, minoritized, and marginalized populations grow and relate to others, and how they might develop their own sense of self. It is impossible for us to thoroughly discuss all developmental models and life experiences that apply to underrepresented populations, but we hope this will offer you a starting point for further discovery.

Before we discuss population-specific developmental models, it is important to recognize that deviating from the developmental pathway that everybody is expected to follow can be challenging and leave people feeling like outsiders. As we mentioned in Chapter 3, the lack of fitting in and the stress it can cause are referred to as *minority stress* (Meyer, 2003). Again, context matters, and it is hard to separate the developmental models we discuss from the world we live in that can be hard on or even ignore people who do not fit in. Remember that we also talked about how people are very complex and hold a wide range of *identities* all at the same time, which is often referred to as *intersectionality* (Crenshaw, 1991). Counseling psychologists have to consider key identities and contextual variables when they are thinking about their clients, because they recognize that people with multiple identities have unique experiences based on those identities. We are about to take you through an overview of several identity-related developmental processes. These identity development models do not negate or replace other models; rather, they interact with and enrich, expand, and better explain other developmental theories or models. Let us tell you, there is a plethora of identity development models, which seek to describe and explain how people form different identities. There are way too many to talk about here. We only talk about LGBTQ+ and racial identity development below, but there are tons of different models about religious development and other social identities too.

Racial Identity Development

How often do you think about your culture, background, race, and ethnicity? Your answer probably depends on a lot of factors. For example, if the people around you hold racial identities closer to your own, you may not think about race much at all. However, if you immigrated to your current country from a different one, you may notice racial, cultural, and ethnic differences all the time. As a wise student studying counseling psychology, you are probably already thinking about the different stress levels a person might feel if they are regularly reminded of differences between their own culture, norms, and appearance and the people around them. Racial, ethnic, and cultural similarities and differences can be both a source of stress and resilience, as we discussed in Chapter 3. Whether you regularly think about it or not, you are undergoing your own racial, ethnic, and cultural identity development process as you read this chapter.

Like the developmental models we reviewed so far, the most common racial identity development models include phases that a person might move through as they develop a deeper understanding of who they are in the world. However, racial identity development is not tied to specific ages or stages of life. A person's process of exploring, understanding, and embracing can be lifelong and does not always follow a linear path. People can move between stages at different times in their lives, based on a lot of contextual factors. To facilitate a deeper discussion of these models

Table 4.2 Common racial identity development models

Black Racial Identity (Cross)	*Ethnic Identity (Phinney)*	*White Racial Identity (Helms)*
Pre-encounter: Assimilation	Diffuse/foreclosed: Adoption of others' views	Contact: Lack of awareness of racism/privilege
Encounter: Challenging event	Moratorium: Active exploration/questioning	Disintegration: Awareness of racism
Immersion-emersion: Embrace of Black culture	Achievement: Clear, secure ethnic identity	Reintegration: Assertion of racial superiority
Internalization: Secure sense of Black identity		Pseudo-independence: Intellectualized acceptance
Internalization-commitment: Investment in social justice		Immersion-emersion: Commitment to anti-racism
		Autonomy: Internalized anti-racist identity

and the ways they function, we provide an overview of common racial identity development models in Table 4.2. Common models include the Model of Black Racial Identity (Cross, 1991), Model of Ethnic Identity (Phinney, 1990), and Model of white Racial Identity (Helms, 1990) (Note: APA suggests that when discussing race, "White" should be capitalized. But Helms disagreed with that and used lower case w "white" to recognize the impact of white supremacy on racism). We encourage you to read more about the details of these different models and their stages. But overall (very generally speaking), the stages include first, a sense of not-knowing or blindness about one's identity; then, some kind of encounter or event that makes one start thinking or noticing that their identity is different; usually followed by some self-exploration, often characterized by strong emotions; and then, hopefully, coming to accept and celebrate one's identity. But the stages don't necessarily go in order. They can repeat, and people don't always go through all of the stages.

Common themes in the racial identity development models in Table 4.2 are their focus on self-acceptance or self-concept and acceptance of others. You might notice that this approach to development is consistent with other models we have discussed so far. For example, Kohlberg's Moral Development model (Kohlberg, 1981) examines ways that people understand themselves, the expectations of others, and work to fit into society in ways that maximize their health, safety, and social connections. Counseling psychologists recognize that health is not just an internal process that can be fixed by medications or interventions focused solely on one person. Rather, health takes shape in community, is transmitted between people, and is maintained through rich social connections with others (Berkman & Glass, 2000).

Racial identity, especially for historically marginalized populations, can take shape in an oppressive environment (Cross, 1991; Helms, 1990). Racial identity development will differ for people with different racial identities and involves increased complexity for people with multiple marginalized identities, for example someone who is biracial and gay (Cole, 2009; Crenshaw, 1991). Racism has an impact on racially minoritized people, and social justice and self-acceptance can be key parts of developing wellness across the lifespan (Sue et al., 2022). Think about why racial identity development might be important for a counseling psychologist to understand. How do you think those differences might show up in the therapy room? As you can see, the right approach can depend on a person's developmental stage and needs. The same can be true for other populations such as LGBTQ+ people (Meyer, 2003).

LGBTQ+ Identity Development

People may also go through unique stages of development related to their gender or sexual identities (this is true for people who identify as straight and/or cisgender as well as people who identify as LGBTQ+). Many of the LGBTQ+ identity development models were built from or based on the racial identity development models. For that reason, there are many common themes and points of connection between common LGBTQ+ development and racial identity development models that you are likely to notice as you read this section. You will also notice how outdated some of the terminology related to LGBTQ+ identity has become. Counseling psychologists have been key players in the continual work to better understand, respond to, and discuss the identities and experiences of marginalized people. For that reason, our use of terms is constantly evolving.

Table 4.3 provides an overview of common developmental models. Cass developed the Model of Homosexual Identity Development (Cass, 1979) by interviewing gay men later in life, so it is not something to apply to other people with LGBTQ+ identities and is a little out of date. You can see that the Model of Lesbian, Gay, and Bisexual Identity Development (D'Augelli, 1994) and the model of Transgender Identity Development (Bilodeau, 2005) have similar phases but are separate

Table 4.3 Common LGBTQ+ identity development models

Homosexual Identity (Cass)	*LGB Identity (D'Augelli)*	*GL Identity (Fassinger & Miller)*	*Transgender Identity (Bilodeau)*
Identity confusion: Initial awareness	Exiting heterosexual identity	Awareness: Recognizing differences	Exiting a traditionally gendered identity
Identity comparison: Acknowledging possibility	Developing personal LGBTQ+ Identity	Exploration: Investigating attractions	Developing a personal transgender identity
Identity tolerance: Seeking out others	Developing LGBTQ+ social identity	Deepening/ commitment: Internalizing identity	Developing a transgender social identity
Identity acceptance: Embracing identity	Coming out to family	Internalization/ synthesis: Integrating identity	Coming out to family
Identity pride: Active expression/advocacy	Developing LGBTQ+ intimacy status		Developing a transgender intimacy status
Identity synthesis: Integration with self	Entering a LGBTQ+ community		Entering a transgender community

to recognize that sexual orientation identity development is different than gender identity development. We are also including the Model of Gay and Lesbian Identity Development (Fassinger & Miller, 1996) which was initially developed based on work with lesbian women and then later included work with gay men, but note that it does not include LGBTQ+ identities other than people who identify as gay men or lesbian women, so again it is a little out of date.

As you read over Table 4.3, you may find common developmental themes showing up again. You may start to notice that wellness over the lifespan takes place in relationship with others, involves self-discovery, and includes self-understanding and self-acceptance. There are lots of ways to explain and describe the ways people grow up to be healthy, thriving members of society and each person is likely to experience and navigate the developmental process differently.

Again, take a moment to reflect on what you have learned about identity development for people with marginalized identities. How might knowing about identity development change the way you work with culturally diverse populations? You might notice yourself feeling thoughtful, introspective, and empathetic. Like we discussed in Chapter 3, counseling psychologists work to cultivate cultural humility, or thoughtful openness to other cultures and perspectives. In other words, you are thinking like a counseling psychologist!

The Role of Age

So far, we have talked about the fact that standard developmental models may leave specific groups of people or populations out or may not fully account for their experiences. The importance of cultural humility and awareness of specific needs and challenges extends to working with all sorts of clients, including those who are much younger or much older than you.

If you have ever been dismissed or looked up to because of your age, you are already familiar with what a major role age (or perceived age) can play in the work of a counseling psychologist. At some point, you have probably had a younger person look up to you or an adult think you were not ready for something or responsible enough. Early in their career, young counseling psychologists often encounter older adults who ask, "Aren't you too young to be a counseling psychologist?" (Implying: What could you possibly know about life?) The truth is that counseling psychologists know a lot about life because they have intense professional training in human development and mental health. And: It is a myth that someone has to experience something to be able to empathize, listen, or understand. This just isn't possible! In fact, many counseling psychologists specialize with different age groups and focus on specific stages of life such as infancy, childhood, adolescence, and older adulthood. You may find yourself drawn to a specific age group or stage of life as well. Some people absolutely love working with children and other people are passionate about working with older adults. Some people refuse to work with specific age groups. One of the authors of this book, Julie, has even heard a counseling psychologist say that college students were "intimidating." As you read about the different developmental stages that counseling psychologists might specialize in working with, we encourage you to reflect on your own passions and interests.

Pediatric Psychology

Counseling psychologists who are also pediatric psychologists focus on psychological practice with children and their families. For the sake of this section, we are going to refer to them as *pediatric counseling psychologists*. Some pediatric counseling psychologists work at hospitals with infants and their caregivers. Other pediatric counseling psychologists work in outpatient clinics embedded in communities. There are some things that distinguish most pediatric counseling psychologists from other pediatric psychologists (APA, 2023). For example, school psychologists work with children, but as we discussed in Chapter 1, they tend to focus heavily on behavior change using behavioral interventions and may work closely with schools to improve the learning environment. School counselors also work with children and families, but they work in schools and often do psychoeducation and prevention in large groups. On the other hand, pediatric counseling psychologists usually spend more time working directly with children and their families, providing therapeutic services that leverage a wide variety of techniques and skills (APA, 2023). They often work in hospitals or health settings.

Some pediatric counseling psychologists use play therapy and other interactive approaches to help children and their families process through stressful experiences, resolve trauma, and identify opportunities for positive change (Landreth, 2012). Play therapy can involve something as simple as allowing children to act out through puppets or as resource-intensive and complex as sand tray therapy. Regardless of the type of play therapy a pediatric counseling psychologist uses, the general idea is that children reveal their thoughts, needs, relationship patterns, and other key information when they play (Landreth, 2012). Some pediatric counseling psychologists and other behavioral health providers focus their careers almost entirely on play therapy research and practice.

Play therapy is not the only approach to working with young children, but it can be very effective in some cases, because developmentally, children are often unable to express their thoughts or feelings. For example, imagine you are watching a four-year-old girl play with two dolls. She tells you that one doll is the brother and the other doll is the sister. She hands you the sister doll and holds onto the brother doll. Then she proceeds to use the brother doll to yell at the sister doll and hit her on the shoulder. Where do you think she might have gotten the idea that this is the way brothers and sisters interact? Children use play as their mechanism of learning, interacting with the world, and expression. The basic principle of play therapy is that the ways that people play and engage in creativity can tell us a lot about them and can allow children to act out or express things they are trying to make sense of. No matter whether a pediatric counseling psychologist is using play therapy or another child-appropriate technique, it is critical that the approach is developmentally appropriate. It would not be appropriate to expect a child (or even an adolescent) to do the same kind of hour-long talk therapy that we expect of adults.

Working with children can be fun and incredibly challenging. It can be very rewarding to help children grow and heal. It can also be hard to hear children share about their experiences of abuse and neglect. Work with children requires work with caregivers, and sometimes caregivers and families can be very resistant to change. Pediatric counseling psychologists take a lot of different approaches to the challenges, rewards, and resistance they face, but they are generally unified by their passion for helping children and families. If you are interested in working as a pediatric counseling psychologist, explore your own passion for the field. What draws you toward working with children and families? What barriers might you encounter? What experiences could you gain now that could help you in your future work?

Adolescents and Emerging Adults

So far, we have focused on young children, but pediatric counseling psychologists and other counseling psychologists also work with adolescents and emerging adults (around ages 18–22). Youth who are minors face a lot of the challenges experienced by other minors or people who are still reliant on their caregivers for their basic needs. When a person is a minor who lives at home, their behaviors, attitudes, and perspectives are still very shaped by their families or caregivers. However, older teens are increasingly able to leave their homes, work, and drive. They tend to have greater autonomy than younger children and they face unique developmental challenges brought on by puberty and other psychophysiological changes. For these and other reasons, some counseling psychologists spend their entire careers focusing on, working with, and researching teens and young adults.

Psychologists who work with adolescents and young adults are embedded in a variety of agencies and organizations such as human services departments, child welfare offices, youth service agencies, juvenile detention centers, and high schools. However, they differ from other professionals who work at youth-serving sites. For example, social workers are often employed at youth-serving government agencies and serve as case managers, court advocates, and develop family support plans. Likewise, counselors often work at youth service agencies where they provide individual therapy for clients in consultation with their families. Counseling psychologists provide similar services, but they are also able to administer assessments, write psychological case reports, and provide more intensive, evidence-based services for youth and their families. Counseling psychologists may serve at inpatient sites focused on specific presenting concerns that impact youth such as self-harm, disordered eating, and psychiatric disorders. Counseling psychologists also work in administrative positions such as clinical director and supervisory roles. In other words, they provide key oversight and support for other providers and workers in the field. Work with minors who are older teens can be delicate as the counseling psychologist balances the autonomy of the client with the responsibilities to the caregivers. For example, caregivers may have the right to know if a young person is at risk of harming themselves, but at what point might a counseling psychologist need to disclose that?

One growing area of focus among counseling psychologists is the age of transition, or when teens turn 18 years old and transition out of their homes to live more independently (Arnett, 2000). In the United States, beginning around age 18, youth usually age out of foster care, leave home for college, or otherwise take greater responsibility for their housing, finances, and needs. Youth who undergo this transition to greater independence between the ages of 18 and 25 years old are generally referred to as transition-aged youth or emerging adults (Arnett, 2000). One of the largest groups of counseling psychologists who work with transition-aged youth are those in counseling centers attached to colleges and universities. Counseling psychologists who work with emerging adults may encounter concerns about beginning life outside their childhood home, learning to cope with greater stress and responsibility, establishing themselves as adults, financial concerns, relationships, and mental health issues like anxiety, depression, and substance use.

Adulthood and Later Life

There are a lot of counseling psychologists who work with adults. Many of the theories, interventions, and services you will read about in this book apply to adults and guide psychological practice with adults. Psychologists who work with adults are employed at a wide range of agencies (see also Chapter 14). However, as adults reach the end of their lifespan, they may need *specialized* services. It goes without saying that older adults live exciting, active, and fulfilled lives, but they are also more likely to experience the loss of a partner, loved one, or friend. They are also more likely to experience a major medical event or receive a terminal medical diagnosis.

APA defines *older adults* as those aged 65 and older. Given the unique challenges that many older adults face, psychologists have developed ways to meet those challenges with a set of guidelines to assist with working with this age group (APA, 2014). In fact, there is an entire group of psychologists who work with older adults called *geropsychologists*. Providers who work in geropsychology usually specialize in providing care for end-of-life issues, grief, loss, and other existential concerns. As you read this paragraph, you might be thinking of losses you have experienced or moments of grief in your own life. As you can imagine, helping older adults work through these challenges can be very hard, but it can also be very rewarding. Some counseling psychologists love working with older adults and are able to offer opportunities for growth and hope even in the most challenging of circumstances.

Practice and Application

Now that we have examined many of the ways that age, identity, environment, and other unique factors can impact development, we can apply that knowledge more directly to therapeutic practice. As we discussed earlier in this chapter, counseling psychologists do their best to consider all of the unique factors that have an impact on the development of their clients. They consider ways that the interaction between a client's context, identities, and experiences shapes the way they navigate life and interact with others. When counseling psychologists write up a case as they begin working with clients, one of the first things they do is note the client's identities. For example, a report might start with, "Jamie (she/her) is 16 years old and identifies as a Black, bisexual, cisgender girl who is able-bodied, middle-class, rural, and attending a public high school."

As you read that opening sentence, please reflect on how the information that was shared with you might impact the discussions, needs, and presenting concerns Jamie might bring to therapy. Then reflect on how those needs might change, based on Jamie's age. You will probably notice that Jamie's needs are likely to change based on how old she is and where she is in her unique developmental journey. You may start to realize that you would need unique tools to work with Jamie to ensure that she gets the culturally and developmentally responsive care she needs. The good news is that counseling psychologists are constantly developing culturally responsive and culturally competent interventions to address the needs and account for the diverse experiences of people across the lifespan.

Summary

As we started this chapter, we asked you to reflect on your own life to this point: your dreams, hopes, goals, achievements, friendships, relationships, and your own sense of who you are. We imagine that a lot of things have stayed the same and even more things have changed with time over your life. We hope that you were able to relate to a lot of what we discussed in this chapter, like the identity development models and different ways that people learn and grow over time. We reviewed common developmental theories and talked about the importance of context in human development. We discussed ways in which counseling psychologists consider human development and the role of age in their applied clinical work with clients. We hope you now have a good understanding now of how lifespan development can interact with mental health and interventions. This was the third core concept of counseling psychology (after focus on strengths and cultural context) that we have reviewed so far, and in the next chapter, we get to another one: the importance of work in people's lives.

What Would You Do?

For this exercise, we will return to our discussion of Jamie. You might remember that Jamie (she/her) is 16 years old and identifies as a Black, bisexual, cisgender girl who is able-bodied, middle-class, rural, and attending a public high school. Jamie's parents take her to therapy because she is "having issues" at school and her grades are "beginning to drop." Her parents made the decision to place Jamie in counseling after she was sent to detention last week for the first time. They share with the counseling psychologist that they have "tried everything they know to do" for Jamie but that Jamie "just keeps shutting down and refuses to talk." They say that the principal called them and said that Jamie seems "angry all of the time at school." When the counseling psychologist talks to Jamie, they discover that she is being bullied at school and is unable to identify a single classmate that she considers a friend. She is not out about being bisexual to their parents. Jamie shares feelings of isolation, fear, and confusion. She reports that she regularly gets blamed for the behavior of other students in her classes. She also says that she does not want to talk to her parents about her concerns because she knows "they already have a lot to deal with" and she does not want to be "a burden on them." She says she thinks things would be better if she could "just get a job," but her parents will not let her because they want to "keep a close eye on her."

- Please pick a traditional developmental model from this chapter and identify which stage Jamie might be in right now. How does the model you selected help you to better understand Jamie's situation?
- Consider Bronfenbrenner's Ecological Systems Model. What are Jamie's systems like and how might they affect her development?
- Please pick an identity development model (racial/LGBTQ+) model from this chapter and identify which stage(s) Jamie might be in right now.
- How might the counseling psychologist's approach to Jamie change if she was 25 years old? What about if she was 80 years old?
- How might getting a job change Jamie's situation? How might the counseling psychologist change their approach to working with Jamie if she had a job?

Counseling Psychologist Spotlight: Child and Adolescent Psychologist

Dr. Jesus "Zeus" Pichardo

When Dr. Jesus "Zeus" Pichardo was in high school and was thinking about what he wanted to do after graduating, a psychologist was never on his list. He always jokes that it happened by accident, because it did! He was originally pre-med and knew that he wanted to work with kids in some capacity. In his sophomore year of college, he took a developmental psychology course and, in that moment, he knew that this was the route that he wanted to go down. He still has that textbook as a reminder of that moment, and he can confidently say that he loves his job and the work that he does now.

Zeus is a Postdoctoral Research Fellow at the Belin-Blank Center at the University of Iowa (but he doesn't just do research). He said every day is a little different for him, which is great! The Belin-Blank Center focuses on gifted education and talent development. In this position, Zeus works mostly with children, adolescents, and emerging adults who are *twice exceptional*. That term refers to people with disabilities (such as autism spectrum disorder but other disabilities as well) who are also gifted. Imagine a child with autism who is a gifted painter. Zeus does assessment, therapy, supervises doctoral practicum students, and consults with the other team members at Belin-Blank. Two days a week, he is often in the observation room watching practicum students take the lead on psychoeducational assessments. This gives him the opportunity to take notes on how they administer the test, give them in-the-moment feedback, and provide any additional support needed for challenging behaviors (from the clients) or test administration. Depending on the case and the concerns, he gets to jump in from time-to-time to give the practicum students the chance to observe him conducting Autism Diagnostic Observation Schedule administrations

Dr. Zeus Pichardo. Photograph by author.

or model how to administer a particular set of tests that may be new to them. His afternoons are generally set aside for therapy cases – his current caseload involves children as young as five and as old as 22, and he loves the diversity, as every client brings something different. When he's not testing or in a session, he usually fills out his day with writing notes, reviewing, or writing reports; doing case review; doing intake or feedback sessions; or meeting with school teams to advocate for accommodations and provide recommendations.

Zeus said there are so many things that he loves about his job that it's hard to narrow it down. He said his favorite parts are building connections and getting to play. He loves having the opportunity to really get to know each client that he works with and building a therapeutic space where they feel safe, supported, and comfortable so that they're able to work together toward their goals. This often involves learning all about them, their friends, and their hobbies and interests – and he tries to include that as much as he can in their work together. He also loves having the opportunity to incorporate play into sessions as much as possible – whether it's a card game like Uno or a game created specifically for therapy, he often walks into sessions with a basket of fidgets and a couple of different game options. Zeus said that celebrating the children/youth he's working with and the progress toward their goals will always be his favorite part of the job. It doesn't matter to him if they just took the first step, made huge progress, or reached the goal – he appreciates the work that the client and their family put in and enjoys taking time to celebrate progress before working toward the next goal.

Zeus finds that one of the hardest parts about his job is that the cases that are referred to the center for assessment are often very complex. They often get referred kids who are suspected of being twice-exceptional (2e), meaning that the client has a disability and is gifted. He said that every kid is at their own unique intersection of giftedness and disability. There are definitely times when making sense of client data and information is easier, but there are a handful of pretty complex cases that require him to sit with the information for a long while before coming to a conclusion. While it can be hard to make sense of all the information provided, he finds it very rewarding to have families share that they feel Zeus has captured their kiddo perfectly in the report he wrote and throughout the feedback he offered them. Zeus said that being a counseling psychologist allows him a lot of flexibility in the work that he is able to do. He finds teaching, assessment, therapy, and supervising students are all professionally fulfilling in their own unique way, and he is thankful that he's able to take on these roles. His training to become a counseling psychologist also helped him understand his relationship to social justice and advocacy and engage with them both in a way that is meaningful to him. Lastly, his training has made him comfortable discussing issues related to identity. He said there were a few specific cases he has had where families wanted to bring up issues around identity but were unsure how to go about that. His ability to initiate these conversations made families feel heard and seen, and that's what he strives for.

Zeus likes to be active in the community. He's currently a Big Brother through Big Brothers Big Sisters (BBBS) of Johnson County, Iowa. BBBS matches "Bigs" (mentors) with children in their local community ("Littles") to provide them with mentorship. His Little is currently nine years old, and at the time of this writing, they were matched for about a year. He says it has been such a great experience to see his Little and their relationship grow and remind his Little that there's always someone in his corner rooting for him and there, no matter what. Being a postdoctoral fellow means Zeus is working toward licensure as a psychologist. He said he has not had as much time as he would like to be involved in state or national psychology organizations but hopes to in the future. When he's not working, you can usually catch Zeus hanging out at home with his partner, Dustin, listening to music (such as Twenty One Pilots, Noah Kahan, and Logic), playing video games (such as Minecraft, Pokémon, and Fortnite), cycling, watching movies or TV, or hanging out with his cats, Winnie and Binx.

Zeus holds a PhD in counseling psychology from the University of Iowa. Throughout his training at the University of Iowa, he completed his practicum training at the Belin-Blank Assessment and Counseling Clinic, the Center for Disabilities and Development's Day-Treatment Clinic for severe and challenging behaviors (which helps manage behaviors such as elopement, physical or verbal aggression, destructive behaviors, and self-injurious behaviors), the Iowa City Community School District, and Center for Disabilities and Development's assessment clinic. He completed his predoctoral internship at the University of Wisconsin – Madison in the School of Medicine and Public Health's Psychiatry Department. While on internship, he completed rotations in primary care/behavioral health, autism assessment, family therapy, eating disorders, adolescent dialectical behavior therapy, and in-school therapy. Although challenging, the family therapy rotation allowed him to practice co-leading sessions with other therapists and navigating interpersonal and training differences. Zeus thinks that the autism assessment rotation through the Waisman Center prepared him for his current role at the Belin-Blank Center and laid a great foundation for understanding the complexities of autism spectrum disorder.

Zeus' MA is in General Psychology from Adelphi University in Garden City, New York. Zeus was able to tailor the courses he took throughout this time to focus on child development, developmental issues, and learning the foundations of interventions that can be used with children. Zeus earned his BS in Psychology from Stony Brook University in Stony Brook, New York. While completing his undergraduate degree, Zeus volunteered in the Social Competence and Treatment Lab which focused on individuals with autism spectrum disorder and provided opportunities for them to engage in social skills groups, connect with other families, get connected to local resources, and participate in brain imaging studies. Zeus looks back at this as the first time that he interacted with folks in a more clinical sense and started to learn the importance of working with the individual in front of him and not just the diagnosis. Throughout Zeus' undergraduate and master's training, he was also a classroom teacher in the local childcare center. He originally started working with the infants and toddlers before transitioning to working with the preschoolers. This first-hand experience made Zeus more comfortable in working with kids and is one of the reasons you'll see him get on the floor and speak to children at eye-level.

References

American Psychological Association. (2014). *Guidelines for psychological practice with older adults*. https://www.apa.org/practice/guidelines/older-adults

American Psychological Association. (2023). *Recognized specialties and proficiencies in professional psychology*. https://www.apa.org/education-career/grad/specialize

Arnett, J. J. (2000). Emerging adulthood: A theory of development from the late teens through the twenties. *American Psychologist, 55*(5), 469–480. https://doi.org/10.1037/0003-066X.55.5.469

Berkman, L. F., & Glass, T. (2000). Social integration, social networks, social support, and health. In L. F. Berkman & I. Kawachi (Eds.), *Social epidemiology* (pp. 137–173). Oxford University Press.

Bilodeau, B. L. (2005). Beyond the gender binary: A case study of two transgender students at a Midwestern research university. *Journal of Gay & Lesbian Issues in Education, 3*(1), 29–44. https://doi.org/10.1300/J367v03n01_05

Bowlby, J. (1982). *Attachment and loss: Vol. 1. Attachment* (2nd ed.). Basic Books.

Bronfenbrenner, U. (1979). *The ecology of human development*. Harvard University Press.

Cass, V. C. (1979). Homosexual identity formation: A theoretical model. *Journal of Homosexuality, 4*(3), 219–235. https://doi.org/10.1300/J082v04n03_01

Cole, E. R. (2009). Intersectionality and research in psychology. *American Psychologist, 64*(3), 170–180. https://doi.org/10.1037/a0014564

Crenshaw, K. (1991). Mapping the margins: Intersectionality, identity politics, and violence against women of color. *Stanford Law Review, 43*(6), 1241–1299.

Cross, W. E., Jr. (1991). *Shades of Black: Diversity in African-American identity*. Temple University Press.

D'Augelli, A. R. (1994). Identity development and sexual orientation: Toward a model of lesbian, gay, and bisexual development. In E. J. Trickett, R. J. Watts & D. Birman (Eds.), *Human diversity: Perspectives on people in context* (pp. 312–333). Jossey-Bass.

Erikson, E. H. (1963). *Childhood and society* (2nd ed.). W. W. Norton.

Fassinger, R. E., & Miller, B. A. (1996). Validation of an inclusive model of homosexual identity formation in a lesbian population. *Journal of Homosexuality, 32*(2), 53–78. https://doi.org/10.1300/J082v32n02_04

Helms, J. E. (1990). *Black and White racial identity: Theory, research, and practice*. Greenwood.

Kohlberg, L. (1981). *Essays on moral development. Vol. 1: The philosophy of moral development*. Harper & Row.

Landreth, G. L. (2012). *Play therapy: The art of the relationship* (3rd ed.). Routledge.

Meyer, I. H. (2003). Prejudice, social stress, and mental health in lesbian, gay, and bisexual populations: Conceptual issues and research evidence. *Psychological Bulletin, 129*(5), 674–697. https://doi.org/10.1037/0033-2909.129.5.674

Phinney, J. S. (1990). Ethnic identity in adolescents and adults: Review of research. *Psychological Bulletin, 108*(3), 499–514. https://doi.org/10.1037/0033-2909.108.3.499

Piaget, J. (1952). *The origins of intelligence in children*. International Universities Press.

Sue, D. W., Sue, D., Neville, H. A., & Smith, L. (2022). *Counseling the culturally diverse: Theory and practice* (9th ed.). Wiley.

Chapter 5

The Role of Work in People's Lives

What Do You Want to "Be"?

Reflect for a minute on this – when you were a child, what did you want to "be" when you grew up? This is a question adults like to ask children. How did you answer this? "I want to be … a firefighter." Or "I want to be … a teacher." Or "I want to be … a basketball player." Now take a few moments to reflect on where you are now. Maybe you are pursuing exactly what you thought you were going to when you were a child. But if not, think about – why are you NOT pursuing that career path? What messages did you get, or what changed in your life, or what experiences did you have in junior high or high school that might have shifted your path in one way or another? For most of us, our ideas about what we want to "be" shift and change as our values change, as we gain new experiences, as we grow, and as we learn more about ourselves and the world of work.

In this chapter, you will learn about vocational psychology, the world of work, and career counseling. Counseling psychologists consider work to be an integral part of all people's lives. Some counseling psychologists focus specifically on career counseling or vocational psychology, but all counseling psychologists will do some career-related counseling in their work at some point. We introduce you to some of the main theories and theorists in vocational psychology. Career counseling is tied to social justice as well as existential issues such as finding one's meaning or purpose. We will address career-related concepts such as "work-life balance" and "find your bliss" and will discuss the roles of vocation and avocation. We will discuss new trends in the field, such as influencers as a vocation, unpaid labor, and working remotely.

Career counseling is one of the cornerstones of counseling psychology. As we discussed in Chapter 1, the emphasis on career and work distinguished counseling psychology as its own field apart from clinical psychology. The focus on work and career is a unique factor to counseling psychology, and most other psychologists (other than perhaps industrial/organizational psychologists) generally do not put the same kind of emphasis on the role of vocation in people's lives and well-being as counseling psychologists do. Through career counseling, counseling psychologists might help clients do any number of things, including:

- Find a career and make career choices.
- Adjust to career transition.
- Apply for and secure a job.
- Expand self-understanding and explore existential issues.
- Manage work stress and demands.
- Navigate workplace conflict.

DOI: 10.4324/9781003439899-5

Although some counseling psychologists specialize in career work, it is important to note that for most, career counseling is not a separate or standalone service limited to those specialists. It is often integrated into regular counseling sessions as counseling psychologists take a holistic approach to their work, similar to multicultural counseling, strengths-based approaches, and a lifespan development approach.

What Is Work?

When you hear the word "work," what is the first thing that pops into your mind? Do you envision an office, someone behind a desk, or a group of people gathered in the hallway dishing on their boss? It may surprise you to know that work is actually a pretty broad concept that can be approached from a lot of different angles. For example, there are a lot of types of clinicians who can provide work-related support and their titles are often used interchangeably, but the work they do is fundamentally different. *Vocational Psychology* is defined as "the study of vocational behavior and its development across the life cycle" (Savickas, 2006, p. 852). You may hear people refer to vocational psychology, career psychology, or work psychology. Some people would argue that those terms have very specific differences, but for the purposes of this chapter, we will use these terms interchangeably.

The point is that the role of work is varied, complex, and interconnected with other aspects of life. Some questions, like "who am I?" and "what do I want to do with my life?" and "what is my meaning or purpose?" can be related to work. In fact, a lot of times, career counselors talk about vocation and *avocation.* Avocation includes things you do when you are not working, like your hobbies or your extracurricular activities. For example, if you are really passionate about dance, but you know you will not be a professional dancer for the rest of your life, you might pursue a career in a different field (for example, dental hygienist). Then you can fulfill your passion for dance through other means like volunteering at a dance school or participating in local dance groups. There are ways you can pursue your hobbies, or avocation, through means other than work, and this often brings people fulfillment.

From Work to Career Development

When counseling psychologists consider the role of work in their clients' lives, they want to understand their clients' *career development.* As we will see in this chapter, different theorists have put forward a number of definitions of career development. Super defined career development as a lifelong, continuous process of developing and implementing a self-concept, as it relates to vocational preferences and competencies (1953). Hansen said that career development was the process of the counselor helping people "clarify their life roles and values, make choices and transitions, and teach them a career decision-making process which they can use at different stages over the life span" (Hansen, 1987, p. 32). Basically, we think of career development as the process that someone goes through, over their lifetime, as they figure out who they are and who they want to be regarding their work. This is something that counseling psychologists can help people learn about, explore, and encourage them to try new ideas. Counseling psychologists may also provide practical, direct guidance like helping people find a good career fit through testing, updating a resume, or role-playing interview skills.

Why is career development important? First, the role of work is a huge part of a person's identity, worth, and social status in US culture. People assume that someone's career or work reflects their values, interests, and personality. I am sure you can think of many instances when you have heard others ask someone they just met, "What do you do?" One of the first questions a person might ask about someone else is "What do they do?" These questions of course refer to what someone does for work (which is implied), and not what they do for fun or fulfillment. Depending on how someone answers that question, others make judgments or decisions about that person. If someone says they are a biochem major, people might assume they are bookish, smart, and interested in science. If someone is an artist, people may assume they are quirky and interested in other arts and cultural events. Give it a try yourself. Read over the list of vocations below and think about the assumptions you may make about each career or job:

- Someone who works in the produce section of a grocery store
- A waitress who is in a local band
- A farmer or rancher
- A bookkeeper
- Someone who owns a small business selling baked goods
- An international law attorney

All of these are jobs or careers that conjure up different images, many of which may not be true. Regardless of whether they are true, though, they impact the people in those jobs. The assumptions we make about people, based on their jobs, shape how we treat them and what we believe them to be capable of, among other things.

The Impact of Work

It makes sense, then, that work can often play a role in people's health, mental health, and well-being (Mental Health America [MHA], 2023, 2024; National Alliance on Mental Illness [NAMI], 2024). For example, in one survey, 33% of participants said their work productivity suffered because of their mental health, and 36% said their mental health suffered because of work issues (NAMI, 2024). Burnout is a particular concern, with female employees and employees under age 50 reporting higher rates of burnout (NAMI, 2024). NAMI (2024) also found that 34% of employees aged 18–29 and 28% of employees aged 30–49 reported that they considered quitting their jobs because of the effects on their mental health. In another survey, results showed that over 80% of all employees said workplace stress affected their mental health and over 70% said workplace stress affected personal relationships (MHA, 2023). Between 50% (those in healthy work environments) and 90% (those in unhealthy work environments) of people said workplace stress affected their ability to sleep (MHA, 2024).

It is also important to note that work issues affect different groups of people differently. Often, we talk about career decision-making as though people have complete autonomy or agency to make these decisions, which is not always true. For example, in early 2024, the unemployment rate for American Indian/Alaska Native people was 6.7%, compared to 3.4% for White people and 2.9% for Asian Americans (U.S. Department of Labor, 2024). Further, three in five workers report experiencing microaggressions at work based on race, and two in five report gender-based microaggressions (MHA, 2023). Workers who identify as female, transgender, or gender diverse report worse mental health related to work than male workers (MHA, 2023). Generational differences exist as well: Gen Z workers were more likely to experience their work environments as unhealthy (71%) compared to Boomers (42%) (MHA, 2024). So, any counseling psychologist who works with human beings, most of whom rely on employment or work to support themselves, is likely to have issues related to work come up in therapy sessions, regardless of the initial presenting concern.

When Work Works

You may have heard or been told something like "If you find a job you love, you'll never work a day in your life." The idea is that if you just find your "dream job," you'll be happy the rest of your life. What do you think about this idea? How realistic is it for you? Do you know people for whom this has been true? Do you know people for whom this has not been true? What are some different aspects of having a job that might make a "dream job" less than ideal? The notion of being able to secure a dream job is in many ways a very privileged idea. You probably know people who have jobs that are not their dream jobs, maybe not what they wanted to do, but they have been doing it for 30 or 40 years.

For most people, around the world, the reason why they have a job is because it is close to their home, or there is good pay, or there are certain benefits, or maybe the job taps into a skillset they have. Many people are limited to geographical regions due to family obligations or partners. Further, a dream job does not guarantee a dream salary, dream commute, dream salary or benefits, dream boss, dream coworkers, dream hours per week, or dream work environment. Most people do not have jobs that are completely blissful. At the same time, for some people, career development overlaps naturally with positive psychology and counseling psychology's focus on strengths and values of clients (Dik & Duffy, 2012).

Some counseling psychologists have argued that work is one way for some people to find meaning and purpose in life; they have talked about vocation as a *calling* (Dik & Duffy, 2012). Dik et al. (2015) proposed that counseling psychologists can apply the principles of purpose and meaning in career development work: by focusing on client strengths, helping clients become aware of positive emotions, increasing gratitude and work hope, learning about job crafting, and living a calling. They noted that these ideas may not apply to all clients and addressed the ways in which sociocultural or systemic barriers may not allow people to gain meaningful work. Later in this chapter, we talk about the concept of decent work (Blustein, 2006), which may address some of these issues.

Values activities (such as values card sorts) are one way that career psychologists can help clients build a connection between their purpose and their work. Career psychologists often like to integrate conversations around personal and professional values with people making career decisions. Career values are beliefs and ideas that are related to your occupation or job. If you can understand what your values are, that can help you solidify your choices. One activity that career psychologists might use is a values card sort; each card has the name of a work value, and people must rank them, in order, from top to bottom. For example, which of these values are more important to you:

- Education or religion?
- Autonomy or financial wealth?
- Prestige or helping others?
- Flexible schedule or security?

Exploration of these values can help people come to good self-understanding and can be a valuable exercise.

Origins of Career Counseling

As we discussed in Chapter 1, and as you have likely learned about in other classes, the Industrial Revolution happened in the United States (and elsewhere) in the late 1800s and early 1900s. People shifted from working in rural and agricultural areas to cities and manufacturing. At the same time, there was an influx of immigrants coming to the United States. Further, the United States experienced migration domestically with people moving from rural areas to cities to get jobs. This is around the same time that women began to enter the workforce outside the home in greater numbers. At the same time, psychology as a field was beginning to develop. Freud was talking about psychoanalysis and using psychology to solve problems. In the early 1900s, the military was beginning to utilize testing to match people with certain skills to certain types of jobs.

There was a large social reform movement beginning at this time, largely aimed at assisting people who were impoverished. To address the needs of workers in Boston, Frank Parsons started the Vocation Bureau (Jones, 1994). He developed the first *trait and factor* model of career guidance. His idea was if a career counselor could determine what people's traits or characteristics are and could determine what factors are at play in certain jobs, and put those two together, it would result in a situation where people can be matched to jobs that will be satisfying for the rest of their lives. He wrote that the purpose of the Vocation Bureau was:

> To aid young people in choosing an occupation, preparing themselves for it, finding an opening in it, and building up a career of efficiency and success. And to help any, young and old, who seek counsel as to opportunities and resources for the betterment of their condition and the means of increasing their economic efficiency.
>
> (Parsons, 1908, p. 3)

So, for example, according to Parsons, if John is really good at using tools to fix things, and we can find an occupation for John where he gets to use tools to fix things, this will set John up to have a job for the rest of his life. Unfortunately, this is unrealistic idea in today's world, but it is not very realistic or practical in today's world. But it is important to know that Parsons was the first person to really come up with this idea and develop this model. Parsons wrote *Choosing a Vocation* (1909) and was interested in training others to do career counseling. One way in which Parsons was revolutionary for his time was that he stressed the importance of providing services to women and immigrants who were newly entering the workforce at high rates. Parsons also suggested that services be offered on weekends and evenings, when people were not working. This focus on accessibility of services is still considered progressive today. Parsons is considered by many to be the founder of vocational guidance or career counseling because of his unique ideas about offering guidance to people about careers (Jones, 1994). As we discussed in Chapter 1, career-focused counseling continued to play a large role in the development of counseling psychology as a unique field, across World Wars I and II and into the present.

Career Theories

Here, we are going to introduce you to four main categories of career psychology theories:

- Trait and factor theories, or the fit between the person and their work environment
- Developmental theories, which have to do with your stage in life related to career work
- Social-cognitive theories, which are related to the interaction of your social context and how you think about things
- Newer theories that incorporate and address recent changes in society

We encourage you to consider these theories with a critical eye. What fits for you or makes sense to you? What seems out of date? What areas are not included or addressed by the theorists?

Trait and Factor Theories

As we mentioned earlier, Parsons introduced the notion of trait and factor, or person-environment fit. Then, over time, other theorists expanded on this idea. One of the most popular and frequently used trait and factor theories was put forward by Holland (1966) and is one of the most commonly used approaches even today. In fact, if you took any career assessments in junior high or high school, they were likely based on Holland's theory. Holland classified jobs into six main areas: Realistic, Investigative, Artistic, Social, Enterprising, and Conventional (RIASEC).

Holland's classification system has been studied all over the world and there are thousands of studies based on hundreds of thousands of people that build on and support his theory. It is the most widely researched occupational classification system, and the US Labor Department uses it to classify occupations in the O*NET database (Greenhaus & Callanan, 2006; U.S. Department of Labor, n.d.). One of the reasons why this approach is so popular is that the system is simple to understand and use.

- Realistic (R) refers to interests in working with your hands, with tools, with animals or plants, and very practical kinds of things. Occupations might be car mechanics, air traffic controllers, cooks, or farmers.
- Investigative (I) often has to do with science; people with a strong I often like to use tools to determine answers to questions. They might be scientists, researchers, or work in a lab.
- Artistic (A) people are creative writers, dancers, producers, directors, musicians, and designers.
- Social (S) refers to helping others and working with others, learning about new cultures, and making new friends.
- Enterprising (E) usually is affiliated with sales, management, business-related occupations, and using persuasive skills.
- Conventional (C) usually refers to interests in things like filing, using spreadsheets, keeping things organized, working with details, or keeping a budget.

Look back over the list you just read through and think about which category or categories fit you best. Do you feel drawn to one job classification more than the others? Do you notice classifications that are a better fit with counseling psychology than others?

Often, people will take an assessment and receive a Holland code that is a combination of three of these types. So, for example, someone might get a code of RIA. There are resources available, such as the US Department of Labor O*NET system, that assist people in learning about the types of occupations that might fit an RIA profile. According to O*NET, jobs that might be a good fit for someone with an RIA code are architects, landscape architects, and commercial and industrial designers. If you ever do take such an assessment and receive your Holland code, it is important to note that the results are not telling you that you should seek a certain type of job. They are saying that, based on job satisfaction data about thousands of people, people who have your same code and certain occupations are likely to be satisfied in their jobs.

Someone with an RIA code may be perfectly happy and satisfied working as an agriculture educator, or in a medical laboratory. But generally speaking, the jobs recommended through your Holland code will offer ways for you to use your interests in your work. Regardless of your code, Holland's theory is based on a few assumptions:

- Interests are the most important aspect of career decision-making.
- People and jobs can be put into categories.
- Job satisfaction is based on matching interests to occupations.

There are a number of commonly used assessments based on the Holland theory, including the Strong 244 (formerly the Strong Interest Inventory; Miller, 2013; Morris, 2023), and the Self-Directed Search (Holland & Messner, 2017).

Have you ever taken a career assessment that used this kind of six-factor typology? What did you think about it? Was it useful to you? Why or why not? In general, how useful do you think Holland's theory is? What are some strengths and limitations of applying this theory with clients? If you want to learn more, we encourage you to go to the US Department of Labor's O*NET website, which can be easily found, and explore the resources there. Also, there is likely a career services office at your campus. Look for its website and review the resources and services they offer.

One historical criticism of this theory is that it assumes that someone's personality is the primary factor in job satisfaction, which may not always be true. It also assumes that personality or interests are static, or in other words, it assumes that these things do not change over time. Holland's theory focuses on interests and not necessarily aptitudes or skills. For example, painting a set for a theater group might sound fun, or writing a play might sound interesting, but are those things that you are actually skilled at? This theory works on the assumption that people will always have a choice or agency in shaping their own career paths. It does not consider contextual, cultural, or societal issues that may restrict or put up barriers for some workers.

For example, a young man may aspire to go to college and become an engineer, but his family financial situation is such that he decides to drop out of high school and take a job at a local grocery store. Over time, he advances from working hourly in the produce department, to becoming manager of the produce section. It never seems financially feasible to him to pursue a GED and go to college, so he remains employed by this store, eventually becoming assistant manager and then manager. Trait and factor theory is also limited by the ever-shifting workplace and societal changes. For example, phone operator is not a job that exists anymore, although at one point in time, there were ample opportunities for people to work as phone operators. Strengths of the theory include the fact that it is so simple to understand and use, it is widely researched, and assessments are readily accessible.

Developmental Theories

Another group of theories is *developmental theories*, which focus on how career choices and experiences change over one's lifespan. Donald Super was a theorist who argued that career decisions were not made at a single point in time (so basically, he disagreed with trait and factor theory). He said career patterns unfolded or developed over someone's lifetime. Super's Life-Span, Life-Space Theory (Super, 1953, 1980) can be visualized as a rainbow. The outermost ring describes life*span* stages as:

- Growth (infancy to adolescence; people are making sense of the world of work through play and looking to role models)
- Exploration (around adolescent to early adulthood; people are learning, exploring, and experimenting about their potential careers)
- Establishment (approximately early 1920s to mid-1940s; people are starting in their chosen careers, stabilizing, and establishing themselves)
- Maintenance (around mid-1940s to mid-1960s; people are focusing on maintaining their skills and contributions in their field)
- Disengagement (around mid-1960s and beyond; people are starting to disengage from their career and transitioning out of the workforce)

Super described life *space*, or roles that people may hold over their lifetime, as:

- Child
- Student (engaging in formal and informal learning)
- Leisure (having leisure-time activities which could include hobbies or even just relaxing)
- Citizen (things like being a voter, or paying taxes)
- Worker (engaging in work)
- Homemaker (taking care of a home or apartment and paying rent or mortgage)

People can have multiple life space roles at the same time, and the ages shown in the rainbow are flexible. In other words, someone can be a student at age 65; a teenager who is not old enough to vote yet can work on an election campaign as a citizen; a child may be a 55-year-old who is navigating elder care for her parents; and so on. Everyone's life career rainbow will look different.

As with any theory, Super's approach has some limitations. Early criticisms of Super's model included concerns about rigidity of ages or roles, which he later clarified to have more flexibility. Earlier models also included roles such as "spouse" and "parent," which do not fit all people. The theory really fits best for someone who has one lifelong career, as opposed to people who might have a second, third, or multiple careers over their lifetime. Super's theory does not take sociocultural factors other than age, such as gender or race, into account. Prior to his death, Super acknowledged in an interview that he hoped future research on his theory would consider the roles of gender and multicultural issues (Freeman, 1993). Some of the strengths of this theory are that it allows people to have more than one role at a time; there is flexibility in the ages at which tasks are done; and it allows for lifelong learning. And everyone loves a rainbow! Someone could easily look at the rainbow to consider what life space or lifespan they are currently in, and it can help counseling psychologists conceptualize the career patterns and development of their clients. Think about your own life space and lifespan:

- What are your current roles?
- What stage do you fit in developmentally?
- Does this theory ring true for you?

Children and Adolescents

Across most of this chapter, we have mainly focused on the career development of adults, but career development in children and adolescents is also important. As we discussed at the beginning of this chapter, children are asked what they want to be when they grow up beginning at an early age. For children and adolescents, career concerns are often connected to their roles as students. Counseling psychologists can provide meaningful support to children and adolescents in these areas, just as they do with adults. Another developmental theory that specifically focuses on children and adolescents is Gottfredson's *Theory of Circumscription and Compromise* (Gottfredson, 1981, 2005).

Gottfredson focused specifically on children and outlined Stages of Individual Development for children. These stages include:

- Orientation to Size and Power (ages 3–5) wherein children understand that adults are the ones who have jobs.

- Orientation to Sex Roles stage (ages 6–8), wherein children begin to develop strong and sometimes rigid gender categories and rules about work, such as "girls can't be construction workers."
- Orientation to Social Valuation stage (ages 9–13) wherein children begin to figure out that status is assigned to certain jobs and they may eliminate potential jobs for themselves if they don't have the level of prestige the child wants. This is where you hear lots of children say they want to be famous singers or professional sports figures.
- Orientation to Internal, Unique Self stage (ages 14+) wherein children begin to figure out what their aspirations are and who they are.

Furthermore, the term *circumscription* refers to children's process of eliminating potential jobs, and *compromise* refers to their recognition that there are external constraints on their job choices (Gottfredson, 1981, 2005). It is important to note that children start to make decisions about who they are, what their skills are, and what their career and educational paths will be as early as seven to eight years old. Try to imagine yourself when you were seven or eight years old. Reflect for a moment on messages you heard in the classroom. You might have heard things like "Logan is a good reader," "Carly can run fast on the playground," "Wes can climb the rope in gym," "I'm not good at math," "The teacher tells me to be quiet all the time," or "I get in trouble all the time for not sitting still." Statements like these make an impact.

As adults, it seems like seven years old is too young for children to begin making these decisions or forming this kind of self-concept. But if you remember what it was like for you as a child, some of this might make more sense. Children make decisions at this age about whether they will drop out of school or continue to college. They are getting messages from their families and from educators and they are making decisions about themselves such as "I'm a good student," or "I'm a bad student." This is also where they start to think to themselves things like "I want to be a doctor, but I've never seen a doctor who looks like me, so I probably can't be a doctor." Children start to figure out and narrow down their career choices. The child's thought process might be:

> I want to be a movie star, but I live on a farm that has been in my family for generations and when I grow up, my dad expects me to help him on the farm, so that dream of being a movie star is probably not going to happen.

This is how children narrow their career choices.

Gottfredson (1981, 2005) argued that often these compromises are based on gender, race, what children perceive their abilities to be, or what their physical abilities are. An important takeaway here is that people who work with children must realize how early children are making these kinds of decisions. Counseling psychologists can help children process some of the decisions they have made, discuss the barriers they have developed internally, offer role models such as Black women scientists, or provide educational material and resources about careers. One limitation of Gottfredson's theory is its being restricted to child development. Another limitation is its reliance on the role of gender stereotypes, which have changed over time. Conversely, one of its strengths is the fact that it is one of the few major theories that specifically focus on childhood, when many career decisions are being made. It was also one of the first theories to consider any issues related to cultural context such as gender or race.

Learning Career Theories

The next group of career theories we will discuss is *learning career theories*, one of which is called Social-Cognitive Career Theory (SCCT) (Lent et al., 1994). This theory is based on Bandura's

Social-Cognitive Theory, which states that people learn and develop beliefs and attitudes in a social context or environment (Bandura & National Institute of Mental Health, 1986). One of Bandura's key concepts was *self-efficacy*, or someone's belief about their ability to succeed in a certain area. Extending that to the world of work, SCCT integrates self-efficacy, as well as other social learning ideas, into its framework (Lent et al., 1994). This theory incorporates a lot of factors that the other theories do not and is more sophisticated, but that also makes it a little complicated.

This theory includes Person Inputs, which are things like predispositions, gender, race, and health, as well as Background and Environmental Influences, such as being raised on a farm that has been in your family for generations. These factors are related to one's Learning Experiences, so for example the person on the farm may have had a small public-school environment with limited resources. People develop Self-Efficacy Expectations, where they might think "I'm good at this" or "I'm not good at this." For example, someone might think to themselves, "As a child, I learned I am pretty good at interacting with people. People still say that about me today." These experiences then increased that person's confidence in their own interpersonal skills. Their Outcome Expectations might be "I will typically have positive interactions with other people." People develop interests, set goals related to career choice, take actions related to career choice, and then develop Performance Domains/Attainments (for example, getting a job or getting a raise or promotion). This is a cyclical process that can stall or shift or change at any step. This theory is very popular because it includes so many different variables or aspects of a person's career development process; it is one of the first theories that really considers someone's cultural context in the process. At the same time, its complicated nature makes it a little hard to fully grasp and apply.

A related theory that also focuses on learning as it relates to work and career decision-making is the Happenstance Learning Theory (Krumboltz, 2009). What do you think of when you hear the term *happenstance* in everyday life? You probably think of some kind of coincidence that occurred. Happenstance Learning Theory (Krumboltz, 2009) states that unplanned events, as related to work, are normal and happen to everyone. Krumboltz (2009) believed that people learn "skills, interests, knowledge, beliefs, preferences, sensitivities, emotions, and future actions" (p. 135) based on planned and unplanned events. We are sure you have experienced this yourself or have heard of others who have.

For example, perhaps your friend Josie was walking her dog and ran into her neighbor who was also walking her dog. Josie told her neighbor she was looking for a summer job, and her neighbor mentioned that the local café was looking for summer help; she saw a sign there that morning. Josie got the job, worked at the café all summer, and shared with some customers that she was going to State College in the fall and was hoping to find a job there. She planned to major in education. The customers knew some people who ran a food truck in that town and connected them to Josie. Josie worked for the food truck business, then started baking cake-pops and selling them at the food truck; soon, she was starting her own cake-pop business and taking entrepreneurship classes at State College. She changed her major to business and started her own cake-pop food truck business.

In this situation, according to Krumboltz (2009), Josie was using flexibility, curiosity, persistence, optimism, and risk-taking as she moved through these various circumstances that eventually led her to being an entrepreneur. Happenstance Learning Theory is a fun one to think about because it literally happens to all of us in different ways. On the other hand, while it may shed some light on how career pathways unfold, it traditionally was not considered something that could be applied in a practical way. Krumboltz himself called the Happenstance theory "a rebellion against traditional counseling theories" (2015, p. 283). He attempted later to share some ideas for practical application, and his first point was that career professionals should not actually help people make career decisions, because the future was not predictable! Rather, he thought they should encourage people to explore, see how the exploration process was going, and document the exploration as learning about the career development process.

Newer Career Theories

Finally, there are several newer theories that have been recently developed that take into account our modern global and societal contexts. Unfortunately, we do not have space in this chapter to cover every new theory or development in this area so we are just going to describe a couple of theories that we think you will be interested in. However, if you are considering a career in vocational psychology or if you are just curious about the future vocational psychology, we strongly recommend that you look into work by Mark Savickas (Career construction theory; 2005), Saba Ali (career development of rural youth; e.g., Ali et al., 2021), and Lisa Flores (career development of women and Latinx people; e.g., Flores et al., 2023).

One recent theory is the *Chaos Theory of Careers*. Pryor and Bright developed this theory in response to traditional theories that they felt were just not realistic in real-life circumstances. They wanted to develop a theory that was consistent with "the way in which the whole universe operated" (2014, p. 4). Along those lines, even the vocabulary terms that Pryor and Bright (2014) use to describe career processes, such as fractals, emergence, phase shift, and attractors, are quite space-y and science-y. We do not have space to go into depth here, but we like this theory because it is new, unique, complex, practical, and realistic. One of its most important concepts is that uncertainty is inevitable, and life is unpredictable, and life and career processes are super complex; therefore, the counseling psychologist should help clients build resilience and flexibility to be prepared for unexpected changes on their life paths (Pryor & Bright, 2014). You might kind of think of this theory as one that includes aspects of social-cognitive theory as well as happenstance theory. They argue that there is no one theory or approach that captures all of the processes of career development. If you like their ideas, we encourage you to look up their work and read more. Research on this theory is still emerging.

As we discussed above, one limitation of more traditional theories is the assumption that people have agency and choice in making career decisions. Also, traditional theories do not attend to societal changes and are based on Western models of work and philosophies, such as "people are independent human beings and can do what they want." They are largely focused on the person's interests, skills, and values rather than their environment, context, or other systemic factors, and as such, often do not include people with lower income, people with marginalized identities, and others for whom context plays a large role in work decisions (Duffy et al., 2016). Psychology of Working Theory (Blustein, 2006; Duffy et al., 2016) was developed as a more inclusive approach that focuses on *decent work*. Rather than trying to achieve a perfect and idealistic person-job fit, decent work refers to all kinds of work, as long as there are safe work conditions, hours that allow for rest, adequate compensation, access to health care, and family and social values are taken into account (Duffy et al., 2016).

Recent Trends

Societal expectations about work are dynamic, particularly around the concept of work-life balance. This notion gained heightened attention in the 1970s related to a large number of women working outside of the home. Women realized that although they were working full-time jobs, they were still expected to fulfill motherhood and homemaker roles expected by society. People started to have discussions about whether women specifically could have both worlds: a fulfilling career and a fulfilling home life. There was talk of whether they could "have it all." In the 1980s, Sunny Hansen developed a theory called Integrative Life Planning (1987) to partially address this issue. She said that people should engage in holistic, purposeful life planning that integrates preferred life roles, physical, emotional, intellectual, and spiritual needs, and vocational needs. These discussions have continued and with heightened expectations at the workplace and outside work (not necessarily "family," but "life"), many people are concerned about how to balance multiple demands.

We got about 22,000 results when we entered the term *work-life balance* into Google Scholar. Recently, this issue especially came to light during the COVID-19 pandemic, when parents were working from home and juggling multiple responsibilities due to childcare centers being closed and schools operating remotely. For example, one study found that working from home during the COVID-19 pandemic was related to lower work-life balance, higher work-family conflict, and higher rates of burnout (Khalid et al., 2024). Now, some workers are back in the office, some work from home, and some work in a hybrid format, but schools have returned to in-person, reducing some of the burden for parents who work from home.

This reminds us that the occupational landscape is constantly shifting. Recently, new career trends have emerged that we could not have predicted even five or ten years ago. By the time this book is published, there may be even newer occupations; can you think of any? For example, social media influencer is an occupation that has only recently emerged in the 2020s. Yet, in a recent study, 57% of Gen Z participants said they wanted to be an influencer (Morning Consult, 2023). Other trends like "the great resignation" and "quiet quitting" have been recently in the news as well (Grensing-Pophal, 2024). Another new hot topic is related to artificial intelligence (AI) and how AI might replace human workers or take over jobs that people currently do (Kelly, 2025). The role of social media in the workplace is also fairly recent development. For example, employers are gathering information about potential or current employees via social media, and there have been implications regarding the rights of employers as well as freedom of speech (Cotriss, 2025). It will be interesting to follow new career and work trends in the future.

Summary

We started this chapter by asking you to think about what you wanted to "be" when you were a child, how that has changed over time, and why it changed. We also asked you to think about your first reactions to the word "work" and what images it brings up. We considered some issues related to work and career, such as work-life balance and whether it is always possible for people to find fulfillment through their work. We also introduced you to the concept of career development and reviewed some historical career counseling theories as well as some newer trends. As you wrap up this chapter, we encourage you to think about how some of these theories relate to your own career development. Which theories are most relevant or applicable for you? Where do some concepts from different theories overlap or conflict for you? We hope this chapter gave you a good understanding of why counseling psychologists consider the role of work to be a core concept for humans in their lives. In Chapter 6, we are moving on to learn more about broader counseling psychology theories.

What Would You Do?

You are a counseling psychologist at a university counseling center. You have been seeing Bo for a few weeks. He sought out counseling to talk about friendships and conflict with his roommates. Bo's parents are from Nigeria and he is the oldest son in the family. His father is a professor of engineering and his mother is a neurologist. Bo said that growing up, he always loved scouts, soccer, and cross-country. He loves to hike and to be outdoors. He is currently a volunteer soccer coach for a local children's league, plays recreational soccer, and goes on long runs when he can. He tells you that he has been angry a lot lately. He shares that he has been a "bad roommate" because he "never wants to do any chores." He discloses that he has had no energy but has been unable to sleep, has no appetite, and has been avoiding his roommates and family. He shares that he recently failed two midterms in his pre-med biochem courses, which he "hates." Bo says he never wanted to be a doctor or do a pre-med major; he was only doing pre-med because his parents have always pressured him to be a doctor. He said he was always good at science classes growing up, but he finds it boring. The only classes he is attending this semester are his environmental history class and his sports management class, and he has A's in both of those. It seems to you that Bo is worried about his anger and roommate situation, but what might be going on is some unhappiness related to his career and college plans.

- How would you approach your work with Bo?
- What guidance might you give him?
- How would his family culture and background play a role in your decision?
- What career theory might be useful in working with Bo?
- How would you apply it?
- What would you do if Bo insists that career/education are not the most pressing concern, and he is not willing to discuss career issues?
- What other information would you want to have to move forward and help Bo?

Counseling Psychologist Spotlight: Career Counseling

Dr. LaRae Jome

Dr. LaRae Jome is a psychologist at Work-Life Directions, PLC. On a daily basis, she works with clients and helps them navigate their careers and working lives (in other words – career counseling!). Prior to this, she was a professor of counseling psychology for 15 years but started to feel burned out and made a career transition to starting her own career counseling business. LaRae is able to integrate her own personal experience with this shift as she supports clients with all kinds of vocational issues and questions. She has individual counseling sessions with adults (a few teenagers but mostly people aged 1920s–1960s) to provide guidance and support for work-related issues. These include career exploration, work burnout, work adjustment, career decision-making, job and career transitions, and job searching. She helps people discover answers to questions like: What should I major in? What career path might fit me? What other jobs or career paths might fit me better than the one I am in now? How do I cope with a difficult job or a difficult supervisor or coworker? Should I stay or leave my job?

LaRae uses quantitative and qualitative assessment tools like career interest inventories, occupational card sorts, values and skills checklists, interview preparation, and resume development

Dr. LaRae Jome hiking in Norway. Photograph by author.

techniques but tailors her assessments and interventions to each individual client's needs. She stays current with trends in career development research and information about the job market and employment trends. As someone who is self-employed, she works to develop her visibility as a vocational psychologist and to market her practice by writing book reviews and blog articles related to work issues.

She enjoys seeing people move from a state of feeling discouraged, lost, trapped, and anxious about their career and work futures, to feeling more curiosity, excitement, sense of control, and readiness to make changes. She uses her knowledge about career development and decision-making and employment trends, but also her counseling skills in working with the depressive and anxious thoughts and feelings that almost always come along with work and career issues. She says she also loves being in control of her own work life; at this stage in her career, she gets to decide when she works, what kinds of clients she sees, and how she wants to use her professional skills. One of her favorite things about her job is when a past client calls or emails with updates about their career and work decisions ("I got a job!" or "I feel a lot less dread about going into work every day.") Another favorite experience is helping people to identify their skills, showcase these skills on their resume and LinkedIn profile, and feel increased confidence about the value that they will bring to an employer.

There are also a lot of challenges in LaRae's work. Because her job is to hear about the jobs of others, one challenge is that she listens to very negative work experiences. People's work lives are full of painful experiences, even traumas, and include negative interpersonal interactions and experiences of being bullied, shamed, fearful, on edge, unvalued, and discriminated against. For example, the experience of being laid off can shake someone's confidence and bring up feelings of demoralization and depression, even when they know that being let go had nothing to do with their performance. She makes sure she has regular consultation meetings with other mental health providers to get support and self-care. In this way, she models reflective practice (see Chapter 12). Another challenging issue is working with people who are unhappy in their working lives but for various reasons are not yet at a place where they are ready to make changes. Even though she works with them to identify their career or job searching goals, they may be unable to take the next steps needed, such as applying for a job. Making major changes, such as applying for jobs, can be such a vulnerable and anxiety-producing experience and there are times that, despite her best efforts, the person is not yet ready to take steps into the unknown and uncertainty. (And when this happens, she says she likes to encourage them to move at the pace that fits for them, as they need to be ready to take action before it can be successful). She sometimes fields calls from parents of adult children who would like their adult child to get some career counseling so they can figure out a career path and perhaps leave the parents' home. If the adult child is not ready for exploration and decision-making, the work is less likely to be successful. She sometimes finds herself doing a few sessions of family career counseling.

In this way, her background as a counseling psychologist is really helpful and valuable. It is embedded in the values and tenets of counseling psychology such that she focuses on prevention and growth rather than pathology. Even though she is working on psychological problems, her focus is on moving toward healing, wholeness, and growth. She brings in larger issues about navigating work in a capitalistic society with embedded oppressions, and this helps her clients heal from some of the negative internalizations they may have related to work (such as – being laid off does not mean that you have done something wrong, it means the system does not value the individual worker). She feels it is a privilege to live out the values of counseling psychology in her daily work.

Outside of work, she loves reading, listening to podcasts, and taking long walks in nature with her family. She supports her local library, art museums, theaters, and music venues. She is active politically, especially around women's health and education. She is active in professional career development associations. She received her PhD in counseling psychology from the University of Akron. She also has an MA in counseling psychology from the University of Akron, and her BA is in psychology and English from Marquette University. She is a licensed psychologist in Minnesota and New York and is authorized to practice telehealth through PsyPACT.

References

Ali, S. R., Garrison, Y. L., Cervantes, Z. M., & Dawson, D. A. (2021). Sociopolitical development and healthcare career interest, self-efficacy, and outcome expectations among rural youth. *The Counseling Psychologist, 49*(5), 701–727. https://doi.org/10.1177/00110000211007440

Bandura, A., & National Institute of Mental Health (1986). *Social foundations of thought and action: A social cognitive theory*. Prentice Hall, Inc.

Blustein, D. L. (2006). *The psychology of working: A new perspective for career development, counseling, and public policy*. Routledge.

Cotriss, D. (2025, May 5). How social media screenings affect hiring decisions. *Business News Daily*. https://www.businessnewsdaily.com/2377-social-media-hiring.html

Dik, B. J., & Duffy, R. D. (2012). *Make your job a calling: How the psychology of vocation can change your life at work*. Templeton Press.

Dik, B. J., Duffy, R. D., Allan, B. A., O'Donnell, M. B., Shim, Y., & Steger, M. F. (2015). Purpose and meaning in career development applications. *The Counseling Psychologist, 43*(4), 558–585. https://doi.org/10.1177/0011000014546872

Duffy, R. D., Blustein, D. L., Diemer, M. A., & Autin, K. L. (2016). The psychology of working theory. *Journal of Counseling Psychology*, *63*(2), 127–148. https://doi.org/10.1037/cou0000140

Flores, L. Y., Hu, X., & Martinez, L. D. (2023). Latinx career psychology: Work and vocational development of Latinx individuals. In W. B. Walsh, L. Y. Flores, P. J. Hartung & F. T. L. Leong (Eds.), *Career psychology: Models, concepts, and counseling for meaningful employment* (pp. 345–365). American Psychological Association. https://doi.org/10.1037/0000339-017

Freeman, S. C. (1993). Donald Super: A perspective on career development. *Journal of Career Development*, *19*(4), 255–264. https://doi.org/10.1177/089484539301900403

Gottfredson, L. S. (1981). Circumscription and compromise: A developmental theory of occupational aspirations. *Journal of Counseling Psychology Monograph*, *28*(6), 545–579.

Gottfredson, L. S. (2005). Applying Gottfredson's theory of circumscription and compromise in career guidance and counseling. In S. D. Brown & R. W. Lent (Eds.), *Career development and counseling: Putting theory and research to work* (pp. 71–100). John Wiley & Sons, Inc.

Greenhaus, J. H., & Callanan, G. A . (2006). Holland's theory of vocational choice. In J. H. Greenhaus & G. A. Callanan (Eds.), *Encyclopedia of career development* (pp. 353–356). Sage Publications, Inc. https://doi.org/10.4135/9781412952675

Grensing-Pophal, L. (2024, February). 2023 Labor trend – the shift from the great resignation to quiet quitting. *HR Daily Advisor*. https://hrdailyadvisor.com/2024/02/16/2023-labor-trend-the-shift-from-the-great-resignation-to-quiet-quitting/

Hansen, L. S. (1987). Changing contexts for career programs. *Journal of Career Development*, *13*(3), 3–91. https://doi.org/10.1177/089484538701300304

Holland, J. L. (1966). *The psychology of vocational choice*. Blaisdell.

Holland, J. L., & Messner, M. A. (2017). *Self-directed search (SDS)* (5th ed.). Psychological Assessment Resources, Inc. https://self-directed-search.com/

Jones, L. K. (1994). Frank Parsons' contribution to career counseling. *Journal of Career Development*, *20*(4), 287–294.

Kelly, J. (2025, April 25). These jobs will fall first as AI takes over the workplace. *Forbes*. https://www.forbes.com/sites/jackkelly/2025/04/25/the-jobs-that-will-fall-first-as-ai-takes-over-the-workplace/

Khalid, A., Raja, U., Malik, A. R., & Jahanzeb, S. (2024). The effects of working from home during the COVID-19 pandemic on work–life balance, work–family conflict and employee burnout. *Journal of Organizational Effectiveness: People and Performance*, *11*(4), 749–766. https://doi.org/10.1108/JOEPP-12-2022-0366

Krumboltz, J. D. (2009). The happenstance learning theory. *Journal of Career Assessment*, *17*(2), 135–154. https://doi.org/10.1177./1069072708328861

Krumboltz, J. D. (2015). Practical career counseling applications of the happenstance learning theory. In P. J. Hartung, M. L. Savickas & W. B. Walsh (Eds.), *APA handbook of career intervention, Vol. 2. Applications* (pp. 283–292). American Psychological Association. https://doi.org/10.1037/14439-021

Lent, R. W., Brown, S. D., & Hackett, G. (1994). Toward a unifying social cognitive theory of career and academic interest, choice, and performance. *Journal of Vocational Behavior*, *45*(1), 79–122. https://doi.org/10.1006/jvbe.1994.1027

Mental Health America. (2023). *Mind the workplace 2023*. https://mhanational.org/2023-workplace-wellness-research

Mental Health America. (2024). *Mind the workplace 2024*. https://mhanational.org/2024-workplace-wellness-research

Miller, M. J. (2013). *Strong Interest Inventory® manual* (3rd ed.). The Myers-Briggs Company.

Morning Consult (2023, September). *Report: How brands can succeed at influencer marketing*. https://pro.morningconsult.com/analyst-reports/influencer-marketing-trends-report

Morris, M. (2023). *Strong 244*. The Myers-Briggs Company.

National Alliance on Mental Illness (NAMI). (2024). *The NAMI workplace mental health poll*. https://www.nami.org/support-education/publications-reports/survey-reports/

Parsons, F. (1908). *The vocation bureau*. The Arena.

Parsons, F. (1909). *Choosing a vocation.* Houghton Mifflin Co.

Pryor, R. G. L., & Bright, J. E. H. (2014). The Chaos Theory of Careers (CTC): Ten years on and only just begun. *Australian Journal of Career Development, 23*(1), 4–12. https://doi.org/10.1177/1038416213518506

Savickas, M. L. (2005). The theory and practice of career construction. In S. D. Brown & R. W. Lent (Eds.), *Career development and counseling: Putting theory and research to work* (pp. 42–70). John Wiley & Sons, Inc.

Savickas, M. L. (2006). Vocational psychology. In J. H. Greenhaus & G. A. Callanan (Eds.), *Encyclopedia of career development* (pp. 852–853). Sage Publications, Inc. https://doi.org/10.4135/9781412952675.n295

Super, D. E. (1953). A theory of vocational development. *American Psychologist, 8*(5), 185–190. https://doi.org/10.1037/h0056046

Super, D. E. (1980). A life-span, life-space approach to career development. *Journal of Vocational Behavior, 16*(3), 282–298. https://doi.org/10.1016/0001-8791(80)90056-1

U.S. Department of Labor, Bureau of Labor Statistics. (2024). *States: Employment status of the civilian non-institutional population by sex, race, Hispanic or Latino ethnicity, and detailed age, 2024 annual averages (Table 14).* https://www.bls.gov/lau/ptable14full2024.htm

Chapter 6

Theories and Approaches in Counseling Psychology

What Is a Theory?

When you imagine a counseling session, what images come to mind? What is the setting like? What actually occurs in the therapy space? You can even enter "therapy" or "counseling" into a search engine to see what images come up. What is similar about these images and how therapy is represented? You may have heard about some different counseling psychology theories like psychoanalysis or cognitive-behavioral therapy, but do you have a good sense of what a counseling theory actually is or how it helps a counseling psychologist? Generally, a theory or *theoretical orientation* if you want to use a fancy term, gives counseling psychologists a framework for thinking about (a) how people's problems develop; (b) how people's problems are maintained; (c) how people's problems can get resolved; and (d) what the role of the therapist is in this whole process.

In this chapter, we offer you an introduction to some of the historic, well-established counseling theories as well as some of the newer approaches that factor context and modern-day demands into account. We discuss the strengths and weaknesses of approaches such as Psychodynamic, Cognitive-Behavioral Therapy (CBT), Humanistic, and Existential theories. We describe constructivist approaches. We also describe modalities other than individual counseling, such as group therapy, family therapy, and partners therapy.

As you are probably aware, there are lots of theories, approaches, and clinical tools that counseling psychologists can use to treat clients. We should clarify a few things before we discuss this further because when counseling psychologists talk about theory and practice, a lot of words get used interchangeably that are related, but do not always mean the same thing. In the simplest terms, a *theory* is a collection of ideas and concepts that are developed through observation, experimentation, and analysis, to explain, understand, and even predict human behaviors and mental processes (American Psychological Association [APA], n.d.)

When a counseling psychologist or a student adopts a *theoretical orientation*, they are saying that they feel a specific theory such as psychodynamic theory or Cognitive-Behavioral Theory (CBT) does a good job of explaining human behavior and offers important tools for addressing client concerns. As scholars research and practice various theories, they identify useful theory-based tools, interventions, and approaches that they offer to other psychologists to use with clients. When a person says they are practicing a theory such as CBT, they mean that they are practicing from a CBT theoretical orientation, and they are using CBT tools to address client concerns. This terminology is similar to other fields. For example, a physician might say they are "practicing" a certain type of "medicine." Counseling psychologists may develop a theoretical orientation based on their own personal and professional philosophy or thoughts about how people develop, grow, get stuck, and change, and how counseling psychologists are able to facilitate the process.

DOI: 10.4324/9781003439899-6

Theories and Practice in Psychology over Time

We discussed some of the history of counseling psychology in Chapter 1, so you know that all of the theories we have today did not just pop into existence suddenly as a suite of options that counseling psychologists could choose from like opening an app and looking at a menu of possibilities. The development of theories is very tied to the history of counseling psychology and many of the long-standing theories like psychodynamic, behavioral, and cognitive theories have a storied past. In different times in history, theories like psychodynamic have been incredibly popular, very unpopular, widely used, taken over by other theories, and so on. We will provide you with a brief overview of the development of theories in the history of psychology but first we want to point out that there are several factors that impact the popularity of a theory:

- How society views the theory: Sometimes theories capture the imaginations of Hollywood producers, authors, actors, influencers, and popular psychologists. In other cases, theories gain popularity through word of mouth or social media testimonials. When clients seek out specific treatments, they tend to get more attention from counseling psychologists and researchers.
- How researchable the theory is: Theories that are easier to research or that are tied to a larger pool of evidence tend to be more prominent. Insurance companies and clients want consistent results, and they tend to invest/gravitate toward theories with a proven track record for improving health and addressing client concerns.
- How vocal, organized, and powerful the theorists are: When leaders of psychological organizations such as the APA or leading APA divisions support a specific theoretical model or approach, other psychologists tend to follow suit. For example, as we mentioned in Chapter 3, key leaders of APA Division 17 Society of Counseling Psychology helped push counseling psychologists toward a greater emphasis on social justice theory and practice (Vera & Speight, 2003).
- How available training and education are: If a theory is popular, more doctoral programs are likely to offer an emphasis in that theory. The more training programs that offer theoretical emphasis, the more future counseling psychologists will be prepared to train others in the theory. The success of a theory very much depends on how many people are practicing it and how many training programs are available to expand the number of available practitioners and trainers.
- How fundable the theory is: Researchers need funding to cover the cost of designing, conducting, and publishing their studies. The availability of funding can impact what researchers are able to focus on. Sometimes, the focus of counseling psychology research is driven by government priorities, federal funding availability, and the interests of private foundations.

Of course, there are many other factors that can impact the popularity of a theory and many of the factors we listed can interact with each other. For example, the Society of Counseling Psychology (SCP, n.d.) calls upon us to consider the theory called *critical consciousness*, which calls for an awareness of and reflection on the impact of racism and other forms of oppression in therapeutic practice. Many psychology training programs include an emphasis on multicultural counseling competencies and work with health disparities populations. But broader society in the United States is currently divided over diversity, equity, and inclusion initiatives. Some corporations and media agencies are stepping back from supporting equity-focused events, and federal and state agencies are pulling funding for research related to diversity, equity, and inclusion initiatives. As you can see, the popularity and practice of a theory is rarely simple or straightforward. There can be hot debates and a lot of factors that influence the rise, fall, and development of theoretical approaches to therapy. That definitely applies to the longer-standing theories that have grown out of the history of psychology.

Psychodynamic Theories

Psychoanalysis

One of the earliest theoretical approaches to the practice of psychology grew out of the work of Sigmund Freud (Shedler, 2010). Freud developed psychoanalysis as a way to access and engage with the unconscious processes that are believed to cause and maintain psychological and behavioral problems. Early in his career, Freud was considered a visionary and his work captured the attention and imagination of Western Europeans and European Americans. You are probably familiar with the image of a person lying on a couch while a therapist sits nearby taking notes on a clipboard. That idealization of therapy grew out of popular interpretations of Freud's approach.

However, Freud's heavy theoretical emphasis on sex and strong unconscious drives eventually became less popular and was replaced by behavioral approaches to clinical practice that were easier to observe and research. Take a moment to reflect on your own feelings about Freud and think about the ways you have heard other people talk about him. Do you hold him in high regard, think he was eccentric, or even find him amusing? To this day, opinions on Freud and his work can be fairly divided. Some people find great promise in the theory he helped build and others find him easy to dismiss.

Regardless of how you feel about Freud, he left a sizeable and lasting impact on the field of psychology, not in small part to his daughter Anna Freud who carried on his legacy, interpreted many of his writings, and expanded his work to apply to therapy with children (Donaldson, 1996). Freud's early theoretical tenets or psychoanalytic theory developed into what is now regarded as psychodynamic theory, a theoretical approach that spawned theoretical tools like the Rorschach test (Rorschach, 1942; see Chapter 9), contemporary psychoanalysis (Shedler, 2010), and Time-Limited Psychodynamic Therapy ([TLDP]; Strupp & Binder, 1984; Levenson, 2004).

What's more, Freud put forward a number of ideas that psychologists still use today and that have become core components of some psychological theories. Many of them have become a part of mainstream psychology that many people are familiar with, such as:

- The idea that there are various states of awareness that he called the *unconscious*, *preconscious*, and *conscious*. If you have ever said something like "I just don't think she is conscious of how much she talks," you are using a concept developed by Freud.
- An approach to categorizing structures of the mind that he labeled the *id*, *ego*, and *superego*. Prior to Freud, no one would have said something like "I think his ego is getting in the way of his doing well at work."
- A way of framing key interpersonal processes that he labeled *transference* (clients' tendency to view the therapist in terms that are shaped by their experiences with caregivers and other significant figures in their life) and *countertransference* (therapist's reaction to the client that provides potentially valuable information about the client).
- A list of *defense mechanisms*, or strategies that are used unconsciously to protect a person from stress or anxiety such as denial, intellectualization, and rationalization (Cramer, 2015). These were originally developed by Freud and expanded upon by his daughter Anna (Donaldson, 1996). If you have ever said anything like "My parents are in denial," or "I think my roommate represses his feelings about everything," you are using Freud's concepts.
- Stages of human psychosexual development, including the oral stage (birth to one), anal stage (one to three years), phallic stage (three to six years), latent period (age six-puberty), and genital stage (puberty-death).

Many of these themes and contributions are key components and treatment targets for psychoanalytic therapy.

Modern Psychodynamic Approaches

So, what is psychoanalysis as it is practiced today? At its inception, psychoanalysis was a fairly time-intensive form of therapy that could involve meetings with a psychotherapist as frequently as three to five times a week over a course of several years. Contemporary forms of psychodynamic therapy can be less time-intensive and dependent on a client's presenting concerns. For example, Time-Limited Dynamic Psychotherapy shares many foundational psychological principles with standard psychodynamic therapy, but it has a narrower focus on specific cyclical maladaptive patterns and is administered over a limited number of about 20 sessions (Levenson, 2004). While engaging in psychoanalysis, a client might be asked to free associate or say everything that pops into their head, share their dreams, revisit their childhood, and reflect on the interpersonal dynamic they share with their therapist.

Behaviorism

Another school of thought emerged in the early 1900s as *behavioral* approaches became more prominent. Supporters and key theorists behind behaviorism argued (and still argue) that it is superior because behavioral science and research focuses on what can be observed and directly treated, as opposed to largely unobservable mental processes and subconscious thoughts. Experiments by researchers like B. F. Skinner (Skinner, 1938) captured the imagination of the public and are interesting to think about even to this day. For example, after the bombing of Pearl Harbor, Skinner worked on a program aimed at creating pigeon-guided bombs (Skinner, 1960). At the time, the technology for computer-guided bombs had not been developed.

The core idea behind behavioral interventions is that behaviors are maintained when they are reinforced, either positively or negatively. Think about some of the things that guide your behaviors. For example, do you tend to do things that cause other people to smile and celebrate you, or do you like agitating people and getting yelled at? If you do things to get positive responses from others, your behaviors have probably been shaped by that positivity. Your behaviors have also probably been shaped by attempts to avoid negativity. As you can see, behaviorists have a good argument for the value and importance of their theory and the way it accurately frames behavioral health dynamics. Today, most counseling psychologists do not practice true behaviorism. Most of the professionals who take a true behavioral path, such as people who do Applied Behavior Analysis, are professionals who focus on changing behaviors, for example in children with autism, people with substance use disorders, or older adults with behavior problems (Behavior Analysis Certification Board, 2025). But what if there was a middle path? What if cognitive and behavioral sciences could be combined to boost outcomes for clients? Those are the sorts of questions that took counseling psychology to the next level.

Cognitive-Behavioral Theories

Cognitive-behavioral therapy (CBT) stems from cognitive and behavioral schools of thought and is largely based on the work of Albert Ellis (Rational Emotive Behavior Therapy, 1962) and Aaron Beck (2011). It is appealing to many clients because CBT therapists follow a clear treatment approach, clients are able to build a sense of mastery or control, researchers have been able to demonstrate the effectiveness of many CBT interventions, and CBT scholars have produced specific therapeutic tools that clients can use to meet their goals (Hofmann et al., 2012). CBT approaches help clients to modify cognitions (thoughts/thinking), behaviors (actions/doing), and emotions (feelings/feeling). Although emotions are not explicitly named in the title of the theory, it does not mean that CBT therapists avoid or overlook emotions. On the contrary, emotions are very much part of the model used by CBT therapists.

In fact, scholars have used the thinking-feeling-doing triangle to describe the powerful interaction between thoughts, feelings, and behaviors. You can create a diagram yourself by drawing a triangle on a piece of paper and placing each of the three modes (thoughts, feelings, behaviors) at a different point. Now consider how these things interact. For example, think about a thought someone might have, like "people don't like me." Related feelings might be sadness or loneliness. Related behaviors might be staying at home or not trying to make new friends. Think about a time you were having a gloomy day and you pushed yourself to get out of the house and do something you enjoy like spend time with friends. Did doing something fun help you feel better? These are just a few of the ways that thoughts, behaviors, and emotions can interact.

CBT is based on a few main principles. First, people's feelings and behaviors are determined by how they perceive events. They develop thoughts, or core beliefs, about themselves and the world. They may have negative thoughts that come to them automatically. A lot of the clinical tools in CBT target these issues and educate clients about how to change their thoughts, feelings, and behaviors. The goal is to learn new behaviors, challenge distorted thoughts about situations, and test out alternatives in the real world (Beck, 2011). CBT is highly structured and time-limited: clients usually engage in one hour of CBT a week over roughly 16 sessions focused on a specific presenting concern like depression, anxiety, and so on. However, this rigidity means that CBT can be directive and formulaic and tends to treat the client as the person who needs to change in order for things to get better. That works for a lot of people, but what if life is rough and depression, for example, is a reasonable response to how bad things are? What if changing your thoughts, feelings, and emotions does not fix the problem in a person's environment? Questions like these have spurred further developments in cognitive-behavioral theories.

Beyond CBT

Scholars and researchers have developed other extensions of CBT to address what they perceive as limitations. One popular approach that extends CBT principles, Acceptance and Commitment Therapy or ACT (pronounced "act" like "I am going to act out a role play"), was developed in the early 2000s by Steven Hayes and colleagues (Hayes et al., 2011). It is based on the assumption that problems are caused and maintained by psychological rigidity, and the goal is for clients to learn flexibility. There are six core processes in ACT theory: defusion, acceptance, attention to the present moment, self-awareness, values, and committed action. Some ACT therapists refer to these six processes as the "hexaflex" (Hayes et al., 2011). You might notice that in some ways ACT therapists place a greater emphasis on what is happening outside of the client and they help clients find greater stability within their environment.

Another popular approach is Dialectical Behavioral Therapy (DBT), developed by Linehan (1993). DBT incorporates mindfulness exercises and assists with emotion regulation or the ability to evaluate, reflect on, and make decisions about how to process an emotion like anger, euphoria, or disappointment. In some ways, DBT splits the difference between CBT and ACT by emphasizing the importance of personal and environmental stressors and equipping clients with the skills to wisely reconcile their internal experiences with the world around them (Linehan, 1993). Scholars continue to identify, modify, and adapt the cognitive-behavioral-based theories and approaches and a full list of current approaches is beyond the scope of this chapter, but if you find yourself wanting to know more, the good news is that there is plenty of room for you to jump in and even contribute to further expansions in this area of the field.

Humanistic and Existential Theories

As we mentioned in Chapters 2 and 3, counseling psychologists tend to place a heavy emphasis on strengths, potential, and cultural context. As someone interested in counseling psychology, you might have noticed yourself thinking "there has to be more" when it comes to theory. You might have picked up on the fact that psychoanalytic, behavioral, and cognitive-behavioral approaches focus on people's problems. If you did, you are not alone. The good news is that scholars offered another cluster of theoretical approaches that place the client at the center of care and take a more positive, strengths-based, and context-aware approach to treatment. That group of approaches is collectively referred to as *humanistic* theories.

Humanistic theory works on the assumption that all people are inherently good and that, given the chance, they will become the healthiest, most fulfilled versions of themselves possible. Humanistic theories developed out of the work of dedicated researchers and transformative thinkers like Carl Rogers (Rogers, 1951, 1957), Irvin Yalom (Yalom, 1980), and Viktor Frankl (Frankl, 1962). We introduced Carl Rogers to you in Chapters 1 and 2, and here he shows up again! Perhaps not for the last time. One of the earliest and well-known humanistic approaches is Person-Centered Therapy, developed by Rogers (1951). The key concepts in person-centered therapy are that people have an innate striving for self-actualization, the client engages in self-healing, and therapy is a journey between two people. Rogers argued that there are three facilitative conditions to help a client work toward change: *congruence* (genuineness, meaning the counseling psychologist has to be genuine); *unconditional positive regard* (meaning the counseling psychologist does not judge); and *empathy* (understanding of the client's situation or feelings). He stated that it was not enough to have these three qualities; the therapist must also be able to communicate them to the client (Rogers, 1957). In person-centered therapy, the therapist does not evaluate, interpret meaning, question in a probing manner, diagnose, reassure, criticize, judge, or praise the client. We believe, and evidence indicates (see Chapter 8), that all counseling psychologists should have this person-centered, understanding, and empathic approach as a foundation, no matter what their theoretical orientation is.

Existential Approaches

Existential Therapies are another cluster of humanistic approaches to work with clients that include Gestalt Therapy (Perls et al., 1951), Logotherapy (Frankl, 1962), and some forms of group therapy (Yalom & Leszcz, 2020). The existential approaches to psychology were drawn, in part, from the philosophical works of historical figures like Kierkegaard (1843/1959) and Nietzsche (1886/1998). Existential counseling psychologists tend to place emphasis on self-knowledge, client autonomy and responsibility, and acceptance (Yalom, 1980). Toward this end, existential therapists might confront clients by pointing out discrepancies in their stories, offer guidance such as exercises and experiments in session, and focus on the present, or what happens between the therapist and client during the actual counseling session. Existential therapists may also help clients face what they consider the four "givens" of existence: death, meaning, isolation, and freedom (Yalom, 1980).

Again, this is just a brief overview of humanistic theories, but there are always new developments and approaches in this area. For example, scholars like Albert Jenkins (2005) have pointed out ways that humanistic theory explains resilience and thriving in Black and African American populations. Scholars have also proposed humanistic-related approaches that are widely practiced like

Emotion-Focused Therapy (EFT; Greenberg, 2011) and Internal Family Systems (IFS; Schwartz, 1995). So, what do you think? Are you satisfied with humanistic and existential approaches, or do you still want something more? If you feel at home in the approaches we have outlined so far, we are excited you are starting to find some theories you like. If not, do not despair! Researchers and scholars are constantly at work developing, extending, and expanding current theoretical approaches. That is one of the things we love about the world of counseling psychology!

Newer Theories: Constructivist Approaches

If you noticed yourself feeling that Person-Centered Theory was too focused on a person's inner experience or if you worried that Existential Theory was too philosophical, you are not alone. You will regularly notice that counseling psychologists are dedicated to understanding how cultural context and the systems within which we live (political systems, economic systems, etc.) impact psychological health. It should come as no surprise, then, that theorists are going a step further by introducing *constructivist* theories, or approaches to psychotherapy that acknowledge the ways people make meaning out of the world they live in and how that impacts psychological functioning (Neimeyer & Mahoney, 1995). Constructivist theories differ from other theories that view reality as fixed and to be discovered and they approach reality as something that is created (or even co-created between the client, therapist, and others). The pool of constructivist theories includes Feminist Therapy (Brown, 2010), Narrative Therapy (White & Epston, 1990), Solution-Focused Brief Therapy (SFBT; de Shazer, 1985), Relational-Cultural Therapy (RCT; Jordan, 2010), and Multicultural Theories (Sue et al., 2022). One of the strengths of constructivist theories is their adaptability to work with people with historically marginalized identities.

Despite what you might assume from its name, Feminist Therapy is not just about women. Feminist theorists borrow and build on key themes that were originally forwarded by feminist theorists such as a focus on power, politics, and social change (Brown, 2010), but any client can benefit from feminist therapy. Feminist counseling psychologists try to remain highly aware of power differentials between themselves and their clients, collaborate with clients to bring about psychological change, and name or highlight the oppressive forces in a client's life that work to keep the client in a place of less than optimal functioning (Brown, 2010). A counseling psychologist might work with a client to increase their awareness about their gender-role socialization experiences, ways they have internalized negative messages about themselves, and help the client build a more empowered existence by pushing back against oppressive systems and power structures. As you might have noticed, Feminist Therapy helps clients to change the world around them as opposed to simply helping them conform to their environment.

As we pointed out in Chapter 3, multicultural theories are a cluster of guiding principles that foreground the value of human difference and cultural resilience (Sue et al., 2022). Counseling psychologists are heavily involved in the development and application of multicultural knowledge, awareness, and skills to practice. In that chapter, we discussed different models of multicultural competence that are relevant to multicultural therapy as well. Counseling psychologists explore key themes of minority stress, microaggression, resilience, and culture and identity-based strengths with their clients.

Theoretical Integration

Sometimes, counseling psychologists do not adhere to just one theoretical orientation. For example, they might feel that it is important to discuss existential issues such as death and meaning with certain clients, while other clients could benefit from a structured approach like cognitive-behavioral therapy. Other times, counseling psychologists will combine or integrate different pieces of different theories in their work. When we talk about *integration*, we are talking about the process of combining multiple theories or approaches to meet the specific needs of each unique client. You might hear some counseling psychologists refer to any approach using multiple theories as *eclectic*, but we usually caution students against using language that implies they randomly use parts of theories willy-nilly and without some kind of intention or plan. On the contrary, theoretical integration is a thoughtful, scientific, and theory-driven process of fitting therapeutic practice to client concerns.

We would say that integrative theorists select a primary theory or theories to guide their overall understanding of the therapeutic process. Having a primary theory, even as an integrative therapist, can help with conceptualizing, or thinking about, client concerns and how best to treat them. Guided by their primary and, in some cases, secondary theory, counseling psychologists are able to create hypotheses about tools that may help their clients succeed and are able to offer those tools to clients to test out those hypotheses. For example, an existential therapist could use the "miracle question" (a SFBT intervention) to help a client explore their fears about death. In other words, the therapist could ask the client to reflect on what life would look like for them if they woke up one morning and had magically been given meaning in life. It might give the client a chance to get past their continual feelings of meaninglessness and envision a future defined by potential.

Integrative approaches also help therapists adjust their practice to address cultural dynamics for clients (Norcross & Goldfried, 2005). For example, a client who identifies as Cherokee might express close ties to her history and community. She might share that she connects strongly with the stories and oral traditions (White & Epston, 1990). As a way to explore power dynamics in the client's life, the counseling psychologist might ask her to tell a story that has deep meaning for her or might use narrative approaches to respect the client's connection with oral traditions. By doing so, the counseling psychologist would be meeting the goals of feminist therapy surrounding empowerment, cultural connections, and community-level change (Brown, 2010). The counseling psychologist might also integrate Indigenous and culturally based healing practices (Sue et al., 2022) into their work with the client.

Systems Theories

At this point, you might be noticing that the theories we have discussed are pretty focused on individual therapy settings. In other words, nearly all of the approaches play out in a therapy room between one therapist and one client. Yet again, you might be wondering, "Is this it? Does therapy have to take place between just two people, or can it be more than that?" Or maybe you are thinking, "Wait, what about family and relationship therapy. I have a friend who sees a therapist with their partner." In any case, you are right, counseling psychologists not only work with individuals, but also with groups of people as well. Sometimes, counseling psychologists will refer to this as the *modality* of treatment: individual, couples or partners, family, or group. In this chapter, we refer to those theories collectively as *systems* theories. You may remember from Chapter 4 that Bronfenbrenner talked about how different systems affect people's development (Bronfenbrenner, 1979). People live within *systems* that are present in society; people work together to produce some kind of system. The idea behind systems theory is that humans exist in systems such as families, friend networks, universities, classrooms, neighborhoods, and communities. A main principle is that doing therapy with other people in a client's systems can be beneficial to see how the whole system works. In group therapy, people who do not know each other come together in a group, and relationships form over time that allow the therapist to see how the individuals relate to others. In this section, we are going to focus on these theories that are used with more than one client simultaneously. Said another way, there are multiple people in the therapy space and they are all considered clients. Common systems theories fall under a few main categories that include IFS (Minuchin, 1974), Partners Therapy (Gottman & Gottman, 2015; Snyder et al., 2006), and Group Therapy (Yalom & Leszcz, 2020). The unifying thread among these approaches is that they address the concerns both within individual clients and issues that take shape between multiple participants in the therapeutic space.

Partners and Family Therapy

In family or partners therapy, the counseling psychologist is able to address the whole family/partners group rather than just one person. Family and partners therapy can help the counseling psychologist see how everyone in the group is feeling and get different perspectives if addressing family- or partners-level problems (Nichols & Davis, 2020). You have likely heard people use the terms *couples counseling* or *marriage counseling*. In this book, we are using the term *partners therapy* to be more inclusive of relationships that might include polyamory or consensual non-monogamy.

Often, if someone is having difficulty, that person may be *scapegoated* or blamed by other members rather than looking at the whole picture (Nichols & Davis, 2020). You might hear someone in the family (of four people) say, "Justin is the problem." Or one member of a couple may say, "This all started when Shannon started working extra hours. It's all her fault." When in fact from the systems perspective, problems are created and maintained through the dynamic between members and the way that everyone in that system works together (Gottman & Gottman, 2015). Looking at the previous examples, Justin may be acting out, but it might be because of other family members' behaviors. Or maybe Shannon took the extra work because their partner has a gambling problem, and they have financial concerns. Families and partners form "rules" for themselves such as "Justin is the troublemaker, Jordan (his older brother) is the good one." Or "Shannon is never home because she doesn't care about (her partner)." In systems therapy, basic assumptions are that people within the system are connected emotionally and that their behaviors affect each other's thoughts and feelings (Nichols & Davis, 2020).

These occur in repeated relationship patterns. The counseling psychologist tries to work collaboratively with the whole system to improve the way systems work between members, promote change, and help members communicate. Typical reasons for seeking family or partners therapy include conflict among members, one member having an issue that is affecting others, trauma, unexpected loss, or adjustment such as a move or divorce. Or partners may have different ideas about what relationships are supposed to look like (Snyder et al., 2006). These kinds of therapy may be challenging if one person does not want to engage in therapy or if the counseling psychologist finds themselves aligning with one member. Often, families and partners do not seek therapy until there is a "last resort" kind of issue, which can make it challenging for the counseling psychologist. On the other hand, partners and family therapy can be highly effective as the counseling psychologist can promote healthy means of communication, changes in behaviors, and empathy and understanding among the members for one another.

Group Therapy

You have likely heard of group therapy, but you might not be completely sure what that means. For example, are Alcoholics Anonymous meetings group therapy? What about a group in a school for kids whose parents are divorcing? What happens in those groups? Another question to consider is: Why would you participate in group therapy if you could do individual therapy? What might be some benefits of working with people in a group rather than individually? In this section, we are going to introduce you to some different kinds of groups and share some of the amazing benefits of participating in group therapy.

First, let's talk about different kinds of group therapy. Some therapy groups may have specific topics, for example, as we mentioned before, in an elementary school, a group for children whose parents are divorcing or a group for children with Attention-Deficit/Hyperactivity Disorder; a university setting might offer a social skills group or an anxiety group (Corey et al., 2018). A counseling psychologist might run a group for children with Type I Diabetes at a local hospital, or a group for caregivers of cancer patients. There are also groups called interpersonal process groups, which bring together people with a wide range of presenting concerns and issues. In a typical group of ten people, clients might have anxiety, depressed mood, romantic relationship issues, family relationship issues, work concerns, self-esteem problems, you name it. In the group, all of these people come together and share and build trust of one another (Burlingame et al., 2013). Research indicates that group therapy is as effective as individual therapy (McRoberts et al., 1998). However, unfortunately, interpersonal process groups can be difficult to find and participate in; there are few opportunities outside of university settings to try it out (Yalom & Leszcz, 2020). A group that has the same membership over time such as an interpersonal process group is called a *closed* group and allows people to build relationships and work through their own concerns in that environment. There are also *open* groups, such as the Alcoholics Anonymous model, that allow members to come and go without obligation or commitment (Alcoholics Anonymous World Services, 2001).

Interpersonal process groups go through some typical stages over time. The American Group Psychotherapy Association (AGPA, 2020) delineates five stages that groups may typically go through:

- Forming: The group is getting to know one another, and they tentatively share some things about themselves.
- Storming: Conflicts begin to arise between members as they compete or vie for power within the group. The group might challenge the group facilitator (which can lead to group solidarity as they challenge the authority figure).
- Norming: The group begins to form a consensus or agreement about their tasks and goals. There is more cohesion and openness.
- Performing: Some people say that this is where the "work" of the therapy happens. Group members can express individual differences and are productive as they exchange ideas and support each other.
- Termination: This is toward the end of the group as they wrap up and complete the work. This can be characterized by satisfaction and gratitude as well as grief and disappointment at the group ending.

If you have ever had to do a group project in school or at work, you may not have a strong belief in how groups can function well. But with a skilled facilitator and motivated members, a group therapy experience can be transformative. Consider this example. Maybe you can think about how to use similar communication skills in a group that you're in. What happens in group therapy can look something like this:

(Shreya is talking, Wes interrupts her.)

Shreya: "Wes, um, I wonder if I could maybe finish what I was saying?"

Carlie: "Yeah, Wes, last week you interrupted me a bunch too."

Wes: "Oh man, I didn't even know I was doing that!"

Carlie: "Well, it's super annoying."

Wes: "That's really hard for me. I get so excited, I just want to share. How can I do better?"

Carlie: "Maybe you can work on listening and waiting until someone is totally done before you jump in."

Group facilitator: "Does anyone else have ideas for how to remember not to interrupt other people?"

— Two weeks later —

(Shreya shares something that happened recently. The group listens. Then Shreya shares her observation.)

Shreya: "Wes! I was able to get through my whole thought without you interrupting! Thank you."

Wes: "Thanks, I've been trying to listen more and not interrupt so much at work too."

Carlie: "I've really noticed a difference the past two weeks. I can tell you're trying hard."

One of the coolest things about group therapy is that it is a *social microcosm* (Yalom & Leszcz, 2020). This is a fancy way of saying that group members act out their real-world behaviors in the group, replicating their everyday life (thoughts, behaviors, and feelings) in the small group. If Wes interrupts people in the group, chances are good that he interrupts people in real life; if Shreya is a little hesitant or shy in the group, chances are this reflects her real-life interactions with others; and if Carlie is direct and no-nonsense in the group, she probably is this way in real life too. Groups like this require skilled facilitators who can allow the group to go through the stages and give the members space, yet direct or redirect as needed (AGPA, 2020).

Yalom outlined 11 specific *therapeutic factors* (Yalom & Leszcz, 2020) that occur in groups:

1) Instillation of hope (members feel a sense of hope as they are inspired and encouraged by other members).
2) Universality (members realize they are not the only ones feeling this way; they are not the only ones struggling in life).
3) Imparting information (members share information, ideas, or coping strategies).
4) Altruism (members experience mental health benefits from helping others in the group).
5) Corrective recapitulation of the family group (allows members to have a healing and corrective experience as they work through past family dynamics in a safe place).
6) Socializing techniques (members learn new social skills as they interact with other people in the group).
7) Imitative behavior or modeling (members observe others in the group and practice behaviors they see other members exhibiting).
8) Interpersonal learning (members gain insight about themselves through feedback from the other members).
9) Group cohesiveness (members experience a sense of belonging, acceptance, trust, and support).
10) Catharsis (members are able to express emotions and feel a sense of relief in a safe place).
11) Existential factors (members can explore issues like finding meaning or coming to terms with death; they gain a deeper understanding of themselves and their place in the world).

Let's stop for a bit to consider some questions. What therapeutic factors might be beneficial to cancer patients participating in a group? What therapeutic factors might be beneficial to *caregivers* for cancer patients? How are the needs of these two groups similar, but different? As you can see, the way group dynamics play out can be nuanced and group-specific.

Table 6.1 Examples of responses to Cassie (p. 92)

Category	*Therapeutic Approach*	*Potential Response*
Psychoanalytic	Psychoanalysis	What is your earliest memory of feeling watched and judged?
	Time Limited Dynamic Psychotherapy	What problematic pattern in your life does this issue with your dad remind you of?
Cognitive-Behavioral	Behavioral	What factors have reinforced your current behavior toward your father?
	Cognitive Behavioral Therapy	What cognitive distortions might be involved in your thinking about the wedding?
	Acceptance and Commitment Therapy	What is within your power to change about this situation?
	Dialectical Behavior Therapy	What strategies could you use to regulate your strong emotions about this?
Humanistic/ Existential	Person Centered Therapy	If you were completely free to act without judgment, what would you do?
	Existential	What are the central fears that are coming up for you as you think about this situation?
	Emotion-Focused Therapy	What does it feel like to be judged?
	Internal Family Systems	What part of you feels judged and helpless?
Constructivist	Feminist	How does being socialized as a woman relate to your feelings of powerlessness?
	Multicultural	What past experiences of oppression or marginalization might have contributed to your worries about judgment?
	Narrative	What is the story you wish you could tell about your relationship with your father?
	Relational-Cultural Therapy	How did the lack of connection with your father shape your view of relationships?
	Solution-Focused Brief Therapy	If you could wave a magic wand and have the outcome you want, how would the perfect wedding play out?
Systems	Family	What is your designated role in your family?
	Partners	How can you work with your fiancé in this situation?
	Psychoeducational	Situations like this are common, and there usually is not an ideal outcome, but it is important to act in line with your values.
	Group	Who else in the group has had a similar experience and how did you navigate it?

Bringing It All Together

We have talked about a lot of theories in this chapter. We have encouraged you to thoughtfully reflect on each cluster of theories, but it is still easy to get overwhelmed. The good news is that just about everyone has that reaction at first. You are not alone. Over time, if you pursue a career in counseling psychology, you will find your primary theory/theories and we are here to help. Table 6.1 offers you the chance to reflect on many of the widely used theories we discussed and how they might be used by therapists. Feel free to keep this table close and refer to it as needed if you continue your education in counseling psychology. It will probably be a helpful tool you will grow to value.

First, let's set up a sample case that we unpack in Table 6.1. Imagine that a client, Cassie, is seeing a counseling psychologist and is discussing her relationship with her father. She says,

> I mean, we didn't really have a relationship when I was growing up, and now all of a sudden he expects to be a part of my life. He wants to come to my wedding and do all the usual daughter-dad stuff, and I just don't know how I feel about that. I hardly know him. But it's not like I have someone else to be in that role at the wedding. And I feel like all these people are going to be watching and judging whatever my relationship is with him

Which approach do you think would work the best? Do you feel drawn to a specific theory or intervention? Why did you pick the intervention or response that you picked?

Summary

At the beginning of this chapter, we asked you to imagine what you thought a counseling session looked like and to reflect on what might actually happen in a counseling session. We hope that this chapter has shed some light on different kinds of theories, approaches, and modalities that counseling psychologists might use. All of these are driven by counseling psychologists' beliefs about how people's problems develop and are maintained, and how people can change. We reviewed the main theories that have been put forward by counseling psychologists over time and introduced you to some theories that you might not have been familiar with before reading this chapter. What theory or theories "speak" to you? What would you like to experience if you were a client? What would you like to practice if you were a counseling psychologist? How are these similar or different, and why? In Chapter 7, we will introduce you to some of the skills that counseling psychologists use so you can see some of these theories come alive in real practice.

What Would You Do?

One of your close friends has been struggling in classes and just went through a very difficult breakup with her boyfriend. She and her boyfriend had been together for three years and the breakup hit her hard. She thinks he broke up with her because she had gained some weight recently. She cries a lot and has started skipping classes to sleep all day. Several people in her life have strongly recommended she see a therapist at the University Counseling Center, but she keeps refusing to go. Finally, she shares with you that she has no idea what to expect and she is afraid counseling will be "weird." She says she has only seen therapists on TV and they are usually unethical, pushy, out of touch, or disconnected. She tells you that every time she tries to imagine going to see a therapist, she just imagines lying on a couch while a person with a clipboard writes down judgmental things about her. You have been taking an introduction to counseling psychology course and know that counseling psychology practice looks a lot different from your friend's imaginary sessions.

- How do your friend's beliefs about therapy differ from the theoretical approaches you learned about in this chapter?
- Which theory(ies) might fit well with the challenges your friend is experiencing and why?
- Would you encourage your friend to consider group therapy and why?
- What group therapeutic factors could your friend benefit from?
- Would your recommendations change if your friend was Native American, lesbian, or held other minoritized identities?

Counseling Psychologist Spotlight: Small Liberal Arts College Professor

Dr. Yun (Yunkyoung) Garrison

Dr. Yun Garrison is an Assistant Professor at Bates College, a small liberal arts college in Maine. She teaches and mentors undergraduate students in innovative ways, such as holding class sessions in community partner organizations' spaces, local art galleries, libraries, and historical sites. Teaching in these spaces allows her to deepen students' engagement with real-world experiences and application of counseling psychology. She runs the c.a.l.m. lab (Community, Acompañamiento, Liberation, and Multicultural) where she leads students in community-engaged research and meaningful projects. In this way, students do not just study research and literature, but they actively listen to, engage with, and learn from local communities. The students' research then can become a tool for change. For example, she collaborates with Maine Community Integration, a Somali-led organization that promotes empowerment of refugee women and girls. She recently hosted a research-based gallery show with Maine Community Integration exploring posttraumatic growth of refugee women. The show integrated psychological theory, research, and the arts. Her work was featured in a special issue of the journal *The Counseling Psychologist*. Yun teaches an introductory course for students considering a career in counseling psychology and has mentored students applying to graduate programs. Yun says that she loves the versatility and creativity that being a counseling psychologist allows her to have in her work. She finds that her background in counseling psychology encourages her to engage in lifelong self-reflection and growth and allows her to express her values of compassion and justice. Yun says that one challenge she experiences in her work is related to sociopolitical issues that affect people in the community – it can be hard to do this work when there is constant and multilayered uncertainty, grief, and systemic challenges. Outside of her academic work, she runs a private practice. In her leisure time, she is active in her community through a community chorale group and she practices pottery in a community studio. She enjoys reading Irvin Yalom's books, novels that she says help her reflect on psychotherapy and human connection. She is also involved in professional networks such as the Korean Psychology Network, the Asian American Psychological Association, and the Society of Counseling Psychology. Yun graduated from the counseling psychology program at the University of Iowa. She is a licensed psychologist and also holds a master's in Educational Measurement and Statistics and a master's in Psychology.

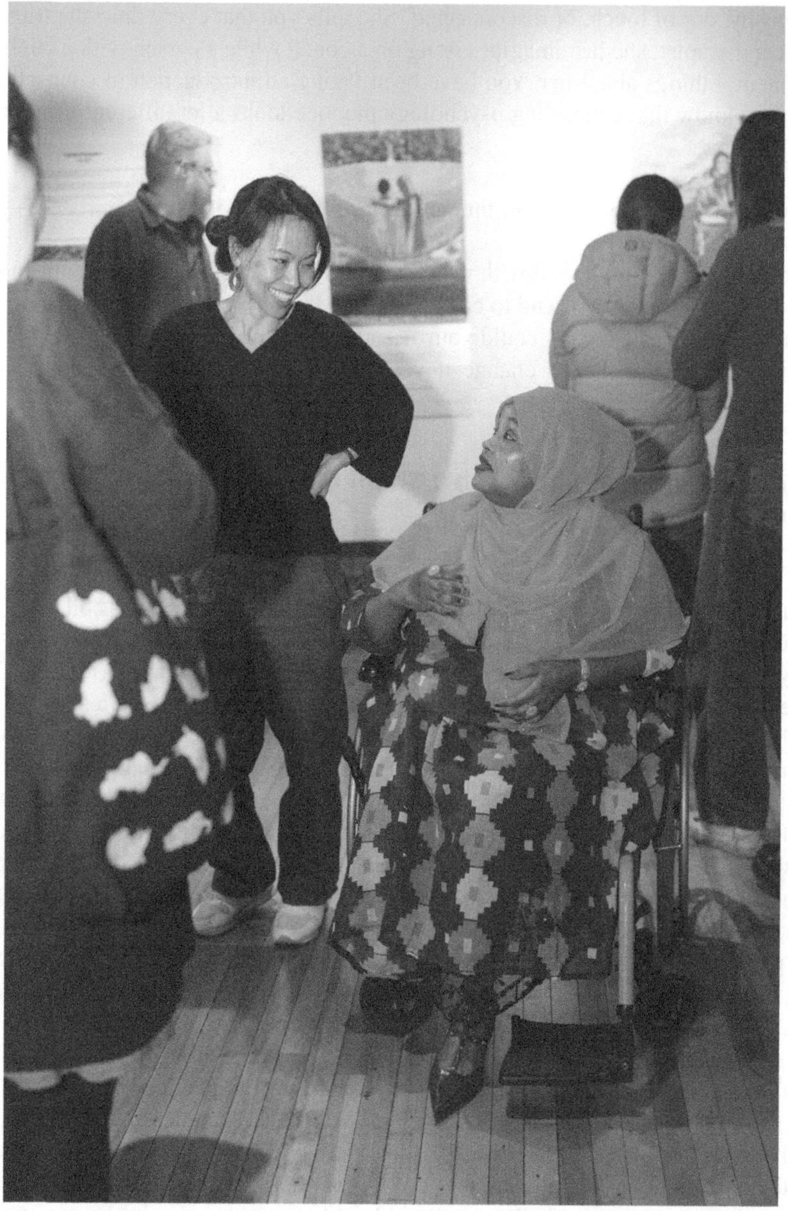

Dr. Yun Garrison with an artist. Photograph by author.

Dr. Yun Garrison with students. Photograph by author.

References

Alcoholics Anonymous World Services. (2001). *Alcoholics anonymous* (4th ed.).

American Group Psychotherapy Association. (2020). *Practice guidelines for group psychotherapy* (3rd ed.). https://agpa.org/guidelines-ethics/practice-guidelines-for-group-psychotherapy/

American Psychological Association. (n.d.). Psychology. In *APA dictionary of psychology*. https://dictionary.apa.org/psychology

Beck, J. S. (2011). *Cognitive behavior therapy: Basics and beyond* (2nd ed.). Guilford Press.

Behavior Analysis Certification Board. (2025). *About behavior analysis*. https://www.bacb.com/about-behavior-analysis/

Bronfenbrenner, U. (1979). *The ecology of human development*. Harvard University Press.

Brown, L. S. (2010). *Feminist therapy* (2nd ed.). American Psychological Association.

Burlingame, G. M., Strauss, B., & Joyce, A. S. (2013). Change mechanisms and effectiveness of small-group treatments. In M. J. Lambert (Ed.), *Bergin and Garfield's handbook of psychotherapy and behavior change* (6th ed., pp. 640–689). Wiley.

Corey, G., Corey, M. S., & Corey, C. (2018). *Groups: Process and practice* (10th ed.). Cengage Learning.

Cramer, P. (2015). Understanding defense mechanisms. *Psychodynamic Psychiatry, 43*(4), 523–552. https://doi.org/10.1521/pdps.2015.43.4.523

de Shazer, S. (1985). *Keys to solution in brief therapy*. W. W. Norton.

Donaldson, G. (1996). Between practice and theory: Melanie Klein, Anna Freud and the development of child analysis. *Journal of the History of the Behavioral Sciences, 32*(2), 160–176. https://doi.org/10.1002/(SICI)1520-6696(199604)32:*2%3C160::AID-JHBS4%3E3.0.CO*;2-%23

Ellis, A. (1962). *Reason and emotion in psychotherapy*. Lyle Stuart.

Frankl, V. E. (1962). *Man's search for meaning: An introduction to logotherapy*. Beacon Press.

Gottman, J. M., & Gottman, J. S. (2015). *The science of couples and family therapy: Behind the scenes at the Love Lab*. W. W. Norton.

Greenberg, L. S. (2011). *Emotion-focused therapy*. American Psychological Association.

Hayes, S. C., Strosahl, K. D., & Wilson, K. G. (2011). *Acceptance and commitment therapy: The process and practice of mindful change* (2nd ed.). Guilford Press.
Hofmann, S. G., Asnaani, A., Vonk, I. J. J., Sawyer, A. T., & Fang, A. (2012). The efficacy of cognitive behavioral therapy: A review of meta-analyses. *Cognitive Therapy and Research, 36*(5), 427–440. https://doi.org/10.1007/s10608-012-9476-1
Jenkins, A. H. (2005). Creativity and resilience in the African American experience. *The Humanistic Psychologist, 33*(1), 25–32. https://doi.org/10.1207/s15473333thp3301_3
Jordan, J. V. (2010). *Relational-cultural therapy*. American Psychological Association.
Kierkegaard, S. (1959). *Either/Or* (D. F. Swenson & L. M. Swenson, Trans.). Doubleday.
Levenson, H. (2004). Time-limited dynamic psychotherapy. In J. J. Magnavita (Ed.), *Handbook of personality disorders: Theory and practice* (pp. 254–279). John Wiley & Sons Inc.
Linehan, M. M. (1993). *Dialectical behavior therapy for treatment of borderline personality disorder: Implications for the treatment of substance abuse* (pp. 201–216). NIDA Research Monograph 137.
McRoberts, C., Burlingame, G. M., & Hoag, M. J. (1998). Comparative efficacy of individual and group psychotherapy: A meta-analytic perspective. *Group dynamics: Theory, research and practice, 2*(2), 101–117. https://doi.org/10.1037/1089-2699.2.2.101
Minuchin, S. (1974). *Families and family therapy*. Harvard University Press.
Neimeyer, R. A., & Mahoney, M. J. (Eds.). (1995). *Constructivism in psychotherapy*. American Psychological Association.
Nichols, M. P., & Davis, S. D. (2020). *Family therapy: Concepts and methods* (12th ed.). Pearson.
Nietzsche, F. (1998). *Beyond good and evil* (M. Faber, Trans.). Dover Publications.
Norcross, J. C., & Goldfried, M. R. (Eds.). (2005). *Handbook of psychotherapy integration* (2nd ed.). Oxford University Press.
Perls, F. S., Hefferline, R. F., & Goodman, P. (1951). *Gestalt therapy: Excitement and growth in the human personality*. Dell.
Rogers, C. R. (1951). *Client-centered therapy: Its current practice, implications, and theory*. Houghton Mifflin.
Rogers, C. R. (1957). The necessary and sufficient conditions of therapeutic personality change. *Journal of Consulting Psychology, 21*(2), 95–103.
Rorschach, H. (1942). *Psychodiagnostics: A diagnostic test based on perception* (P. Lemkau & B. Kronenberg, Trans.). Grune & Stratton.
Schwartz, R. C. (1995). *Internal family systems therapy*. Guilford Press.
Shedler, J. (2010). The efficacy of psychodynamic psychotherapy. *American Psychologist, 65*(2), 98–109. https://doi.org/10.1037/a0018378
Skinner, B. F. (1938). *The behavior of organisms: An experimental analysis*. Appleton-Century.
Skinner, B. F. (1960). Pigeons in a pelican: A case history in military psychology. *American Psychologist, 15*(1), 28–37. https://doi.org/10.1037/h0045345
Snyder, D. K., Castellani, A. M., & Whisman, M. A. (2006). Current status and future directions in couple therapy. *Annual Review of Psychology, 57*, 317–344. https://doi.org/10.1146/annurev.psych.57.102904.190212
Society of Counseling Psychology. (n.d.). *Mission & values*. https://www.div17.org/mission-values
Strupp, H. H., & Binder, J. L. (1984). *Psychotherapy in a new key: A guide to time-limited dynamic psychotherapy*. Basic Books.
Sue, D. W., Sue, D., Neville, H., & Smith, L. (2022). *Counseling the culturally diverse: Theory and practice* (9th ed.). Wiley.
Vera, E. M., & Speight, S. L. (2003). Multicultural competence, social justice, and counseling psychology: Expanding our roles. *The Counseling Psychologist, 31*(3), 253–272. https://doi.org/10.1177/0011000003031003001
White, M., & Epston, D. (1990). *Narrative means to therapeutic ends*. W. W. Norton.
Yalom, I. D. (1980). *Existential psychotherapy*. Basic Books.
Yalom, I. D., & Leszcz, M. (2020). *The theory and practice of group psychotherapy* (6th ed.). Basic Books.

Chapter 7

Key Skills for Counseling Psychologists

What Are Counseling Skills?

Counseling skills is one of our favorite things to talk about! One of the most enjoyable parts of counseling psychology is getting to use all the tools in our counseling skills toolbox. Imagine a client comes in and says:

> I am so mad at my roommate right now. She decided to get a puppy without asking me, but she doesn't know anything about dogs, doesn't take it out as much as she should, and is hardly ever in the apartment! I end up taking care of it and feeding it and walking it all the time.

As a counseling psychologist, how would you respond? In Chapter 6, we provided different responses psychologists might have, based on their theoretical orientation, but there are also key listening skills that nearly all psychologists use. For example, you might just listen and then empathize by saying "Yeah, that sounds frustrating." Or, you could ask a question that opens up the opportunity for deeper reflection like, "How is this affecting you?" Or, you could just say, "Wow, yeah" (we call this a minimal encourager, which we explain more below). These statements are all examples of different types of skills (empathic listening, open questions, minimal encouragers) that a counseling psychologist might use to help a client feel heard and to share in their experience with them.

In this chapter, we will consider the question: What skills are most important for counseling psychologists to implement? We introduce readers to important counseling skills including attending, listening, empathy, unconditional positive regard, genuineness, reflecting content and feelings, paraphrasing, summarizing, asking questions (open-ended and closed-ended), giving information, and others. We also discuss the important role of the intake session and how skills may be utilized for an effective clinical interview. Finally, we will discuss some crisis intervention skills. Throughout this chapter, these skills come alive through examples of real-life dialogues between counseling psychologists and their clients.

Microskills

The first skills that counseling psychologists learn are sometimes referred to as *microskills*, *basic counseling skills*, or *helping skills* (Hill, 2009; Ivey et al., 2019). Like we said earlier, some skills are not tied to a specific theoretical orientation and those are the skills we discuss first in this chapter. There are a lot of advanced counseling skills that counseling psychologists in training develop through their doctoral programs. To start, we will focus on the first set of introductory skills. As you

DOI: 10.4324/9781003439899-7

read these paragraphs, you might keep in mind that (as we have discussed in other chapters) therapeutic practice is a lifelong learning process and counseling psychologists never arrive at perfection. That means, using and developing skills is a lifetime growth experience as counseling psychologists integrate new approaches, figure out what works for them, and identify what works for their clients.

Before applying these microskills, you might want to revisit Chapters 2, 3, and 11, because the foundation for counseling psychology skills includes multicultural competence, ethics, understanding of biological-neurological factors, positive psychology, and resilience (Ivey et al., 2019). In other words, you need to have a thoughtful approach to client concerns before you start trying to use microskills. As we discuss these skills in this chapter, we will act as if you are preparing for a career in counseling psychology, but we understand that you may or may not be pursuing a career in a mental health field. Regardless, even if you are going into law, business, engineering, or other fields, skills such as listening and asking open-ended questions can be beneficial for your career and success. We believe just about anyone can benefit from taking an introductory counseling psychology course.

Before we dig in further, we want to note that discussions about microskills can include an implied or even outright bias against people with disabilities. For example, as you will read, microskills emphasize listening, tone of voice, body movements, and other activities that require sensory and physical components. As you read the following sections, we encourage you to think of what each skill looks like in your own context as well as in an inclusive, equitable context. For example, sign language carries a tone and requires active listening. Minimal encouragers do not require a single word to be uttered and open questions can be communicated with a shrug. By now, you have noticed that we want you to apply this book to your own life, experience, and context. This chapter is no exception. As you read about microskills, we invite you to think, "How would I do that in a way that is comfortable and congruent with my own, unique style and physical capabilities?"

Attending Skills

We refer to the most basic set of counseling skills as *attending skills*, because the counseling psychologist is physically attending to the client with their physical presence and tone. You may hear other people talk about how you communicate with your "body language." In counseling psychology, appropriate body language – or *attending* – is a professional skill that requires expertise and practice. Attending skills include making eye contact, perhaps nodding, verbally tracking what is going on, and posture. You may think these things come naturally to you – which is great! But each piece is critical.

For example, posture is really important. Typically, it is suggested that the counseling psychologist lean in a little bit to communicate listening and interest, but if you lean in too close, the client can feel uncomfortable. On the other hand, the counseling psychologist should not be so relaxed that they slouch back in their chairs as though watching TV or playing a video game. How the counseling psychologist engages, how far they lean in or lean out, sends a message to clients, and that message itself is therapeutic or a key part of the therapeutic process. Think about how you usually engage with other people and how it shapes your relationship with them:

- Do you get close or keep a distance?
- Do you lean in or lean out?
- Do you cross your arms or legs?
- Do you fidget with your hands or feet a lot?

Most likely, your answer was, "It depends." It depends on the specific person, the setting, and so on. In therapy, your posture may depend on the client, what they are saying, and what their emotional presentation is like. These factors should determine how you react or respond. We asked you to reflect on the impact your behavior has because a counseling psychologist's physical presentation can influence a client. For example, if you are fidgety and squirmy, it might be hard for them to feel calm and safe in the moment.

With friends or family talking about casual topics, it is no big deal if you fidget a little. But as a professional, you have to control your body and responses appropriately. Eye contact can also be important. In general, counseling psychologists are encouraged to make eye contact with their clients. However, in some situations, such as with shy teenagers, clients might actually open up and talk more if you're not making direct eye contact, which can feel too intense. Along these lines, we do want to note that posture, body language, and attending are very culturally based notions with different understandings of what is appropriate and professional. In the United States, Western-based norms about body space may be different from other places around the world. Eye contact may have different implications for diverse cultural groups or people of different ages. With all of these skills, there are exceptions and the counseling psychologist has to apply their professional training and judgment to the situation.

Another skill you might not have thought about is vocal tone. If you have a client who comes in depressed and your tone is (excited voice) "Tell me more!" that might not be an appropriate tone to take. Often in working with someone with low mood or energy, counseling psychologists may need to remind themselves to slow down a little and use a quieter, gentler tone of voice. Pacing is also important. Counseling psychologists may come to an understanding or insight about an issue before the client does, but if they bring this up before the client is ready (e.g., "Oh! Now I understand! You are doing all of this because of the way your mother treated you as a child."), there is danger of the client not being ready to leap to the same conclusion or interpretation. The therapist needs to gauge the client's pace and what they are ready for.

This chapter is going to be a little more interactive than other ones. We are going to give you opportunities to practice some counseling skills. Let's try something. Right now, go ahead and get into your counseling posture to the extent you are physically able.

- Put your phone or other electronic devices (unless you're using one to read this) away. Not only face-down, completely away where you cannot see them. If you have a smartwatch, make sure it is on silent or does not give you notifications.
- Put your feet on the ground, legs uncrossed (uncross your ankles too).
- Put your hands on your legs (don't wring them together or clasp them).
- Lean forward a little.
- Imagine someone is sitting across from you, observing you.

How open is your body? Do you feel yourself wanting to cross your legs or arms? Or to clasp your hands together in your lap? Are you jiggling your legs or otherwise fidgeting? Are you dying to check your phone? Now think: Could you sit this way for 55 minutes? How comfortable would it be? How does sitting this way feel to you? Counseling psychologists have to be physically aware of themselves when providing therapy. How might this look different if you are providing services via telehealth?

Active Listening

How can you communicate to someone else that you are actively listening to what they are saying? One way is through nonverbal communication, which might include nodding, gestures, or the posture we discussed earlier. Would it surprise you to know that in counseling psychology, listening is not just about using your ears? Active listening also may include observing the client's body language (how is the body language perhaps communicating something different than the content of what they are sharing?) and energy level. Again this is cultural and nonverbal messages may look different across cultural groups.

You may consider yourself a good listener. In fact, you may be a good listener with friends or family. But keep in mind that again, this is a professional skill that takes practice and intentional action. In truth, it is hard to just sit still and listen to someone for a long time! As a professional, it is important to try not to let your mind wander to the groceries you need to get later, the leftovers in your fridge for dinner, or whether your roommate remembered to let the dog out. This is why this skill is called *active* listening. One mistake that lots of beginning counseling psychologists make is jumping in to share, talking too much, asking too many questions, and not allowing space for their clients to open up or to just be. Often, they feel like they need to fill the space, or ask questions, and they are not comfortable with silence. As a professional counseling psychologist, it is important to offer space, time, and silence to clients as you listen. Counseling psychologists really have to practice being patient, which can be more difficult than it sounds.

Minimal Encouragers

Minimal encouragers are usually very short, brief, one-word encouragements. They might include saying "yeah," "mm-hmm," "sure," "right," or "wow." Minimal encouragers do not interrupt the client; they provide just a small, non-obtrusive communication that you are listening and are present with the client in that moment. A minimal encourager just takes one extra small step beyond listening with your body. Minimal encouragers convey that you are engaged – you are empathizing, encouraging, and reassuring the client. We live in a world where people are so involved with their phones, screens, or other distractions, that having the experience of sitting with a human for an hour and having that person be fully present – in and of itself can really be therapeutic.

Why is this therapeutic? In part, because it is a rather uncommon experience. Take a moment to ask the question, "Who else do you get that with?" Even if you are talking to your best friend, mom, partner, or sister, the conversation will go in a lot of different directions. These people may jump in to try and fix the situation, problem-solve, share other examples of how that happened to them or to someone else, and so on. So, therapy is this unique experience where you can be completely heard – it is all about the client. The counseling psychologist's job is to make it all about the client. We mentioned a few minimal encouragers, but what others can you think of? As you practice, you may be surprised at what emerges.

In a recent class, when one of the authors of this book, Julie Koch, taught these skills and the whole class was practicing together, a student shared that she said "Oh gee" to her partner, which is a word she does not frequently use, but it seemed appropriate at the time. Another student shared she was pulled naturally to use words she would typically use in her daily life, like "valid," "period," or "slay." She worried that maybe these weren't good minimal encouragers. We think that depending on who the counseling psychologist is working with, these are great examples of minimal encouragers. The more you get to know your client and the stronger the relationship, you may be able to use other words or terms that the client uses (such as "damn"). We once heard someone joke that counseling psychology is the only place where you can get a degree for learning how to say "mm-hmm, uh-huh, and ohhh."

Reflecting Content

Another basic skill used by counseling psychologists is *reflecting content*. Here, the counseling psychologist is basically taking whatever the client has said and feeding it right back to them, often using their own words. With reflecting content, the counseling psychologist is taking one small step further than attending, listening, and encouraging but they are not going so far as to get into feelings. They are not solving or fixing anything. This skill involves just reflecting the actual content of what the client said, which shows that you have heard what they said, and you get it. Here's an example.

- Client: "I was really mad at my roommate, and it sucked."
- Counseling psychologist: "Yeah that sucked."

Now you try – How would you reflect this content?

- Client: "My dad is being so annoying. He expects me to text or call multiple times a day and wants to know everything about all of my classes."
- You: ______________________________

Here are some examples of responses that might fit on the line above: "Your dad is being so frustrating." "Your dad wants you to call and text a lot." "Your dad is trying to reach you a lot." "Your dad has high expectations about being active in your life."

Are you getting the hang of it? Try responding to another example:

- Client: "My family members keep asking me when I'm going to get pregnant ever since I got married. They really want a grandbaby and even though I tell them I want to get adjusted in my new job and new town, they ask about it a lot and I don't know what to do."
- You: ____

Check your response against these options: "Sounds like they are pressuring you." "They are rushing you and not letting you take things at your own pace."

Reflecting Feelings

With the skill *reflecting feelings*, the counseling psychologist is mirroring what the client might be experiencing emotionally. It may seem obvious, but it can actually be a bit complex. To build this skill, it is important for the counseling psychologist to have a strong, healthy vocabulary of feeling-related words. Often, clients have a limited vocabulary to express their feelings: they may just use "mad," "bad," or "good." In US society, it is often not considered appropriate or acceptable to feel or express anything other than "good" except under certain circumstances.

Right now, how many words can you think of to express emotions? Try writing some down. Now, use your favorite search engine to look for something called a "feeling wheel" or "emotions wheel." There are many of these available online (*Side note: A feeling wheel is a great resource; we encourage you to print one out – in color! – and keep it handy to build your own emotional vocabulary, for journaling, or for self-reflection). You may be amazed by the number of options someone may have to express a feeling that they may have previously described as "mad." There are: frustrated, angry, pissed off, furious, enraged, fuming, seeing red, and so many others.

Clients may not have the words to describe their feelings, so reflecting feelings can express empathy for what is going on for the client. Doing so can also help expand clients' ways of describing their experiences, which allows them to get deeper in touch with what is actually going on for them. Reflecting feelings helps clients gain insight and helps them feel validated. Consider this example of a counseling psychologist reflecting feelings:

- Client: "My co-worker forgot to do her part of the project again, ugh! She always leaves me hanging and then I have to scramble at the last minute. It makes me so mad."
- Counseling psychologist: "That sounds so frustrating." "How infuriating." "Ugh, you must have been so angry."

Sometimes, reflecting feelings is not that obvious, as clients may not be in touch with how they are feeling or may not have the vocabulary to express their feelings. Often, we hear clients use words that aren't exactly emotion words to express something – like "gross" or "awkward." Reflecting feelings can help the client figure out what all of their feelings are, give them permission to feel lots of different ways, and determine how intense different feelings are. Consider this example and look over the different ways a counseling psychologist could respond, based on the desired therapeutic impact or outcome:

- Client: "My friend's boyfriend got drunk, was causing a scene, and it was really gross."
- Options:
  - If the counseling psychologist wants to invite client to use other words than "gross" to describe emotions/feelings about the situation, they might say: "I wonder if you can use a different word than gross?" Or "Can you elaborate?"
  - If a counseling psychologist wants to go deeper, they might say: "Okay you said it made you feel gross, but what I'm hearing is that it made you feel confused and upset and maybe even frustrated because you've said this has happened lots of times before." Gives lots of options for clients to expand their feeling vocabulary.
  - If a counseling psychologist wants to check in about what they suspect the client is feeling, reflecting feelings can also be in the form of a question or can be phrased tentatively. "Sounds like you were really frustrated." "This has happened a lot – do you think your anger towards him is building?"

Keep in mind, people can have multiple feelings at the same time. They can be: excited, proud, and nervous; exhilarated and frightened; they can feel love, care, and anger toward the same person. Now it is your turn to try. How would you reflect feelings in this situation?

- Client: "I love my dad so much, he is so supportive and great. But his bugging me all the time is adding to my anxiety and pressure and I just want to have some time to enjoy college and my friends without feeling like he is so overbearing. But I also feel bad because I know he's lonely since my stepmom died."
- You: ________________________________

Some counseling psychologist responses might be: "Sounds like you're having a lot of conflicting feelings about this." "Wow, that is really overwhelming." "Sounds like you feel a little guilty about wanting some space."

Open-Ended and Closed-Ended Questions

Counseling psychologists use open-ended and closed-ended questions to gather information from their clients when needed and appropriate. It is important for the counseling psychologists to be intentional in their use of questions and to be sure a question is needed at that moment, as opposed to another response or skill. Questions may be open-ended or closed-ended. Closed-ended questions usually have a specific answer, and, although sometimes necessary, often have the effect of halting the conversation or requiring further questioning. Here are some examples of closed-ended questions:

- Counseling psychologist: "When did you go to Colorado?"
- Client: "In 2020."
- Counseling psychologist: "Where did you grow up?"
- Client: "Lincoln, Nebraska"
- Counseling psychologist: "Did you talk to your boss?"
- Client: "No."

In this example, the counseling psychologist is collecting specific information, but not really inviting or allowing the client to share or expand. The result is that the counseling psychologist is not really getting any detailed or descriptive information about the client and is acting more like a detective than a therapist. Even though the client expanded a little bit, it is really limiting the client to respond only to the counselor's prompts.

Open-ended questions allow the therapist to hear more from the client's perspective. The idea is that open-ended questions are open invitations to the client to talk and share without the counselor necessarily leading the conversation. Here are some examples of open-ended questions.

- Example one:
  - Counseling psychologist: "How are you feeling about your upcoming trip to Colorado?"
  - Client: "Well, I'm not really sure, ..."
- Example two:
  - Counseling psychologist: "What was your upbringing like?"
  - Client: "Overall, I'd say I had a happy childhood, but ..."

Open-ended questions may also be used to clarify a point. Clarifying questions invite clients to elaborate and affirm that what the counseling psychologist is hearing is correct. Examples might be:

- "I'm not sure I fully understand – am I hearing you say that you're thinking of quitting your job?"
- "Am I getting this right, you're asking for advice on how to get your family to stop asking you these questions?"

It is important for counseling psychologists not to over-rely on questions, to ask too many questions, or to ask them rapidly, because that can make the client feel as though they are being "grilled." When asking questions, counseling psychologists should particularly be cautious of multipart, leading questions such as: "How were you feeling? Angry? Jealous? Upset?" because this does not allow for the client's own thoughts and feelings to emerge.

Table 7.1 Examples of skills in action

Client: "I am just so tired of all the stress and drama at work lately. I don't seem to be able to do anything right! It is so frustrating."	
Skill	*Example of counseling psychologist response*
Attending	(Open posture, eye contact, no physical barriers)
Active listening	(Nodding, tilting head)
Minimal encourager	Hmm.
Reflecting content	Sounds like work is really stressful for you right now.
Reflecting feelings	Ugh, that sounds so frustrating.
Open-ended question	How are you handling all that stress?
Closed-ended question	What part do you think is the most stressful?
Summarizing	So, it sounds like you're dealing with a lot at work and are feeling frustrated because you aren't feeling successful in your role.

Summarizing

Summarizing is a skill that may be used by a counseling psychologist throughout a session or at the end of a session. Summarizing is a way to ask the client if the therapist is fully understanding what the client is sharing to that point. An example midway through a session might be:

> Okay, so to summarize what you've talked about so far, just so I'm clear … you talked about the error you made in data entry at work, and then your boss was yelling at you, and that felt really intimidating, and now it sounds like you're wanting me to help you figure out what to do

Sometimes clients will go off on tangents, and a summary can be used to bring them back to the topic:

> Okay, I hear you, but I want to take you back to what you said earlier. This sounds like it was significant for you. What I heard happened was that your car broke down and you were really scared because your phone battery was dead and you couldn't reach anyone. Is that right?

At the end of a session, a counseling psychologist might summarize to wrap up and to make sure they got the main gist of what the client wanted to bring to the session. "It's time to wrap up, but just to summarize, it seemed like today you really wanted to focus on your relationship with your old friend from elementary school and how you want to reconnect with her."

There are so many microskills that a counseling psychologist could pull upon. There is generally not a "right" or "wrong" skill to use in a given situation, but it is important for the counseling psychologist to think intentionally about what might be best to use with their professional judgment. Table 7.1 gives examples of different microskills a counseling psychologist might use in response to a client.

The Intake: Clinical Interview Skills

One set of specialized skills that counseling psychologists must have is clinical interview skills. Often, these are used in an *intake session*, or the very first session with the client. An intake session is a way for counseling psychologists to gather information and history about the client. It helps the counseling psychologist to get the big picture, begin to form a sense of what is happening for the client, and perhaps set some treatment goals. Even before an intake, clients are usually asked to fill out all kinds of forms with personal information like date of birth, names and pronouns, demographic information, insurance information, emergency contact, any medications, any past history of suicide, and questions about why the client is seeking counseling now.

Often the intake just requires one session but if the client is particularly talkative, is in crisis, or has an extensive history, it could take two sessions or more. Other times, for example if the counseling psychologist is working with a reticent teenager who doesn't talk much, it might only take 20 minutes and then they may have to probe to get more information. Depending on the agency or setting, the client may first see an intake counselor rather than the therapist who they will work with longer term. Some agencies have employees who are intake counselors and all they do is complete intakes, and then the staff meet and discuss the client, and decide which therapist might be a good fit. For example, if a client comes in with concerns about disordered eating and body image issues, an agency might assign them to one therapist with that special interest and expertise, but if a client comes in and wants to process an issue related to stress at work, there might be several different therapists who could work with them. How do you think having one person doing the clinical interview/intake and then another person for therapy affects the client? What are the pros and cons to this approach? If the intake counselor will likely be different from the assigned therapist, it is very important to explain to the client up front that the person doing the intake might be different.

There are several purposes behind an intake session, including screening, assessment, and emergency situations. Screening allows an intake counselor to meet with the client before assignment to a therapist to determine best fit with a therapist at that agency or setting. For group therapy, it allows the therapist to assure that the client is a good fit with the group. Another purpose of the intake is for assessment. Therapists may provide an initial diagnosis based on the clinical interview. So, based on the background information the client provides and the intake interview, a therapist may be able to offer an initial diagnosis of, for example, major depressive disorder. This diagnosis may change across the course of therapy depending on how issues arise and present. Intakes may also be used for initial consultation with other therapists or for emergency situations.

At the beginning of the intake, it is important for counseling psychologists to go over the informed consent document together with the client so they understand what their rights are. Informed consent helps them understand what they might want to share with the counseling psychologist (or not). The informed consent document shares a lot of information with clients – such as fees, hours, what to do in an emergency, cancellation policies, risks and benefits to therapy, confidentiality, and privacy. It is not sufficient for a counseling psychologist to say something like "I see you have read the informed consent, any questions? No? Okay let's begin."

Clients may sign the informed consent document without reading and paying close attention to every detail. However, it is crucial that clients understand risks and benefits of counseling, what counseling might look like, and confidentiality as well as limits to confidentiality. It is best practice for a counseling psychologist to ask if there are any questions about the informed consent, and then verbally describe, at a minimum, limits to confidentiality. That might look something like this:

> Before we begin, I want to review this section about confidentiality. As it states, what we discuss is confidential, with a few exceptions. Those exceptions include things like if I believe you are in danger of harming yourself or someone else, if I learn that a child or vulnerable adult is being abused or neglected, for insurance purposes, or if I am subpoenaed.

Different states have different limits to confidentiality. So you might also say:

> Also, in the State of [fill in your state here], there is a requirement that if I know a person who is pregnant is using alcohol or illicit substances, I have to report that. Do you have any questions about any of this?

Some counseling psychologists may incorporate a mental status exam, or mini-mental status exam, into the intake session. These brief exams can help establish a baseline of cognitive functioning, can assess or screen for any kind of cognitive impairment, and can monitor clients' changes or progress over time. Counseling psychologists will often report this in the intake notes as "client was orientedx3" or "oriented to person, place, and time" meaning the client was able to state their name, the date, and the location. Full assessment may be used more for people showing some psychotic symptoms. Here, the counselor is really just looking for anything that might be unusual. If not unusual, can just say "nothing noticeable" but if there is something unusual, "Client spoke rapidly and loudly, got up and down from chair throughout session, highly agitated."

Counseling psychologists must have strong clinical interview skills to complete an intake session well. An intake session requires counseling psychologists to gather a large amount of information in a short amount of time, as they are getting a full psychosocial history within 55 minutes to an hour. The intake counselor or counseling psychologist must establish rapport and build trust so the client feels comfortable with the agency and feels like they can get help there. The intake counselor must utilize the microskills that we described earlier in this chapter. They will attend to verbal and nonverbal information from the client, will need to consider pace so they don't go too fast or too slow. They need to balance gathering information with being in tune with the client's needs and emotions in session.

Often, clients who have never been to therapy (and some who have) are really frightened or anxious in their first therapy session. It is important to attend to any of these emotions in the intake. It is also important to explain to the client what will happen during this first session and set the tone for the intake. Starting with something like:

> Hi, I'm Bobbi, my pronouns are he/him and today we're going to spend about an hour together. I'm going to be asking a lot of questions about your background, for example I might ask about your childhood, but I'm also going to ask about health. Some of the questions may seem a little unusual, but I want you to do the best to answer them so we can get a full, good picture of what's going on for you. Toward the end of the session, I'm going to check in with you and share some thoughts that I'm having and then we'll talk about next steps. How does that sound to you?

During the intake session, the counseling psychologist will usually take copious notes or perhaps record the session because they are gathering so much information. Now it is your turn, take a minute to write down a brief intro you might use to start an intake session. How would you want to introduce yourself? What information would you want to convey to the client? What wording would you use to let them know what is going to happen in the session?

Identifying the Presenting Concern(s)

Counseling psychologists use the term *presenting concern* to refer to the issue that is bringing someone in for counseling. If you were a client, and someone asked what your presenting concern was, would you know what they were referring to? This is a term that real people in the real world in real life do not use. So, one of the first things that a counseling psychologist wants to get from the client is for them to describe in their own words what is going on. Counseling psychologists must keep in mind that sometimes, what the client initially shares as the presenting concern is not what they really want to work on. For example, a client might state that their presenting concern is conflict with their roommate, but as they begin to trust the therapist more, they disclose that they have been having some obsessive-compulsive thoughts and behaviors that are worrisome, but they have been too embarrassed to tell anyone else about.

Keeping in mind that the client has already filled in paperwork and has probably shared why they are coming in, one way for a counseling psychologist to initiate discussion of the presenting concern in the intake session is to say something like "Okay, I've read through your paperwork and what's going on, but if you could, just in your own words, please describe for me why you're seeking counseling right now." Or "If you were to tell someone what your concerns were, how would you do that?" There are also important pieces to understand about the presenting concern. If someone comes in and says they've been having anxiety, the counseling psychologist might ask about how long it has been happening. For example, if someone answers, "I've been super anxious the last two months," the counseling psychologist might understand this has fairly recent onset. However, if someone states, "My mom described me as a really anxious and worried child," it is likely the client has been struggling with anxiety their whole life. It is also good to know whether the client has sought treatment for anxiety in the past, how they are coping with it now, how they coped with it in the past, what impact is it having on the client's life right now, and how they are currently functioning. A client might share: "I haven't been able to study, I can't leave my room, and I'm afraid to drive." That kind of information is useful and different from "I'm having a hard time concentrating and I forget things sometimes."

Psychosocial Factors

In addition to setting the tone, building rapport, going over informed consent, telling the client what they're going to do today, and finding out about the presenting concern, the counseling psychologist has to gather lots of information about psychosocial factors (history and background to what is going on). Why do we ask about all these different factors? For example, if you have someone who comes in and they talk about feeling really low-energy, but they didn't have any depression as a child or high school student, and it doesn't run in the family at all, asking about the last time they had a physical check-up with a doctor could be really important. There could be a health concern such as thyroid issues or anemia. So, if the client says "Yes, I saw a doctor a couple months ago, and they ran bloodwork and everything is looking good," you might consider that differently from a client saying they haven't seen a doctor in five or so years and about a year ago switched to a new type of diet.

Here are some of the typical psychosocial factors that a counseling psychologist will ask about in an intake session.

- A counseling psychologist should ask about *childhood and development*, for example "Can you tell me a little about your family background? What was it like for you growing up?" This could be a two-minute conversation like "Oh I had a great childhood!" or could take 40 minutes.
- Another topic could be *friendships or romantic relationships/history and other social supports.* "What is your social support system like?" "Do you have people you can talk to?"
- It is also important to ask about *work and academic history*: "Tell me a little bit about your job." "Tell me how you do in school – what is school like for you?"

- As mentioned earlier, counseling psychologists should ask about *health and medical concerns* including pain concerns, such as how many hours of sleep is the client getting per night? How many actual meals (not including chips and cookies) are they getting per day? Are they engaging in any physical activity?
- Counseling psychologists also ask about *alcohol or substance use*: "Do you ever drink alcohol? How many drinks per day/week?" One question that may make clients nervous is asking about illicit substance use, so it can be good to remind them that the session is confidential – "Do you use any other illicit or recreational substances?"
- A counseling psychologist may ask about *identity,* such as "I see on your paperwork that you identify as Muslim. Is your faith an important part of your coping?"
- A counseling psychologist usually asks about *legal and judicial history*, which might include any arrests or current lawsuits. "Do you have any history of any kind of legal concerns?" "Yeah, I have three DUIs." Or "I'm being sued for child support and I'm going to ask you to write a letter about my parenting skills."
- It is important to ask about *trauma history* delicately and with sensitivity – in an intake, it is good to clarify, for example, "I see you noted a traumatic event that happened a couple of years ago. Today we won't be able to get into the full history of that event, but is that something that you are wanting to dive into in therapy more?" or "Is that event related to what you're coming in for?"
- Counseling psychologists may ask about *current symptoms* and how they may be interfering with functioning, "What do you see going on?" "What's happening for you as a result of your concerns?" Clients may respond with something like "I'm angry at my roommate all the time," or "I'm not sleeping," or "I don't feel like eating or going to work," or "I'm seeing things when I walk into a room since my husband died."
- Another important aspect of the informed consent process is *risk assessment and history*, including risk to self and others. This allows the counseling psychologist to determine whether the client might need a higher level of care or immediate crisis intervention. "Do you self-harm?" "Have you ever attempted suicide? Are you thinking about it now?" "Gosh, you're describing a lot of rage. When you feel like that do you ever want to hurt someone?" or "Are you thinking about hurting someone?" Clients will often be honest: "I'm not going to do anything but if something happened, they would be getting what they deserved."
- Counseling psychologists may also ask about *safety*, especially if working with populations such as vulnerable youth or people in interpersonal violence situations, such as: "Do you have a safe place to go? Do you have money, gas, and food? Are your children safe?"

Can you think of any other factors or issues that might be important to ask a client?

At the end of the session, the counseling psychologist may offer a diagnosis. It is helpful to collaboratively discuss diagnostic impressions with the client to get clarity of the client's understanding of, and agreement with, the diagnosis. "I am thinking that you might have generalized anxiety disorder, I want to ask you some more questions about that next time, but does that make sense to you? Does that align with what you've been thinking or experiencing?" And then the counseling psychologist may work collaboratively with the client to think about treatment, goals, and next steps.

Crisis Intervention Skills

There are more advanced skills that counseling psychologists might utilize based on their theoretical orientation, the presenting issue of the client, the number of sessions they have to work within, and other factors. We can't describe all of these different skills in this chapter – books have been written about skills! But we feel it is important to note that one additional set of skills that all counseling psychologists must have is crisis intervention skills (James & Gilliland, 2016). Crisis intervention is a short-term approach intended to address immediate psychological distress, ensure client safety, and restore stability (Roberts & Ottens, 2005). In these situations, counseling psychologists work to problem-solve in a practical way.

In a crisis situation, clients are sometimes experiencing *acute stress*. Acute stress disorder is a short-term condition that occurs immediately after a traumatic event (American Psychiatric Association, 2022). People experiencing acute stress may have disturbing memories of the event, nightmares, extreme distress when reminded of the event, or feelings of emotional numbness. ASD is different from post-traumatic stress disorder (PTSD) because acute stress refers to the initial, immediate symptoms after a traumatic event (up to a month afterward), and PTSD is more like the long-term aftermath (with symptoms lasting at least a month) after a traumatic event. Sometimes, if acute stress can be addressed, it is possible to prevent it from developing into PTSD (Bryant, 2019).

There are all kinds of traumatic events that people could have an acute stress reaction to – death or injury of a loved one, experiencing a sexual assault, interpersonal/domestic violence, and other events – we cannot offer an exhaustive list here. Counseling psychologists also refer to suicide intervention as crisis intervention (James & Gilliland, 2016). If a counseling psychologist believes a client to be actively planning suicide, they will work to ensure safety and stability of the client (Roberts & Ottens, 2005). We give an example of this below. It is also important to note that what one person considers a crisis, someone else might not. (Roberts & Ottens, 2005). For example, many people might experience sadness at the loss of a beloved pet. For others, this could be a much more distressing or disturbing event that could be at the level of a crisis.

There are numerous models of crisis intervention, but one useful model is James and Gilliland's (2016) six-step model in which the helping professional works to:

1) Define the problem: A counseling psychologist might respond differently to vague statements ("I wish I would never wake up") as opposed to urgent ones ("I want to die") by assessing:

   - Plan: Do they have a plan? A timeline?
   - Means: Do they have access to the method?
   - Lethality: A firearm is much more lethal than some pills.
   - Contributing Factors: Impulsivity, substance abuse, and other things.

2) Ensure client safety: May involve direct inquiries about things like: Will they call a friend and have the friend take them safely to the emergency room for a safety evaluation?
3) Provide support: May involve encouragement and reminders about the client's value and importance.
4) Examine alternatives: May involve identifying coping skills like running around a track rather than toward the street.
5) Make plans: May involve more frequent sessions or phone calls between sessions.
6) Obtain commitment: May involve something called a "safety plan," which could involve spelling out (often on paper that the client can take with them) what the client can do if they are feeling particularly at risk, such as calling friends (with phone numbers), the psychologist or doctor (with phone numbers), or crisis helplines. It may also include a written commitment from the client to not kill themselves, with signatures from the client and counselor. Generally, there is evidence that safety plans such as these can be effective in reducing suicidal behavior and ideation (Nuij et al., 2021).

Conversations about suicide can be heavy and tough, but they can also be turning points for clients. The steps we outlined often help clients make changes in their lives that reduce their focus on suicide. Counseling psychology is not an easy profession, but it saves lives. As we said at the beginning of this chapter, we love talking about microskills and interventions because they have the power to make a huge difference.

Summary

At the beginning of this chapter, we gave you this scenario: A client says:

> I am so mad at my roommate right now. She decided to get a puppy without asking me, but she doesn't know anything about dogs, doesn't take it out as much as she should, and is hardly ever in the apartment! I end up taking care of it and feeding it and walking it all the time.

In this chapter, we described all kinds of skills that a counseling psychologist might use. Based on what you know now, how might you respond to the client? We hope you learned new skills that you can utilize in your own life, not only if you pursue a career as a helping professional, but really in any future career or even in your own relationships. We also described a clinical interview and briefly discussed crisis intervention skills. Now that you have read Chapter 6 about theories, and this chapter, you might be wondering what actually works to help people get better in therapy. We talk about that in Chapter 8!

What Would You Do?

Imagine you are lying in bed enjoying the latest Romantasy book from your favorite author. You are just getting to the part where the dragon and the fairie queen are going to reveal who their secret love child is when your best friend texts: "Hey what the heck. Look at this." They send you a screenshot of a social media post from their own counseling psychologist's public account. The post describes exactly what your friend told you they were just talking to their therapist about last week! They said the only other person they talked to about it was you! It doesn't include your friend's name or any other identifying information, but your friend recognizes it immediately as being about them. In the post, the counseling psychologist shares that they were "so proud" of their client who "finally became vulnerable" and "allowed themself to cry" this week about some family issues. Your friend had just shared some super private stuff about their family. Your friend is appalled and upset, and so are you! You cannot believe that your friend's counseling psychologist would put this on a social media post!

- We have not yet discussed ethics and legal issues in detail, but what does your gut instinct tell you: Do you think this is ethical? Do you think it is legal?
- Even if it is ethical and legal, do you think it is actually okay? Why or why not?
- You thought things people discussed with their therapists were confidential but what does that actually mean?
- What kind of advice or guidance would you give your friend?
- Is there anything else you might do?

Counseling Psychologist Spotlight: Corrections

Dr. Ashlee Jayne

Dr. Ashlee Jayne is a Sex Offender Program Psychologist for the Federal Bureau of Prisons. Ashlee never guessed when she started her training that she would have to wear a law enforcement uniform, stab-resistant vest, and carry handcuffs with her in her future work. She fell in love with corrections work when she did a doctoral practicum placement at her local county jail. She liked seeing and supporting the resilience in the people she worked with. She said it was inspiring to see people adjust and work through the hardest times in their lives. She also enjoyed the challenges of *coordinating groups with custody* (this term refers to collaborating with all the different units or agencies that are cooperating to handle the care of a person who is in custody), responding to crises, learning how to de-escalate dangerous situations, and providing treatment to people whom many others avoid. In her current work in the prison, on a daily basis, she does group treatment, individual treatment, crisis intervention, training, supervision, mentoring newer staff, risk assessments, and psychological testing, and she serves on correctional support teams for the region and

Dr. Ashley Jayne with her very good dog, Kronk. Photograph by author.

her local institution. You might also want to refer to Chapter 13, Counseling Psychology Applied to Special Settings, for a description of the kind of work counseling psychologists do in corrections settings.

One thing she loves about her job is working with her team. As a very team-oriented person, she considers herself fortunate to have an amazing team to work with. She also likes the challenges of her job. She says there is never a dull moment and her job requires adaptability, flexibility, and creativity. She is always moving and learning and never stands still for long. She has had a lot of amazing experiences in her job. As we discuss later in Chapter 12, environments like corrections, law enforcement, and first responders are high stress and intensity. Not surprisingly, staff experience burnout and stressors at a higher level than in other environments. So, Ashlee created a wellness program that was offered to all staff such as correctional officers, medical staff, executive staff, educators, case managers, and others. She began this program from scratch and included teaching about wellness and exercises for improving wellness. She provided the training and included individuals who support the staff such as family and friends. She also co-created a three-day leadership course for people who were interested in seeking promotion, advancing their careers, or supervising other employees. This course included interactive scenarios and simulations. The training focused on leading with empathy. Participants engaged in difficult dialogues and were trained on cultural competence with a heavy emphasis on active listening. She also loves her role as a supervisor and mentor. She says she has been fortunate to train newer staff and students and appreciates how much she learns from her supervisees. These are ways in which Ashlee is applying her counseling psychology training not only to the individual clients who she works with, but also to her coworkers and to improve the overall climate of her workplace.

Ashlee said that one of the challenging parts of her job is that the integration of corrections and psychology is always difficult. She knows amazing psychologists with much more experience than her who continue to have difficulty providing therapy in an environment where there are lockdowns, searches of cells, and rule-breaking behavior. She learned early on that boundaries and rules are central to her job as a prison psychologist. While this is the case in many areas of counseling psychology, she finds it to be much more rigid in the prison setting. Ashlee also said that humor is one of her major secrets to her success. Being able to laugh at herself has been a huge help to developing into who she is today and her resilience in her line of work.

Ashlee shared that having dyslexia and not liking school as a kid, she went from barely graduating high school and a B/C average undergraduate student to getting her doctorate and Board-Certified Behavior Analyst credential. She says that she learned early on that obstacles show her how badly she wants a goal. In other words, if she was willing to quit given the obstacle, then maybe she did not truly want it. Now, Ashlee has succeeded in her work as a counseling psychologist and said she loves the versatility that being a counseling psychologist offers. She says that many of her friends do different things, and their lives are vastly different even though they have the same degree. Working in corrections, she is surrounded by individuals with clinical, forensic, and criminal justice backgrounds. She appreciates that she has a more generalist training and focus and often finds she can see the "big picture" or have a more holistic point of view about a client. Being trained as a counseling psychologist also allows her to work from a strengths-based model rather than focusing just on mental health diagnoses and problems her clients might have.

Outside of her job, Ashlee enjoys time with her husband and dogs (not necessarily in that order). She says there are lots of dog-friendly events in her area and she participates in them as much as possible. She enjoys dog training and teaching fun skills to dogs such as service animal skills, scent training, and tricks just for fun. She also enjoys building Legos. She loves to be outside, "even with her allergies." She says that organizing and baking are two hobbies that bring her peace.

Ashlee earned her PhD in counseling psychology from Oklahoma State University (OSU). She also holds a BS and MS from OSU. She is a licensed psychologist and is a Board-Certified Behavior Analyst. *Note: Kronk, Ashlee's dog, consented for his photo to be included.

References

American Psychiatric Association. (2022). *Diagnostic and statistical manual of mental disorders* (5th ed., text rev.; DSM-5-TR). American Psychiatric Publishing.

Bryant, R. A. (2019). Early intervention for post-traumatic stress disorder. *Current Opinion in Psychology, 14*, 112–115. https://doi.org/10.1016/j.copsyc.2019.01.002

Hill, C. E. (2009). *Helping skills: Facilitating exploration, insight, and action* (3rd ed.). American Psychological Association.

Ivey, A. E., Gluckstern Packard, N., & Ivey, M. B. (2019). *Basic attending skills: Foundations of empathic relationships and problem solving* (6th ed.). Cognella Academic Publishing.

James, R. K., & Gilliland, B. E. (2016). *Crisis intervention strategies* (8th ed.). Cengage Learning.

Nuij, C., van Ballegooijen, W., de Beurs, D., Juniar, D., Erlangsen, A., Portzky, G., O'Connor, R. C., & Smit, J. H. (2021). Safety planning-type interventions for suicide prevention: Meta-analysis. *The British Journal of Psychiatry, 219*(2), 419–426. https://doi.org/10.1192/bjp.2021.50

Roberts, A. R., & Ottens, A. J. (2005). The seven-stage crisis-intervention model: A roadmap to goal attainment, problem solving, and crisis resolution. *Brief Treatment and Crisis Intervention, 5*(4), 329–339. https://doi.org/10.1093/brief-treatment/mhi030

Chapter 8

Counseling Psychology Processes and Outcomes

What Works?

What Makes Therapy Effective?

In Chapter 6, you learned about different theoretical orientations and approaches that counseling psychologists might use with clients. In Chapter 7, you reviewed a wide variety of counseling or helping skills that counseling psychologists may employ in session. But all of this may have left you with more questions than answers. Do counseling psychologists have to pick one theoretical orientation and stick with it? Is it okay for a humanistic counseling psychologist to employ cognitive-behavioral techniques with clients? Is there one theory or approach that has the best outcomes for clients? What does it depend on? How do counseling psychologists know if their clients are getting better? In this chapter, we are going to discuss what research indicates about the effectiveness of therapy and try to come up with some answers – although you may be left with even more questions!

In this chapter, you will be challenged to consider some important questions, such as: What is more important: what a counselor *does* or how they *are*? How do we know if counseling is effective? Why is it important to study or measure outcomes? Are there some theories that have better outcomes than others in all situations? In specific situations? Who are the most effective counseling psychologists? What contributes to clients getting better? We introduce the concept of common factors, or concepts that may be effective across theoretical approaches, modalities, and skills. We also talk about how counseling psychology outcomes can be tied to things like the number of sessions, whether or not clients return, and health insurance, among other factors. We describe the importance of therapeutic alliance and attendance to ruptures, and the roles of readiness for change and stages of counseling.

Let's start with a little activity. Rank-order the following therapeutic factors, based on what you think is most impactful on client outcomes:

- The client's motivation to change/get better
- The therapist's skills
- The therapist's level of training (MS vs. PhD)
- The theory/approach used
- The client's willingness to take medication
- Something else

We will come back to this later at the end of this chapter and see if you have any changes to your list. For now, set your list aside, but as you read this chapter, try to be a detective and look for clues as to what primary or common factors make therapy effective.

DOI: 10.4324/9781003439899-8

History

To start, it might be good to dig into a little history about counseling outcomes. That is because history is often a source of clues regarding what works and what does not work. As you might remember from Chapter 1, Freud developed psychoanalysis in the late 1800s. Then other theorists developed new approaches like Person-Centered Therapy (Rogers, 1940s) and Rational-Emotive Behavior Therapy (Ellis, 1950s). But all these theorists were putting forward new theories, without a lot of solid evidence of their effectiveness (at least to begin with). Much of what was written was personal accounts by psychologists about their perception of whether clients got better.

In the first half of the 20th century, there just was not much research or understanding of the effectiveness of therapy, but because these amazing theorists were saying it was effective, it was largely believed to be so. In 1952, a psychologist named Hans Eysenck published an article that rocked the psychology world. He did a review of studies of therapy outcomes and concluded that patients showed no more improvement from therapy than those who had no therapy. In other words, he asserted that psychotherapy was ineffective. He brought attention to the lack of adequate data and research and called for "properly planned and executed experimental studies" (Eysenck, 1952, p. 323). Bad news, right?

Eysenck's findings and call to the profession sparked a wave of research on psychotherapy outcomes. In 1963, in the very first issue of the new journal *Psychotherapy*, Strupp reiterated Eysenck's concerns and drew attention to "staggering research problems" in trying to examine the effectiveness of psychotherapy (p. 2). For a long time, there were arguments, discussions, and speculations about whether therapy actually worked to help clients improve. Finally, in 1977, Smith and Glass published a meta-analysis of 375 therapy studies.

If you haven't heard the term *meta-analysis* previously, think of it as a study of studies: researchers compile a large group of studies examining a similar variable or outcome (in this case, psychotherapy outcomes). They look at the studies to determine their rigor and whether they are high quality enough to be included in the meta-analysis. Then they run statistical analyses to compare the findings and make conclusions from this large group of studies. In this case, Smith and Glass' findings offered optimism for the field of applied psychology. They reported that, on average, a client who participated in therapy had outcomes that were better than 75% of people who did not seek therapy.

They also found that there were no real differences in outcomes across therapy types; in other words, there was no a clear "winner" or "best" therapy. Specifically, in spite of behavioral and cognitive-behavioral advocates arguing that behavioral interventions had the best outcomes, in reality, behavioral interventions and nonbehavioral interventions did not differ in terms of effectiveness. This finding was actually first put forth in 1936 by a psychologist named Rosenzweig, who called it the *Dodo Bird Verdict*. Rosenzweig was referring to Alice Carroll's book Alice's Adventures in Wonderland, in which there is a scene after a race, when the Dodo Bird exclaims, "Everybody has won, and all must have prizes!" (Carroll, 1865, p. 27). Since that time, the *Dodo Bird Verdict* refers to the idea that all effective psychotherapies are about equivalent, in other words, the actual theoretical approach is less important to outcomes than things like the relationship between the counselor and client.

So we are pretty much right back to the conclusion that therapy works, but we are still not able to say what makes different therapeutic approaches work differently. We must be careful here to note that the Dodo Bird Verdict applies to all *effective* psychotherapies. There is a danger in thinking that any willy-nilly therapy goes. There is a history of psychologists experimenting or implementing therapies that they thought would be helpful but turned out to be quite harmful to clients.

For example, there was a trend in the late 1990s/early 2000s where attachment therapists did an aggressive treatment called *attachment therapy* that involved *holding therapy* or *rebirthing* (Lilienfeld, 2007). The idea was that children with attachment problems and anger must re-experience infant attachment experiences. In holding therapy, therapists or caregivers would physically hold or restrain children until they made eye contact. Rebirthing involved wrapping the child in a blanket and squeezing them to simulate the birth process. There is record of several children dying from this process, and no evidence of its effectiveness (Lilienfeld, 2007).

Another caveat is that the Dodo Bird Verdict applies to therapy in general. General therapy helps with general problems. On the other hand, for some specific disorders, there is evidence that specific kinds of treatments are better. For example, for specific phobias (such as fear of flying/aerophobia, spiders/arachnophobia, or public speaking/glossophobia), counseling psychologists know that the most effective form of treatment is exposure therapy, specifically systematic desensitization, in which the client creates a hierarchy of the least-scary situation to the scariest, and with relaxation techniques, gradually works toward increasing comfort and decreasing fear of the stimulus. In fact, lately, there have been some really cool innovations in this kind of treatment, such as using 3D games and virtual reality to treat phobias (Lopes et al., 2025). So, when we discuss common factors across therapy in a later section of this chapter, it is important to keep in mind that this does not mean any therapy works at any time. At this point, what clues are you picking up about the effectiveness of therapy? Are you starting to form some hunches? If you are, it is time to add some more nuances to your conclusions by introducing you to more psychotherapy research.

Empirical Support

Smith and Glass's (1977) study was super important to help get psychotherapy established as effective healthcare treatment. Something else happening around that time was that health insurance companies were beginning to gain more power as they decided what they would or would not cover as treatment for health care. Most insurance companies did not begin offering coverage for mental health care until the late 1950s and were not required to cover mental health treatment until 1996; addiction treatment was added in 2008 (Barry et al., 2010). In the United States, insurance companies have a lot of control over how and why people seek treatment and what kind of treatment they can have access to or afford.

You may have heard the term *managed care*, which refers to the idea of trying to have high-quality health care while keeping costs low. Insurance companies do not want to take the risk of covering a treatment if they are not certain it will work. So, consider a counseling psychologist in 1980: She knows counseling psychology treatments are effective (based on Smith & Glass, 1977, and other studies), but can only see the few clients who have insurance coverage for psychotherapy or who are wealthy enough to pay for therapy out of their own pocket.

To help legitimize mental health treatment as something that should be considered necessary health care, a group of psychologists worked hard across the 1990s to develop and publicize a list of *empirically supported treatments* (ESTs) (American Psychological Association [APA], 1995; Chambless & Hollon, 1998). Empirically supported treatments are defined as "clearly specified psychological treatments shown to be efficacious in controlled research with a delineated population" (Chambless & Hollon, 1998, p. 7). Since that time, other terms have been used: empirically-based treatment, empirically valid treatment, and so on. Let's pause for a second to consider:

- Why is it so important to have evidence (empirical support) that therapy is valid and effective?
- Why do you think research on therapy took so long to produce?

- In other words, why is research on therapy so complicated?
- Why is it hard to do research on therapy, compared to medical treatments?

There are a lot of reasons for this – in therapy, unlike medical treatments, evidence of client change is not always readily apparent or immediately observable. For example, a client may gain insight that helps them understand themselves, but it could take a lot longer for their behavior to change. And how do you measure constructs like empathy? Or unconditional positive regard? There are some very concrete theories, such as cognitive behavioral therapy (CBT), that are so systematic and step-by-step that they lend themselves well to observation and measurement.

There are other theories that are perhaps a little fuzzier, like humanistic therapy, that may take more effort or time to measure and study. And then there are all kinds of factors that may come into play that are so incredibly complicated: perhaps the therapist reminded the client of their uncle, and they terminated early. Perhaps the client has to take a long, crowded bus ride to get to therapy and winds up being cranky at the beginning of every session. There are just too many human variables to be able to reasonably measure or account for. But that doesn't mean we give up – it just means it is complicated and is not as clear-cut to engage in research as with some medical treatments. As Miller et al. (2005, p. 22) concluded, "psychotherapy does not work in the same way as medicine."

The APA currently recommends that psychologists use evidence-based practice in psychology, which refers to psychologists practicing using, considering, and integrating: (a) the best available research; (b) their clinical expertise and judgment; and (c) the context of client characteristics, culture, and preferences (APA, 2005). This is a reasonable approach that we really like because it allows the psychologist flexibility and accountability at the same time.

Let's say that a client, Nita, presents with anxiety, but tells the counseling psychologist right off the bat that she does not want to participate in homework activities usually used by cognitive-behavioral therapists. She said her last therapist always wanted her to do it, but she never did, and she stopped going to therapy because it made her feel so guilty. The counseling psychologist knows that research (evidence, empirical support) indicates that CBT is pretty effective for anxiety work in therapy, but it is not the only effective anxiety treatment, so they decide to start with a feminist approach to allow Nita to feel empowered in her therapy. In other words, the counseling psychologist takes into account Nita's preferences and her past history (she disliked homework), with the understanding of different types of approaches that can help lessen anxiety, and they used their expertise and professional clinical judgment to move forward in collaboration with Nita.

Readiness for Change

As you have been collecting clues about what makes therapy work, you might have noticed a major theme in counseling psychology: it depends. How, when, and why therapy works can be impacted by a bunch of variables and factors. One idea that people have put forward about whether or not counseling is effective is *readiness for change.* You can imagine that some people are more ready to change, or seek out treatment, or look for therapy, than others. Think about a time when you might have wanted to make a change. Maybe you wanted to stop chewing gum so often, or limit your energy drink intake, or wanted to be better about cleaning your bedroom or doing laundry more often. What spurred you to action? Did you end up making the change? Was it sustainable? There are a lot of factors that go into someone's readiness for change. The *transtheoretical model of change* is based on the notion that how a client changes, or gets better, depends on their readiness to actually change (Prochaska & DiClemente, 1983).

Imagine three potential clients: Josie, age 45, has been suffering from depression and generally feels low every day; when she goes to therapy, she reiterates the same complaints and symptoms but does not seem willing to try any new behaviors. Franklin, age 38, has also been suffering from depression. With encouragement from his counseling psychologist, over time, he learns to reframe some thoughts in which he blames himself or criticizes himself and realizes that he is not the "failure" that he had previously labeled himself. He begins to feel better and has more confidence in himself at his work. Finally, we have Carlos, age 14, who is in therapy because his family just moved to a new city and his parents made him go because he's been skipping school. He is furious that he is being forced to spend his time in therapy.

He spends most of the sessions not engaging with the counseling psychologist, doodling in his notebook, because he is not allowed to take his phone into sessions. In looking at these three cases, we have three people at very different levels of readiness for changes. It seems that Franklin was most ready to change and engage in the "work" needed to change, whereas Josie seemed to be more passive and wanted the change to magically occur for her. Carlos, on the other hand, did not seem to think anything needed to change at all. Research indicates that the further along someone is in the stages of change (the more ready they are to change), the better their treatment outcomes will be (Krebs et al., 2018).

Stages of Change

Scholars who study readiness for change suggest there are different stages people go through or levels of readiness they pass through as they work to change a behavior or outcome. The six stages of change are (Prochaska & Velicer, 1997):

- *Precontemplation:* The client does not intend to take action in the foreseeable future; they are not aware of how change could help them or they have tried changing in the past and felt it didn't work.
- *Contemplation:* The client intends to take action in the next six months; they are weighing the pros and cons of changing.
- *Preparation:* The client intends to take action in the immediate future, usually within the next month; they have some kind of plan for change.
- *Action:* The client has made steps toward change in the last six months; they have done some things to change their behavior.
- *Maintenance:* The client is working to maintain the changes they saw in the action stage; they are confident that they can keep up with the changes but are not as active as they were in the action stage.
- *Termination:* The client has completely changed the previous behavior.
- Based on the three examples we gave you previously (Josie, Franklin, and Carlos), where do you think each of those people fits in the stages of change?

Processes of Change

Prochaska and Velicer (1997) also proposed some *processes of change*, which are the strategies or actions that move people toward change. All of these are processes that can be utilized by the counseling psychologist if someone seeks help. These include:

- *Consciousness raising:* The client has increased awareness of the issue or problem; this could be because of education such as reading a book, feedback they received from other people, or media campaigns.

- *Dramatic relief:* The client experiences some kind of emotional catharsis or sense of relief, possibly through things like sharing with others or through a grieving process.
- *Self-reevaluation:* The client considers their own image, how others perceive them, how they perceive themselves, and how they might want to change. Engaging in activities like clarifying values or goals, or modeling after role models, can assist with change.
- *Environmental reevaluation:* The client thinks about how their environment might be playing a role in their behavior, thoughts, or feelings, or they consider the effects of their behavior on their environment, such as their family life.
- *Self-liberation:* The client feels a sense of motivation or willpower to change. It helps if there are multiple options or choices for change so the client has freedom to choose which direction they want to go in.
- *Social liberation:* The client experiences a shift or change in their social environment that promotes change. This is particularly applicable to people who have experienced oppression or who would benefit from social advocacy.
- *Counterconditioning:* The client learns new behaviors or coping techniques that can take the place of previous unhealthy techniques. For example, relaxation techniques can help manage stress, or assertiveness training can help people appropriately express themselves.
- *Stimulus control:* The client removes or changes some kind of stimulus or cue that previously would have triggered them into doing an unwanted behavior. In this case, avoidance is an okay technique – for example, if someone is trying to quit drinking as much alcohol, making plans to participate in an alcohol-free game night instead is a positive change.
- *Contingency management:* The client receives or provides themselves with some kind of appropriate and realistic reinforcement (positive is best) for changing the behavior. Positive self-statements are an example: "Wow, I did all my reading for the week. I am feeling more excited about my philosophy class now!"
- *Helping relationships:* The client has supportive, positive relationships – with a peer, mentor, counseling psychologist, or trusted friend or family member – that assist in making the change. One of the reasons groups like Alcoholics Anonymous are so successful is the support from mentors and others who have been in similar situations and who can relate to the client.

So how does all this information apply to therapy and what hypotheses are you forming about the key factors that lead to therapeutic success? Let's go back to our three examples – Josie, Franklin, and Carlos. Josie is likely "stuck" in the contemplation stage. She took the step of seeking therapy but does not seem ready to make more changes. How could a counseling psychologist help get her "unstuck?"

- One thing could be consciousness raising. The counseling psychologist could say something like, "Josie, you have been in therapy for about three months now and it seems like we are where we were at the beginning. It seems like you are a little stuck. How does that sit with you?"
- The counseling psychologist could provide a trusting helping relationship to encourage Josie to experience her feelings in session more deeply, which might allow for dramatic relief.
- The therapist could process how Josie sees herself and how others see her and could discuss things like how Josie has been pressuring herself with how she "should" behave rather than how she "wants" to behave, which might allow her some self-liberation.

Now, let us turn to Franklin. Franklin was pretty ready for change! We think he is likely in the action stage and will be moving into maintenance soon. Franklin experienced some self-reevaluation with a helping relationship with his counseling psychologist. For maintenance, he may want to engage in contingency management, reminding himself of the good change he has seen in himself. Perhaps he also realized that one of the things that was bringing him down at work was that he was hanging out with a group of people who were all "negative Nancys." People who did nothing but complain and vent and moan about their work. Franklin realized he actually enjoys his job and has begun to distance himself from this group during lunches. Instead, he engages in stimulus control by going outside for walks.

Finally, let's consider grouchy Carlos. Carlos says he does not want to go to therapy, does not want to talk about anything, and based on what we know, we would definitely place him in the pre-contemplation stage (in fact, if there was an anti-change stage, he would be in it). At the same time, it is clear that Carlos is hurting. He is so visibly angry that the counseling psychologist knows if they are able to find the pain that Carlos is experiencing, they might be able to help him. The counseling psychologist recognizes that Carlos likes to draw so asks him to draw various things such as his school, home, family, and dog. Over time, Carlos shares small things that allow the counseling psychologist to conclude that Carlos is being bullied at his new school but does not want to talk to his parents about it. First, his parents are nurses who both work the night shift and sleep during the day, and they are always so tired and stressed that he doesn't want to bother them. Also, he thinks he should be able to handle what is happening at school on his own.

The counseling psychologist also learns that Carlos, who is African American and Latino, is the only non-White kid in his class so:

- The counseling psychologist supports Carlos through a helping relationship (that was definitely built over time) and they discuss how his angry mood could be affecting the rest of his family (environmental reevaluation).
- The counseling psychologist shares information with Carlos about a local Black community organization offering a drawing class to youth, where he could meet other kids with similar backgrounds (social liberation).
- Finally, the counseling psychologist role-plays some ways for Carlos to talk to his parents about what is happening at school (counter conditioning).

In all of these examples, the counseling psychologist first assesses the client's *readiness for change* and then, using their theoretical orientation and their counseling skills, can implement some different strategies or *processes of change* to assist with moving toward change and improvement–whether that change is related to something like depression, anxiety, a problem at work, a relationship issue, or something else.

Stages of Counseling

So far, we've talked a lot about the role the client plays. Client readiness for change is not the only variable that impacts counseling processes and outcomes. Another factor that influences counseling psychology outcomes is the process of counseling from beginning to end. There are various models of what counseling can actually look like from the time someone begins therapy to the time they wrap up. For example, Clara Hill developed a three-stage model of counseling, sometimes called the Process Model of Helping (Hill, 2001). She said that counseling consists of three stages, which are *exploration*, *insight*, and *action*.

- In the exploration stage, the counseling psychologist helps the client explore their thoughts and feelings.

- In the insight stage, the counseling psychologist helps the client understand the reasons for their thoughts and feelings and how they developed.
- In the third stage, action, the client learns how to make changes.

This is not to say that the focus is entirely on the therapy and nothing else. In fact, the therapeutic process is client-centered, collaborative, and culturally grounded.

Other stage models with different steps have been proposed as well. Some models are based on specific theories or other factors. For example, Ridley et al. (2021) based their model on the concept of multicultural competence. They developed the *multicultural competence process model* with three stages: preparation, intake and in-sessions, and termination. This model has five components or what they call *clinical operations*, which are:

- Grounding in cultural competence
- Preparation
- Building a therapeutic relationship
- Adapting interventions (using skills and theories)
- Evaluating the process and outcome

In general, we think many of these models have benefits to counseling psychologists, but they are a little hard to grasp because they are theoretical. In real-life terms, based on our own clinical experiences in working with clients, we think the ideal counseling experience might look like this.

Imagine a shallow bowl shape, where the therapy starts a little on the edge, goes into the shallow end, and then gets deeper over time. As therapy winds down, the work gets a little less deep and moves back toward the shallower edge.

- First, even prior to counseling, which we will call *pre-counseling*, the client and counseling psychologist or agency communicate. Perhaps the client uploads documents in a portal or fills out other paperwork and answers a bunch of questions that help the counseling psychologist get some background information that will help guide the first session and the course of therapy. Even before they meet, these interactions set the tone for the therapy.
- Then we have the intake and early sessions. Here, the client and counseling psychologist begin to get to know one another and build trust. The counseling psychologist works from a holistic base foundation that is person-centered (communicating empathy and unconditional positive regard), ethical, culturally aware, and strengths-based. The counseling psychologist gathers a bunch of information and tries to form a diagnostic impression to figure out how best to work with the client. A lot of times, what the client initially presents with as the issue they want to discuss can shift and change over sessions as they begin to build trust.
- Once the relationship is built, the "work" of counseling begins. (Sometimes these things happen simultaneously). The middle sessions, and those toward the end of therapy, are typically where a lot of the change happens. As they get deeper, clients may feel uncomfortable and may want to go back up to the shallow part of the bowl occasionally.
- Counseling psychologists call the end of a therapy relationship "termination" (which is a horrible word that reminds us of The Terminator but it's the standard). As the client changes, or gets better, or the goals have been met, ideally, the counseling psychologist will talk to the client about termination and sustaining change outside of therapy in the real world. This is ultimately the goal of counseling!

We want to note that all of this is what an ideal counseling relationship looks like, but therapy does not always go to plan. A lot of times, a client will come to an intake and then never show up for another appointment! Maybe it made them uncomfortable. Maybe they got busy. Maybe they realized it would be too expensive. Maybe they thought the counseling psychologist's office smelled overwhelmingly like essential oils. Often, the counseling psychologist will not know and is left with ambiguity about the situation. Other times, a counseling psychologist might think therapy would be about three or four months, but a client might just decide in the fourth session that they're doing a lot better and want to wrap up.

So even with all these process models, it is just important to know that every therapy relationship is different; sometimes they are in a nice bowl shape, sometimes they are zig-zaggy, sometimes they might jump to the super deep zone right away. Likewise, every session is different. Sometimes, a counseling psychologist may think they are going to talk about a certain topic based on the previous session, for example llama grooming as a future career path, and the client jumps in with wanting to discuss something their brother did that made them mad. Or the counseling psychologist may be ready to go deeper and talk about the client's relationship with their brother, but the client needs a break and brings up their recent weekend foraging for mushrooms. The counseling psychologist has to be flexible, adapt, and adjust, and use their best professional judgment in moving forward. That is why we asked you to be detectives and collect clues about therapeutic effectiveness in this chapter. Working as a counseling psychologist is rarely a direct path from point A to point B. It takes a lot of data gathering, adaptability, and an ability to spot common themes. As you read this chapter, you are actually exercising counseling psychologist skills!

Common Factors

Okay, we discussed earlier about how historically there is mixed information about the effectiveness of therapy. And we talked about how it is super important that therapeutic approaches have empirical evidence to support that they are effective. We have considered different factors such as the client's readiness for change and the overall process of therapy. But what about specific theories? In other words, is there one theory or therapy approach that is the best? Do some theories have better outcomes than others? Going back to the Dodo Bird Verdict, remember that there is some understanding that overall, most well-established and well-researched therapies are effective, with some being better than others for specific diagnoses, and some unestablished therapies being harmful. Once it was established that therapy is, in fact, effective in producing positive client outcomes, people began to do more research related to the debate about whether or not one kind of therapy is "best." A number of scholars, including Hubble, Duncan, Miller, and Wampold, have been doing research over the past 20 years or so on something called *common factors* to try to figure this out (e.g., Hubble et al., 1999; Miller et al., 2005; Wampold, 2015; Wampold & Imel, 2015).

The term *common factors* refers to the notion that across therapies (humanistic, existential, CBT, Gestalt, dialectical behavior therapy, etc.), there are some pieces that are similar or shared that contribute to client outcomes. Over the years, there have been lots of studies on common factors using meta-analyses and other methods, and although the researchers have had different findings, in general, we know that there are factors common across therapies that account for change. Duncan et al. (2009) found four main things that contribute to client change:

- Client and extra-therapeutic factors
- Models and techniques
- Therapeutic relationship/alliance
- Therapist factors

These are not mutually exclusive; any of these factors can influence the others in a therapeutic relationship, they may change over time or even within a session. They don't work apart from one another, in other words. Let's start with *client and extra-therapeutic factors*. This is something that is not examined very closely, but it should be! Imagine a client sees a counseling psychologist once a week (if they go every week) for a one-hour session. There are 168 hours in a week. That means that every week, there are 167 hours *not* spent in therapy. All kinds of life things that have nothing to do with therapy can happen in those 167 hours. Things change! A client gets a new boss to replace the boss who she initially came to therapy to talk about. Life is better for her now! And it has nothing to do with therapy. Another client started running at the recommendation of his friend, and he has met a new group of runners, and life is better for him now! And it has nothing to do with therapy. And so on. It is also important to note that the client is a human being, who has choice and autonomy. Counseling psychologists cannot work from a model of knowing what is correct for the client – they have to work in collaboration, in a client-centered way. Research shows that when client feedback is sought out, and when counseling psychologists take into account the client's opinions about how therapy is going, outcomes are better.

The second factor, *models and techniques*, includes theories and skills. This is what the majority of psychotherapy research has focused on, forever. And it does in fact contribute to client outcome – but it is not the only thing, and it is not even the biggest thing. And, a large part of the effectiveness of models and techniques is not necessarily in the use of them, but in the therapist's and client's belief that they work. Some scholars have referred to this as the expectancy effect; it is the effect that if a client expects that treatment to work, it likely will have a positive outcome. Again, revisiting the danger of some harmful psychotherapies, we are referring here to studied models and techniques that have some evidence behind them. Duncan et al. (2009, p. 37) said: "Models and techniques work best when they engage and inspire the participants."

The third factor, *therapeutic relationship/alliance*, refers to the partnership between the client and the counseling psychologist. A positive relationship is a strong predictor of positive client outcomes. Think about your own interactions with helping professionals – teachers, doctors, perhaps counselors – what made your interaction with them a positive one? Often, it is a positive relationship where you feel heard, respected, and that you had some choice. The relationship/alliance goes hand in hand with some of the other factors here, such as models and techniques. This is a professional relationship, not just a friendly or personal one, so the treatment, or the therapy, must go along with the relationship. Along those lines, the counseling psychologist must actively and intentionally work to establish a genuine, collaborative, working relationship for it to be effective.

The final factor, *therapist factors*, focuses on the person as a therapist (see also Chapter 12). Duncan et al. (2009) said that research indicates that the therapist is the most robust factor accounting for client outcomes – which is saying a lot! They also said that perhaps this notion is a bit taboo, that some therapists are more effective than others, and the things you might think would account for differences, like age, gender, race, experience, or credentials, of the therapist do not actually account for that effectiveness. A lot of people think that if they can find a counseling psychologist with years of experience, that will be the best person for them. Or, they think that if they can find someone with a similar racial or ethnic match, that counseling psychologist will be the most effective. Actually, there is no evidence that these kinds of demographic factors contribute to client change and outcomes. Unfortunately, there isn't a clear understanding of what amazing therapists do that makes them so good. There are a few hints, though, that we will dig into further below.

The Contextual Model

Based on years of common factors research, Wampold put forward the Contextual Model (Wampold, 2015; Wampold & Imel, 2015) to help people understand what contributes to positive therapeutic outcomes. First, let's revisit something you read about in Chapter 6, about humanistic theories. Humanistic theory is based on the idea that people are essentially good, have the capacity for self-direction and choice, and you may recall that Rogers' person-centered therapy talked about the need for a positive relationship with empathy, genuineness, and unconditional positive regard. This sounds a lot like the common factors we described earlier! In fact, Wampold asserted that all psychotherapies are humanistic (Wampold, 2012). Likewise, the therapeutic relationship plays a big role in his Contextual Model. The Contextual Model states that first, before any change can happen, there must be work toward an initial therapeutic relationship. This initial relationship or bond is critical. A lot of clients do not return after the first session. So the counseling psychologist must intentionally work to develop trust and rapport. Then, there are three pathways to change through therapy.

Pathway One: The Real Relationship

The *real relationship* involves the client and therapist being genuine with each other and perceiving the other in ways that are beneficial. The real relationship also includes unique aspects of a therapy relationship. First, it's confidential, so it's different from a relationship with your mom, friend, or roommate. Also, it includes disclosure of difficult material. If the client discloses difficult content, that does not disrupt the relationship the way it might a friendship or other close relationship. Often a client might think "I have been a bad client, I haven't done my homework" and when the counseling psychologist responds with "Oh, that's totally cool, we were just going to try it and see what happened, no biggie" and then processes the issue – "Are you worried about me thinking differently of you or judging you because you didn't do your homework?" – this can be a corrective experience for someone who fears they're going to be criticized for not being perfect, for not always achieving what they're supposed to achieve. This is also a reminder that this is a professional, nonjudgmental relationship.

Pathway Two: Expectations

The second pathway is *expectations.* Clients seek out therapy having already developed some kind of explanation for what is going on with them or beliefs about their distress. In therapy, the counseling psychologist can explain and share their beliefs about how the distress might have developed or what is going on with the client and how the counseling psychologist can treat it. If the client believes that therapy is going to be helpful because the counseling psychologist is laying it out for them and telling them that therapy is going to be helpful, it can create an expectancy effect. The client and therapist need to be in agreement about the treatment and the goals of therapy.

So, if a client comes in and says, "I want to work on making friends," but the counseling psychologist says, "Well, really, I think you need to work on issues related to conflict with your mother," they are not in agreement or alignment about the goals of therapy. The counseling psychologist needs to be able to explain their theoretical orientation or theory of change for the client – they need to be able to explain how this is going to help them get better. For example, if the counseling psychologist says, "I believe that cognitive-behavioral therapy, where we are going to work on your behaviors, thoughts, and feelings, is going to be the best kind of treatment for you" and the client agrees, they will be in alignment and can begin the good "work" of therapy. This instills confidence in the client, who believes they will have some control.

Pathway Three: Health-Promoting Actions

The third pathway is *health-promoting actions*. These are the specific ingredients, or specific parts of the therapy, that a counseling psychologist uses or things that the client does, such as practicing things in real life. For example, using CBT, a health-promoting action might be helping the client think about the world in a less maladaptive way. So, if a client goes about their day thinking, "I'm not going to fit in, other people are going to reject me," the counseling psychologist may help them shift that thought pattern. Or using some dynamic therapies, the skill might be improving interpersonal relationships; in emotion-focused therapy, it might be naming and expressing difficult emotions; in feminist therapy, it might be helping clients feel empowered to enact change. The important part is not the tool itself but rather that the counseling psychologist does have specific tools that they are using and a rationale for their use.

What Does All This Mean for Clients?

We have spent a lot of time talking about what the counseling psychologist needs to consider in thinking about psychotherapy effectiveness and outcomes, but from a client perspective, it is good to know that it is important to have good fit with therapist. When seeking out a therapist, clients will get lots of advice to see someone who uses this therapy or that one, to only see someone with certain credentials, and so on. But keeping in mind how important that relationship is, ultimately, the client is the consumer and should look for someone who they will feel comfortable with, and who they trust.

Clients often don't know that it is okay to shop around, to ask questions before making an appointment, or to consider requesting a 15-minute consultation with a therapist before committing to doing therapy with them. Upon meeting, it is also okay to say, "I don't think this is the best fit, is there someone else (within this agency) you could refer me to?" Let's try something. Using your favorite search engine, do a search for *therapist* (or *counseling psychologist*) *in my area*. What kinds of links show up? Select a profile and see if you can find out the following:

- What is their licensure status?
- What is their theoretical orientation?
- How much do they charge per session?
- What insurance do they take?
- Are there issues or populations they specialize in?

Based on the images in the profile (of the therapist, office setting, or other) and the description you can find, would you feel comfortable seeking services from this person or referring a friend or relative to them?

Ruptures

Before we wrap up, we want to talk about one more issue related to counseling processes and outcomes, something counseling psychologists call *ruptures*. Things can occur in therapy where the relationship or bond can be broken, or the trust can be broken. This could be because of something the therapist did or said, or something the client did or said. It could also be something random like something that happened in the waiting room, or an issue related to payment. Ruptures happen. For example, if a client tells the counseling psychologist they looked up her home address, drove by her house, and thought their house looked really nice, this could create an issue with trust. Or, a counseling psychologist might make a comment or joke that unwittingly hurt the client's feelings, and the client was upset. The important thing to know is when a rupture happens, it is always best to openly process it with the client. For example, the counseling psychologist could say, "Well gosh that makes me feel uncomfortable, it feels like you're checking me out or like you're wanting information about me and how I live." And ideally, if a client is upset or angry, they will feel okay to bring it up with the counseling psychologist: "You know last week when you joked about what I was going to do over the weekend? It really upset me because it seemed like you were belittling me." Processing through the conflict, and coming to a better place together, can actually really help the relationship and create more trust. Unfortunately, what often occurs is a client becomes frustrated, disappointed, or angry, or the therapy becomes intensely emotional and uncomfortable, and the client just stops coming to therapy. So, there is no chance to work toward repairing the rupture. It is always best for the counseling psychologist to invite clients to discuss any issues they have with the therapy. It is better to figure out what went wrong and work through it, which can be a wonderful corrective experience.

Bringing It All Together

It is finally time to return to the activity we had you do at the beginning of this chapter. You have had a chance to collect a lot of details about the effectiveness of therapy. Now you get to test your learning by doing the activity again and identifying differences between your first list and your second. As a reminder, we asked you to rank-order the following therapeutic factors, based on what you thought was most impactful on client outcomes:

- The client's motivation to change/get better
- The therapist's skills
- The therapist's level of training (MS vs. PhD)
- The theory/approach used
- The client's willingness to take medication
- Something else

Based on what you know now, would you change this rank-order list at all? How would it look different? Do you find yourself thinking, "It depends?" If so, you are starting to sound like a counseling psychologist.

Summary

In this chapter, we started off by asking you to consider a bunch of questions about what makes therapy effective: Is it something about the client? The counselor? The theoretical orientation or skills used? We talked you through the history of research on therapy effectiveness. We reviewed aspects of readiness for change and stages and processes of change as well as stages of counseling. We introduced you to common factors and how they can play a role in change regardless of theoretical orientation. Finally, we emphasized the importance of the therapeutic relationship and how ruptures can actually strengthen that relationship. We hope you have a better understanding of the complex interactions of factors that can actually encourage change in a client. In Chapter 9, we are going to dive into a very specific aspect of counseling psychology that can also have a huge impact on people's lives: psychological assessment.

What Would You Do?

A couple of your friends, Jennifer and Sam, have been seeing therapists in the local community at different agencies. Jennifer has been seeing a doctoral student who is in training and has only been practicing psychotherapy for two years. Sam is seeing a well-established counseling psychologist who has been licensed for 20 years. You are shocked by how different their experiences are because before reading this chapter, you would have assumed that more experienced therapists are just better. However, Jennifer cannot quit talking about how much she loves her therapist and how much better she feels after going to therapy. She says, "My therapist just gets me. He listens, asks thoughtful questions, and every week he shares a new skill he found for me to try out." Sam, on the other hand, is thinking about quitting therapy. He shares, "My therapist seems to be set in his ways. I keep getting the feeling that he tells everyone the same thing. He even just told me to read his book." Jennifer and Sam know you are taking a class about counseling psychology. At dinner one night, they ask you why their experiences have been so different.

- How would you explain the reason for different therapy outcomes?
- What are essential elements of effective therapy that might be missing for Sam?
- What are essential elements of effective therapy that might be part of Jennifer's experience?
- What could Sam do to address the concerns he has expressed to you?
- If Sam decides to seek a different counseling psychologist, what recommendations might you give him in his search?

Counseling Psychologist Spotlight: Veterans Affairs

Dr. Alex Alvarez

Dr. Alex Alvarez joined the US Army after graduating high school and served for four years, reaching the rank of Sergeant (E5) before his honorable discharge. He joined the military on August 27, 2001 and had been in basic training for about two weeks when 9/11 happened. Being in the military made him realize the need for mental health services for veterans, and set his path to becoming a counseling psychologist at the Veterans Affairs St. Louis Health Care System. He now works in the Spinal Cord Injury Center. On a daily basis, he does individual psychotherapy, cognitive testing, and leads team meetings with an interdisciplinary team. This team includes physicians, nurse practitioners, nurses, social workers, physical therapists, occupational therapists, recreational therapists, creative arts therapists, chaplains, respiratory therapists, pharmacists, and dietitians. He is amazed at how this team can come together, learn from each other, and provide high-quality care for the veterans. He does in-person and virtual psychotherapy with individual veterans and with their family members. One of his favorite things about his job is getting to train predoctoral interns and postdoctoral fellows in the medical inpatient unit and an outpatient primary care clinic. This role as mentor allows him to observe their work and engage in deep and meaningful conversations around diversity, strengths and areas of growth, and ways to heighten their confidence and intervention skills. Alex is passionate about training future psychologists as the Psychology Training Director for the psychology residency program at the St. Louis VA. He deeply values the opportunity to guide postdoctoral fellows during one of the most transformative years of their professional development – the final step before licensure.

Dr. Alex Alvarez. Photograph by author.

Alex says he enjoys working with veterans with spinal cord injuries as he can address the psychological effects of the injury as well as helping them accept and adjust to new ways of living. Through his work, he sees veterans improving their quality of life. He works hard to destigmatize mental health care, promote mental health awareness, and enhance access to care for veterans and their families. Even though the work is rewarding, Alex says there are also challenges: the losses that come with a spinal cord injury are complex and it can be challenging to help these veterans work toward realistic goals and grieve. Alex loves helping people learn they are stronger and more capable than they realize and feeling like he is trusted with his clients' hardest moments.

Alex has two active children, a three-year-old son and a six-year-old daughter, who take up most of his "free" time outside of work. He said they love to make obstacle courses and play at the park. When he has time to himself, Alex hikes, kayaks, runs, and SCUBA dives. He recently completed his first marathon! Alex graduated with his PhD from the counseling psychology program at Oklahoma State University and is a licensed psychologist. He holds a master's in counseling from Oklahoma State and his bachelor's degree is in psychology from the University of Florida.

References

American Psychological Association Presidential Task Force on Evidence-Based Practice. (2005). Evidence-based practice in psychology. *American Psychologist 61*(4), 271–285. https://doi.org/10.1037/0003-066X.61.4.271

American Psychological Association Task Force on Promotion and Dissemination of Psychological Procedures. (1995). Training in and dissemination of empirically validated treatments: Report and recommendations. *The Clinical Psychologist, 48*(1), 3–23.

Barry, C. L., Huskamp, H. A., & Goldman, H. H. (2010). A political history of federal mental health and addiction insurance parity. *Milbank Quarterly, 88*(3), 404–433. https://doi.org/10.1111/j.1468-0009.2010.00605.x

Carroll, L. (1865). *Alice's adventures in wonderland.* Macmillan.

Chambless, D. L., & Hollon, S. D. (1998). Defining empirically supported therapies. *Journal of Consulting and Clinical Psychology, 66*(1), 7–18. https://doi.org/10.1037/0022-006X.66.1.7

Duncan, B. L., Miller, S. D., Wampold, B. E., & Hubble, M. A. (Eds.). (2009). *The heart and soul of change: What works in therapy* (2nd ed.). American Psychological Association.

Eysenck, H. J. (1952). The effects of psychotherapy: An evaluation. *Journal of Consulting Psychology, 16*(5), 319–324. https://doi.org/10.1037/h0063633

Hill, C. E. (2001). *Helping skills: Facilitating exploration, insight, and action* (1st ed.). American Psychological Association.

Hubble, M. A., Duncan, B. L., & Miller, S. D. (Eds.). (1999). *The heart and soul of change: What works in therapy.* American Psychological Association. https://doi.org/10.1037/11132-000

Krebs, P., Norcross, J. C., Nicholson, J. M., & Prochaska, J. O. (2018). Stages of change and psychotherapy outcomes: A review and meta-analysis. *Journal of Clinical Psychology, 74*(11), 1964–1979. https://doi.org/10.1002/jclp.22683

Lilienfeld, S. O. (2007). Psychological treatments that cause harm. *Perspectives on Psychological Science, 2*(1), 53–70. https://doi.org/10.1111/j.1745-6916.2007.00029.x

Lopes, I., de Almeida, R. S., Gomes, P. V., & Marques, A. (2025). A gamified virtual reality exposure therapy for individuals with arachnophobia: A pilot study. *Virtual Worlds, 4*(2), 15. https://doi.org/10.3390/virtualworlds4020015

Miller, S. D., Duncan, B. L., & Hubble, M. A. (2005). Outcome-informed clinical work. In J. C. Norcross & M. R. Goldfried (Eds.), *Handbook of psychotherapy integration* (2nd ed., pp. 84–102). Oxford University Press. https://psycnet.apa.org/doi/10.1093/med:psych/9780195165791.003.0004

Prochaska, J. O., & DiClemente, C. C. (1983). Stages of change and counseling interventions. In W. R. Miller & S. Rollnick (Eds.), *Motivational interviewing: Helping people change* (pp. 11–27). Guilford Press.

Prochaska, J. O., & Velicer, W. F. (1997). The transtheoretical model of health behavior change. *American Journal of Health Promotion, 12*(1), 38–48. https://doi.org/10.4278/0890-1171-12.1.38

Ridley, C. R., Sahu, A., Console, K., Surya, S., Tran, V., Xie, S., & Yin, C. (2021). The process model of multicultural counseling competence. *The Counseling Psychologist, 49*(4), 534–567. https://doi.org/10.1177/0011000021992339

Rosenzweig, S. (1936). Some implicit common factors in diverse methods of psychotherapy. *American Journal of Orthopsychiatry, 6*(3), 412–415. https://doi.org/10.1111/j.1939-0025.1936.tb05248.x

Smith, M. L., & Glass, G. V. (1977). Meta-analysis of psychotherapy outcome studies. *American Psychologist, 32*(9), 752–760. https://doi.org/10.1037/0003-066X.32.9.752

Strupp, H. H. (1963). The outcome problem in psychotherapy revisited. *Psychotherapy: Theory, Research, & Practice, 1*(1), 1–13. https://doi.org/10.1037/h0088565

Wampold, B. E. (2012). Humanism as a common factor in psychotherapy. *Psychotherapy, 49*(4), 445–449. https://doi.org/10.1037/a0027113

Wampold, B. E. (2015). How important are the common factors in psychotherapy? An update. *World Psychiatry, 14*(3), 270–277. https://doi.org/10.1002/wps.20238

Wampold, B. E., & Imel, Z. E. (2015). *The great psychotherapy debate: The research evidence for what works in psychotherapy* (2nd ed.). Routledge. https://doi.org/10.4324/9780203582015

Chapter 9

Assessment in Counseling Psychology

What Is Your Experience with Psychological Tests?

If you are a college student reading this book, it is likely that you have taken some kind of psychological test or assessment in your life, even if it was not specifically labeled that way. What do you think of when you hear the term *psychological test?* Can you think of any psychological tests you have taken? Some examples might be:

- An achievement test in school (like a benchmark to move on to the next level of math).
- A career interest test.
- A pre-college test: the American College Testing examination ([ACT]; ACT, n.d.), Scholastic Aptitude Test ([SAT]; College Board, n.d.), or Armed Services Vocational Aptitude Battery ([ASVAB]; ASVAB, n.d.).
- A set of questions administered by a counselor or clinic: an anxiety or depression screen.

All of these are psychological tests or assessment tools. Now think of the specific logistics surrounding the test. What was it like for you to take the test and then get the results? Did anyone explain the results to you? How did you understand the results? The answers that pop into your mind may be different depending on the test you took. You might have been anxious about your ACT scores but barely remember the depression screen you took when you saw a counselor.

In this chapter, you will learn about the wide range of assessments that counseling psychologists do, and why. We describe the harms and benefits of psychological assessment, as well as some historical factors. The role of cultural factors is crucial to assessment, and you will see how counseling psychologists select appropriate tests and consider whether or not they are valid for certain populations. In this chapter, we introduce several groups of assessment tools, including:

- Work/vocational tests (aptitude, skills, interests, and values)
- Objective personality tests
- Projective personality tests
- Intellectual/academic tests
- Other kinds of measures like the Beck Depression Inventory II (BDI-II; Beck et al., 1996 and screeners to determine risk for suicide

We also talk about how counseling psychologists might use tools to monitor their clients' progress over time. Finally, we describe how assessments and tests are introduced to clients, administered, and then processed with clients afterward to integrate into a treatment plan.

DOI: 10.4324/9781003439899-9

Testing and assessment comprise a big part of what psychologists do. You may hear the terms test, measure, instrument, inventory, or assessment used interchangeably. But what is the difference between psychological testing and a psychological assessment? There is actually a big difference. Technically, a psychological test is a standardized tool used to measure some psychological feature: aptitude, intelligence, interests, personality, and so on. Many different professionals might administer a psychological test.

For example, a teacher, school counselor, or school administrator might be qualified to administer an academic achievement test. In other words, lots of professionals can give a test or a measure. An example is the ACT (ACT, n.d.). When people take the ACT, at a local high school or other community center, the people administering those tests aren't usually psychologists. They may be paid professionals who have training in administering the ACT. Note the use of "a/an" before these words: a test, a measure. This means only one dimension of a person's functioning or performance is being measured and that usually is not enough to produce an assessment. In some cases, people may refer to the ACT as an assessment, but unless the results are integrated with other information, a full assessment has not taken place. Strictly speaking, at least in psychology, a single assessment instrument is a test and (like when you take the ACT) you just get a score that tells you one thing (like your likelihood of succeeding in college).

Psychological *assessment*, on the other hand, is a skill used by counseling psychologists to collect information, analyze it, and offer some kind of conclusion based on the counseling psychologist's expertise, training, and judgment. Compared to testing, psychological *assessment* is much more complex and holistic. It is an approach that might include a test or tests but will also include other information such as medical information, psychosocial background, or clinician observations. It requires the professional, subjective judgment of the counseling psychologist (so it cannot just be administered by anyone). That is because assessments take a high degree of skill and require complex interpretation of many data points and outcomes. Imagine what would happen if psychologists decided to use a single test, such as how quickly you can put together a Lego set, to measure intelligence. That makes no sense! It would make a lot more sense to include how someone is doing in their classes, how they do on multiple measures of intelligence, memory, and problem-solving, what their family members or teachers report, what the person reports, and the psychologist's observations of the person. Matarazzo (1990, p. 1000) puts it this way:

> The measurement of intelligence (or personality, memory, or other psychological functions) is not, even today, a totally objective, completely science-based activity. Rather, in common with much of medical diagnosis, … the assessment of intelligence, personality, or type or level of impairment is a highly complex operation that involves extracting diagnostic meaning from an individual's personal history and objectively recorded test scores. Rather than being totally objective, assessment involves a subjective component. Specifically, it is the activity of a licensed professional, an artisan familiar with the accumulated findings of his or her young science, who in each instance uses tests, techniques, and a strategy that, whereas also identifying possible deficits, maximizes the chances of discovering each client's full ability and true potential.

So, if a counseling psychologist needed to complete an intelligence assessment, they would likely use a lot of different tests.

They might administer intelligence quotient (IQ) tests, academic achievement tests, and so on, but they would also observe the client and talk to them about their experiences. The counseling psychologist would then use all of that information to offer some kind of assessment report that integrates all of that information and offers the client ways of understanding the results. All this to say, you will still hear people refer to a single test as "an assessment," and you will also hear people say they did "an assessment," meaning a battery of tests and other information that they analyzed, integrated, and made conclusions on. So yes, we understand it's confusing and lots of terms can be used interchangeably, but just know that in this chapter, when we talk about a single test, we will say test or measure, and if we are talking about the fancier integration-of-everything assessment, we will say assessment.

One other thing to note: as we mentioned in Chapter 1, assessment is an area that often differentiates PhD-level counseling psychologists from master's-level counselors. Generally, there are some tests and measures that counseling psychologists are qualified to administer that most master's-level counselors are not. For example, counseling psychologists may be trained to assess intelligence, learning disabilities, attention-deficit/hyperactivity disorder (ADHD), autism, and psychological disorders like personality disorders. Most master's-level counselors may use career tests, or they may give a brief measure like the Beck Depression Inventory (we use this as an example a lot because it's used pretty frequently), and they are trained to know how to interpret test results, but they usually do not have the lengthy and in-depth training in psychological assessment that counseling psychologists have.

How Psychological Tests Work

Think back again to the questions we asked you at the very beginning of this chapter. We asked you to reflect on tests you have taken in the past. If you started thinking of academic tests like final exams or reading comprehension quizzes when you started reading this chapter, you were identifying a very specific sort of test that is designed to measure learning outcomes or a person's ability to remember educational content and concepts. The reality is that there are a lot of different kinds and categories of tests. Some psychological tests are designed to measure progress over time, therapeutic change, or even how much knowledge participants gain from a cultural competency training. However, a larger number of psychological tests are designed to get at things that are less concrete or harder to detect than just asking, "What queen of France is remembered as uttering the phrase, 'Let them eat cake?'" Many psychological tests try to measure the degree, intensity, duration, and other aspects of behavioral health disorders, presenting concerns, and other aspects of mental and psychological functioning.

You may be wondering, "Why does measuring psychological experiences take so many questions or a test? Couldn't a psychologist just ask someone, 'Are you depressed?'" That is a good question, but getting an accurate picture of psychological states is not that easy. Psychologists are not like other behavioral health providers (physicians, nurses) who are able to assess health disorders and presenting concerns (a broken arm, a swollen toe) more directly. If they suspect you fractured your arm, they can order an X-ray to confirm their hypothesis. Maybe someday scientists will design an affordable, widely available way of scanning for and confirming mental health concerns, but for now, it is not affordable or possible to X-ray for depression and then put a cast on it. Counseling psychologists and other scientists are working hard to identify neurochemicals and hormones that are elevated or depressed when a person is anxious, experiencing attention deficits, or managing hyperactivity, but those approaches are still under development and not widely available. Instead, scientists have developed psychological tests to assess and inform treatment for "invisible" health concerns. They administer assessment tools or conduct an assessment to see inside a person's head, so to speak.

To do this, psychological tests ask a series of questions, require a series of tasks, or present clients with a set of prompts to respond to. Based on a client's responses, psychologists can rule out certain disorders (this is not depression) or identify specific disorders that may need treatment (the client is endorsing symptoms consistent with generalized anxiety). For example, the BDI-II (Beck et al., 1996) asks a series of questions about feelings, thoughts, and behaviors. Clients give a response that is converted to a number and all of the responses are added up to give an overall depression score. Higher overall numbers indicate higher levels of depression. In other words, all of the responses taken together are part of the X-ray that is designed to look inside a person and detect their depression. The BDI may not exclusively confirm the presence of depression, but it contributes to the data that a psychologist collects to support a depression diagnosis, such as the client's symptoms (persistent sadness, sleepiness, and lack of interest), presentation (downturned eyes and sluggish movements), and history (recent loss of a family member).

You probably noticed right away that this is a high-stakes process in some cases. For example, you would not want to diagnose someone with ADHD and have their doctor prescribe stimulants unless they really needed them. That is why a lot of thought goes into the development of psychological tests and a bunch of strategies are used to make sure that those tests actually detect and measure what they are supposed to. Also, this is why, in conducting a psychological assessment, counseling psychologists will use multiple data points to come to a conclusion.

We will discuss this more later in this chapter (and as we noted in Chapters 2 and 3), but it's important to remember that not all tests are valid and reliable with all populations or across all cultures. Validity and reliability can be highly dependent on a wide range of factors. It is important to consider the client's cultural context as well as validity and reliability when selecting a test for a client. For example, will the client feel the test is valid or connected to their experiences and needs? If not, they may stop taking the test or give random answers that invalidate the test results. We are sure you can remember surveys you have taken that felt frustrating and like a waste of time. Clients can feel that too if they are not invested in or optimistic about the testing process. Another thing that can impact client trust and optimism about the testing process is the history of psychological testing and how tests have been used with various populations.

History of Psychological Tests

Some historians have dated the origins of psychological testing for skills or intelligence back to Ancient Chinese and Greek civilizations anywhere from 2,000 to 2,500 years ago (Matarazzo, 1990). For example, thousands of years ago, the Chinese empire employed basic proficiency testing to select civil service officers and Greek philosophers forwarded theories about human abilities and temperaments that laid the groundwork for later tests of personality and other individual assessments. It took some time for those early developments to trickle down into a more standardized and expanded form of testing theory, but philosophy played a large role in the early development of psychological principles and schools of thought.

In the 20th century, psychologists developed interest in how to measure intelligence and learning, vocational interests and aptitudes, and personality and psychological functioning. Modern interest in testing for intelligence began around the same time that psychology as a field was developing in the late 1800s–early 1900s (Schultz & Schultz, 2016). For example, Wilhelm Wundt was one of the first people to formalize experiments in psychology. He helped to move psychology out of the philosophical and conceptual realm and into laboratory science so that psychological principles could be tested (Schultz & Schultz, 2016; Wundt, 1904/1874). Other contributors to psychological science and testing theory like Sir Francis Galton (1883) and James McKeen Cattell (1890) began developing sensory and motor measures that quantified reaction times, muscle strength, and other aspects of human performance. Their work laid the foundation for the emergence of intelligence tests that could be used to assess the performance of grade school children.

Alfred Binet, Théodore Simon, and Henry Goddard hoped using these assessments could provide extra learning support to underperforming students (Binet & Simon, 1905/1916; Goddard, 1911). However, it is important to note that early intelligence tests were also used to further racist, classist, and xenophobic efforts both during their early development and well into the modern era. For example, Henry Goddard applied the tests to immigrants at Ellis Island based on the notion of eugenics (Goddard, 1912; Gould, 1981), an unscientific concept that has been discredited. Given this history and use of tests, you can probably see why some clients may be wary of psychological tests.

World War I marked a turning point in the history of psychological testing. Around this time, intelligence tests were developed to facilitate the quick evaluation and classification of large groups of drafted and volunteer soldiers (Yerkes, 1921). Following the war, achievement and aptitude tests were developed and used to evaluate vocational and academic dynamics (Brigham, 1926; Strong, 1927). *Achievement* tests measure what someone has learned so far; *aptitude* tests measure what they are capable of doing or learning. Many counseling psychologists trace the origins of the counseling branch of psychological practice back to the development of vocational psychology and assessment that took shape around this time, as we mentioned in Chapter 1. These interests in academic, vocational, and intelligence testing continued through the 20th century and are ongoing now.

Research and development in the mid-20th century also gave rise to an interest in *personality* tests used by counseling psychologists and other behavioral health professionals. In the mid-20th century, psychologists realized it would be efficient and helpful to develop standardized measures of psychological functioning and personality that could be given to many clients, rather than spend hours and hours interviewing clients to gain all of the information they might need to make a diagnosis. One of the most important tests developed around this time was the Minnesota Multiphasic Personality Inventory (MMPI), which is still in use today as the MMPI-3 (it has been updated a lot since then) (University of Minnesota Press, 2019). Other personality tests, such as the Rorschach (ink blot test), started to gain more popularity and use in the United States around this time. We go into more depth about different kinds of personality tests later in this chapter.

Moving into the 21st century, the field of psychological assessment continues to expand and develop. Counseling psychologists are at the forefront of the efforts to enhance psychological assessment tools and procedures. For example, counseling psychologists have been leaders in the development of culturally adapted and culturally informed testing (Sue et al., 2022). Additionally, assessment *batteries* or collections of psychological tests used to identify and rule out a broader range of presenting concerns are becoming increasingly common in psychological practice (Groth-Marnat & Wright, 2016). These assessment batteries can detect and more accurately represent the behavioral health concerns of a wider range of diverse, marginalized, and underrepresented populations and individuals. Finally, the fast-moving development of new technologies and artificial intelligence (AI) has strongly affected psychological assessments recently. Tests that formerly could only be given in a paper-and-pencil format are now computerized and often can be taken in the comfort of someone's home. Some new tests use virtual reality or gaming systems. Other tests may be scored and interpreted via AI systems, and AI might assist with more accurate diagnosis and decision-making. But these processes still require the oversight of a psychologist or other trained professionals because, as we mentioned earlier, this is a high-stakes and complex process that can have a huge impact on a person's life.

Culturally Appropriate Assessment

One of the biggest historical criticisms of psychological testing is bias. Bias can occur for a lot of different reasons, but one of the most controversial contributors is cultural bias. There is long-standing evidence that people with different racial backgrounds score differently on IQ tests, for example (Reynolds et al., 2021). Likewise, there have been heated debates about whether college entrance exams like the SAT and ACT are culturally biased, with strong opinions on both sides (e.g., Friedman et al., 2024; Ruhalter & Rath, 2024). There has been a lot of discussion recently about whether or not college admissions tests are fair. Given that you have probably completed a college admissions test or gone through the admissions process recently, take a moment to reflect on your own experience.

- What have you heard about these tests?
- Why do some colleges require them?
- Do you think they are culturally biased?
- Are they easier for some people to take than others?
- Do they actually work?

Prior to the COVID-19 pandemic, almost all colleges or universities required either the SAT or ACT as part of the admissions application. However, around the time of the COVID-19 pandemic, there was heightened awareness about issues related to fairness, accessibility, and cost of these tests. Due to the pandemic, it was also really difficult to administer these tests, and as a result, many colleges and universities dropped the SAT or ACT as a requirement. However, lately, they seem to be realizing that not including these scores may also introduce bias that they did not previously expect, due to grade inflation and the inability to compare, for example, a grade point average (GPA) of 4.0 at a rural Nevada high school versus a GPA of 4.0 at a highly competitive, private school in Massachusetts. There is mounting evidence that college admissions tests scores are actually better predictors of whether or not students will succeed in college than GPAs are (Friedman et al., 2024).

However, historically, there has been a lot of cultural bias in tests. For example, the MMPI was long considered a gold standard in personality assessment and mental health diagnostics (Butcher, 2010). However, it was also long criticized because the samples on which it was normed predominantly identified as White, heterosexual, cisgender, and were fluent in spoken and written English (Sue et al., 2022). Because of the huge problems related to potential cultural bias, test developers have worked hard to develop assessments that minimize the role of cultural bias for all test-takers. For example, when developing a test, they will take multiple steps such as:

- Make efforts to ensure the use of language is inclusive and broadly understandable.
- Consult with experts from a wide range of cultural backgrounds.
- Run all kinds of pilot tests or development tests prior to releasing a test for use.
- Try to *norm* the test with a large sample that represents the population that it would be used with.

These are some of the ways that test developers have made significant improvements in the recent updates to the MMPI-3, for example.

Validity and Reliability of Tests

In addition to wanting tests to be culturally fair, we also want them to be accurate, consistent, and theoretically and statistically valid. If we give someone a test to determine if they have depression, it is important for the inventory to accurately detect depression (and not something else) or they might be diagnosed and treated for a problem they are not experiencing. One way to ensure accuracy is to make sure the test is *reliable* or stable and consistent. Beck et al. (1996) worked hard to

Table 9.1 Types of test validity

Type	*Explanation*	*Reflection Question*
Content validity	The items/tasks should make sense being included together in a test about a certain topic (e.g., depression) and should cover all the bases when it comes to the topic.	Would you feel confident about a test of anxiety if one of the questions asked you what book you read two weeks ago?
Criterion validity	The test should actually measure the topic (e.g., depression).	Would you feel confident about a test that concluded that workers at a factory were highly motivated, but in actuality, managers reported that their workers had low morale and high absence rates?
Criterion validity (predictive)	The test results should predict future performance if appropriate.	Would it make sense if a group of people who scored high on work commitment all quit their jobs two weeks later?
Criterion validity (concurrent)	The test results should check out when compared to other approaches to measuring the same topic or issue.	How likely would you be to use a test that found that a person's stress was high but their psychological well-being was also high?
Construct validity	The test results should make sense, based on current theories and scientific outcomes.	What would you think if a test for depression actually picked up on anxiety levels?
Construct validity (convergent)	The test results should correlate to other similar tests.	Would you trust a new test of resilience that produces results similar to a preexisting resilience test that is supported by ten years of research?
Construct validity (discriminant)	The test should not correlate to other tests that measure unrelated issues.	How accurate would you consider a test of depression that produces similar results to a test of creativity?
Face	The wording of the test should make sense, given the topic or issue it is designed to test.	Let's say someone is designing a test and wants you to look at it. It is riddled with grammatical errors and misspellings. Would that inspire confidence that this is going to be a high-quality test?

Note. Table content was drawn from current testing theory discussed in American Educational Research Association et al. (2014).

ensure that all of the prompts for the BDI-II, for example, consistently relate to depression (what we call *internal consistency reliability*) and are stable over time (*test-retest reliability*). Earlier, we talked about what it would be like to have an X-ray to test for depression. If we circle back to that here, we would want the X-ray to consistently generate accurate images of those bones every time the X-ray machine is used.

Another way psychologists ensure that psychological tests work is by confirming their *validity*. Just like there are different types of reliability, there are also several forms of validity when it comes to psychological tests (see Table 9.1). We do not have the space to dig too deeply into testing theory in this chapter, but it is important for you to know the basics so that you understand how counseling psychologists look for high-quality tests. Basically, when we are talking about validity, we are saying we want the test to measure what it's supposed to measure and no other random things. Using our X-ray analogy, we want the test to pick up bones, but not other random things that aren't necessary to diagnose a fracture.

Common Types of Assessments

How is assessment useful to counseling psychologists? There are a lot of different reasons why a counseling psychologist might want to (or need to) conduct psychological assessment. For example, if a client has not made much progress over time, or if a counseling psychologist is feeling "stuck" on how best to help the client move forward, they could do an assessment to help better pinpoint exactly what is going on for the client. Likewise, if a client seems to present with multiple different issues and diagnoses, it can assist with something called *differential diagnosis*, or parsing out what the different issues are. Assessment can also help clients better understand themselves; often, clients may feel like there is something wrong, but they aren't sure what it is; going through the process of assessment, discussing the results and potential diagnoses, can often be a relief and give them hope to move forward. Assessment may assist with educational placement and services in schools as well as give people some sense of what kind of career they might want to pursue. Assessments can also be useful for monitoring progress over time in a therapeutic relationship. Below, we go into further description about all kinds of assessments like career development and decision-making; personality assessment; aptitude, achievement, and intelligence assessment; and progress monitoring, behavior, and symptom checklists.

Work and Vocational Assessment

We talked quite a bit about the role of work in people's lives, including different kinds of tests that counseling psychologists might use to learn more about people's vocational interests, skills, and aptitudes, in Chapter 5. You might remember that career *interest* tests are often based on Holland's theory and codes, such as the Strong Interest Inventory, which has been normed on tens of thousands of people globally (Donnay et al., 2012), the Self-Directed Search (Holland & Messer, 2013), and the Kuder Occupational Interest Survey (Kuder & Zytowski, 1991). In that chapter, we also talked about career decision self-efficacy. There are several scales designed to measure this construct, such as the Career Decision Self-Efficacy Scale (Betz & Taylor, 1983) and the Career Decision-Making Indicator (Al-Kalbani & Salleh, 2010). These individual tests may be administered by lots of different professionals, including counseling psychologists, vocational psychologists, certified career counselors, or master's-level mental health counselors who specialize in career counseling. They may be used in colleges to help make decisions about majors or minors; they may be used to help people understand what kinds of occupations exist; and they may be used to help people determine what their values are related to their career. Remember that there is a difference between giving people career tests and conducting a more holistic *assessment*. Counseling psychologists might interview a client and ask them to complete a number of different career measures, then they will discuss the results with the client and integrate their findings in a vocational assessment report.

Personality Assessment

Personality assessments are often quite complex and require specific, advanced training. This is one type of assessment that is usually completed by a doctoral-level psychologist and not someone with a master's degree, unless there are special circumstances and the master's-level professional has some kind of special training or credential. Personality assessments are often considered high-stakes assessments, as they can have a huge impact on someone's life. For example, if a client undergoes a personality assessment and the counseling psychologist determines that a potential diagnosis is a personality disorder, this could have really critical consequences for the client. It might influence the way the client sees themselves, the way others view them, and the way future health professionals might form opinions about them. A diagnosis like this can stay with someone for life. So, it is something that must be taken very seriously and handled extremely professionally and ethically.

One of the first things that a counseling psychologist would do in conducting a personality assessment is a full and detailed clinical interview, similar to the intake interview we described in Chapter 7 on skills. Ethically, it is important not to ever make a psychological diagnosis based on the results of one single test. But there are personality tests that can assist a psychologist in understanding what is happening for the client. These tests are usually split into two different kinds: *objective* and *projective* tests (Anastasi & Urbina, 1997; Groth-Marnat & Wright, 2016). Objective tests are similar to the ones we have discussed so far, with specific items, prompts, or tasks that have a specific systematic method of scoring. Projective tests are assessment tools that allow clients to respond to test materials in a more open-ended way that allows for more subjective interpretation by the psychologist.

There are several different well-researched objective personality tests. One of the most popularly used is the MMPI (MMPI-3; University of Minnesota Press, 2019). The MMPI-3 has over 300 items and takes about an hour to administer. The MMPI-3 has features built into it to determine if someone is trying to make their symptoms seem worse than they really are or better than they really are. There are patterns that a psychologist can look at to determine what potential diagnoses might be appropriate for the client. Often psychologists use the MMPI-3 to help home in on what is going on for someone or for differential diagnoses. For example, if a client reports that they experience some mood highs and lows, and have difficulty maintaining relationships over time, a psychologist may administer the MMPI-3 to determine if the client is experiencing something more related to mood (such as bipolar disorder) or personality (personality disorder), or perhaps both. Another objective personality measure is the Millon Clinical Multiaxial Inventory (MCMI-IV; Millon et al., 2015), which generally is used when a counseling psychologist already knows that someone has more severe mental health issues or a personality disorder.

At some point, you have probably seen a photo or movie of a psychologist showing a client a large image of a blot of black ink on white paper. This is a well-known projective personality test, the Rorschach test (Exner, 2003; Rorschach, 1921/1942). There is a series of images that a counseling psychologist will show to the client and ask, "What might this be?" Although clients will answer in an open-ended way, similar to objective tests, client responses to projective tests are also organized, scored, and interpreted, and can be very useful as a guide for treatment. However, there is some subjectivity to the interpretation of projective tests, and often, projective tests require extensive training for psychologists to be competent to administer them. Another projective test is the Rotter Incomplete Sentences Blank (Rotter et al., 1992). There are several open-ended prompts that a client must respond to, such as "My greatest fear…" or "A mother…" Other projective tests include the House-Person Tree Test (Buck, 1981) and the Thematic Apperception Test (Bellak & Abrams, 1997; Murray, 1943). Based on how the participant responds, the psychologist will make some interpretations. Remember that a projective test would only be used in combination with a clinical interview and objective tests – these tests are not used in isolation to make any decision or diagnosis.

You may have heard of other types of personality tests like the Myers-Briggs Type Inventory (MBTI; Myers et al., 2018). The MBTI measures personality preferences in four different areas:

- Extraversion-Introversion (E-I; how people focus and get energy: with others or alone).
- Sensing-Intuition (S-N; how you take in information: concrete details or big-picture information).
- Thinking-Feeling (T-F; how you make decisions: logic and analysis or emotions).
- Judging-Perceiving (J-P; how you live your life: with control and structure or with flexibility and spontaneity).

There are 16 personality type combinations. You may have come across these before, such as ISFJ (meaning someone who prefers Introversion, Sensing, Feeling, and Judging) or ENTP (Extraversion, Intuition, Thinking, Perceiving). There is some controversy about whether these tests are valid, but they remain highly popular, especially in educational and workplace settings. They may be used in various contexts for better self-understanding or understanding of people in relation to others. However, these tests are generally not used for any kind of psychological diagnosis purposes.

Intellectual Assessment

In conducting intellectual assessment, a counseling psychologist might include all kinds of academic data, including school records as well as IQ tests, aptitude tests, achievement tests, or other academic tests. They may also include client self-report, parent report, or educator/teacher report. Intellectual assessment is used to assess potential or strengths as well as learning difficulties. It can also be used in comprehensive testing for ADHD. The goal of these tests is to help people, children, or adults to determine if there is some kind of challenge or barrier and figure out how counseling psychologists can help them learn and thrive. *Achievement* tests measure what someone has already learned, and *aptitude* tests measure someone's future potential to learn. It is fairly common for a technician or diagnostician to administer intellectual tests. However, usually a psychologist – clinical, school, or counseling – will be the one to consider all of the information together holistically to determine what is happening for the client and to make recommendations.

The most common intelligence tests, or IQ tests, measure a person's intelligence in four areas:

- Verbal comprehension
- Perceptual reasoning
- Working memory
- Processing speed

Based on the results, the psychologist scores an IQ. IQs generally range from 50 to 150; the average IQ is 100. An IQ below 70 could indicate developmental delays, intellectual disabilities, or cognitive impairment. An IQ of 130+ indicates higher intelligence. Most commonly, intelligence testing is used to determine learning disabilities, usually in school settings. A psychologist might look for differences in IQ and achievement. For example, if someone is doing really poorly in English/Language Arts classes, but they have a high Verbal Reasoning IQ, it could indicate some kind of learning disability that needs further examination. The most commonly used IQ tests in the United States are the Wechsler Adult Intelligence Scale (WAIS-V; Wechsler, 2008), the Wechsler Intelligence Scale for Children (WISC-IV; Wechsler, 2003), the Stanford-Binet (Roid & Pomplun, 2012), and the Woodcock-Johnson (Schrank & Wendling, 2018). Julie once had a student ask her, "Can you go online and take an IQ test?" Take a moment to reflect on the answer Julie might have given that student. What do you think? Knowing what you know now, what might be some issues or problems with taking an IQ test online?

Counseling psychologists may also consider achievement and aptitude tests in conducting intellectual assessment. There are a number of achievement tests, often which are state or school-district specific, such as the Iowa Test of Basic Skills or the Stanford Achievement Test. A commonly used *aptitude* test is the ASVAB (ASVAB, n.d.). You may have taken this test or known others who took it in high school. It measures aptitudes in general science, arithmetic reasoning, verbal reasoning, word knowledge, paragraph comprehension, mathematics knowledge, electronics information, auto and shop information, mechanical comprehension, and assembling objects.

Progress Monitoring, Screeners, and Symptom Checklists

The last category of psychological tests that we will discuss here includes progress monitoring, screeners, and symptom checklists. These may or may not be used in a holistic psychological assessment. More frequently, they are used as a kind of quick check-in to see how someone is behaving, thinking, or feeling. Over time, they can be used to see if there are changes or to monitor progress (or decline). These may be used in counseling every session, pre-post treatment, or at regular intervals to indicate change in the client. For example, a counseling psychologist might ask their clients to answer five or six questions every single session and will track progress over time. Or a counseling psychologist might ask clients to complete something like the OQ-45.2 (45 questions; Lambert et al., 2004) every month or two for more thorough understanding. Routine outcome monitoring has been found to increase treatment effectiveness, decrease dropout rates, and shorten treatment length (see also Chapter 8 on Outcomes). Another example of a symptom checklist is the Adult ADHD self-report scale (ASRS-v1.1; Kessler et al., 2005); as an adult, if you are being assessed for ADHD, you might complete this checklist in addition to other measures. For children, counseling psychologists will often ask parents/guardians or teachers to complete behavior checklists based on observations of the child who is being assessed for ADHD.

Screeners are generally extremely brief measures specifically designed to see if someone might need further assessment or if a referral for counseling might be in order. For example, they might be used on college campuses across the United States for events like National Depression Screening Day, where college/university counseling centers might set up tables with brief depression screeners, and students can stop by to complete the screener and speak to a counselor about whether or not they might like treatment. Other examples of brief measures are the Generalized Anxiety Disorder 7-item scale (GAD-7; Spitzer et al., 2006) or the Patient Health Questionnaire-9 (PHQ-9; Kroenke et al., 1999).

Assessment in Psychological Practice

Okay, so now you know about the history of assessment, the kinds of assessments that counseling psychologists do, and the kinds of tests they use. But what does it actually look like in practice? Let's say you are a counseling psychologist and have been working with a client for a while and have been thinking that personality assessment could help with pinpointing a diagnosis and improving your treatment. First, you would need to bring up the idea of assessment with your client. Also, if the client is a minor, there are special considerations you would need to make like whether to involve caregivers, family members, educators, and possibly physicians or other professionals. Sometimes clients might want to be tested and that may be why they reached out to you in the first place, other times they might be suspicious or concerned about being tested and what will happen with the results. And with minors, just because a parent wants a test and gives consent, that doesn't mean the child will give *assent* or agree. So, there are a lot of things to consider in deciding whether or not to do an assessment. But that process usually starts with a conversation about what assessment is, what it does, and what possible outcomes to expect.

McHenry (2018) wisely reminds us that although *testing* can be administered in groups, psychological *assessment* happens at the individual level, with one human being. This human being, as we have discussed in previous chapters, is an autonomous person with unique cultural background, lifespan development, interests, needs, desires, and characteristics. Counseling psychologists approach any assessment with that in mind, in an ethical and professional way, respecting the client with dignity. Administering psychological assessment, including observation, self-report, and formal and informal tests, "requires expert knowledge of the tools, techniques, and standards by which an individual's results are being measured/compared" (McHenry et al., 2018, p. 1). So, counseling psychologists must have extensive training and competence in administering and interpreting psychological assessments in a way that is ethical, collaborative, and culturally responsive. One of the most important points, which will mirror what you have heard throughout the rest of this textbook, is that assessment is not done *to* someone, but rather *with* someone, a human being. It is important to have conversations with the client prior to, during, and after any test administration and interpretation.

Let's say that you have had a conversation with the client, who is eager to participate in psychological assessment to help form a clear diagnosis, which will help inform and improve their treatment plan and goals. You are good to go, but now you need to actually administer the test(s). First, you will need to know the answers to several questions and key considerations such as: What goes into setting up a testing environment? What are the optimal conditions for testing? What are best practices?

There are all kinds of things that could affect testing outcomes. Think back to a big test you have taken in the past. Maybe it was the ACT or SAT test for college admissions or some kind of academic achievement test. Think through the following questions that apply to taking a test.

- Did you have to take an ACT/SAT test for college admissions?
- How much did it cost?
- How easy was it to register for the exam?
- Where did you take it?
- What were the testing conditions like?
- Were you in a large cafeteria, for example, or in small classrooms?
- Did you have to wake up really early and drive a long distance to take the exam, or was it just a few miles away at the school you attend?

- Did you have access to a test prep course or training through your school, or did you pay a tutor or test prep agency to get ready?
- Did you take the test multiple times (were you or your family able to afford to pay for multiple administrations), or did you have a fee waiver due to financial constraints and were only able to take the test once?
- What was your health like? Did you have a big meal the morning of the test, or did you go on an empty stomach?
- What was your mood like that day? Your stress level?

All of these factors play a role in test outcomes, and this is why we do not look at just one test result and make any kind of decision. We always consider multiple data points. Ideally, optimal conditions are common sense and should be similar if possible. The environment should be free of obstructions (loud noises, hot temperatures), the client should be as prepared as possible (good night's rest, healthy diet), and the clinician should be professional and appropriate (McHenry, 2018).

Once tests (including observation, checklists, or other measures) are complete, the counseling psychologist will interpret the results of the assessment. Keeping in mind what we mentioned above, that there are always variables that can influence the results, the counseling psychologist should spend some time checking in with the client and discussing what they found. McHenry (2018) calls this "meaning making," which means the counseling psychologist consults and asks the test-taker their perspective. The counseling psychologist is basically saying, "This is what the tests indicated, how does that fit for you?" or "With all of this information coming together, I am thinking about this diagnosis, what do you think?" and allows the client to respond. The client might disagree: "Well, I can see how it looks that way, I was in a super bad mood when I took that test though because I just wrecked my car." Or they might have some new insight: "Wow, I've always known that I have more difficulty relating to people than others seem to. This makes so much sense now." Or, the client might argue against the results because they indicate something that they are unaware of and do not like the test interpretation. As McHenry (2018) says, "assessing clients is an act of discovery" (p. 6). A skilled counseling psychologist can work with the client to explore this new information and how it fits, or doesn't fit, with the client's perception of themselves. In other words, the X-ray may indicate a need for help, but it is still up to the counseling psychologist to determine the best course of treatment (a cast, a brace, a sling, and so on) as well as monitor and make adjustments if needed (keep the cast on longer than usual).

Summary

At the beginning of this chapter, we asked you to think about any psychological tests you might have taken yourself. Knowing what you do now, are there any changes you would have made to the test setting, how you prepared, or the way the test was given? We hope you now have a strong sense of the importance of high-quality psychological assessment. We reviewed the history of psychological assessment and emphasized the importance of cultural appropriateness, reliability, and validity in assessment. We introduced you to different kinds of psychological assessments that counseling psychologists might do with a client and talked through some of the practical logistics of actually conducting a psychological assessment. In Chapter 10, we are going to move on to common types of research methods that counseling psychologists do and why research is so important to counseling psychologists.

What Would You Do?

Your feisty and cute little sister, Maggie, is seven years old. Her teacher recommended her for an accelerated reader program. Maggie is a voracious reader; she has had to get permission from your parents to check out more advanced books from her elementary school library because she is reading books that are designated for readers in higher grades. The teacher told your parents that to qualify for the program, Maggie would have to be tested at her elementary school by the person in charge of the program, Mrs. Pickle. Your parents readily agreed to give permission. Maggie was excited about the possibility of being in a program with other children who love to read. One day, Maggie came home and gave your parents a note from the school. It was a letter stating that Maggie was tested for the program and did not qualify. Your dad spoke to Maggie's teacher, who was really surprised and recommended that your dad speak to Mrs. Pickle. The next day, your dad told you that he spoke to Mrs. Pickle to try to figure out what happened. She said she was not sure, but Maggie just finished the test really quickly and when Mrs. Pickle scored it, it did not meet the threshold for the program. So, you and your dad sat down with Maggie to see if she could tell you what happened. Maggie said she did not know why Mrs. Pickle was having her do worksheets when all the other kids went out to recess before lunch. She did not know it was the test for the reading program. She said she could see out the classroom window all her friends playing and her friend Junie showing off her new sneakers that light up. Also, she was excited because it was fried burrito day at school, and she was hungry for lunch. So, she just tried to answer the questions as fast as possible so she could go play. Your dad told Maggie that it all made a lot of sense, and he wouldn't want to have to stay inside either, but he was going to see if Mrs. Pickle would be willing to test her again. If she did that, Maggie should take it seriously and try not to rush. Maggie said she would try.

- Knowing what you know now about testing, administration, and interpreting results, what recommendations would you give your dad if he reaches out to ask Mrs. Pickle to test Maggie again?
- What steps should Mrs. Pickle take in the future to ensure the most accurate outcome?

Counseling Psychologist Spotlight: Health Care

Dr. Courtney Gunn

Dr. Courtney Gunn is a psychologist at the Baton Rouge location of Ochsner Health System, a leading nonprofit healthcare organization headquartered in New Orleans, Louisiana. On a daily basis, she uses evidence-based practice and clear communication in her individual psychotherapy with adults and adolescents. She also conducts psychological and psychoeducational assessments with children, adolescents, and adults, and enjoys providing clients with clarity through the assessment and diagnosis process. She says that this often provides clients with relief and validation, alleviating their anxieties and uncertainties – it gives them answers they have been looking for. She works hard to build a strong therapeutic alliance with her clients, using active listening skills and empathy to ensure her clients feel heard and understood. She also sees a positive impact on clients' families, which promotes intergenerational mental wellness and increases utilization of mental health services. She works hard to destigmatize and improve access to mental health care.

One of the favorite parts of her job is mentoring a predoctoral intern student through an American Psychological Association (APA)-accredited psychology internship program. She finds mentoring emerging professionals and witnessing their growth to be incredibly rewarding. Through this mentorship, she gets to share her expertise and learn from the students' different perspectives,

Dr. Courtney Gunn. Photograph by author.

which enhances her own professional development and energizes her commitment to advancing the field of psychology. Some of the most challenging aspects of her job involve having conversations with parents about their child's suicidal thoughts or attempts, as well as making the difficult decision to recommend hospitalization. These discussions are emotionally demanding and require compassion and sensitivity. She explains that her location is facing a shortage of mental health professionals, making it difficult to keep up with demand while already managing a full caseload. She notes that systemic barriers, including insurance limitations and financial hardships, affect both providers and the individuals seeking care. In her role at Ochsner, she takes advantage of opportunities to engage with the community and advocate for mental health awareness. She is deeply committed to serving others, particularly racially minoritized populations who are less likely to seek mental health services. As a Black woman, she appreciates when clients express feeling safe and understood because of their shared identity, which underscores the importance of representation and cultural competence in building trust and rapport.

Courtney stays active in her community through a wide variety of mental health initiatives. She has written blogs on mental health topics and has participated in television interviews to reach a broader audience. She has spoken at conferences about topics such as bullying, holiday depression, the benefits of therapy, meditation, maintaining mental health during the COVID-19 pandemic, dangers of social media, and advice to parents about back-to-school stress. Being in Louisiana, she has also discussed things like preparing for hurricane stress with children and mental health considerations during Mardi Gras.

Courtney prioritizes activities that help her recharge and support a balanced lifestyle. She enjoys riding her Peloton bike, which doubles as a powerful stress reliever, as well as reading and traveling. Time with her husband, son, parents, sister, and friends is especially meaningful and plays a key role in her overall well-being and happiness. She emphasizes the importance of setting boundaries, getting enough rest, staying physically active, nurturing a fulfilling life outside of work, and maintaining strong connections with loved ones. She says these all help her sustain her passion and resilience in this demanding field. In this way, Courtney embodies a counseling psychologist who is reflective and intentional in her self-care (See Chapter 12!). Courtney earned her doctorate in counseling psychology from Howard University. She completed her undergraduate degree in psychology from Xavier University in New Orleans, LA and obtained her master's in clinical psychology from Northwestern State University in Natchitoches, LA.

References

ACT (n.d.) *ACT test*. https://www.act.org

Al-Kalbani, M. S., & Salleh, A. (2010). Developing a career decision making indicator (CDMI). *Procedia – Social and Behavioral Sciences, 5*, 2146–2153. https://doi.org/10.1016/j.sbspro.2010.07.428

American Educational Research Association, American Psychological Association, & National Council on Measurement in Education. (2014). *Standards for educational and psychological testing*. American Educational Research Association.

Anastasi, A., & Urbina, S. (1997). *Psychological testing* (7th ed.). Prentice Hall.

Armed Services Vocational Aptitude Battery. (n.d.). *Armed services vocational aptitude battery*. https://www.officialasvab.com.

Beck, A. T., Steer, R. A., & Brown, G. K. (1996). *Beck depression inventory–II (BDI-II)*. Pearson.

Bellak, L., & Abrams, D. M. (1997). *The thematic apperception test, the children's apperception test, and the senior apperception technique in clinical use* (6th ed.). Allyn & Bacon.

Betz, N. E., & Taylor, K. M. (1983). The relationship of career self-efficacy expectations to perceived career options in college women and men. *Journal of Counseling Psychology, 30*(3), 385–392. https://doi.org/10.1037/0022-0167.30.3.385

Binet, A., & Simon, T. (1916). *The development of intelligence in children* (E. S. Kite, Trans.). Williams & Wilkins.

Brigham, C. C. (1926). *A study of American intelligence*. Princeton University Press.

Buck, J. N. (1981). *The House-Tree-Person technique – revised manual*. Western Psychological Services.

Butcher, J. N. (2010). The MMPI-2: History, interpretation, and clinical issues. In J. N. Butcher (Ed.), *MMPI-2: Assessing personality and psychopathology* (2nd ed., pp. 1–50). Oxford University Press.

Cattell, J. M. (1890). Mental tests and measurements. *Mind, 15*(59), 373–381. https://doi.org/10.1093/mind/os-XV.59.373

College Board. (n.d.). *SAT*. https://www.collegeboard.org.

Donnay, D. A. C., Morris, M. L., Schaubhut, N. A., & Thompson, R. C. (2012). *Strong Interest Inventory® manual supplement: Occupational scales update 2012*. CPP.

Exner, J. E. (2003). *The Rorschach: A comprehensive system* (4th ed.). Wiley.

Friedman, J., Sacerdote, B., & Tine, M. (2024, January). Standardized test scores and academic performance at ivy-plus colleges. *Data Insight*. https://opportunityinsights.org/wp-content/uploads/2024/01/SAT_ACT_on_Grades.pdf

Galton, F. (1883). *Inquiries into human faculty and its development*. Macmillan.

Goddard, H. H. (1911). The Binet-Simon measuring scale for intelligence. *Training School Bulletin, 8*, 56–62.

Goddard, H. H. (1912). *The Kallikak family: A study in the heredity of feeble-mindedness*. Macmillan.

Gould, S. J. (1981). *The mismeasure of man*. W. W. Norton.

Groth-Marnat, G., & Wright, A. J. (2016). *Handbook of psychological assessment* (6th ed.). Wiley.

Holland, J. L., & Messer, M. A. (2013). *John Holland's Self-Directed Search: Professional manual* (5th ed.). Psychological Assessment Resources.

Kessler, R. C., Adler, L., Ames, M., Demler, O., Faraone, S., Hiripi, E., Howes, M. J., Jin, R., Secnik, K., Spencer, T., Ustun, T. B., & Walters, E. E. (2005). The World Health Organization Adult ADHD Self-Report Scale (ASRS): A short screening scale for use in the general population. *Psychological Medicine, 35*(2), 245–256. https://doi.org/ 10.1017/s0033291704002892

Kroenke, K., Spitzer, R. L., & Williams, J. B. W. (1999). *Patient Health Questionnaire*-9 *(PHQ-9)* [Database record]. APA PsycTests. https://doi.org/10.1037/t06165-000

Kuder, G. F., & Zytowski, D. G. (1991). *Kuder Occupational Interest Survey®, Form DD: General manual* (3rd ed.). CTB/McGraw-Hill.

Lambert, M. J., Morton, J. J., Hatfield, D., Harmon, S., Hamilton, S., Reid, R. C., … Burlingame, G. M. (2004). *Administration and scoring manual for the OQ-45.2 (Outcome Questionnaire)*. OQ Measures.

Matarazzo, J. D. (1990). Psychological assessment versus psychological testing. *American Psychologist, 45*(9), 999–1017. https://doi.org/10.1037/0003-066X.45.9.999

McHenry, B., (2018). Introduction. In B. McHenry, K. C. MacCluskie & J. McHenry (Eds.), *Tests and assessments in counseling: A case-by-case exploration* (pp. 1–13). Routledge. https://doi.org/10.4324/9781315279534

Millon, T., Grossman, S., & Millon, C. (2015). *Millon Clinical Multiaxial Inventory–IV [Test]*. Pearson.

Murray, H. A. (1943). *Thematic apperception test: Manual*. Harvard University Press.

Myers, I. B., McCaulley, M. H., Quenk, N. L., & Hammer, A. L. (2018). *MBTI manual for the Global Step I and Step II assessments* (4th ed.). The Myers-Briggs Company.

Reynolds, C. R., Altmann, R. A., & Allen, D. N. (2021). *Mastering modern psychological testing*. Springer. https://doi.org/10.1007/978-3-030-59455-8_15

Roid, G. H., & Pomplun, M. (2012). The Stanford-Binet intelligence scales, Fifth Edition. In D. P. Flanagan & P. L. Harrison (Eds.), *Contemporary intellectual assessment theories, tests, and issues* (pp. 249–268). The Guilford Press.

Rorschach, H. (1942). *Psychodiagnostics* (P. Lemkau & B. Kronenberg, Trans.). Grune & Stratton.

Rotter, J. B., Lah, M. I., & Rafferty, J. E. (1992). Rotter Incomplete Sentences Blanks--Second Edition (RISB-2). [Database Record]. APA PsycTests. https://doi.org/10.1037/t15153-000

Ruhalter, K., & Rath, A. (2024, January). *Standardized tests aren't biased, says new data – but scores reflect society's biases*. All Things Considered. https://www.wgbh.org/news/education-news/2024-01-23/standardized-tests-arent-biased-says-new-data-but-scores-reflect-societys-biases

Schrank, F. A., & Wendling, B. J. (2018). The Woodcock–Johnson IV: Tests of cognitive abilities, tests of oral language, tests of achievement. In D. P. Flanagan & E. M. McDonough (Eds.), *Contemporary intellectual assessment: Theories, tests, and issues* (4th ed., pp. 383–451). The Guilford Press.

Schultz, D. P., & Schultz, S. E. (2016). *A history of modern psychology* (11th ed.). Cengage.

Spitzer, R. L., Kroenke, K., Williams, J. B. W., & Löwe, B. (2006). *Generalized Anxiety Disorder 7 (GAD-7)* [Database record]. APA PsycTests. https://doi.org/10.1037/t02591-000

Strong, E. K. (1927). *Vocational interests of men and women*. Stanford University Press.

Sue, D. W., Sue, D., Neville, H. A., & Smith, L. I. (2022). *Counseling the culturally diverse: Theory and practice* (9th ed.). Wiley.

University of Minnesota Press, Test Division. (2019). *MMPI-3 development update*. University of Minnesota Press.

Wechsler, D. (2003). *Wechsler Intelligence Scale for Children, Fourth Edition (WISC-IV)* [Database record]. APA PsycTests. https://doi.org/10.1037/t15174-000

Wechsler, D. (2008). *Wechsler Adult Intelligence Scale--Fourth Edition (WAIS-IV)* [Database record]. APA PsycTests. https://doi.org/10.1037/t15169-000

Wundt, W. (1904). *Principles of physiological psychology* (E. B. Titchener, Trans.; 1st English ed.). Swan Sonnenschein.

Yerkes, R. M. (1921). *Psychological examining in the United States Army*. U.S. Government Printing Office.

Chapter 10

Common Research Methods That Counseling Psychologists Use

Why Research?

You hear a lot about psychologists doing research. What is the purpose of research? How might the kind of research that counseling psychologists do differ from the kind of research that psychologists (broadly speaking) do? Do you have any research interests or have you ever had a question that you thought you could answer using research? We have found that the idea of doing research is intimidating and overwhelming to many students. Even if they have participated in a research lab or heard about a faculty mentor's research, it feels big and scary. Students often think all research must be some kind of multi-year study with thousands of participants, a control or experimental group of some kind, funded by a large granting agency. Those studies do exist, and they are potentially great studies! But really, research can look like a lot of different things. We are hoping to slightly demystify the research process to make it more accessible to you.

In this chapter, readers will learn about the different kinds of research that counseling psychologists do. Research can be a lot of fun because counseling psychologists can develop research questions based on their interests, figure out the best way to try to find an answer, and then test it to see if what they found was important or valid. Counseling psychologists typically do human subjects research, which is overseen by institutions' Human Subjects Review Boards. In this chapter, we will expand on the term *scientist-practitioner* and describe what that means for counseling psychologists. We describe quantitative methods, usually using data and numbers to solve a problem, as well as qualitative methods, usually exploring a problem or question in an exploratory way without a hypothesis. We briefly introduce other approaches such as mixed methods and participatory action research. We wrap up by providing examples of some recent interesting studies done by counseling psychologists.

What is "research?" Basically, it is just trying to find an answer to a question, using a systematic method. What is something you are curious about related to mental health? Perhaps you wonder how birth order is related to mental health. Or how different kinds of social media apps are related to mental health. Or maybe you wonder if energy drinks are related to anxiety or depression at all. We could go on endlessly with wonderful questions! There is, literally, not enough time to find answers to all the questions we have. Where do we start? For starters, to do a research study, we are looking for two main things: whether the study has been done before and whether it will have a meaningful contribution.

First, has the question been explored before? Has anyone ever tried to answer the question with some other kind of study? Sometimes we refer to this as the research "gap" or "gap in the literature," meaning no one has published a study about it before. Even if someone has done a similar study before, you could still replicate it; replication studies are important to see if the findings are

DOI: 10.4324/9781003439899-10

alike. But in general, researchers want to make a new contribution to the literature. What do we mean by *the literature*? (Please pronounce this using a fancy voice.) Basically, that is a term that refers to the scholarship or the body of knowledge around an idea. We encourage you, as you think about research and research questions, to think critically. In other words, try not to take things as they are presented to you at face value. Sometimes, the authors will explicitly lay out what they perceive as issues or concerns about the study in a limitations section, but you may think of limitations or concerns that the author has not explicitly named. Perhaps you notice that the sample does not represent a wide range of cultural groups or age ranges. Or perhaps there are problems with the measures the researchers used. As you read the literature to find out what kind of studies have occurred in the past, try to think about what the strengths and limitations of those studies are.

Now consider: Is it enough for a study to not have been completed before? Does that make the study important to conduct? Let's think about this: Has anyone ever done a research study on why you like to eat a certain breakfast cereal? Or why you like to wear your pink footie pajamas to bed on Fridays? Or why your cat prefers to sleep on the green blanket your parents have but not the blue blanket? Well, probably not. It might be interesting to you to find answers to these questions (and we definitely encourage you to experiment with different blanket colors and textures to find your kitties' preferences), but we also hope that research will *contribute something meaningful* that will help us understand a phenomenon better, that will help people's psychological well-being, or that will make the world a better place. So that is the second part: it might not be enough that a research study has not been done before. It also needs to be a good and meaningful contribution that will help counseling psychologists in their work some way. We sometimes call this the *rationale* or *justification* for the study, and the researcher should be able to make a strong argument (rationale or justification) for the need for the study, usually based on a review of previous studies or literature related to that topic.

Counseling Psychologists' Research

As we mentioned in Chapter 1, most counseling psychologists, and in fact clinical psychologists, are *scientist-practitioners*. In this case, *science* refers to research – in other words, we have some kind of question and use systematic methods to investigate and potentially answer that question. Counseling psychologists, as scientist-practitioners, have four main roles related to research. They may (1) consume research, (2) do clinical practice based on research, (3) produce research, or (4) mentor others doing research – or a combination of some or all of these. Being a scientist-practitioner means that science (research) informs the practice, and practice (psychotherapy) informs science. Some counseling psychologists, for example those in private practice, may be consumers of research – they may read and interpret journal articles, or may attend professional development trainings or conferences based on evidence-based (research-based) practice to better serve their clients. As you read in Chapters 6 and 8, it is important for counseling psychologists to use therapy approaches that are supported by evidence and known to be effective. Some counseling psychologists, for example those who are professors in research institutions, may produce research as part of their work. They may apply for grants to fund their research, may mentor students in the research, and may disseminate research through publications and conferences. They may also do public outreach to try to share with the public, in nonacademic terms and language, about the significance of their findings.

Unlike some other areas of psychology where researchers might study rat or other animal behavior, most of the research that counseling psychologists do is with human beings, or *human subjects*. In counseling psychology, we often refer to subjects as *participants* to indicate a more collaborative and egalitarian kind of relationship. Human subjects research is generally overseen by the human subjects review board, or *institutional review board* (IRB), at an institution to ensure that participants and the public are not harmed by the research study. IRBs protect participants' rights and welfare by conducting independent reviews of the research plan before the study begins. Before a study can begin, a researcher will give detailed plans to the IRB for review, including the literature, background, and rationale for the study; ways that the researcher will obtain consent and protect privacy of participants; step-by-step methodology, including any measures or interview protocols; and so on. IRBs may deem a study *exempt*, for example if a researcher wants to use preexisting data; *expedited*, meaning there is little risk or harm to participants, such as when participants just take a few surveys; or *full review*, for example in a study using more intense interventions like biofeedback or with control/experimental groups. IRBs largely developed after World War II as researchers became more concerned about the rights and welfare of participants (Grady, 2015). Researchers must participate in trainings and continuing education on research ethics and IRB requirements, and they must be sensitive to the needs of vulnerable research populations and participants' cultural context.

Most of the research that counseling psychologists do largely falls into two categories: quantitative, which is probably what you are most familiar with; and qualitative, which may be new to you. In this chapter, we will mostly focus on quantitative and qualitative research methods but will also briefly talk about mixed methods and participatory action research.

Quantitative Research

The kind of research you are probably most familiar with is quantitative research. Quantitative researchers have some kind of research question (for example, does social support – like friendships, family relationships, or community relationships – impact depression?) and hypothesis about the answer to that question (for example, lower levels of social support will be associated with higher rates of depression). They test their hypotheses systematically using statistics. They use high-quality measures (surveys, instruments, or tests) that are valid and reliable to examine their variables of interest (e.g., social support and depression). They might use *descriptive* statistics to describe a phenomenon or they might use *inferential* statistics to look at differences between groups (Betz & Fassinger, 2012). When studying people, it is not possible to study every single human who has ever experienced depression. However, we can take a sample of 1,000 people who represent the general population and survey them about their emotional states. Then, we can make *inferences*, or educated guesses, based on their responses.

You are probably very familiar with descriptive statistics even if you aren't aware of it! Descriptive statistics include things like the mean, median, mode, and range. When you hear on the news that the median age of onset of depression is 31, you are engaging with descriptive statistics. When you hear something like "people who have higher levels of social support report less depression," you are reading a study that used inferential statistics. These researchers probably took a group of 1,000 people and asked them questions about social support and depression. Then they analyzed how responses about social support related to responses about depression and found that, overall, people who reported high levels of social support also said their depression was low and people who reported low levels of social support also said that their depression was high. Assuming the sample they collected was representative of the general population (the people they surveyed share similar dynamics and characteristics as the rest of society), they can conclude with 95% certainty, for example, social support and depression are closely related for people in the United States. Some of the most common kinds of quantitative studies try to prove cause and effect, or what we call *causality*, or they try to prove relationship, or *correlation*. If you have taken any courses specific about research methods, you know one important thing to note is that correlation is not causation! Based on our social support study, for example, we cannot state that low social support *causes* people to be depressed. It might be equally true that people who are depressed a lot tend to isolate and disconnect from others. We can only conclude that there is a likely association. (So beware when you hear a news outlet saying, "A specific factor all by itself causes depression!" Often, they are misinterpreting the results reported by researchers.)

Researchers are also highly concerned about the study design, or what we also sometimes call *methodology* or *procedures*. Honestly, there are too many different types of designs to describe them all here so we are going to focus on a few main concepts. Traditionally, quantitative research has been labeled as either experimental or descriptive, and field or lab.

- *Experimental* means that there is some kind of intervention or variable being manipulated, while *descriptive* means that the researchers are looking to describe something that is happening. (Note that descriptive statistics are different than a descriptive study. We know, that is confusing.) In experimental, some kind of intervention might occur or some kind of variable might be manipulated (for example, half of the domestic violence agency clients receive individual therapy and half receive group therapy), whereas with descriptive studies, the researchers might be more interested in relationships between variables (whether socioeconomic status relates to levels of psychological distress in domestic violence agency clients).
- *Field* just refers to something that happens in the real world and not in a *lab* or simulated type of environment. So, for example, field studies might occur at a local domestic violence shelter, whereas in *lab* studies, the participants might travel to a university building for the study.

Regardless of study design, researchers may use surveys (e.g., scales, measures, tests, or assessment tools) to collect data from participants about things like social support levels, depression intensity, anxiety-related behaviors, and so on. The difference is not so much in how the data are collected, but rather the conditions under which they are collected. For example, in a lab study, very strict controls are maintained to ensure that all participants have the same experience in the same environment (sometimes even down to the temperature in the room and the speed at which questions are asked). In a descriptive study, controls may be less important and participants might

Table 10.1 Examples of different kinds of research methods

	Experimental	Descriptive
Field	**Experimental Field** Domestic violence shelter clients participate at the shelter. There are two comparison groups, people who get individual therapy and people who get group therapy.	**Descriptive Field** Domestic violence shelter clients participate at the shelter. They take two surveys, one measuring socioeconomic status and one measuring psychological distress.
Lab	**Experimental Lab** Domestic violence shelter clients go to a research lab on a university campus to participate. There are two comparison groups, people who get individual therapy and people who get group therapy.	**Descriptive Lab** Domestic violence shelter clients go to a research lab on a university campus to participate. They take two surveys, one measuring socioeconomic status and one measuring psychological distress.

even complete surveys online, in the comfort of their own home. In choosing a research design, quantitative researchers try to use a design that will help their study be valid. We describe this in Table 10.1.

Considering these examples, how do you think being in a naturalistic or field environment, such as the shelter, would affect the results of the study compared to being in a lab? What kind of findings might the researchers get from an experimental study versus a descriptive study? What might be the benefits and challenges of each of the four approaches?

The Importance of Validity in Quantitative Research

As you noticed and might have heard elsewhere, the validity or accuracy of research can be impacted by a lot of factors (remember how lab studies may try controlling the temperature of a room). Even after researchers do their best to control for every single confounding variable or factor that impacts their results, there is usually some unexpected variable they were unable to fully control for (maybe people were more likely to report being angry because the room was 80 degrees). That is why it is so important for researchers to do their best to increase the validity of their research using several strategies. When counseling psychologists use research to make decisions about mental health and treatment approaches, the research they use needs to be accurate. As a researcher and future clinician, you need to know how to evaluate research, so we devote a large portion of this chapter to discussing approaches to accurate research design.

Researchers want to conduct good, valid studies. In quantitative research, *validity* refers to the extent to which a study's findings are genuine and accurate (as opposed to some extraneous variable). When thinking about doing research, we first want to note that it is not possible for any researcher to design a completely perfect study. In any study, researchers weigh the potential risks and benefits of any method and try to limit *threats to validity*, or things that would make the study flawed, but all studies have some flaws. In designing a quantitative study, researchers try to control the study as much as possible to show that there are not alternative explanations for their findings. Sometimes this is referred to as the MAXMINCON principle: Researchers try to *maximize* variance of the variables (they want their variables to be strong and distinct), *minimize* potential error, and *control* for weird extra variables that could influence the study (Heppner et al., 2016; Kerlinger & Lee, 2000). This allows them to conclude that the findings are valid.

Another aspect researchers are often concerned about is *external validity* or *generalizability*, which refers to whether the results, which were found with a sample can generalize to the larger population. This generally has to do with the sample of participants and how much they represent the larger population of interest. So, if researchers conduct a study about athlete mental health only with a sample of 18–22-year-old hockey players, the results are probably not generalizable to all athletes in the United States. But they might be generalizable to other hockey players in the United States. One of the best ways to ensure external validity is through a random sample, but this is not always possible in studies.

Internal validity refers to how sure a researcher is that the conclusions they make are valid. As we said earlier, the researcher wants to be sure that the findings are about the findings, and not about something else. There are all kinds of things that can threaten internal validity. For example, *selection bias* refers to the participants, or the sample, already having some differences before the study begins. Let's say a researcher is going to compare students from two different high school English classes (first period and fourth period), but is unaware that the students in fourth period are almost all student-athletes because they have athletics/team practice during first period, whereas the students in first period are mostly students in vo-tech courses because they leave school at noon for work and cannot take the fourth period English class. These factors could contribute to differences between the two different groups; it would be better if the researcher took all the students in first and fourth periods and randomly assigned them to comparison groups.

Another threat to internal validity is *attrition*, which refers to participants dropping out or not completing the study. This can happen if the study is time-consuming or requires too much energy or commitment on the part of the participant. *Maturation* refers to changes that occur naturally over time to the participant group. For example, in a study on an intervention to help anxiety in college students, if anxiety levels decreased at the end of the academic year compared to the beginning of the year, was that because of the anxiety intervention being studied, or because the students naturally matured and grew over the course of a year?

History effects are when a sample has something happen that is unique to them that can affect their results. One example might be in a four-year study of the effectiveness of school counseling on fifth graders. One year, the school being studied had to undergo major construction, so all the fifth graders were bused to a totally different school. Their results might be due to the busing and not the school counseling. *Instrument error* means errors that can occur with the test itself (or measure, or instrument). For example, we know of someone who forgot to enter an item in an online survey. So instead of completing a psychometrically valid 60-item survey, all of the participants completed a 59-item survey, and the error was not found until the study was completed. Other things can occur such as a page being missing from a test booklet, testing conditions not being the way they are supposed to, and so on. These are all potential threats to internal validity and can affect how certain a researcher can be that their findings are about their findings and not something else. There are many other factors that might threaten internal validity; this is not a comprehensive list. For example, with many research studies using new technology, artificial intelligence, digital recruitment systems, and so on, there may be new threats to validity that have not been seen historically (such as bots pretending to be human participating in a study).

There are all kinds of other validity issues that researchers need to consider. For example, there is something called *statistical conclusion validity*. This is basically about whether the researcher has come to the right conclusion based on their analysis. How sure can they be, based on their statistical analyses, that when they say "the hypothesis was met," that it was actually met? In talking about statistical conclusion validity, researchers don't want to say they found something when in fact they did not, and don't want to conclude that they didn't meet the hypothesis or find something when in fact they did. There are all kinds of statistical issues that can contribute to these errors. One of these is low statistical *power*, which refers to whether or not the sample size was big enough to statistically make a conclusion. Researchers usually will run a power analysis using some kind of statistical analysis software program prior to beginning the study to determine what number of participants they will need to have strong statistical conclusion validity. Another issue is use of *unreliable measures*, which refers to use of a measure (test, instrument) without strong psychometric properties. This occurs sometimes when a researcher cannot find a good measure (or perhaps the good measure is too expensive and they are a student) for their variable of interest and decides to develop their own scale or question items without testing their psychometric properties.

Another type of validity is *construct validity*, or whether the researcher is measuring what they say they are measuring. Let's say a researcher wants to study the relationship between how much someone reads fiction and that person's psychological well-being. They measure "how much someone reads fiction" by number of books checked out from the local public library. In this case, however, if a family member is checking books out for several people in their family, the number of fiction books would be higher, and would not actually represent the individual's fiction books read. Further, books checked out might not necessarily equal books completed. There are a number of threats to construct validity, but this is probably the most common issue – when the way a variable is measured or defined is not accurately captured through the study.

An Example of Quantitative Research

Let's consider an example of a quantitative research study. Just because it is a fun study, we are going to review Taracuk and Koch's (2021) study, about the use of a media intervention to increase positive attitudes toward transgender and gender diverse people. Based on current research, Taracuk and Koch hypothesized that they might be able to change people's attitudes toward transgender and gender diverse people by having them watch a TV show. They recruited a convenience sample of 223 college students from one university. (So right away, we know that the sample is not representative of all adults in the United States and maybe not of all college students in the United States.) Then they randomly assigned participants to one of four groups (random assignment is great!). They checked to make sure all four groups were about equal in size and in terms of demographics and found there were no major differences between their sub-groups.

Then they applied the intervention. They had the students watch one of two episodes of Star Trek. In one, the characters encounter an open-minded and affirming society where people do not express the gender binary. In other words, members of the society were all non-binary and appeared androgynous. The other episode had nothing to do with gender or anything having to do with human demographic characteristics.

- One group took a pre-test (or survey), watched a Star Trek episode about gender, then had a post-test.
- One group took a pre-test, watched a neutral Star Trek episode, then took a post-test.
- One group watched a Star Trek episode about gender, then took a post-test.
- One group watched a neutral Star Trek episode, then took a post-test.

This different way of testing participants helped to control for testing effects, which is where taking the test once influences your later results. Take a moment to think about the reason for this. If you were asked questions about your feelings about gender and then watched a video clip with gendered themes, would you be more likely to focus on gender while watching the video? Maybe, but withholding the pre-test from participants helps researchers look at whether the pre-test had an effect.

The authors ran their statistical analyses and found that their first hypothesis, that watching the Star Trek episode about gender would change attitudes, was met. In other words, people who watched that episode had significantly higher positive attitudes than the people who watched the neutral one. But their second hypothesis, that watching the episode would change people's willingness to engage in social action, was not supported. In other words, their statistical tests were not significant. You might notice that there are very specific ways of talking about research results. Rather than saying, "Our study definitively shows that watching videos changes attitudes," researchers simply acknowledge that, within the bounds of their study, their hypothesis was not supported.

Part of the reason that researchers are very careful about how they discuss their results is because every study involves limitations. We already talked about one limitation or the fact that the sample was not representative. Another is that, because the post-test occurred within a week after watching the TV episodes, it was not possible to conclude that the changes in attitude that follow watching a show last for a long time. Nevertheless, it was possible to say that there is some promise in using media like television and film to influence societal attitudes for the better. We could write an entire book (or even multiple books) about quantitative research, but then where would we fit crucial discussions about qualitative research? The cool thing about counseling psychology is that counseling psychology researchers are open to using a lot of different methods to answer deep and meaningful questions about behavioral health and human beings. Counseling psychologists are leaders in the area of qualitative research as well.

Qualitative Research

Qualitative research differs from quantitative research in that it seeks to explain and understand phenomena. Qualitative researchers are looking to gather detailed, descriptive information about lived experiences. Qualitative research in counseling psychology really started to grow in the 1990s–2000s. Qualitative researchers often use terms to describe the data like deep and rich – they can gather information that quantitative measures often cannot or do not intend to capture. With qualitative research, there is more researcher participation in the data collection process and researchers usually collect smaller samples of participants (12 instead of 200+). This also means that there is a strong likelihood of researcher bias and subjectivity, and that the findings are not generalizable to large populations. Because of this, some psychologists and other scientists are very skeptical and even critical of qualitative methods, but when people talk negatively about qualitative research, it is usually because they are using quantitative standards (generalizability, hypothesis testing) to judge qualitative approaches (thematic coding, data interpretation).

Of course, there are some common concepts that are shared between qualitative and quantitative study designs, but some of those concepts and terms have different meanings. For example, qualitative researchers also consider validity, but in a different way from quantitative researchers. In qualitative research, people often use the term *trustworthiness* to indicate whether findings are truthful, accurate, and representative (Morrow et al., 2012). Researchers often engage in something called *reflexivity* (Morrow, 2005), meaning that they consider their own biases and how their own background or their *positionality* (Goundar, 2025) might affect the findings and how the findings are interpreted. Good qualitative researchers must have good interaction and interpersonal skills, the ability to organize and synthesize many different types of data, and the ability to gain

Table 10.2 Qualitative versus quantitative research methods

Qualitative	*Quantitative*
Focus on texts and narratives	Focus on numbers and statistics
Flexible, semi-structured, unstructured	Rigid, structured design; Participants are limited to predetermined responses
Explore phenomena/ideas	Test hypotheses
Open-ended questions around focus topic; Probing questions	Closed-ended questions
In depth data help us to find out HOW and WHY; seeks to explain and understand; sequence of events	Generalizable data to find out WHO, WHAT, WHERE, WHEN; easily replicated
Researcher participation – intimately involved	Researcher participation – uninvolved observer
Small sample sizes	Large sample sizes

the trust of individuals and groups. Table 10.2 expands on comparisons between qualitative and quantitative research.

One qualitative method that is often used by counseling psychologists is Consensual Qualitative Research ([CQR]; Hill, 2012). In CQR as with other qualitative methods, researchers do not start with a hypothesis and conclusions are built from the data. Instead, pose a research question, collect data, and then draw themes and ideas from the data through an analytic process. In CQR, the term consensual refers to the fact that there is a team of researchers who, as they analyze the data, come to a consensus about the themes of the findings. That approach is intended to somewhat limit the bias inherent in qualitative research. Other qualitative research methods often used by counseling psychologists include grounded theory and phenomenology (Morrow et al., 2012). There is some flexibility in these methods and you will find that different researchers introduce or adapt some qualitative methods in unique ways, but it is important for them to explain any modifications they make and even explain why the method they use is the best one to answer their research questions.

In one example of how CQR could be used to conduct research, a researcher wants to understand the potential mental health benefits of forest bathing (a traditionally Japanese practice where people immerse themselves in the atmosphere of a forest; they do not actually bathe in water). She puts together a team of one other faculty member, two graduate students, and two undergraduate students to help her conduct her research. The team secures human subjects review approval from their institution and recruits 15 participants who actively forest bathe on a regular basis. Are you noticing how the research question shapes who is invited to participate in the study and that the group of participants is small when compared to quantitative studies?

Before the research starts, the team meets to discuss their biases and expectations and discuss any power differences to encourage all to share and come to consensus. Then the graduate students interview the participants about their forest bathing experiences using open-ended questions, and these interviews are recorded and transcribed. Next, everyone on the team reads the first interview transcript and they work together to start making a *domain list*, or a list of themes that they see emerging from the transcript. As they identify more and more domains, they collect examples, generate definitions, combine domains that seem related, and break apart domains that seem too broad. Eventually, (usually after coding a couple of transcripts) their domain list gets established and their list stops going through major changes and edits.

After the domain list stabilizes, they may start reading the transcripts on their own and then just get together (usually at coding meetings) to discuss any places their codes do not match up so that they can discuss their interpretations and come to consensus about the correct code or codes. Some CQR researchers also include an external auditor who reviews their work at different points in the process to further limit bias and increase trustworthiness of the results).

After they have coded all of the transcripts using their domain list, the research team comes together to conduct a cross-analysis to identify categories that are taking shape within the broader domains and then count how many participants are captured by a given category (how representative that category is across participants). So, for example, if the category is "Reduces Anxiety," and all 15 participants said something about this, the team might consider that category differently than the category "Physical Complaints (bugs, sticky sap, heat)" that was brought up by only two participants. Ultimately, the team develops a list of several themes, or domains, that assist others in understanding potential mental health benefits reported by these participants about forest bathing and they include representative quotes to support and illustrate their findings. (By the way: we definitely encourage you to try out forest bathing, even if you don't live near a forest; anywhere outdoors could work.)

Other Research Methods

Mixed methods studies integrate quantitative methods, data, and analysis with qualitative methods, data, and analysis (Hanson et al., 2005). Creswell et al. (2003) said that mixed methods research is:

> the collection or analysis of both quantitative and qualitative data in a single study in which the data are collected concurrently or sequentially, are given a priority, and involve the integration of the data at one or more stages in the process of research
>
> (p. 212)

A mixed methods approach allows researchers to make statistical conclusions as well as gain a deeper understanding of their variables of interest. There are lots of ways researchers can combine quantitative and qualitative studies that can get pretty complex, and you will probably learn about those specifics if you take a research methods course. In this chapter, we will take a more general view of mixed methods approaches by focusing on how qualitative and quantitative approaches can be interpreted side-by-side to give a broader view of a phenomenon or association between variables.

For example, our research question might be: What is the relationship between time spent outdoors and psychological well-being? We would use quantitative and qualitative methods to explore and analyze the data. For the quantitative portion, perhaps we would survey 300 people with questions about the time they spend outdoors and a measure of psychological well-being. We would use statistical analyses to find out whether there is a positive association between the two. For the qualitative portion, we might conduct hour-long interviews with 15 people using open-ended questions. We could use CQR to analyze the data. Then, we would look at the results together, see how they compare, and interpret their meaning.

Let's say that we found, based on our survey, that there is a strong positive relationship between being outdoors and psychological well-being. Because we are just looking at whether they're related, we can't tell whether people who have high psychological well-being just tend to spend more time outdoors, or whether being outdoors has any kind of effect on psychological well-being. All we can conclude is that they're related. But looking at the qualitative data, we see that all participants specifically reported that they felt their mood lift and anxiety lessen after spending time outdoors. Now we can take those findings together and although we still can't conclude that being outdoors causes better psychological well-being, we have a better understanding and insight into how being outdoors and psychological well-being may relate to one another.

Counseling psychologists may also use qualitative research methods in which they work collaboratively to actively engage and involve members of the community toward change, such as participatory action research (Kidd & Kral, 2005) or *community-based participatory research* (Collins et al., 2018). These approaches are not necessarily considered methods as much as they are a perspective or worldview about how research should be conducted. They emphasize doing research *with people* as opposed to doing research *on people*. Using these approaches, people or community members who might be considered participants in other forms of research become co-researchers. The community helps drive the need for the study, the research questions, what interventions or activities might be implemented, interpretation of results, and other aspects of the study design. Using these methods gives an opportunity to approach a research question in a collaborative way that emphasizes community outreach and social justice, but it often takes a long time to build relationships and to implement a participatory or community-based approach, and that can be a challenge.

The Role of Cultural Context

Issues related to culture are highly important to counseling psychology research, whether the research is explicitly focused on cultural variables, or whether it is related to other issues. Some research does explicitly seek to understand the role of cultural variables related to health and mental health. For example, a researcher might be interested in comparing the effects of social media on teenagers versus people older than 65. Or a researcher might examine and compare levels of anxiety in people in rural areas versus urban areas after a flood.

In all studies, though, some cultural background information, or *demographic* information, should be shared and reported. As we mentioned in Chapter 3, APA has Journal Article Reporting Standards for race, ethnicity, and culture, and other demographic characteristics, called JARS-REC. These standards are to be applied in disseminating findings, whether researchers are conducting qualitative, quantitative, or mixed methods studies (APA, 2023). For example, the JARS-REC encourages researchers to use resilience and strengths-based frameworks especially when working with or describing marginalized populations, critically review the literature and its appropriateness for the sample or population of interest, discuss how cultural factors were considered in developing methodology, describe the composition of the sample, use measures that are culturally appropriate, and interpret findings within the context of the study (APA, 2023). APA especially emphasizes the problems inherent in conflating the terms race, ethnicity, and culture (APA, 2023; See also Chapter 3 of this book).

Likewise, Cokley and Awad (2016) emphasize the importance of operationalizing, or clearly defining, cultural concepts, variables, or groups, as there are some terms that authors use interchangeably, such as sex and gender, race and culture, or socioeconomic status and social class. They also discuss the role of *distal* versus *proximal* explanations for human behavior. Distal essentially refers to things that are distant or far away, and proximal refers to things that are close or nearby. In considering multicultural issues, distal explanations might include demographic information like race, age, or disability, but they may not really explain what is happening in the study. Proximal explanations might be things like racial identity, values, or spirituality/religiosity, and might have a closer or more direct meaning for the results. For example, whether a person fits into the (distal) racial category Black does not describe proximal explanations like the education level of their parents, where in the United States they grew up, extracurriculars/interests in high school, whether their family has been in the United States for hundreds of years or whether they recently immigrated, and so on. Therefore, researchers are cautioned against interpreting results based on large and broad distal categories such as race (Cokley & Awad, 2016).

Designing a Study

Here are some typical steps that a researcher might follow in developing, planning, and implementing a study, and sharing the results.

1) Dive into the literature – The researcher will read all kinds of published studies to find out what has been done before and what still needs to be done related to the topic. They may especially look for "calls" for future research. They will critically consider aspects of past studies, such as sample size, measures used, methods and results, and the kinds of conclusions past researchers made.
2) Consider the variables – This is particularly important in a quantitative study, but even with a qualitative study, there may be specific factors or variables that researchers are interested

in learning more about. The researcher identifies independent and dependent variables of interest. Independent variables are those that the researcher may manipulate in order to see a change in a dependent variable. Sometimes researchers refer to defining the variables as *operationalizing* the variables, which is just a fancy way of clearly stating how you're defining the variables.

3) Develop the research question – The research question, if quantitative, should be specific and measurable. If qualitative, it should be open and exploratory in nature. An example of a quantitative research question is: Do people who spend at least an hour outdoors five or more days a week have different levels of depression and psychological well-being than people who spend time outdoors two days a week (or fewer)? A qualitative research question might be: How do people relate their time outdoors to their mental health?
4) Develop hypotheses (if quantitative) – The researcher should offer hypotheses that are related to the research question(s) and state what they think their findings will be. Qualitative studies do not typically have hypotheses. So, related to the research question above, the hypothesis could be: People who spend at least an hour outdoors five or more days a week will have lower levels of depression and higher levels of psychological well-being than people who spend time outdoors two days a week or fewer.
5) Plan research methods and study design – In this step, the researcher would consider recruitment, potential interventions, measures, or interview protocols. If they are going to ask participants demographic questions, these would be developed as well. Here, the researcher weighs all the potential issues related to internal validity and tries to make the best choices possible in designing the study (using MAXMINCON). For our study, would it be better to recruit members of a local hiking club (would be inexpensive, convenient, might not get a large sample) or to try to recruit nationally through an online network of outdoor enthusiasts (might be more expensive, time-consuming, might take longer to get a good sample size)? Should we take paper surveys out to a local conservation fair or Earth Day event? Or send out electronic surveys (taking the chance that we might have bots complete the survey)?
6) Consider any ethical and cultural implications and seek out human subjects review approval – As discussed earlier, the researcher must be transparent about all aspects of the research, its need, and method with their institution's IRB. Typically, the IRB will have questions or feedback for revisions before the researcher may proceed. This can be a lengthy process, so it is helpful for the researcher to plan accordingly.
7) Recruit participants, secure informed consent, and implement study – The researcher will work to recruit an adequate sample size to meet the power analysis they ran prior to the study. They will make sure participants are adequately informed of their rights, risks, and benefits to participating in the study. They will make sure the participants consent to the study, either in writing or using *passive* consent (where a participant indicates consent by completing a survey, for example). In qualitative studies, the researcher will conduct interviews, focus groups, or engage in observations of participants or settings.
8) Analyze results – In a quantitative study, the researcher will use statistical analyses to come to conclusions about their findings. They will examine any anomalies or problems with the data. They will determine whether their results were statistically and meaningfully significant and whether their hypotheses were met. In qualitative analysis, the researcher will adhere to a coding process as outlined by their approach to develop themes.
9) Consider limitations – It is important for the researcher to consider and report limitations of the study. This transparency allows readers to understand how the researchers approached MAXMINCON or tried to minimize bias (if appropriate) in a qualitative study.

10) Share findings – Researchers can disseminate findings in a number of ways. One way is through presenting their findings at a professional conference of some sort, such as a state psychological association, American Psychological Association convention, or a specific conference related to the topic of the research, like APA's Division 34: Society for Environmental, Population, and Conservation Psychology annual virtual conference. Presentations might be an oral talk about a paper, a symposium (a panel of speakers all talking about similar topics), or a poster session. Researchers might also disseminate findings through submitting manuscripts to a peer-reviewed journal such as *Journal of Counseling Psychology*, *The Counseling Psychologist*, or *Journal of Environmental Psychology*. Finally, there are ways of disseminating findings to the public, such as a researcher being interviewed for a local news channel or writing for a more mainstream publication such as national newspapers, magazines, blogs, or podcasts.

Imagine that you were able to design a research project on a topic related to mental health benefits of physical exercise or spending time outdoors. What would your research question be? What would your hypotheses be? How would you design the study? What method would you use? How would you use the results? How would you share the results?

Summary

In this chapter, we tried to demystify the research process for you a little bit. We started this chapter off by talking a little about what research is and why it is important to counseling psychologists. We described the differences between quantitative and qualitative research methods and introduced you to some other methods as well. We emphasized the importance of considering cultural context in any research study. We talked through the steps someone might go through if they were actually designing a research project. We hope that sharing some real-life examples of counseling psychology research has helped you see that real people (like you!) do this kind of research and it's not that difficult. Did it work? Are you thinking about some fun research ideas? In Chapter 11, we move on to the topic of ethics – ethics in practice, research, and everything else a counseling psychologist does.

What Would You Do?

You are in a research lab overseen by a professor in the counseling psychology program. The lab focuses on women's mental health related to fertility issues. For one of the projects, your lab offers $1,000 to participants to complete a year-long study. This includes completing weekly checklists and monthly interview check-ins. Participants must be women and must have experienced issues related to fertility. You have been trained to do monthly interview check-ins with some of the participants. However, during your first set of interviews, you get the feeling that some of the participants do not fit the criteria and are just doing the research to get the $1,000. You know the project is on a tight timeline and your professor is under a lot of pressure to complete the study. In lab meetings, you and other research staff have been pressured to move as quickly as possible on your research tasks and you worry that raising your concerns might upset your professor, slow down the study, and limit your opportunities to apply for the counseling psychology graduate program at your school.

- What are your responsibilities in this case?
- What are the implications of inaction on your part (for research, your professor, and your career)?

- What steps might you take toward notifying your professor if you decide to do so?
- What sources of support are available to you to help you chart a path forward?

Counseling Psychologist Spotlight: Research

Dr. Mike Parent

Dr. Mike Parent is a principal researcher at Hopelab, a nonprofit organization that works to improve mental health outcomes for young people with a specific focus on Black, Brown, and Queer young people. On a daily basis, he develops and fosters collaborative research

Dr. Mike Parent. Photograph by author.

relationships, manages research projects, speaks with external partners, and develops public-facing assets from research projects. In his job, he likes being able to develop projects from scratch that lead to new research collaborations and opportunities to speak with industry and nonprofit leaders. He loves the ability to directly influence policy and knowledge pertaining to youth mental health and the ability to uplift and support other researchers in his work. He said that a challenging part of his job can be focusing and supporting multiple partnerships – he has lots of asks for his time and energy.

Mike's research interests are related to gender, sexuality, and behavioral health. Recently, he has become more interested in the role of technology, artificial intelligence, and social media and their relationship to mental health. Mike enjoys applying his counseling psychology training in social justice and empirical research, which are skills and knowledge sets that he uses daily. Outside of work, he stays active in local sports organizations like his local CrossFit gym and is a competitive bodybuilder. He enjoys building furniture in his workshop, reading, and writing.

Mike earned his PhD in counseling psychology program from the University of Florida. He earned his undergraduate degree in psychology from the University of Manitoba, a master's in psychology from the University of Florida, and a master's of business administration from Lamar University. Before joining Hopelab, he was an Associate Professor at the University of Texas at Austin. He is a licensed and board-certified psychologist and is active in professional organizations like the Society of Counseling Psychology.

References

American Psychological Association. (2023). *Journal Article Reporting Standards—Race, ethnicity, and culture.* https://apastyle.apa.org/jars/rec-table-1.pdf

Betz, N. E., & Fassinger, R. E. (2012). Methodologies in counseling psychology. In E. M. Altmeier & J. C. Hansen (Eds.), *The Oxford handbook of counseling psychology* (pp. 237–269). Oxford University Press. https://doi.org/10.1093/oxfordhb/9780195342314.001.0001

Cokley, K. O., & Awad, G. H. (2016). Diverse perspectives: Conceptual and methodological considerations. In P. P. Heppner, B. E. Wampold, J. Owen, M. N. Thompson & K. T. Wang (Eds.), *Research design in counseling* (4th ed., pp. 187–219). Cengage Learning.

Collins, S. E., Clifasefi, S. L., Stanton, J., The Leap Advisory Board, Straits, K. J. E., Gil-Kashiwabara, E., Rodriguez Espinosa, P., Nicasio, A. V., Andrasik, M. P., Hawes, S. M., Miller, K. A., Nelson, L. A., Orfaly, V. E., Duran, B. M., & Wallerstein, N. (2018). Community based participatory research (CBPR): Towards equitable involvement of community in psychology research. *American Psychologist, 73*(7), 884–898. https://doi.org/10.1037/amp0000167

Creswell, J. W., Plano Clark, V. L., Gutmann, M. L., & Hanson, W. E. (2003). Advanced mixed methods research designs. In A. Tashakkori & C. Teddlie (Eds.), *Handbook of mixed methods in social and behavioral research* (pp. 209–240). Sage.

Goundar, P. R. (2025). Researcher positionality: Ways to include it in a qualitative research design. *International Journal of Qualitative Methods, 24.* Advance online publication. https://doi.org/10.1177/16094069251321251

Grady, C. (2015). Institutional review boards: Purposes and challenges. *Chest, 148*(5), 1148–1155. https://doi.org/10.1378/chest.15-0706

Hanson, W. E., Creswell, J. W., Clark, V. L. P., Petska, K. S., & Creswell, J. D. (2005). Mixed methods research designs in counseling psychology. *Journal of Counseling Psychology, 52*(2), 224–235. https://doi.org/10.1037/0022-0167.52.2.224

Heppner, P. P., Wampold, B. E., Owen, J., Thompson, M. N., & Wang, K. T. (2016). *Research design in counseling* (4th ed.). Cengage Learning.

Hill, C. E. (Ed.). (2012). *Consensual qualitative research: A practical resource for investigating social science phenomena.* American Psychological Association. https://psycnet.apa.org/record/2011-09578-000

Kerlinger, F. N., & Lee, H. B. (2000). *Foundations of behavioral research.* Harcourt.

Kidd, S. A., & Kral, M. J. (2005). Practicing participatory action research. *Journal of Counseling Psychology, 52*(2), 187–195. https://doi.org/10.1037/0022-0167.52.2.187

Morrow, S. L. (2005). Quality and trustworthiness in qualitative research in counseling psychology. *Journal of Counseling Psychology, 52*(2), 250–260. https://doi.org/10.1037/0022-0167.52.2.250

Morrow, S. L., Castañeda-Sound, C. L., & Abrams, E. M. (2012). Counseling psychology research methods: Qualitative approaches. In N. Fouad (Ed.), *APA handbook of counseling psychology: Vol. 1 Theories, research, and methods* (pp. 93–117). American Psychological Association.

Taracuk, M. D., & Koch, J. M. (2021). Use of a media intervention to increase positive attitudes toward transgender and gender diverse individuals. *International Journal of Transgender Health, 24*(1), 1–13. https://doi.org/10.1080/26895269.2021.1878479

Chapter 11

Shades of Gray

Ethics in Counseling Psychology

The Importance of Ethics

Before today, what did you think of when you heard the term *ethics*? Did you ever think to yourself, "Gosh, I want to learn about ethics! It sounds so exciting!"? Probably not. Most people think of "ethics" as dry or boring rules and policies. But having an ethical foundation is possibly the most important part of being a counseling psychologist. Ethics come into play every single time a counseling psychologist meets with a client, does an assessment, conducts a research study, supervises doctoral students, or engages in a prevention activity. And, we are here to tell you, ethics can be super interesting, so we invite you to join us to consider some of the most important aspects of ethical behavior and decision-making as a counseling psychologist.

In this chapter, you will first learn about the moral and philosophical principles that underlie the ethical code of the American Psychological Association. We will describe the APA Ethics Code and will introduce you to APA Practice Guidelines, what HIPAA compliance means, state laws and federal laws, licensure standards, and the new PsyPACT. We offer examples of ethical decision-making models that you can put into practice with illustrations of real-life ethical dilemmas. We discuss the role of licensing boards and supervision. "Shades of Gray" refers to the notion that, often, there is no "right" or "wrong" answer to dilemmas that counseling psychologists are faced with, and how counseling psychologists must deal with some ambiguity in these situations. Eek! Are you ready? Let's go.

What Are Ethics?

First, it is helpful to reflect on the question, "What are *ethics*?" Merriam-Webster (2025) defines ethic(s) a few ways:

1) a) A set of moral principles: a theory or system of moral principles
   b) The principles of conduct governing an individual or group
   c) A consciousness of moral importance
   d) A guiding philosophy
2) A set of moral issues or aspects
3) The discipline of dealing with what is good or bad and with moral duty or obligation

This then means we need to figure out what *moral(s)* are. Again, Merriam-Webster (2025) has answers:

DOI: 10.4324/9781003439899-11

1) a) Of or relating to principles of right or wrong in behavior: ethics
   b) Expressing or teaching a conception of right behavior
   c) Conforming to a standard of right behavior
   d) Sanctioned by or operative on one's conscience or ethical judgment

Whelp, that makes it pretty clear, right? These definitions may make sense on the surface but take a moment to do a deeper, more critical dive into words and terminology (a common practice when it comes to ethics). For example, how clear is the statement, "ethics are related to morals and morals are related to ethics." What does that actually mean? And who decides what is "right" behavior? What are moral principles based on?

Moral principles are usually based on cultural and religious beliefs, so what is ethical or moral in one society might not be considered ethical or moral in another society (Chaddha & Agrawal, 2023; Velasquez et al., 1992). In other words, there is no moral or ethical code written somewhere that is followed by all people at all times. Morals and ethics are negotiated, agreed upon, and revisited across time (the ethical codes we talk about in this chapter have been revised and updated). Throughout this chapter, we refer to the Ethical Principles of Psychologists and Code of Conduct, which is written and published by the American Psychological Association ([APA], 2017), and has been updated many times since its first publication in 1953 (in fact, it is being rewritten currently and we expect to see a new Code in the next few years). So, it is important to note that when we discuss the ethical expectations of psychologists, in the United States, those ethics and morals are based on a Western, Judeo-Christian tradition (Parham, 2009; Pettifor, 2001).

Other countries or groups whose origins are not in Western Europe may have ethical codes that differ significantly. For example, the Association of Black Psychologists (ABPsi, 2019) has its own Ethical Guidelines for Black Psychologists based on "African Centered Philosophy" (p. 7) and offers psychologists 42 commitments such as "I will not pollute the environment," "I will take care not to cause future generations to be deprived of their needs," and "I will always respect that which is sacred" (p. 24). Likewise, the National Latina/o Psychological Association (NLPA, 2018) has the NLPA Ethical Guidelines. NLPA states that their foundations include "The law of In Lak'ech Ala K'in (I am you and you are my other me)" and "collective consciousness," or the notion that "people are extensions of one another and therefore have a responsibility to respect, care, and love one another as cultural beings" (NLPA, p. 3). Tassell et al. (2012) published a set of Indigenous ethical principles and interventions based on Māori culture. These principles emphasize "genealogy and historical links; relationships and sharing between individuals, families, and communities; cooperation and coexistence with environments and sources of food; and the recognition that some tribal knowledge is not accessible to all" (p. 178). Some themes common to these ethical guidelines that differ from APA's include emphasis on community, the natural world, context, and damage done by colonialism.

Established ethical codes are up for debate and can generate a lot of discussion that leads to future revisions and expansions. For example, the Society of Indian Psychologists published a response to APA's 2010 Ethical Guidelines, pointing out that the values system inherent in the APA Guidelines differs from those held by Indigenous peoples in the Americas (Garcia & Tehee, 2014). They state:

> This Commentary is based upon those shared values. They are often different than those apparently assumed, but not stated, in the APA Ethics Code. It is the position of this Commentary that the correct ethical behavior depends upon the framework of the culture of the community in which the psychologist is operating. Ethics are indeed influenced by the prevailing sociocultural

> context in which they are applied. Difficulties and challenges arise when ethics are assumed to be so universal that no provisions are made for different cultural contexts.

The authors then offer stories and illustrations that demonstrate challenges with the APA Ethics Code.

As we move forward in our discussion about ethics, and share some examples with you, we want you to know that this textbook adheres closely to the APA ethical standards. For example, we are guided by APA Ethical Standard 4.07: Use of Confidential Information for Didactic or Other Purposes (APA, 2017), that psychologists do not disclose information about clients or other situations unless they intentionally deidentify or disguise the person or situation. Here and elsewhere, we use fictional examples of cases and situations that are not based on any real people. We also want to point out that at the time we were writing this book, the APA Ethics Code was in the process of being revised by the APA Ethics Code Task Force. It is possible that as you are reading this, a new code has been released or will be released soon. You can find the most recent developments by searching for a key phrase like "APA Ethics Code revisions" in your favorite search engine.

Setting the Tone: An Ethical Dilemma

We talked about how ethics are constructed, but how are they used? To set the tone for the rest of the chapter, and to give you a sense of what we mean by ethical dilemmas, put yourself in the following scenario. You are a counseling psychologist who works at a university counseling center. You are on a well-earned camping trip with a friend in a national park. You are so happy to have time off from work and to relax, hike, eat some marshmallows, and see some wildlife. It is the busy season, so you are grateful you landed a camping spot at this park. You just arrived, scoped out your site, and are setting up your tent. You look over, and at the next campsite, you see that one of the people sitting next to the fire is a client who you saw for a few months. What? All the way out in Yellowstone Park? Yep, it happens, and now your relaxing vacation becomes an opportunity to reflect on ethics.

There might be a few ethical issues here, with the biggest one related to confidentiality. Seeing clients in public can draw attention to your relationship, which you can't really explain to other people. It might invite scrutiny from people around you. Another issue might be your own professional boundaries and being able to "be yourself" while possibly being observed by a client. You will need to be prepared to answer questions like:

- What if your client decides to approach you?
- How do you handle this situation?
- What do you do? Do you stop setting up your tent? Request a different campsite?
- Do you restrict your cold beverage intake?
- How do you explain to your friend why you might be acting weird?
- Do you pretend you do not know who the client is, or say hello? Or wait to see what they do and then respond?
- What might the risks be to the client's privacy?

This is an example of an ethical dilemma that counseling psychologists might encounter and all of these questions point back to central questions about ethics such as: What tools would you use to guide your ethical behavior as a counseling psychologist? What ethical standards might come into play?

We have experienced running into clients in a number of public places. Some see us and turn away immediately, trying to avoid or act like they did not see us. Others approach us and give us a long, 15–20-minute update on everything that has happened in their lives since the last time we saw them. In fact, someone once asked us if we prefer our clients to run away or if we look forward to engaging with our past clients. As with many ethical dilemmas, the answer is "it depends," but our answer is always driven by a concern for our clients, which is an ethical way to think about things. If the occurrence is in a public place, there is the risk of other people overhearing the conversation and confidentiality being broken. Hopefully, you, as the counseling psychologist, had initiated a conversation early in the relationship about what might happen if you ran into each other outside of therapy. However, if this conversation did not occur, and if you acted like you did not recognize the client, the client's feelings could be hurt. On the other hand, if you say hi, it might put the client in an awkward position of having to explain to their friends how you know each other. Remember how we said ethics can be gray and complicated?

Who Has to Behave Ethically?

If ethics are complicated and, in some cases, a downright challenge, there must be a reason for them. There must be a reason why ethics are such a key component of the work that counseling psychologists do. To answer this conundrum, you can look to other professions. Can you think of other professions that must also adhere to confidentiality and similar standards? Some that might come to mind are doctors, attorneys, and accountants. What do these professions have in common? These are fields in which professionals are trusted with extremely private information and the care of people who may be vulnerable. Other fields have also recently begun to develop ethical codes, such as teachers and engineers. Ethical standards are needed when working with vulnerable people and their private information to protect them and the public, to promote trust between the client and the professional, and to ensure trust in the profession by the public. As we move on to discuss the APA Ethics Code, think about how and why counseling psychologists must behave ethically. We are going to use three related terms: code(s), principles, and standards. *Code(s)* refers to the APA Ethics Code (2017) in its entirety. It is split into two parts: *principles* at the beginning, which are followed by numbered *standards*. We explain more in the next section.

APA Ethics Code: Principles

Essentially, there are two main kinds of ethical behavior: aspirational and mandatory (APA, 2017; Corey et al., 2022). *Aspirational* ethics, sometimes referred to as virtue ethics, are what we as counseling psychologists aspire to in our behaviors. Here, we are considering: This is how I want to behave; this is how I want to serve the profession and the public. These are my aspirational behaviors. Aspirational ethics or principles are not actually enforceable, largely because they may be difficult to interpret or measure. The APA Ethics Code (2017) starts with five General Principles that are aspirational in nature and underlie the mandatory Standards that follow (see our next section, below). The Code says that the intent of the Principles "is to guide and inspire psychologists toward the very highest ethical ideals of the profession" but also states they "do not represent obligations" (p. 3). As we mentioned earlier, these Principles are largely based on Western Judeo-Christian moral philosophy and principles (Parham, 2009; Pettifor, 2001). They are:

- Beneficence and Nonmaleficence
- Fidelity and Responsibility
- Integrity

- Justice
- Respect for People's Rights and Dignity

Here and throughout this section as we discuss the APA Code, we recommend you also refer to the Code itself, which is easily found on the APA website or through your favorite search engine. You could even print it out and have it next to you as you work through this chapter.

Beneficence and Nonmaleficence essentially boil down to *do good* AND *do no harm.* These go hand in hand. It is not enough to just do good without doing no harm, and it is not enough to do no harm without also doing good. Still, the two concepts do not always mean the same thing. For example, in some situations, not doing anything at all might be doing no harm, but it also might not be doing good. For example, if a client states that they are feeling worthless and hopeless, listening and being empathic probably does not do any harm. However, it might do more good if the counseling psychologist were to probe these feelings by assessing if the client is considering suicide and then working to ensure the client's safety.

Fidelity and Responsibility refer to a counseling psychologist's responsibility to society, to protect others, and to keep an eye on the behavior of our colleagues, supervisees, and clients. You may have a responsibility, for example, to have a conversation with a colleague if you are worried that they are impaired because of a severe depressive episode after recent loss and grief. You may remember that we consider a client's safety when we see them in public. That is an example of being guided by a responsibility to our clients.

Integrity refers to honesty, truthfulness, and accuracy. For example, psychologists should represent themselves and their competencies accurately. They should be honest and truthful in their informed consent document about fees and limits to confidentiality.

Justice means that psychologists treat people fairly, and people have equal access to services. For example, a psychologist should not discriminate against a client who depends on Medicaid and show preference to a client with higher paying insurance coverage. We talk about related concepts like social justice as an essential activity for counseling psychologists in Chapter 13 and throughout this book.

Respect for People's Rights and Dignity is extremely critical. This principle refers to the human right to autonomy and self-determination, including the client's right to privacy and the right to make their own decisions about their lives. This principle underlies the need for confidentiality because people have the right to privacy and to decide what they want to share with a psychologist and what they do not. They have the right to live their lives the way they want to, even if you do not agree with it. This principle also includes respecting individual and cultural differences. This principle can often be difficult to implement in practice. For example, if a client shares that they are currently doing something illegal, unless it meets the criteria for a limit to confidentiality, the client has the right to engage in that behavior, as damaging as it may be to their own life, and the psychologist may not report it. Let's say a client tells you they had been stealing $50 from the cashier till at their job once a week. Another coworker was blamed for it and lost their job. It is the counseling psychologist's role to discuss the risks and help the client process the behavior – not for the counseling psychologist to report this to the police, the workplace, judge the client, or tell them they should stop the behavior. Even if you have these feelings and process them internally (or with a trusted supervisor or colleague), externally it is important to respect the client's autonomy.

APA Ethics Code: Standards

Now, let's move on to talking about the *Standards* of the APA Ethics Code, which are organized into ten sections. Unlike the Principles, these are considered mandatory or obligations. In other words, psychologists are expected to adhere to these and if they do not, there could be serious ramifications. The most important negative outcomes include not only harm to the client but also harm to the public. These problems could also result in the psychologist being disciplined by their licensing board and possibly losing their license. As we discuss the Standards, again it is helpful for you to have the Code easily accessible as a reference. What we share below is not an exhaustive list or a description of the Standards, because the Standards are already clearly outlined in the Code. We highlight several key considerations for counseling psychologists below.

Resolving Ethical Issues

This section offers psychologists guidance on how to resolve conflicts between ethics and law or organizational policies. It provides steps for psychologists to resolve issues with colleagues, such as discussing the issue with that colleague informally, and then making a more formal kind of action if needed. For illustration purposes, we are going to use Grace, a counseling psychologist working in private practice. Her colleague Frances, who works in the same office space, tells her that they are really far behind on writing up case notes. In fact, Frances says they don't think they have updated notes in at least a couple of months. In counseling psychology, staying on top of writing notes is important for a lot of reasons. States usually mandate how soon notes need to be written. If therapists wait too long, they won't remember what occurred or was discussed in the session. It is also important to have current notes in case some kind of crisis arises.

For example, if Frances had a client who came in on a crisis walk-in call, another counselor would not be able to access notes to know whether or not Frances had made any kind of plan for that client. Or if Frances became ill and could no longer see her clients, there would be no notes for continuity of care. Grace knows Frances has been struggling with a lot of personal issues lately. The first thing Grace would need to do in this situation is express concern and point out that this is an ethical and legal problem. If Grace learns that this continues to be an issue, however, she might consider reporting it to the state licensing board. See also the Record Keeping and Fees Standard (below).

Competence

This section states that psychologists work within the bounds of their training and competence. It offers guidance for what to do if, for example, a psychologist is asked to provide services in an area in which they might not have training and expertise. It discusses delegating work to other people, such as employees or assistants, and what to do if psychologists become aware that they might be impaired in some way, such as personal problems getting in the way of providing competent treatment. Sometimes it seems quite clear: psychologists do not practice beyond their competence. So, for example, let's consider Grace again. if Grace does not have expertise, experience, or training in working with disordered eating, she would generally not take on clients who present with a diagnosis of an eating disorder. Sometimes, though, the circumstances can make things a little muddier: What if Grace has been working with a client for a year and they have a strong relationship built, and then the client reports that they have been so stressed out that they have been engaging in some disordered eating behaviors like they used to in the past? What are some options for Grace? Or, would you think the situation is different if Grace and the client live in a fairly rural, isolated area where the closest eating disorder treatment center is at least a three-hour drive?

Human Relations

This section states that psychologists do not discriminate, engage in sexual or other harassment, hold multiple relationships, exploit relationships, or do work that would be a conflict of interest. It states that they do their best to avoid harm to their clients. They obtain consent for the work they do with clients, cooperate with other professionals, and make plans for interruption of services (such as a move or the client losing insurance coverage). *Multiple relationships* refer to situations in which a psychologist might be in a professional role as well as another role with a client. An example of this might occur when Grace has a client who is an elementary school teacher. Grace just learned that her daughter will be in her client's second-grade class next year. How might Grace handle this situation? Again, would it be different if Grace lived in a large city? If this was a large elementary school? Or if she lived in a rural area and there was only one second-grade class for the whole area?

Privacy and Confidentiality

This section, one of the most important for counseling psychologists, says that psychologists protect the confidential information of their clients. It requires counseling psychologists to discuss limits to confidentiality (times when confidential information will not be maintained) with their clients. Psychologists minimize intrusions on privacy. Limits to confidentiality generally include (a) if the counseling psychologist believes the client is in danger of suicide; (b) if the counseling psychologist believes the client may harm someone else; (c) if the counseling psychologist learns of abuse or neglect of a child or vulnerable adult; (d) insurance records; and (e) if records are subpoenaed or court ordered. States may have different, unique limits to confidentiality, as we discussed earlier.

Maintaining confidentiality may sometimes be tricky and may depend on a lot of factors like age. For example, Grace has a client who reports some self-harm (cutting) behavior. Does self-harm meet the criteria for breaking confidentiality? What if the client states that sometimes he thinks about cutting deeper and "ending it all?" In another situation, Grace's client is a young adult, 22 years of age. He is still covered by his father's health insurance. The client's father calls to give Grace new insurance information and to pay a balance for the client. Can Grace speak to the client's father? In what circumstances might this be okay or not okay?

Advertising and Other Public Representations

This section states that psychologists do not make deceptive statements or mislead about their credentials. They do not solicit testimonials. Before Grace was licensed as a health service psychologist in her state, but after she completed her doctoral program, she worked at an agency that listed her title on their website as "staff psychologist." Grace informed them that they would need to change this because she was not a licensed psychologist yet. Grace also felt uncomfortable about a practice that the agency did, which was to email any clients regularly asking them to give the agency a five-star review. While this was not quite a testimonial, Grace wondered if it was okay. Take a look at this section of the APA Ethics Code (5.0) and see what you think.

Record Keeping and Fees

This section provides guidance for how psychologists create, maintain, and dispose of records, how they discuss fees and payment with clients, and how fees are accepted. Psychologists take steps to maintain confidentiality of records and make plans in case there will need to be a transfer of records. They inform clients early about fees and payments and come to agreement about this. This section also talks about bartering or exchanging psychological services for goods or services. Let's say Grace has been seeing a client for a while and their financial situation recently changed. They tell Grace, "I am not able to make payment this week, but I wonder if you might be interested in a couple chickens for your farm." This section (6.05) states that bartering may only occur if "(1) it is not clinically contraindicated, and (2) the resulting arrangement is not exploitative" (p. 9). Would accepting chickens be clinically problematic or exploitative? What if, instead, the client says, "I am not able to make payment this week, but I will come and do yardwork at your house, and my wife will clean your house for you." Would this be different? How or why?

Education and Training

This section requires psychologists to ensure high-quality education and training programs that descriptions are accurate and that teaching and curriculum are accurate. It states that psychologists and psychology training programs do not require students to disclose personal information about things like sexual history, trauma history, past therapy, and so on. It offers guidance about how to handle when therapy is a course or program requirement. For example, Grace is an adjunct professor at a local college that offers a group therapy course. As part of the course, the training program requires students to participate in an interpersonal therapy group that Grace is supposed to run after each class meeting, one evening a week. According to this standard, when this is a requirement, "psychologists responsible for that program allow students the option of selecting such therapy from practitioners unaffiliated with the program" (p. 10). When Grace pointed this out to the department chair of the program, he said it would be fine because Grace was not technically affiliated with the program; she was hired as an adjunct (meaning she would not teach the students in any other classes). What do you think about this? Why does the APA have this as a standard and is this department meeting this standard? Why or why not?

Research and Publication

This section offers standards for counseling psychologists who actively engage in research. It says that research may not be conducted unless they have sought approval through their institution. Psychologists should obtain informed consent for research with some exceptions. It talks about incentives for research, whether or not participants in research may be deceived, the use of animals, and reporting and publishing research. It is important to note that, historically, psychologists have not always conducted research in ethical and humane ways, and many of the factors in this section are intended to prevent harm to research participants. Often, academic and other settings will have rigorous human subjects review processes that are intended to protect participants and ensure high-quality research. When Grace was a doctoral student, she planned to survey undergraduate students. Her advisor taught a large undergraduate counseling psychology course and said he would be willing to announce the study in class and offer extra credit to students who participated. Grace was not so sure if this was a good idea. She worried that students would feel pressured to participate and would not be able to say no – perhaps they might think their grade would be affected if they did not participate. What do you think? When can extra credit be offered for participation as an incentive? When might this be okay or not okay? See Standard 8.04 for help.

Assessment

This section gives guidance about the use of psychological assessments. It states that psychologists use high-quality instruments (tests or measures) in appropriate ways. It tells psychologists how to offer informed consent, release test data, and interpret results. It says that counseling psychologists do not use tests that are out of date or that are not appropriate to the client population. It also talks about the qualifications of people who administer and interpret tests. When Grace was a doctoral student, she learned to administer tests to youth to determine whether someone might have a learning disability. One time, she had a young client who spoke only Spanish. Grace is bilingual and was happy to use her Spanish skills, but her agency gave her a Spanish-language achievement test that was over 30 years old! When she said that the test might not be the best to use, the agency said that it was the only Spanish-language test they could find and that was available. They said the newer test was extremely expensive and they did not want to charge the client the much higher fee, which would have been hundreds of dollars. What should Grace have done? If she insisted on the newer test, her client would have had a much bigger financial burden (and might not have been able to complete the testing at all). On the other hand, if she used the old test, her results might not have been accurate. What are the ethical principles involved and how could she decide how to move forward?

Therapy

This section about therapy states that psychologists provide information to their clients about the therapy process and receive informed consent from the clients. It offers guidance about working with families and couples. Much of this standard surrounds the notion of dual or multiple relationships, which is when a psychologist might have more than one role with a client (such as – therapist but also the client's child's little league coach; therapist for a couple but also individual therapist for one member of the couple). It recommends that psychologists avoid such conflicting multiple relationships. It clearly states that psychologists do not engage in sexual activities with clients or people close to their clients and do not terminate treatment to engage in sexual activities with these people. It offers guidance for transfer of services or termination of services. Grace has a case load of about 20 clients per week. She just learned that her father has a terminal illness and she needs to go to South Korea to help her mother for a few months. How can she best approach this lapse, or interruption, of services for a few months? Should she try to wrap up with most of her clients? Try to refer them to other counseling psychologists? Could she see them long distance from South Korea via telehealth (this might depend on laws in South Korea as well as laws in her own state)?

APA Practice Guidelines

The APA also publishes Professional Practice Guidelines that are not mandatory or enforceable unless adopted or used for enforcement by a state legislature (see more on licensing boards, below). These Practice Guidelines describe best practices for special populations (e.g., older people, military service members) or issues (e.g., custody hearings). Related to the previous example, APA published Guidelines for the Practice of Telepsychology (APA, 2024). There are also Guidelines related to work with military service members, older adults, men and boys, women and girls, guidelines for forensic psychology, and so on. You might be interested in checking some of these out on the APA website.

The Role of Laws and Policies

We also want to point out that counseling psychologists are governed by a variety of state and federal laws. Some examples you have probably heard of are HIPAA and FERPA.

- The Health Insurance Portability and Accountability Act (HIPAA; US Department of Health and Human Services, n.d.) (Side note, this is spelled HIPAA, not HIPPA, which reminds us of a HIPPO) is a regulation that governs protected health information. Basically, it is a federal law that says health providers (including psychologists) cannot share health information with people who do not have the right to see it. So, a counseling psychologist cannot share a client's diagnosis with their employer, spouse, or anyone else unless the client has given explicit permission to share.
- FERPA, on the other hand, refers to the Family Educational Rights and Privacy Act (US Department of Education, n.d.). FERPA gives parents (and caregivers/guardians) the right to students' educational information if they are under 18. Once a student turns 18, however, it protects the student from others accessing their educational records.
- In addition to federal mandates, some states have specific laws that are unique to licensure in that state (see state-specific policies by visiting state licensing boards and websites). For example, under the federal law FERPA, a counseling psychologist who works at a community college could not share information about their clients with the clients' parents or other family members. In at least one state, if a therapist learns that another therapist sexually exploited a client, they must report that to law enforcement (something not covered in FERPA but required by state law).
- Some clinics and organizations have site-specific policies as well. Counseling psychologists and students in training should pay close attention to the handbook or policy manual at any site at which they work.

Ethical Decision-Making

Often, there are some disagreements between Ethical Codes, laws/statutes, and policies. For example, you may live in a state that has a rule that you believe would actually do harm to your client. Or if you follow one of the standards of the APA ethical code, it might be in conflict with another standard. Some aspects of the APA ethical code are vague and it can be difficult to determine a course of action. When these conflicts arise, you find yourself in a bit of a pickle. We refer to this as an ethical dilemma. So, how do you decide to move forward?

The Code states that when there are conflicts between the Code and the law, psychologists "make known their commitment to this Ethics Code and take steps to resolve the conflict in a responsible manner in keeping with basic principles of human rights" (p. 3). Luckily, a lot of psychologists have been thinking about this for a long time. Something that counseling psychologists may turn to for assistance in making a decision about an ethical dilemma is an *ethical decision-making model*. There are a lot of great models that have been posed over time. Generally speaking, they offer some steps for counseling psychologists to follow to make sure they are systematically and thoroughly considering all aspects of the problem.

Johnson et al. (2022) recently reviewed a bunch of these models and found some commonalities. Typically, the models include some or most of these components:

1) Review, which involves gathering information, defining the problem, and identifying standards, laws, and literature.
2) Intrapersonal, which is when the psychologist takes into consideration their own values and competence and engages in self-reflection.

3) Interpersonal, which is when the psychologist consults with others or seeks supervision from another psychologist. In some models, this also includes candid conversations with the client about the situation.
4) Deliberation, which refers to identifying the problem, considering courses of action, and identifying what the best outcome would be.
5) Prediction, in which the psychologist considers the consequences and feasibility of potential solutions.
6) Perspective taking, where the psychologist thinks about the cultural context, cultural values, and different perspectives.
7) Action, which is when the psychologist decides what they want to do, moves forward with those steps, informs others, and implements the plan.
8) Self-Monitoring, which refers to the psychologist reviewing and reflecting on the process and the outcome, documenting the steps they took, and possibly reengaging with the process if needed.

So, for example, thinking about the situation we described earlier related to seeing a client on a camping trip, the counseling psychologist would first try to name the problem. What exactly is the issue here? They would consider the moral principles as well as the specific standards in the APA Ethics Code (2017). They would self-reflect on how this is affecting them and which of their own personal values might come into play. They would reach out to consult a trusted peer or supervisor to see what they think. They would perhaps consider options and what the risks and benefits of each action might be. They would take into account any cultural context of the client or the situation. Then, ultimately, they would decide what to do and do it. This process might all occur in the counseling psychologist's head really quickly, with some steps omitted (such as consultation). Or, it could occur over a period of hours, days, or weeks. Finally, they would reflect on the whole process, being sure to document all the steps including the consultation they did. Once, talking about this in a class, a student asked Julie: What if you go through all these steps, do the best you can, and you still get in trouble for it? And, in fact, that can happen. Ultimately, counseling psychologists make the best decisions they can, but the theme of this chapter is "shades of gray." There is never a 100% right solution, and there is always some give and take.

Accountability: The Role of Licensing Boards

So how are counseling psychologists accountable for behaving ethically and legally? Usually, the state in which a psychologist is licensed is responsible for that. They handle requirements to become licensed, to maintain licensure, and complaints when they occur. Each state has its own licensing board. For example, in Texas, it is the Texas State Board of Examiners of Psychologists; in Washington, it is the Examining Board of Psychology. These boards generally communicate with each other and are members of the Association of State and Provincial Psychology Boards (this includes the United States and Canada).

There are a lot of laws that govern licensure as a psychologist; in the State of Iowa, you actually have to apply for a psychology license, but you then also have to apply for a Health Service Provider certification if you want to practice. In the past, it was difficult or impossible for someone licensed in one state to see a client in a different location (even via telehealth) unless they were licensed in the second state. Recently, an agreement called "PSYPACT," which allows psychologists to apply and obtain authority to practice across jurisdictions. This agreement can increase access to mental health services, benefits people such as college students who might move across states, and allows people in isolated or rural areas more options for mental health providers (PSYPACT, 2024).

Summary

At the beginning of this chapter, we asked you to reflect on what came to mind when you heard the term ethics. Now, after reading this chapter, has anything changed in your understanding of ethics for counseling psychologists? We offered definitions of ethics and discussed how these are related to cultural norms and understandings. We reviewed the APA Ethics Code and the role that federal and state laws can play. We offered ethical dilemmas to consider throughout the chapter and provided steps toward ethical decision-making. We hope you have a strong understanding now of the complexity and importance of ethical principles. In the next chapter, we move on to another topic: the role of the self and the person in counseling psychology.

What Would You Do?

You are a counseling psychologist at a local community agency. You have been seeing a client for a while to discuss their father's recent death. One day, they share that they live in the upstairs of a home owned by their landlord. They tell you that something adding to their stress is that they can hear yelling and what seems to be other loud noises coming from downstairs. They sometimes babysit for the landlord's children. Recently, they were playing outside and the scarf one of the children was wearing blew off and the client noticed bruising around the child's throat. They are worried that the child might be abused by the parent but also are not totally sure and cannot take the chance of losing their deposit or apartment right now – they would not have anywhere else to live. The client does not want to share any other information with you. What would you do in this situation? Use the components of the decision-making model to:

- Review and define the problem
- Engage in self-reflection
- Consult with someone else
- Consider different options
- Predict possible risks and benefits to courses of action
- Consider different perspectives
- Decide on a course of action
- In this situation, you will not be able to see actual outcomes but go ahead and reflect on what this decision-making process was like for you

Counseling Psychologist Spotlight: University Counseling Center

Dr. Ted Pickett Jr.

Dr. Ted Pickett Jr. is the Associate Director of the University of Maryland Counseling Center. Some of his responsibilities include collecting and reviewing data about the clinical services the counseling center provides, developing policies and procedures for the counseling center, providing clinical consultation services to other clinicians and assistant directors, and of course attending meetings. He loves mentoring staff and creating a space for them to grow at the counseling center. He says he loves that he "gets to laugh with folks every day." He also enjoys the process of

Dr. Ted Pickett Jr. Photograph by author.

problem-solving when the center is developing or maintaining different kinds of systems. One of the more difficult aspects of his job is the personnel management piece.

Ted loves being a counseling psychologist because of its emphasis on multiculturalism and the holistic, strength-based approach to the work. His professional interests include training and supervision; multicultural issues in supervision and training; men and masculinity; and working with Students of Color. He enjoys using different theoretical approaches with clients, including multicultural counseling, psychodynamic theory, and cognitive-behavioral therapy.

In his time outside of work, Ted has a long-time hobby of bonsai. He has trees of his own and volunteers at the National Bonsai and Penjing Museum in Washington, D.C. He says he also enjoys collecting and learning about fountain pens and watches. Ted earned his PhD in counseling psychology from the University of Iowa. His bachelor's degree is in psychology from Wittenberg University. He is a licensed psychologist and is involved in the Association for the Coordination of Counseling Center Clinical Services.

References

American Psychological Association. (2017). *Ethical principles of psychologists and code of conduct*. https://www.apa.org/ethics/code

American Psychological Association. (2024). *Guidelines for the practice of telepsychology*. https://www.apa.org/practice/guidelines/telepsychology-revision.pdf

Association of Black Psychologists. (2019). *Ethical standards of Black psychologists*. https://www.abpsi.org/pdf/EthicalStandardsofBlackPsychologists2019.pdf

Chaddha, R., & Agrawal, G. (2023). Ethics and morality. *Indian Journal of Orthopaedics, 57*(11), 1707–1713. https://doi.org/10.1007/s43465-023-01004-3

Corey, G., Corey, M. S., Corey, C., & Callanan, P. (2022). *Issues and ethics in the helping professions* (11th ed.). Cengage.

Garcia, M. A., & Tehee, M. A. (2014). *Society of Indian Psychologists commentary on the American Psychological Association's ethical principles and code of conduct*. Society of Indian Psychologists.

Johnson, M. K., Weeks, S. N., Gimpel Peacock, G., & Domenech Rodriguez, M. M. (2022). Ethical decision-making models: A taxonomy of models and review of issues. *Ethics & Behavior, 32*(3), 195–210. https://doi.org/10.1080/10508422.2021.1913593

Merriam-Webster (2025a). *Ethics*. https://www.merriam-webster.com/dictionary/ethic

Merriam-Webster (2025b). *Morals*. https://www.merriam-webster.com/dictionary/moral

National Latina/o Psychological Association. (2018). *NLPA ethical guidelines*. National Latina/o Psychological Association. https://www.nlpa.ws/assets/docs/ethical%20guidelines%20nlpa_adopted%20jan%201st.pdf

Parham, T. A. (2009). Ethics and multiculturalism: Synthesizing apparent opposites into responsive treatment. *Professional Psychology: Research and Practice, 40*(4), 432–434.

Pettifor, J. L. (2001). Are professional codes of ethics relevant for multicultural counselling? *Canadian Journal of Counselling, 35*(1), 26–35.

PSYPACT. (2024). *Advancing the Interjurisdictional practice of psychology*. https://psypact.gov/resource/resmgr/legislative_resources/what_is_psypact_11.2024.pdf

Tassell, N. A., Herbert, A. M. L., Evans, I. M., & Young, P. T. A. (2012). 13 principles of Indigenous ethics and psychological interventions. In M. M. Leach, M. J. Stevens, G. Lindsay, A. Ferrero & Y. Korkut (Eds.), *The Oxford handbook of international psychological ethics* (pp. 176–190). Oxford University Press. https://doi.org/10.1093/oxfordhb/9780199739165.001.0001

U.S. Department of Education. (n.d.). *34 CFR Part 99 – Family educational rights and privacy*. https://studentprivacy.ed.gov/ferpa

U.S. Department of Health and Human Services. (n.d.). *Health information privacy*. https://www.hhs.gov/hipaa/index.html

Velasquez, M., Andre, C., Shanks, T., & Meyer, M. J. (1992, August 1). *Ethical relativism*. Markkula Center for Applied Ethics, Santa Clara University.

Chapter 12

The Person as a Therapist

Use of the Self in Counseling Psychology

The Difficulty of the Work We Do

In our Introduction to Counseling Psychology undergraduate courses, we often invite guest speakers who are counseling psychologists in a range of settings to speak to our students. Often, students will ask the speakers about their career journey, and how they trained for the hard work. One of the most common questions that our students ask is "How do you manage to not take work home?" Or, "How do you manage not to be affected by the work that you do all day and the stories you hear?" This is clearly a concern that people considering a career in the helping fields, and specifically counseling psychology, have about their own future quality of life. It is true that the work that counseling psychologists do is hard. Counseling psychologists and other helping professionals hear stories of people's struggles, may intervene in crisis situations, or may sit with clients as they share past trauma experiences. They may feel particularly moved by their clients' stories but also by their clients' willingness to be vulnerable and put their trust in the psychologist. So, how can a counseling psychologist sit with people in their pain and struggle and maintain their own mental health? What do you think this would be like for you?

In this chapter, you will learn how, in the field of counseling psychology, the qualities and experiences of the person doing the work (the counseling psychologist) matter and play a large role in the work itself. Counseling psychologists must engage in self-reflection and self-understanding of their values, their motivations, and their own strengths and weaknesses not only as therapists, but also as human beings. Unlike many other fields, the highly intense and emotional work that many counseling psychologists do can lead to burnout. Burnout prevention and self-care are crucial to a counseling psychologist's well-being. We will describe some of the issues that can lead to burnout and how counseling psychologists can offer empathy and care while maintaining their well-being. We discuss models of therapist development as well as ways counseling psychologists can engage in self-care.

Self-care is a skill that students learn in their training programs and that develops gradually. So first, we think it is important to examine the ways in which counseling psychologists change and grow over time through their training programs and across their career trajectories. As you read this, consider how these models of development fit you. Can you relate to any of the experiences we describe below?

Therapist Development

There is research that shows trends in how therapists develop and grow from beginning students to senior professionals or expert/advanced practitioners (Rønnestad & Skovholt, 2003;

DOI: 10.4324/9781003439899-12

Skovholt & Jennings, 2016). Some researchers have categorized this growth process into stages of therapist development. Here is a list of the stages identified by Rønnestad and Skovholt (2003) that we unpack in this section:

- Lay helper
- Beginning student
- Advanced student
- Novice professional
- Experienced professional
- Senior professional

These categories offer a broad overview of therapist development, but researchers also focus on development at different stages or groups of stages as well (e.g., Chambers-Baltz et al., 2021).

The *Lay Helper* phase is the first stage that happens even before someone becomes a therapist and captures the sorts of non-professional help a person gives to those around them (Rønnestad & Skovholt, 2003). Lay Helpers may be sought out for advice or may try to fix others' problems quickly based on their own experiences (Rønnestad & Skovholt, 2003; Trotter-Mathison et al., 2010). Skovholt and Jennings (2016) described experiences that advanced therapists had in their early personal life. They asked these advanced therapists whether there were experiences or developmental elements in their foundational years that might have been related to their professional development. They found that, often in early years, advanced therapists:

- Were attuned to understanding human relationships or particularly good at understanding the thoughts, feelings, needs, and experiences of other people and at connecting with them.
- Often described some kind of stress or distress – but not necessarily trauma – in their early lives, and they tended to want to process or respond to these experiences rather than avoid them.
- Talked about taking on the role of the helper early in their lives, whether this role was assigned or taken on voluntarily.
- Understood in their foundational developmental years that suffering was an inherent, and perhaps even helpful and positive, part of the human experience.

If you are currently an undergraduate student considering a career in a helping profession, you may find yourself in this phase. You may have been thinking, "Me too!" as you read over the bullet points above. We often hear students say things like "I am the one everyone goes to for help" or "I am a good listener." You may enjoy giving advice or helping friends or siblings problem-solve, and you may have already participated in some kinds of helping activities, such as a peer counselor or crisis hotline volunteer. Of course, these experiences are not required and there are lots of pathways into counseling psychology, so please do not get discouraged if you are unable to place a check mark next to each experience listed above. There is still space for you in counseling psychology.

The *Beginning Student* stage usually starts when students embark on their journeys to becoming therapists by starting a graduate training program. The Beginning Student phase is usually characterized by high anxiety – lots of worries and fears (Rønnestad & Skovholt, 2003; Trotter-Mathison et al., 2010). Students may worry they will do something wrong and harm a client, or they may worry about their counseling skills being appraised and judged. In this stage, students prefer clear instructions and clear feedback and need positive reinforcement and encouragement from their instructors and supervisors. Students often realize that the theories and concepts they have read about in textbooks may not suffice, or they may not know how to apply them in real-world, ambiguous situations.

In "Voices from the Field" (Trotter-Mathison et al., 2010), a counseling psychologist later in his career, Guy Manaster, recalled when he was a Beginning Student and was struggling with a client. When he discussed it with his supervisor, the supervisor was able to see clear and straight to the problem. Guy told his wife about his struggles and being frustrated that his supervisor figured it out right away. His wife reminded him that he had been doing therapy for four months, and his supervisor had been doing it for 50 years. She told him, "Maybe you'll get better" (Manaster, 2010). This is the exact kind of message that beginning therapists need to hear. One skill that students need to tackle as they grow is *comfort with ambiguity*. What we mean by that is the not-knowing, the lack of certainty, about what to do in certain situations, and whether or not any change is happening as a result of the therapy. Therapists may see clear growth and improvement in their clients, but often it is not clearly evident, so there is ambiguity about whether or not the therapy is doing any good. The student may wonder if they are totally awful as a therapist or if they are even helping at all.

Students enter the *Advanced Student* phase as they become more comfortable with ambiguity, more confident that their skills are improving, and gain more experience with a wide range of clients. In this phase, they may require less feedback from supervisors and prepare to begin independent work. Typically, Advanced Students have a couple of years of experience under their belts, are wrapping up coursework, may be completing requirements for their program like their dissertation, and may be completing a predoctoral internship. This can cycle, however. For example, a student may feel comfortable working with adults but then shift back to a beginner viewpoint if they start working with children. Or a student may feel confident providing individual therapy and then feel more of a beginner at facilitating group therapy. This can actually be highly beneficial as the student learns and recognizes what their strengths and growth areas are.

Therapists enter the *Novice Professional* phase as they complete their graduate degree and begin to work independently (Rønnestad & Skovholt, 2003; Trotter-Mathison et al., 2010). Novice Professionals may experience imposter syndrome, or the sense that they do not deserve to do the work or that their skills are not legitimate. They may have mixed feelings about not having the community support they previously had as a student, depending on their work setting. As Trotter-Mathison et al. (2010) said, "The novice professional is plagued by two different sentiments. The good news: Hooray! One has graduated and can begin to practice independently. The bad news: Oh no! One has graduated and has to begin to practice independently" (p. 195). Novice Professionals begin to form their identities as clinicians and adjust to finding their own path and trusting their own professional judgment. In this phase, professionals learn the most from actual practice and from their clients.

Therapists enter the *Experienced Professional* phase as they gain confidence over time (kind of like moving from beginning to advanced student stages) and establish their own unique counseling style. They may begin to teach others or provide training through clinical supervision. They become even more comfortable with uncertainties in therapy and come to terms with the fact that there often are no perfect answers to dilemmas or issues faced by clients. They learn to value a stance of not knowing and become grounded enough to practice authentically in a way that fits with their own values, personalities, and interests.

Eventually, therapists will move into the *Senior Professional* phase that is usually occupied by people who have gained a wealth of experience (perhaps 20 years or more) working with clients (Rønnestad & Skovholt, 2003; Trotter-Mathison et al., 2010). They may find teaching and mentoring gratifying and may look for new ways to stay engaged, through continuing education, learning new counseling techniques, or specializing in working with a new population. Or they may take on leadership roles, for example on state psychology boards or with the American Psychological Association (APA).

What common themes do you notice between the different stages or phases of student/therapist development? Do you notice a common theme of human connection and lifelong learning? How do the skills and experiences described by therapists reflecting on their work as Lay Helpers create a foundation for later stages? How might your experiences and values set the tone for you to grow as in your future career?

Counseling Psychologist: Know Thyself

Now that we have discussed the ways therapists develop, it is time to go back to the topic of self-care and well-being. Just like therapist excellence is something that develops over time, we believe self-care and well-being maintenance are skills that students will learn and improve upon in their training programs and then develop across their lifespan. Across courses, practicum experiences, in supervision, etc., students will have the opportunity to develop resilience and an ability to compartmentalize their work. Just like there are foundational experiences and values for early therapists, there are also foundational activities that increase a person's ability to maintain wellness and self-care as a counseling psychologist. One of the first steps to maintaining wellness is for the therapist to have a good understanding of themselves, their strengths, their growth areas, and areas that might cause difficulty for them.

Let's reflect on examples that bring this point home. You might imagine a farmer with a tractor and a barn full of tools that she loves. Each implement was expensive, serves a specific purpose, includes memories, and she has taken good care of each one over the years. Every time she uses her tiller, she cleans and stores it with care. Why? Because the equipment she has collected over the years has great value and needs to last. In counseling psychology, the psychologist's "self" is the "tool" of the work (Aponte, 2022). You probably see where we are going with this, but if counseling psychologists use their own experience and being as tools, they need to be cared for and cultivated as well. It is hard to last long in the profession of counseling psychology if you do not care for yourself.

For counseling psychologists, this means there is great importance in self-understanding, reflexive practice, lifelong learning, and maintaining psychological well-being. In fact, self-awareness is considered an ethical aspiration and imperative. The APA Code of Ethics Principle A states: "Psychologists strive to be aware of the possible effect of their own physical and mental health on their ability to help those with whom they work" (APA, 2017, p. 3). What do you think this means? How might a counseling psychologist's physical health influence their work? How could these things affect their ability to provide clinical services? And the word *awareness* can be fuzzy or hard to completely hold people to. How can you be aware of something if you're not already aware of it?

For one thing, stuff like sleeplessness or poor sleep hygiene, chronic illnesses, and other things that impact a person's overall wellness are associated with ethical risk and professional impairment (Barnett et al., 2007; Posluns & Gall, 2020). This is one thing that training programs can really help with. In a graduate training program, students will learn a lot about themselves through feedback from peers, faculty and supervisors, self-reflection, and even from their clients. Let's say, for example, that you are someone who gets really eager and excited to talk and share, but you get feedback in your training program that this actually causes you to interrupt clients when they are talking. You want to be a better counseling psychologist so you start building awareness and working on your own approach to counseling by focusing on things like:

- You try to maintain your awareness and monitor for these behaviors as you enter counseling sessions.
- You remind yourself to be patient, to listen, to focus on the client, and to interrupt or speak only if it is helpful and needed.
- You learn about things that cause you distress that you thought you had worked through previously, and you may increase your awareness of biases you might hold.
- You might even realize that there are some populations that you do not feel comfortable working with.

This kind of self-reflection is crucial to a counseling psychologist's professional development and personal well-being. In fact, there is research indicating that therapists who engage in reflective practice (in other words, intentionally stopping to think about how they could improve or how they can grow) have better client outcomes than those who do not engage in this kind of regular practice (Wampold & Owen, 2021).

Further along in the APA Ethics Code, APA Standard 2.06 Personal Problems and Conflicts states:

a) Psychologists refrain from initiating an activity when they know or should know that there is a substantial likelihood that their personal problems will prevent them from performing their work-related activities in a competent manner.
b) When psychologists become aware of personal problems that may interfere with their performing work-related duties adequately, they take appropriate measures, such as obtaining professional consultation or assistance, and determine whether they should limit, suspend, or terminate their work-related duties. (APA, 2017, p. 5)

Consider this a little more. Does the standard seem clear? What do you think APA means here? What is the significance of "when they know or should know?" What kind of personal problems might prevent someone from working in a competent manner?

Maybe this will help. Reflect on whether you have experienced some personal problems that perhaps affected your ability to perform work, volunteer, or extracurricular activities.

- How did you know there was a problem?
- How did you examine and better understand the problem?
- How do you feel about the way you handled things?
- How might you handle it in the future?

As a counseling psychologist, how would someone know that they are at a point where they need to take "appropriate measures?" For example, let's say a counseling psychologist experienced the loss of a longtime friend. Meanwhile, while providing therapy, they notice that they are feeling less patient with their clients. How would they know if their lack of patience was due to the loss and subsequent grief? Or if it was due to something else, like a recent financial stressor, a boss who is stressing them out, or migraines that have been annoying lately? Where would a counseling psychologist need to draw the line? We do not want helping professionals to be short-tempered and impatient with their clients; on the other hand, do helpers always need to be "100%?" Where is there room for some imperfection or normal shifts in mood? What crosses the line into impairment of competence or even burnout?

Burnout and Other Risk Factors

Imagine that Josephine is a counseling psychologist who works in a community agency serving clients who are survivors of domestic violence, sexual assault, and other forms of violence. When she first began her work a few years ago, she was enthusiastic and energetic about serving her clients. Over time, however, the agency has lost some funding, and her caseload has increased. She is feeling overwhelmed at work and finds herself feeling frustrated with the agency and even a little testy with her clients if they are late or not "working" as hard at therapy as she thinks they should. She has noticed that when she gets home, she does not want to talk to her partner; she just wants to go to her bedroom to decompress, play games on her phone, and be left alone for a couple of hours. She has not been interested in her usual activities.

What might be going on? It is likely that, over time, Josephine has experienced stress and *vicarious trauma*, leading to *burnout*. The World Health Organization (WHO) included burnout in the International Classification of Diseases (2022). The WHO stated that it is a workplace phenomenon, and not a medical condition, defined as:

> A syndrome conceptualized as resulting from chronic workplace stress that has not been successfully managed. It is characterized by three dimensions: feelings of energy depletion or exhaustion; increased mental distance from one's job, or feelings of negativism or cynicism related to one's job; and reduced professional efficacy.
>
> Burn-out refers specifically to phenomena in the occupational context and should not be applied to describe experiences in other areas of life.
>
> (WHO, 2022, n.p.)

O'Connor et al. (2018) found that about 40% of all mental health professionals experience burnout.

Why are mental health professionals more vulnerable to burnout? It is likely because of the giving nature of the work: Skovholt and Trotter-Mathison (2024) suggest that one of the dilemmas or double binds that contributes to burnout is the pull that helping professionals feel between caring for others and caring for themselves. Further, helping professionals have to engage in what they call the cycle of caring over and over again. In other words, helping professionals develop a relationship with a client, maintain that relationship, and then at some point terminate the relationship as a natural part of the counseling process. This cycle can be emotionally exhausting if not managed well. Skovholt and Trotter-Mathison's (2024) book, *The Resilient Practitioner*, focuses on "the great dilemma: How to have an open heart without being trapped in the quicksand of human despair? Not once but over many years of work as a practitioner" (p. 5). Burnout can be damaging to the therapist and impact their competence; harm the safety and well-being of their clients, students, or other people with whom they work; and hurt their organization and the profession of psychology (Duncan & Pond, 2024). Burnout can occur when the burden or stress of a job outweighs its rewards or benefits (Demerouti et al., 2001). There is evidence that early-career psychologists experience more stress and burnout than later-career psychologists do (Page et al., 2024). What do you think accounts for this difference? Have you ever known someone who was experiencing burnout? How did you know? What did this look like? How did it get better?

In addition to burnout, psychologists face other common issues and stressors in their workplace, some of which are related to their clients and some of which are related to the workplace. For example, clients can place emotional demands on the psychologist, especially if there is risk of suicide or suicide attempts or completion (Barnett et al., 2007). Clients with chronic mental health issues that do not seem to improve can also create stress and distress for the counseling psychologist (Barnett et al., 2007). Workplace issues not only include the hassles of dealing with insurance companies and complicated payment systems (Barnett et al., 2007) but could also include high demands on time, difficult coworkers or supervisors, or experiences of systemic oppression. Some counseling psychologists have a greater number of clients in crisis or who have experienced trauma, putting the psychologists at risk for experiencing *vicarious trauma*, sometimes also called *compassion fatigue*, meaning that they experience trauma themselves through the experiences of their clients (Newell & MacNeil, 2010). Other stressors might be concerns about adherence to laws and ethical codes, supervision of trainees, and the experience of isolation in a private practice (Duncan & Pond, 2024).

Counseling psychologists are also human beings who experience the same issues other people do at about the same rates as the general population – depression, grief, anxiety, substance use, suicidal ideation, non-suicidal self-injury, and other issues (Victor et al., 2022). These issues can be compounded if the counseling psychologist has a marginalized identity or identities (Hobaica et al., 2021). For example, they may experience microaggressions and discrimination in their workplace, from clients, colleagues, or supervisors (Kelly & Green, 2010; Porter et al., 2015; Sackett et al., 2023). Often, students do not get training about how to handle these kinds of experiences. For example, Abby is a Latina woman who is a counseling psychologist. Her client makes racist remarks about African American people. Should Abby address this? How? No matter how Abby addresses it, she is bound to be affected by the comments and it will likely affect her ability to relate and work with the client with a strong therapeutic alliance. Whether and how Abby addresses it with the client can depend on a number of factors like what the presenting concern is, what her theoretical orientation is, and how strong the alliance is. In a situation like this, it can also help to consult with a supervisor or peer in a confidential manner to consider ethical implications. If the alliance is strong, Abby can likely share how the comments have affected her in a way that the client is able to hear, and hopefully they can process the experience together.

Protective Factors and Self-Care

With so many potential stressors, how and why do counseling psychologists do the work they do?! It is important to know that helping work can be extremely gratifying and rewarding, and researchers have found that some things can prevent burnout and promote thriving in the workplace. There are workplace factors such as feeling a sense of control, having good support from coworkers or supervisors, or having a sense of accomplishment that can buffer negative factors that might cause burnout (Rupert et al., 2015). Personal factors like self-care activities and cognitive coping strategies can also help (Duncan & Pond, 2024; Posluns & Gall, 2019; Rupert et al., 2015). Furthermore, people who study self-care and burnout may also study *resilience*, or the capacity to recover from difficulties. Our favorite definition of resilience comes from Skovholt and Trotter-Mathison (2024, p. 7): "You can just think of the term resilience in this way: the capacity to bounce back from a negative force – like a fishing bobber, pushed under water, pops back up."

You have probably heard a lot about self-care. So, what is it and why is it helpful? Baker & Gabriel defined self-care as "an ongoing process of caring for yourself; maintaining a conscious effort to do things that maintain, improve and repair your mental, emotional, physical, and spiritual wellness" (2021, p. 436). A lot of experts believe that counseling psychologists – in fact, all helping professionals – must engage in self-care and attention to their own psychological well-being and personal risk factors (Barnett et al., 2007; Duncan & Pond, 2024) and that, as we discussed earlier, it is an ethical obligation (APA, 2017). It is best to engage in proactive, intentional actions to prevent burnout, because once it begins, it can be harder to manage or remediate (Duncan & Pond, 2024). Skovholt and Trotter-Mathison (2024) suggested that helping professionals should work toward sustaining the professional self and the personal self. Professional self-maintenance includes balance between caring for others and the self, social support, receiving care from others, being playful and finding joy, setting boundaries, and increasing intellectual excitement. They also recommend that helping professionals nurture different aspects of themselves: their emotional self, financial self, humorous self, nutritious self, physical self, recreational self, solitary self, and others.

Duncan and Pond (2024) identified nine strategies that can assist psychologists in burnout management and prevention. They encouraged training programs to incorporate education about these methods in their curriculum:

- Time off, including vacation time, paid days off, and breaks throughout the workday.
- Leisure activities that are enjoyable and not work-related, including socializing and hobbies.
- Exercise such as yoga, hiking, or gardening.
- Perspective, or having a particular worldview, mindset, or attitude toward helping work. This includes having hope, optimism, and a positive attitude.
- Support and connections with family, friends, colleagues, and supervisors.
- Boundaries and work-life balance around things such as hours worked, caseload, and time spent outside of work.
- Awareness or mindfulness of one's internal state and the impact of work. This includes reminders about who is responsible for the counseling work and change.
- Spirituality or meditation, including faith and prayer, finding meaning, and being connected to something greater than themselves.
- Professional growth and a love of learning, as well as self-use of clinical approaches.

What do you think about this list? Is there anything else you might add? What stands out to you personally as something that could be really beneficial for yourself? What have you seen other people implement that has been helpful? Are there any things here that you think would be less helpful or not helpful?

Another potential self-care activity is for counseling psychologists to engage in their own personal therapy. There is a lot of discussion in helping professions about therapists seeking therapy. Many have argued that someone cannot be an effective therapist without having undergone their own therapy (Norcross, 2005; Orlinsky et al., 2005; Ziede & Norcross, 2020). For example, Norcross (2005) was a huge proponent of participating in therapy. Norcross argued that personal therapy is "emotionally vital, interpersonally dense, and professionally formative" and that all people training to become healthcare psychologists should participate in their own personal therapy (2005). In fact, when people are training to do psychoanalysis (you may recall we discussed this type of therapy in Chapter 6), they have to engage in years of their own psychoanalysis (American Psychoanalytic Association, 2024). However, Bearse et al. (2013) found that sometimes it is difficult for a psychologist to find a psychologist! This may be especially true in a smaller city or town where the counseling psychologist knows all of the other psychologists nearby. Hopefully, the emergence of telehealth and PsyPACT may help with this (See also Chapters 13 and 15). Psychologists also report that finding time to receive therapy can be a barrier to getting treatment (Bearse et al., 2013). Therapy can also be expensive, and financial constraints may limit someone's ability to receive treatment even though they are therapists themselves. (We realize this makes no sense...but that is why we are so excited that you are interested in a career as a counseling psychologist. There is a major shortage in providers that you could help solve!)

We hope this chapter has been helpful to you in illustrating the path of developing counseling psychologists. We talked about the importance of self-awareness and reflective practice. You learned about challenges that counseling psychologists can experience and ways to prevent burnout and thrive as a practitioner. After considering all of these ideas, what do you think these mean for your own potential future as a helper? What are some of your growth areas or biases you might need to work on? What are some strengths that you might bring to the counseling profession? What are some self-care strategies you can use now to take good care of yourself?

Summary

At the beginning of this chapter, we shared that one of the biggest concerns of people considering a career in counseling psychology is how to not be overly negatively affected by the work and the stories that clients share. Is this a concern that you have? If so, after reading this chapter, do you have some ideas about how to maintain or build your own resilience? We hope that you have a better understanding of how the person or the self of the counseling psychologist is like a tool that has to be well-maintained to function well. We reviewed models of therapist development and the importance of counseling psychologists having a strong sense of self-understanding. We discussed the harms of burnout as well as protective factors and self-care. If you do choose to pursue a graduate degree in the helping professions, the good news is that you will have plenty of peers, mentors, and supervisors who are all going through – or have gone through – the same kinds of things. In the next chapter, we move on to ways that counseling psychologists can flourish as leaders and as advocates for social change to improve mental health.

What Would You Do?

Mark is a doctoral student in his late 40s who is studying counseling psychology. He came to this as a second career after a long time working as a retail manager. He is doing a practicum placement at the university counseling center. He has been working with a client, Shaun, for a few weeks. Shaun is a freshman who sought counseling to discuss a breakup with his long-term girlfriend. Over time, Shaun discloses that he has been going out, partying, and drinking a lot to "move on" from his breakup. Mark's father is a recovering alcoholic. He received therapy in his late teens/early 20s to deal with some of his family history and upbringing, and he is aware that he has strong feelings about people who drink a lot. He realizes that he is starting to have some negative feelings toward his client, Shaun, and dreads going to their sessions. He is not sure whether he should discuss any of this with his supervisor and has thought about going back to therapy but is not sure where he could go. Most of the local counseling agencies where he could go are places where other students in his program are doing practicum placements. Also, he doesn't want to hurt his chances of being able to do a practicum placement at one of those agencies in the future. He is so much older than the other students in his cohort and program that he does not feel comfortable discussing these feelings with them or in his practicum courses. He worries he might get a bad evaluation at his practicum site. He wonders if maybe he should just try to wrap up his work with Shaun or try to refocus on the breakup and refer Shaun somewhere else for substance use counseling.

- What do you think Mark should do?
- If you were his friend and he opened up to you, what advice might you give him?
- How might you handle this if you were his supervisor at the counseling center and he shared what was going on with you?
- Are there any ethical concerns about this situation?

Counseling Psychologist Spotlights: Private Practice

Dr. Sandra Eng and Dr. Michelle Trotter-Mathison

Dr. Sandra Eng and Dr. Michelle Trotter-Mathison both work in private practice in a shared office space in St. Paul, Minnesota. They both attended the Counseling and Student Personnel Psychology PhD program at the University of Minnesota. They were in the same cohort, meaning they entered the program at the same time and developed a lasting friendship. Although their practices are independent of one another, they have cultivated a warm, shared space in which they can easily collaborate and consult with each other between clients, enjoy lunch together, and offer mutual support as needed. They participate in a peer consultation group that meets monthly. They also enjoy running together each week.

Dr. Sandra Eng

Sandra says that she spends most of her time on a daily basis meeting with individual clients for therapy. As part of having a private practice, she also spends time writing notes, billing insurance, and attending to other logistics like scheduling, communication with clients, and continuing education. She says she feels privileged to have the opportunity to accompany and assist clients through difficult periods in their lives. She considers clients' trust and engagement to be a gift that she gets to experience every day. She loves it when she and the client are connected in a state of flow. She says it is moving when she can join clients in ways that foster them feeling seen and met, and it is rewarding to observe clients experience a "click of recognition" – about themselves, their relationships, or their histories. The most challenging part of the job is the work with insurance companies – which has nothing to do with the clients themselves. She says that although the work with insurance companies to get paid is frustrating, she continues to accept insurance because of the accessibility it provides to clients.

Sandra loves being a psychologist because of the opportunity it provides to work one-on-one with individuals in a depth-oriented and relational manner. She especially loves the counseling psychology focus on strengths and development rather than pathology or problems. She utilizes a therapeutic approach called Accelerated Experiential Dynamic Psychotherapy (AEDP), which emphasizes the drive toward growth inherent in all humans. This recognition of individuals' innate potential is congruent with their own philosophy of counseling psychology.

When she is not at work, Sandra enjoys spending time with her kids, partner, and friends, attending local events, exploring the outdoors, and connecting over coffee. She stays active through running, walking, and weightlifting. She also enjoys reading, crocheting, and traveling. She even wrote a book of crochet patterns called Crochet Kaleidoscope (Eng, 2018).

Before she started her doctorate, Sandra earned a master's in counseling from the University of Denver. She has an undergraduate degree in physics from the University of Wisconsin (yes, physics! As we mentioned in Chapter 5, no one's career path is completely linear, and this is a great example). She is a licensed psychologist in Minnesota and is a founding member of AEDP Minnesota, an organization that hosts trainings and events to share about AEDP with the therapy community in Minnesota.

Dr. Sandra Eng (left) and Dr. Michelle Trotter-Mathison (right). Photograph by author.

Dr. Michelle Trotter-Mathison

Dr. Michelle Trotter-Mathison also sees clients for individual therapy in her private practice. In addition to therapy, she conducts vocational assessments for candidates in ministry. She speaks, conducts workshops, and writes about the topic of burnout prevention and resilience in the helping professions (we mention her work in this chapter!) and is co-author of the book The Resilient Practitioner (Skovholt & Trotter-Mathison, 2024). Michelle loves working with people and the ongoing learning required for her work. She loves helping people to develop warm and supportive relationships with themselves as a foundation to support them throughout their lives. She also enjoys the variety of the work and opportunities to cultivate different areas of interest. Michelle especially appreciates when a client internalizes self-compassion after struggling with issues related to self-worth and shares with her that they are starting to relate to themselves differently. A challenging part of the work is that the caring/helping nature of therapy can be depleting over time so she makes sure to check in with herself and her self-care needs to thrive in her job.

Outside of work, Michelle spends time volunteering at her kids' schools and is active in their parent-teacher organizations. She loves to run, strength train, sew, grow flowers in her garden, try new restaurants, travel, and spend time with her friends and family. She enjoys storytelling and has shared her work at Listen to Your Mother Twin Cities, a live, on-stage show where women share their stories of motherhood. Michelle earned her bachelor's degree from St. Olaf College in Minnesota and her MA at the University of Minnesota in Counseling and Student Personnel Psychology.

A final note: You might also enjoy a book that Michelle, Sandra, and Julie (co-author of this textbook) wrote together with one of their former professors from the University of Minnesota, Dr. Thomas Skovholt. It is called Voices from the Field: Defining Moments in Counselor and Therapist Development (Trotter-Mathison et al., 2010). The book is a compilation of brief stories from real therapists about defining moments in their personal and professional lives that impacted their work, and it is organized according to stages of counselor development that we highlighted in this chapter.

References

American Psychological Association. (2017). *Ethical principles of psychologists and code of conduct*. American Psychological Association. https://www.apa.org/ethics/code/ethics-code-2017.pdf

American Psychoanalytic Association. (2024). *Standards and principles for psychoanalytic education*. American Psychoanalytic Association. https://apsa.org/wp-content/uploads/2023/04/Standards-PrinciplesForPsaEducation-APsA.pdf

Aponte, H. J. (2022). The soul of therapy: The therapist's use of self in the therapeutic relationship. *Contemporary Family Therapy, 44*(2), 136–143. https://doi.org/10.1007/s10591-021-09614-5

Baker, C., & Gabriel, L. (2021). Exploring how therapists engage in self-care in times of personal distress. *British Journal of Guidance & Counselling, 49*(3), 435–444. https://doi.org/10.1080/03069885.2021.1885010

Barnett, J. E., Baker, E. K., Elman, N. S., & Schoener, G. R. (2007). In pursuit of wellness: The self-care imperative. *Professional Psychology: Research and Practice, 38*(6), 603–612. https://doi.org/10.1037/0735-7028.38.6.603

Bearse, J. L., McMinn, M. R., Seegobin, W., & Free, K. (2013). Barriers to psychologists seeking mental health care. *Professional Psychology: Research and Practice, 44*(3), 150–157. https://doi.org/10.1037/a0031182

Chambers-Baltz, S., Knutson, D., Becerra, M., Hughes, A., Cantu Cantu, L., & Cadaret, M. (2021). Determined to improve: An exploration of therapist perspectives about their development. *Psychotherapy, 58*(4), 437–448. https://doi.org/10.1037/pst0000399

Demerouti, E., Bakker, A. B., Nachreiner, F., & Schaufeli, W. B. (2001). The job demands-resources model of burnout. *Journal of Applied Psychology, 86*(3), 499–512. https://doi.org/10.1037/0021-9010.86.3.499

Duncan, S., & Pond, R. (2024). Effective burnout prevention strategies for counsellors and other therapists: A systematic review and meta-synthesis of qualitative studies. *Counselling Psychology Quarterly, 38*, 525–555. https://doi.org/10.1080/09515070.2024.2394767

Eng, S. (2018). *Crochet kaleidoscope: Shifting shapes and shades across 100 motifs*. Krause Craft.

Hobaica, S., Szkody, E., Owens, S. A., Boland, J. K., Washburn, J. J., & Bell, D. J. (2021). Mental health concerns and barriers to care among future clinical psychologists. *Journal of Clinical Psychology, 77*, 2473–2490. https://doi.org/10.1002/jclp.23198

Kelly, J. F., & Green, B. (2010). Diversity within African American, female therapists: Variability in clients' expectations and assumptions about the therapist. *Psychotherapy: Theory, Research, Practice, Training, 47*(2), 186–197. https://doi.org/10.1037/a0019759

Manaster, G. J. (2010). A novice, an expert, and common sense. In M. Trotter-Mathison, J. M. Koch, S. Sanger, & T. Skovholt (Eds.), *Voices from the field: Defining moments in counselor and therapist development* (pp. 102–105). Routledge. https://doi.org/10.4324/9780203886052

Newell, J. M., & MacNeil, G. A. (2010). Professional burnout, vicarious trauma, secondary traumatic stress, and compassion fatigue: A review of theoretical terms, risk factors, and preventative methods for clinicians and researchers. *Best Practices in Mental Health: An International Journal, 6*(2), 57–68.

Norcross, J. C. (2005). The psychotherapist's own psychotherapy: Educating and developing psychologists. *American Psychologist, 60*(8), 840–850. https://psycnet.apa.org/doi/10.1037/0003-066X.60.8.840

O'Connor, K., Muller Neff, D. M., & Pitman, S. (2018). Burnout in mental health professionals: A systematic review and meta-analysis of prevalence and determinants. *European Psychiatry, 53*, 74–99. https://doi.org/10.1016/j.eurpsy.2018.06.003

Orlinsky, D. E., Norcross, J. C., Rønnestad, M. H., & Wiseman, H. (2005). Outcomes and impacts of psychologists' personal therapy: A research review. In J. D. Geller, J. C. Norcross, & D. E. Orlinsky (Eds.), *The psychologist's own psychotherapy* (pp. 214–234). Oxford University Press.

Page, C., Stamm, K., Assefa, M., Bethune, S., Wright, C. V., Fortunato, L., Weng, J., Novak, K., & Richman, A. (2024). When are psychologists most at risk of burnout? *Monitor on Psychology, 55*(3), 23. https://www.apa.org/monitor/2024/04/psychologists-career-burnout

Porter, J., Hulbert-Williams, L., & Chadwick, D. (2015). Sexuality in the therapeutic relationship: An interpretative phenomenological analysis of the experiences of gay therapists. *Journal of Gay & Lesbian Mental Health, 19*(2), 165–183. https://doi.org/10.1080/19359705.2014.957882

Posluns, K., & Gall, T. L. (2020). Dear mental health practitioners, take care of yourselves: A literature review on self-care. *International Journal for the Advancement of Counselling, 42*(1), 1–20. https://doi.org/10.1007/s10447-019-09382-w

Rønnestad, M. H., & Skovholt, T. M. (2003). The journey of the counselor and therapist: Research findings and perspectives on professional development. *Journal of Career Development, 30*(1), 5–44. https://doi.org/10.1177/089484530303000102

Rupert, P. A., Miller, A. O., & Dorociak, K. E. (2015). Preventing burnout: What does the research tell us? *Professional Psychology: Research and Practice, 46*(3), 168–174. https://doi.org/10.1037/a0039297

Sackett, C. R., Mack, H. L., Sharma, J., Cook, R. M., & Dogan-Dixon, J. (2023). A phenomenological exploration of counselors-in-training's experiences of microaggressions from clients. *The Professional Counselor, 13*(2), 145–161. https://doi.org/10.15241/crs.13.2.145

Skovholt, T. M., & Jennings, L. (Eds.). (2016). *Master therapists: Exploring expertise in therapy and counseling* (10th anniversary ed.). Oxford University Press. https://doi.org/10.1093/med:psych/9780190496586.001.0001

Skovholt, T. M., & Trotter-Mathison, M. (2024). *The resilient practitioner: Burnout and compassion fatigue prevention and self-care strategies for the helping professions* (4th ed.). Routledge. https://doi.org/10.4324/9781003221388

Trotter-Mathison, M., Koch, J. M., Sanger, S., & Skovholt, T. M. (Eds.). (2010). *Voices from the field: Defining moments in counselor and therapist development*. Routledge. https://doi.org/10.4324/9780203886052

Victor, S. E., Devendorf, A. R., Lewis, S. P., Rottenberg, J., Muehlenkamp, J. J., Stage, D. L., & Miller, R. H. (2022). Only human: Mental health difficulties among clinical, counseling, and school psychology faculty and trainees. *Perspectives on Psychological Science, 17*(6), 1576–1590. https://doi.org/10.1177/17456916211071079

Wampold, B. E., & Owen, J. (2021). Therapist effects: History, methods, magnitude, and characteristics of effective therapists. In M. Barkham, W. Lutz, & L. G. Castonguay (Eds.), *Bergin and Garfield's handbook of psychotherapy and behavior change: 50th anniversary edition* (7th ed., pp. 297–326). John Wiley & Sons, Inc.

World Health Organization. (2022). *ICD-11: International classification of diseases* (11th revision). https://icd.who.int

Ziede, J. S., & Norcross, J. C. (2020). Personal therapy and self-care in the making of psychologists. *The Journal of Psychology: Interdisciplinary and Applied, 154*(8), 585–618. https://doi.org/10.1080/00223980.2020.1757596

Chapter 13

Counseling Psychologists as Leaders and Advocates

Why Leadership and Advocacy?

Let's imagine that you are a counseling psychologist in a small city. You learn from friends that it is possible that the local youth agency that provides free counseling services to youth in the area ages 8–18 might close due to funding issues. The state has appropriated funds for this agency in the past but is considering making cuts. You know that this agency serves hundreds, if not thousands, of youth in the area because they have student trainees providing services, they do lots of group work, parenting classes, and outreach to the community. You are so upset that this agency, that provides such needed services, could close! But what can you do? You are just one person. Do you have any ideas about how you, as a counseling psychologist, could do anything to support this agency?

In this chapter, we discuss the importance of developing leadership and advocacy skills as a counseling psychologist. You will discover ways in which counseling psychologists can advocate to reduce mental health disparities in society. You will learn what advocacy means and how and why counseling psychologists can affect policy and systemic change. We also describe why counseling psychologists make great leaders. Counseling psychologists hold leadership roles in higher education settings, hospitals, and corporations. We will offer ways in which you can engage in small or large action steps to advocate for better mental health practices and policies.

Healthcare Access and Disparities

You may have heard the term *health disparities*. What do you think that refers to? What causes health disparities? The Centers for Disease Control (CDC, 2025a) defines health disparities as "preventable differences in the burden of disease, injury, violence, or opportunities" and says that they are "directly related to unequal distribution of social, political, economic, and environmental resources" (paras. 1–2). In plain language, that means some people have access to better health conditions than others. For example, people with lower education have more health problems like obesity, substance use, and intentional injury than people with higher levels of education (CDC, 2025a). Health disparities can result from a lot of factors. They might be related to where you live given that there are sometimes fewer health resources in rural areas than in urban ones. Health disparities are also related to socioeconomic status, race, gender, immigration status, and other sociopolitical factors. A subset of health disparities is *mental health disparities*, or differences between groups of people in terms of mental health concerns, resources, and access (Safran et al., 2009). An example of this is the higher level of suicidal ideation among LGBTQ + youth than among heterosexual/cisgender youth (Johns et al., 2020). After reading most of this book (especially early chapters like two, three, and four), it probably comes as no surprise to you that counseling psychologists

DOI: 10.4324/9781003439899-13

are very involved in efforts to prevent and reduce health disparities in clients, communities, and globally. You already read about some examples of these efforts in Chapter 3 where you were introduced to the developmental models and distress reduction research and practice led by counseling psychologists. Take a moment to think back over the chapters you have read so far and consider ways that discussions of strengths-based practice, multicultural competence, and prevention strategies help counseling psychologists target and address health disparities throughout their work.

One major issue related to mental health disparities is *access* to health care, specifically mental health care. Ask yourself the following questions and take a moment to jot down your answers:

- What do you think is the status of mental healthcare access in your state or city?
- How easy is it to make an appointment with a psychiatrist?
- Are you familiar with whether you can quickly see a therapist, or are there waitlists at agencies that might serve your community?
- What is pricing like in your area?
- What resources are available for someone who does not have health insurance?

Now, pause for a moment and reflect on what it is like to have to answer all of these questions on the spot. Is it stressful? Are some of the answers hard to find? Imagine being in the midst of a mental health crisis and trying to figure all of this stuff out! It is not hard to see how even finding services and getting help can cause stress and impact a person's health. It can even dissuade people from seeking help in the first place, even if they badly need it. In fact, beliefs about help-seeking and access and barriers to care are regularly written about and researched by counseling psychologists and others (e.g., Koch & Knutson, 2016). We will dig into specific access barriers and dynamics later in this chapter.

According to Mental Health America (Reinert et al., 2024), there are 340 people for every one mental health provider in the United States, but this number may actually overestimate the number of mental health providers because it may include people who are no longer practicing or accepting clients. The American Psychological Association Center for Workforce Studies has some really cool interactive maps on its website (https://www.apa.org/workforce/data-tools) where you can see geographic distribution of licensed psychologists at the county or state level across the United States and compare to mental health indicators, rates of substance abuse, or rates of drug overdose and suicide mortality (APA, 2020a, 2020b, 2020c). For example, if you select the state of Pennsylvania, you can see that, in 2018, there were 43 licensed psychologists per 100,000 people, higher than the national average, and about 18% of the population had a mental health issue, lower than the national average (APA, 2020b). Compare that to the state of Idaho, where there were only 14 licensed psychologists per 100,000 people, lower than the national average, and about 24% of the population had a mental health issue, higher than the national average (APA, 2020b). What might account for these differences?

In rural areas, access to mental health care is of critical concern right now in the United States. To use Iowa as an example, there is a workforce shortage of mental healthcare providers compared to other states. As of 2018, Iowa had 16 licensed psychologists per 100,000 people, and the national average was about 32 licensed psychologists per 100,000 people (almost double) (APA, 2020b). Yet, the number of people with mental health issues was 20%, and the national average was about 19% (APA, 2020b). Iowa also experienced higher than national average rates of severe mental illness, major depressive disorder, alcohol use disorder, and suicide mortality (APA, 2020a, 2020b, 2020c). But, if you look at the actual utilization of mental health services, people in Iowa used mental health resources greater than the national average (APA, 2020b). So, in Iowa, there are people experiencing higher levels of depression, greater serious mental health concerns; they have half the number of psychologists compared to the rest of the country on average; and yet, people are wanting these services and are utilizing them more than the average person in the United States (APA, 2020b). If we take a closer look and examine the distribution of psychologists at the county level, we can see that there are a few places in Iowa where psychologists cluster (for example, Iowa City), and there are many places across the state with no psychologists at all. Consider this: Why might this be? Why might a state like Iowa have fewer psychologists than the rest of the country? Why might the people in this state report greater level of mental health concerns than the rest of the country? What are some factors that would contribute to that? What are your reactions? What is the situation like in your state?

There are all kinds of factors that contribute to the distribution of licensed psychologists across the United States. In Chapter 15, we mention that part of the required training for doctoral applied health psychology programs (counseling, clinical, or school) is one year of full-time predoctoral internship. One issue that arises then is the number of predoctoral internship training sites and opportunities in Iowa. As of 2025, Iowa only has three APA-accredited internship sites throughout the whole state; compare that to Pennsylvania, which has 38 (Association of Psychology Postdoctoral Internship Centers [APPIC], 2025). You can find out more about APA-accredited, APPIC-member internship sites on the APPIC website. So, psychology trainees in Iowa often must leave the state and continue training elsewhere, which starts the process of putting down roots and getting established in another state. To increase access to mental health care, we need to have a large and thriving workforce. That is why we want you, the reader, to pursue a mental health career! What's more, we need psychologists who share key attributes with the communities they serve. The psychologist workforce we do have is largely comprised of White women (APA, 2022). So, we not only need more psychologists, but we also need a more diverse, representative workforce that mirrors the racial, gender, and religious fabric of the state and of the United States.

The Health Belief Model

There are also individual factors that contribute to access to mental health care. Health professionals use the *health belief model* (Alyafei & Easton-Carr, 2024; Rosenstock, 1966), a highly researched framework, that helps them to understand, anticipate, and predict individuals' help-seeking behaviors. It has largely been utilized in medical settings to help understand whether a person is likely to seek healthcare services but also has been applied in mental healthcare settings (Nobiling & Maykrantz, 2017). The model considers six health-related dimensions: perceived susceptibility, perceived severity, perceived benefits, perceived barriers, cues to action, and self-efficacy (Alyafei & Easton-Carr, 2024).

- *Perceived susceptibility* refers to an individual's understanding or belief about the likelihood they might have an issue, for example, "How likely is it that I could be depressed?" There are gender and other cultural components to this also. But if someone doesn't believe that they're susceptible to depression, this will impact the likelihood that they will seek help.
- *Perceived severity* refers to the threat of the disease or mental health issue posed to or experienced by the individual: "If I were to experience depression, how bad would it be? Really, I've just been feeling down for a couple of days." This will impact their willingness or likelihood to seek help.
- *Perceived benefit* and *perceived barriers* refer to specific dynamics involved in seeking help or taking preventative actions: "I could be experiencing depression. My friend Mary said therapy

helped her depression, so it helped her, but I don't know if I would have time in my busy schedule, and I'm not sure therapy would really help me." Higher perceived barriers than benefits will decrease the likelihood of seeking treatment. Benefits and barriers are also related to individual cultural factors like race or religion that contribute to the person's likelihood of seeking help.
- *Cues to action* refer to whether there are messages in someone's environment about seeking help. For example, are there current mass media campaigns? Does the person have trusted loved ones who have sought mental health care, that they could look to as a model? These are cues that treatment is a good thing to do, and other people do it, and that directly impacts the likelihood of seeking treatment.
- *Self-efficacy* refers to someone's belief that they could do something effectively. Someone might consider, "Can I navigate the health insurance system and find a decent therapist? How well would I navigate all of this? And if I did get therapy, would I follow through and benefit from it?"

All of these six pieces interact with each other and impact whether or not someone will seek mental health care (Alyafei & Easton-Carr, 2024; Nobiling & Maykrantz, 2017).

Let's consider an example: Josefina is a 52-year-old mother of three who works at a manufacturing plant in rural Minnesota. Her husband was recently diagnosed with pancreatic cancer and is now unable to work. She has been crying a lot lately, has not been sleeping, has lost a lot of weight, and has been getting to work late. She is worried she is going to be fired from her job, which is the only source of health insurance for her family. Let's break it down:

- Perceived susceptibility: Josefina does not really consider herself to "have" anxiety or depression, she thinks that life is just hard sometimes, and she and her family will get through this together.
- Perceived severity: Josefina thinks she is just a little stressed out.
- Perceived benefits and barriers: Josefina trusts her doctor, who has referred her to a therapy group for spouses of cancer patients, but worries about taking more time off from work.
- Cues to action: Her husband's oncology nurse gave her some brochures about the therapy group. Josefina's daughters have expressed worry about her and have encouraged her to join the group.
- Self-efficacy: Josefina, like most people, finds the insurance and referral system confusing and complicated, but her oldest daughter is a medical biller and said she can help her figure out what it would cost. Josefina is usually outgoing and friendly and can see herself connecting with other people in the group.

What are some other factors or considerations that might affect Josefina's willingness to seek mental health care? How might all of the factors we listed interact to further impact Josefina's mental healthcare access?

Mental Health Stigma

Another factor influencing whether or not someone will seek treatment is *mental health stigma*. Mental health stigma refers to "negative attitudes, beliefs, and stereotypes people may hold towards those who experience mental health conditions" (CDC, 2025b). Consider these questions:

- How is mental health stigmatized in our society?
- How have you experienced mental health stigma?

- How have you potentially contributed to it?
- How have people talked about mental health within your life?
- What cultural factors may contribute to stigmatization of mental health?

Contributors to stigma are complex and may include gender norms, cultural norms, the role of the media, societal messages, and use of language, such as saying things like "he's just crazy" or "she's so bipolar." Take a moment to reflect on how mental health stigma shows up in your daily language. Do you call things "lame" or say things like "that's crazy!"? If so, you might be inadvertently making it harder for people to identify and experience self-efficacy (or empowerment) related to their mental health challenges and disabilities.

In general, there's a sentiment that people should be able to "get over" mental illness, that they have control over it, and that mental health issues can be solved by thinking positively. Going to a physician is normalized and legitimized in our society, but going to a therapist is not. We wouldn't tell someone to "get over your broken arm," but there is a notion that if an issue is related to mental health, such as depression, people should be able to manage it and get better. It goes without saying that depression is just as legitimate as a broken arm and can be just as harmful if it goes untreated. If you take a look at the difference between a functional magnetic resonance imaging graphic of the brain of a person with clinical depression as compared to a person who is not clinically depressed, one glance will tell you that depression is as real, measurable, and physically impactful as a broken arm. Nevertheless, societal stigma toward mental health issues impacts policy and research in important ways. For example, the amount of funding for breast cancer research is high (which is wonderful and needed), but funding for research on suicide is much lower (Ax, 2018; Fortgang & Knox, 2021). Yet, individuals die by suicide at greater rates than breast cancer (Ax, 2018; Fortgang & Knox, 2021). Often, these funding priorities are heavily linked to some of the stigma around mental health issues.

Sociocultural Considerations

A final factor affecting access to mental health care is sociocultural considerations. Even if we have positive attitudes and can overcome stigma, and there is care available, not everyone has the exact same access to or trust in that care. Differences in provider access and trust are often related to multicultural variables such as race, gender, socio-economic status, and other cultural factors. For example, a group of researchers found that mental health providers provided positive callback voice messages to potential "clients" with a stereotypically-sounding White name at a 12% higher rate than they did to a client with a stereotypically-sounding Black name (Shin et al., 2016). Take a minute to think about how these differences might impact your own engagement with a provider or clinician. You might be less likely to follow up with your healthcare provider if you got a dismissive, uninvested, or less-than-positive message from your provider. Another study that highlighted cultural factors was done in the Washington, D.C., metropolitan area (Ronzio et al., 2006). The researchers used geospatial mapping to find out the location of psychiatric providers in comparison to the demographics of the communities in which they are located. They found that, basically, locations where mental health providers work were the exact opposite of locations with high levels of poverty and higher concentrations of African American residents and they provided some maps showing this discrepancy (Ronzio et al., 2006). So, even if someone does get a positive call back from a provider and they want to follow up about their health care, they may have to travel all the way across town to get care. This research is very sobering and really brings home the importance of multicultural education and training for mental healthcare providers. It also further reinforces our suggestion that it is important for psychologists to be accessible to the communities they serve.

Possible Solutions

With all of these barriers to accessing mental health care, what are some possible solutions? There are some things that the field of counseling psychology has been doing that have proven successful. For example, you may have heard of *integrated behavioral health care*. This is an approach to health care that includes both behavioral and physical health care and is becoming increasingly common within hospital and medical settings. Integrated behavioral health care tries to ensure that if you go to a doctor, it is a "one-stop shop;" you can also meet with a mental healthcare provider or behavioral health specialist. For example, let's say a patient is noticing that they have been overly fatigued and haven't had an appetite. They might think that something is going on physically with their hormones or thyroid. They see a doctor who runs some diagnostic tests and, after some conversations and visits, the doctor thinks it might actually be depression. In an integrated behavioral health model, the doctor can easily suggest to the patient that there is a behavioral health consultant and can refer the patient to them.

In this way, mental health professionals and physicians are working together to reduce the barriers to mental health care, by bringing these services together, to serve a larger number of individuals and address stigma. Another example is at a large university, there is an in-house healthcare clinic, where students can go if they have a cold, or the flu, or something like that. The physicians have partnered with a counseling psychology program so that students studying counseling psychology are on-site during office hours. At least one counseling psychology student is always there when the clinic is open. So, if a doctor or nurse had a patient who came in and who said they were feeling sick and shared other personal things or any mental health issues (they just broke up with their boyfriend, they can't pay their bills, etc.), the healthcare provider can see if the student is interested in talking to someone. They might say something like "Okay after we wrap up, I'm going to walk you down the hall, and you can talk to a counselor who can visit with you. The counselor can provide referrals or offer other assistance."

Telepsychology or telehealth is another potential solution to improving access to mental health care. Since the COVID-19 pandemic, telepsychology has gotten a lot more attention and use. Telepsychology is the use of telecommunication (phone, videoconferencing, even texting) to deliver and receive mental health care. It provides access for people who are maybe in a rural location or area with fewer providers; for people who do not have a lot of physical mobility; or even for people without transportation. This is a growing field and is becoming an important piece of the puzzle to help with access issues. Take a moment to reflect on your own experience and feelings about telehealth.

- Would you feel comfortable texting with a therapist?
- Would you feel comfortable talking with a therapist over the phone?
- Would you prefer telepsychology in a virtual format over going in person to a counseling psychologist?
- What do you think are the pros and cons of in-person versus telehealth mental health care?

Researchers are still trying to understand how effective some telepsychology services are compared to each other and compared to in-person therapy. In some cases, technology-based therapeutic interventions can expand access to care and help clients who are in crisis. Counseling psychologists are actively developing and testing mobile mental health interventions and other research-based, technology-mediated approaches to mental health care for health disparities populations (e.g., Knutson et al., 2021). We remain a little cautious, however, about some of the large corporations that promise a quick fix or solution as we are not sure how therapeutic or helpful these are in the long run. Unfortunately, some states and some insurance companies are placing limits on telehealth services. This is an emerging area of research with lots of space for development and innovation.

Advocacy

Another way that counseling psychologists are working to reduce health disparities and improve access to mental health care is through *advocacy*. It is no longer enough for counseling psychologists to limit their work providing individual therapy only (Kozan & Blustein, 2018; Vera & Speight, 2003). To truly alleviate human suffering, they must also work to advocate for changes in society. This section might call to mind our earlier discussion about prevention in Chapter 2. Prevention and advocacy sometimes work hand in hand, but they are not synonymous. Advocacy can include prevention efforts, but not all prevention work is inherently driven by a spirit of advocacy. The idea of advocacy implies a focus on health disparities populations that may lack the power, resources, and social capital to stand up for themselves.

Counseling psychologists can engage in advocacy at different levels. They might engage in client advocacy, social justice advocacy, professional advocacy, or other forms of advocacy. This is important enough that many counseling psychology doctoral programs now include training on advocacy, public policy, and social justice education (Alexander & Allo, 2021; Mallinckrodt et al., 2014). One definition of advocacy is "the act of speaking up or taking action to make environmental changes on behalf of our clients" (Bradley & Lewis, 2000, p. 3). However, there is some danger in a rescuer-type mentality of doing things for a group. Instead, we like the advocacy competencies described below, which encourage people to consider different levels of advocacy and how we might advocate with a group (alongside health disparities populations) rather than just for (or in place of members of health disparities populations).

The American Counseling Association (ACA, 2018) developed a set of advocacy competencies that describe the necessary skills, attitudes, and behaviors that counselors need to engage in advocacy for students, clients, or groups of people. The competencies are organized by two domains:

- Extent of client involvement In advocacy (In other words, with the client? Or on behalf of the client?)
- Level of advocacy intervention (Is the intervention with an individual? A family? A group of people such as a class, school, or workplace? A community? Or for the public in general?)

The ACA guidelines allow for multiple advocacy approaches to be taken at the same time so the two main domains should not be viewed as separate categories but rather as overlapping or interactive components. The intersection of these two domains produces six possible kinds of actions, illustrated in Table 13.1.

Table 13.1 Intersections of advocacy level with client involvement

Level	*Advocating For*	*Advocating With*
Client/student	Direct advocacy for client	Empowerment of client to self-advocate
Community/ school/ organization	Direct advocacy aimed at changing the system	Collaboration with community to enact change
Public	Direct advocacy aimed at social/ political structures	Collective action taken with affected parties

So far, these ideas may feel aspirational and hard to practice. The good news is that scholars have offered specific steps that psychologists can take and behaviors they can engage in to enact these advocacy competencies. For example, at the individual level, a counselor might go through the following steps (Ratts & Hutchins, 2009, pp. 271–273):

1) Identify strengths and resources of clients/students.
2) Identify the social, political, economic, and cultural factors that affect the client/student.
3) Recognize the signs indicating that an individual's behaviors and concerns reflect responses to systemic or internalized oppression.
4) At an appropriate development level, help the individual identify the external barriers that affect his or her development.
5) Train students and clients in self-advocacy skills.
6) Help students and clients develop self-advocacy action plans.
7) Assist students and clients in carrying out action plans.
8) Negotiate relevant services and education systems on behalf of clients and students.
9) Help students and clients gain access to needed resources.
10) Identify barriers to the well-being of individuals and vulnerable groups.
11) Develop an initial plan of action for confronting these barriers.
12) Identify potential allies for confronting the barriers.
13) Carry out the plan of action.

The American Psychological Association encourages psychologists to engage in advocacy and they are so serious about the importance of advocacy for psychologists that they even created a branch of psychologists called the APA Services Advocacy Team. This team is specifically geared toward supporting psychologists who want to learn how to advocate more or want to get more involved (APA, 2025). They have resources to help people advocate at the state and federal levels. DeAngelis (2018) put together a great list of eight ways psychologists can engage in advocacy. Some of these are things that you could do as a student now and others are more geared toward professionals who are psychologists. These suggestions may feel overwhelming! Even the most seasoned psychologist can find some of these strategies challenging to enact. For now, just read over them and reflect on your openness to using these strategies. Which strategies fit with your advocate identity and which ones feel harder to do?

1) Communicate with lawmakers. This might feel intimidating, but your elected officials are there to serve you, their constituents. Anyone can call, send an email, write a letter, or meet with their legislators (although for US Senators or Representatives, you might meet with their staff).
2) Volunteer for a cause or a candidate. This could be at different levels – attending a one-day event or participating more heavily in a long-term campaign, for example.
3) Run for office. Yes, you! Any adult can run for public office at the local, state, or national level. You may be inspired by one of the several mayors of towns in the United States who hold this role at the age of 18!
4) Write an op-ed. Op-ed stands for "opposite the editorial page," which historically meant pieces written for a newspaper that would literally show up on the page opposite the page where editorials were written. Nowadays, it most commonly refers to an opinion or commentary piece written by someone outside of newspaper (or magazine or other journalist work) staff. You can write a piece about any topic that is important to you and submit it to a newspaper for consideration.
5) Raise your voice on social media. Social media outreach can allow you to join with others to support a cause or candidate.

6) Support student advocacy. This point was written for psychology faculty, but you, the student reader, can take this to mean to support and encourage other people to get involved. Encourage your friends, family members, and community to engage in advocacy.
7) Serve as an APA Fellow. Again, this point is for current psychologists to work with APA on specific interests, including reducing health disparities and clinical work with children.
8) Become a citizen psychologist. APA recognizes psychologists who are active in their communities and who serve the public good. They volunteer for a wide range of causes and do good work beyond their careers. For example, a counseling psychologist who serves on the board of a local public library could be a citizen psychologist.

Leadership

In many ways, engaging in advocacy requires leadership skills. According to Fassinger and Shullman (2017), counseling psychologists make great leaders because of:

- Their focus on strengths (See Chapters 1 and 2);
- Their background and training in multicultural issues (See Chapter 3), because of the need for leaders to understand growth and development (See Chapter 4);
- Their interpersonal skills needed to be effective listeners (See Chapters 6, 7, and 8);
- The importance placed on ethical considerations (See Chapter 11);
- Their self-awareness to lead with genuineness and authenticity (See Chapter 12).

How does it feel to reflect on your progress through this book so far and to realize that you have been following the path of a leader in counseling psychology? We designed this book to help you explore a future career as a counseling psychologist and as you near the end of the text, you will have many of the tools necessary to take the next step in your career!

Becoming a leader in psychology may feel daunting. You may be thinking, "Hold on…I just started exploring this career path. How am I supposed to be a leader in the field?" The good news is that many of the principles of strong counseling psychology leadership are not just for psychologists. They are for clients, students, teachers, and community members, and that includes you! You can start acting as an advocate and leader right where you are, in your university, dorm, program, community, and so on. Fassinger and Shullman (2017) gave some examples of ways in which counseling psychologists and others can act as leaders in their current context (you) and as their careers develop (future you). Keeps an eye on what sets counseling psychology leaders apart from other types of leaders. Can you spot the differences?

- Seeking out leadership opportunities with a focus on collaboration: Counseling psychologists who are leaders may focus more than other people would on collaboration, the cultural context of group members and stakeholders, and how research supports the work they are doing. They may use their strong interpersonal skills and some basic counseling skills such as listening and reflecting content.
- Inclusive approaches to research: Counseling psychologists who lead research projects might consider short-term cost-effectiveness at the same time as long-term impact of the projects. They bring a strong understanding of the ethics involved in research. They are likely to treat community members as collaborators and co-researchers.
- Identifying strengths in healthcare settings: Counseling psychologists who are leaders in healthcare settings will bring to a team of providers a focus on the patient's strengths, cultural context,

and development. They might remind the team of the patient's potential rather than focus on their problems or pathology.

- Foregrounding educational opportunities: Counseling psychologists who work in educational settings are attuned to their students' and trainees' cultural context, help trainees explore client strengths and assets, and model for trainees how to integrate issues related to vocational or work concerns. Here, too, they are likely to take a collaborative and cooperative approach with trainees rather than a hierarchical approach (Fassinger & Shullman, 2017).

Take a moment to reflect on the kind of leader you hope to be. Do terms like collaborative, inclusive, strengths-based, and education-focused describe your approach to working in teams and leading groups? How could you work to make your leadership style more empowering and cooperative? When you reflect on these questions, you are doing the work of a counseling psychologist.

Summary

At the beginning of this chapter, we posed a scenario to you: A local youth agency was losing funding and would no longer be able to provide therapy services. We asked if there was anything you could do to advocate for the agency. Now, hopefully, you have lots of ideas about ways that you – or you and a group of others – could advocate to maintain this important agency in your community. We discussed different factors that get in the way of access to mental health care, like healthcare beliefs, stigma, and sociocultural issues. We also introduced you to potential solutions, like telehealth, and gave you ideas for ways you can advocate for change. Before reading this chapter, you might not have considered that psychologists can be leaders toward change, but hopefully you now have a good understanding of how psychologists are often great advocates because of their expertise. Even if you are not planning on pursuing a career as a counseling psychologist, we hope that you now have some models and strategies to work toward change if you are inspired to do so. In the next chapter, we are going to introduce you to a wide range of settings where counseling psychologists practice, research, and advocate for change within their agencies and larger systems.

What Would You Do?

Recently, you learned that the school district in your hometown is cutting funding for its theater/drama, music, and arts programs. As a student, you benefitted greatly from the band program; you played the drums starting in 6th grade, played all through your senior year of high school, and got a scholarship to college to play with the marching band. In fact, you attribute the good grades you got in high school to being in band, and the rigorous requirements that the band directors had for keeping up with homework and grades. All of your best friends are people you met through band. You also think that being involved in music programs helps students' mental health. It upsets you to learn that this program could potentially lose its funding, and students will no longer get to benefit from marching band or other arts and music programs. You decide that you want to advocate against this budget cut. You start by writing a letter to the superintendent of the school district and the school board. From communicating with them, you learn that the cuts are because the state congress has cut back on allocations to public schools across the whole state. At this point, you decide to reach out to your state congresspeople. Here are some steps you can take:

- Gather information. Can you find any statistics or research about the benefits of involvement in music and arts programs for students' mental health or academics?

- Reach out to your community. Congresspeople like a story. Interview current and past students, faculty, and community members about what these arts programs mean to them.
- Provide resources or a solution. Rather than just telling the congressperson what NOT to do, think of potential solutions and encourage them to consider other options.
- Share your personal information, give them a way to contact you. Be sure you let them know that you are a voter and how you can be reached. See if they are willing to meet with you to discuss the issue.
- Even if you do not actually mail this letter, we hope this is a helpful exercise for you to engage in. Perhaps you have a different topic that you are passionate about, such as your local youth agency, school counseling resources, or a domestic violence agency. Consider how to make a compelling argument and advocate for solutions for change.

Counseling Psychologist Spotlight: Leadership

Dr. Gayle Skawen:nio Morse

Dr. Gayle Skawen:nio Morse is a Professor and Internship Director in the Psychology Department at Russell Sage College in Troy, NY. She says she loves her students and colleagues in the Psychology Department. Her students inspire her with their energy, their hope, and their desire to help people and their community. She says her colleagues are kind, thoughtful, and look forward to seeing each other at regular department meetings. At the end of the semester, their whole department meets to share a meal and regroup before they take a break prior to heading into the next semester! When we asked her about her favorite aspect of her job, she said, "All of it is my favorite. I am so blessed to have the work I love with the people I love and doing the teaching, research, and writing I love." One challenging aspect of her job is balancing teaching in evenings with administrative meetings, student meetings, and research work during the daytime. But it is all worth it – her favorite part of her work is watching her students grow from hopeful first-year graduate students into mature professionals. She loves seeing people achieving their dreams. Gayle says that being a counseling psychologist has allowed her to explore an infinite variety of professional interests while actually enjoying and being entertained by the work she is involved in!

> Being a counseling psychologist has been a dream come true and has opened doors for me to travel the world and meet with other psychologists. I have spent a summer in the south of France, several summers in Australia, and had speaking engagements in Canada, New Zealand and throughout the United States. A tiny factoid, due to my counseling psychology activities I have met my goal of traveling to all 50 States of the U. S.!

Gayle says,

> My Kanienkehaka (Mohawk) background has given me the foundation to do the work that I love. The Kanienkehaka principles of Skennen, Kariwiio and Kasastensera – or peace, good mind and strength – are achieved by respecting the environment and people, and are what fuel my efforts

Gayle lives these values through her leadership. She has been active as a leader in the American Psychological Association and the Society of Indian Psychologists for over 20 years. She has served in leadership roles such as President of the Society of Indian Psychologists and Chair of

Dr. Gayle Skawen:nio Morse. Photograph by author.

the Board for the Advancement of Psychology in the Public Interest. She is a Fellow of Division 35 (Society for the Psychology of Women) and Division 45 (Society for the Psychological Study of Culture, Ethnicity, and Race). She is the past Editor of the *Journal of Indigenous Research.* In 2020, she co-chaired the Division 45 Warrior's Path Task Force, whose mission was to consider ways in which Division 45 could "protect and care for the most vulnerable, such as children, elders, refugees, immigrants, and the sick. In other words … the guardian of the vulnerable – those who cannot stand up for themselves" (APA Division 45 Warrior's Path Presidential Task Force, 2020).

Gayle considers herself an "accidental leader." She was asked to fill a leadership role, so she did.

> I took a deep breath for courage, reminded myself to be humble, then took a tentative step into the unknown. What I learned was that anyone can be a leader if they put in the time. But I am also thankful for my training as a counseling psychologist which prepared me to be a leader in an organization because it requires one to view all nuances of a problem, consider the needs of the people around you, and to tolerate confrontation graciously.

Outside of work, Gayle fosters abandoned and abused dogs and cats. She said that being able to provide a safe place to heal and help them learn to trust a human again is both gratifying and humbling. Gayle also enjoys cooking as a hobby and says that cooking for family and friends "is sublime." She enjoys creating new and innovative dishes.

> When I look around my table while serving my friends and family a warm loving bowl of steaming soup with a slice of warm bread right out of the oven, my day is made! It is a beautiful thing to be able to nurture and nourish loved ones – or, actually, anyone who needs it!

Gayle is a member of the Mohawk Tribe. She was honored in 2020 by the American Psychological Association's Society for the Psychology of Women's Sweetgrass Award, which recognizes a professional who advanced Indigenous values through outstanding professionalism and service. In 2021, she received the Joseph E. Trimble & Jewell E. Horvat Award for Distinguished Professional in Native/Indigenous Psychology. Gayle received her PhD in counseling psychology from the State University of New York, Albany. She also holds a master's degree in Clinical Psychopharmacology that she earned after her doctorate. She graduated with a BA in Psychology and Native American Studies from Kennesaw State University. She is a licensed psychologist in New York.

References

Alexander, A. A., & Allo, H. (2021). Building a climate for advocacy training in professional psychology. *The Counseling Psychologist, 49*(7), 1070–1089. https://doi.org/10.1177/00110000211027973

Alyafei, A., & Easton-Carr, R. (2024). *The health belief model of behavior change.* In StatPearls. StatPearls Publishing. https://www.ncbi.nlm.nih.gov/books/NBK606120/

American Counseling Association. (2018). *Advocacy competencies.* American Counseling Association. https://www.counseling.org/docs/default-source/competencies/aca-advocacy-competencies-updated-may-2020.pdf

American Psychological Association. (2020a). *County-level interactive map: Distributions of licensed psychologists, drug overdose mortality rates, and suicide mortality rates.* https://www.apa.org/workforce/data-tools/geographic-distribution

American Psychological Association. (2020b). *Distribution of licensed psychologists and mental health indicators.* https://www.apa.org/workforce/data-tools/mental-health-indicators

American Psychological Association. (2020c). *Licensed psychologists, population substance abuse, and unmet need.* https://www.apa.org/workforce/data-tools/substance-abuse-unmet-needs

American Psychological Association. (2022). *Demographics of U.S. psychology workforce.* https://www.apa.org/workforce/data-tools/demographics

American Psychological Association. (2025). *Advocacy.* https://www.apaservices.org/advocacy

APA Division 45 Warrior's Path Presidential Task Force. (2020). Protecting and defending our people: Nakni tushka anowa (The warrior's path). *Journal of Indigenous Research, 9*(8). https://doi.org/10.26077/2en0-6610

Association of Psychology Postdoctoral Internship Centers (2025). *APPIC Directory.* https://www.appic.org/

Ax, J. (2018, June 8). U.S. suicide prevention programs say more funding needed. *Reuters*. https://www.reuters.com/article/business/healthcare-pharmaceuticals/us-suicide-prevention-programs-say-more-funding-needed-idUSKCN1J42WE/

Bradley, L., & Lewis, J. (2000). Introduction. In J. Lewis & L. Bradley (Eds.), *Advocacy in counseling: Counselors, clients & community* (pp. 3–4). ERIC Clearinghouse on Counseling and Student Services.

Centers for Disease Control. (2025a). *Health disparities*. https://www.cdc.gov/healthy-youth/health-disparities/index.html

Centers for Disease Control. (2025b). *Mental health stigma*. https://www.cdc.gov/mental-health/stigma/index.html

DeAngelis, T. (2018). 8 ways to advocate for psychology. *Monitor on Psychology, 49*(3), 34. https://www.apa.org/monitor/2018/03/cover-advocate

Fassinger, R. E., & Shullman, S. L. (2017). Leadership and counseling psychology: What should we know? Where could we go? *The Counseling Psychologist, 45*(7), 927–964. https://doi.org/10.1177/0011000017744253

Fortgang, R. G., & Nock, M. K. (2021). Ringing the alarm on suicide prevention: A call to action. *Psychiatry, 84*(2), 192–195. https://doi.org/10.1080/00332747.2021.1907871

Johns, M. M., Lowry, R., Haderxhanaj, L. T., Rasberry, C. N., Robin, L., Scales, L., Stone, D. M., & Suarez, N. A. (2020). Trends in violence victimization and suicide risk by sexual identity among high school students—Youth Risk Behavior Survey, United States, 2015–2019. *Morbidity and Mortality Weekly Report, 69* (Suppl 1), 19–27. https://doi.org/10.15585/mmwr.su6901a3

Knutson, D., Kertz, S., Chambers-Baltz, S., Christie, M., Harris, E., & Perinchery, R. (2021). A pilot test of a text message based transgender and non-binary affirmative cognitive behavioral intervention for anxiety and depression. *Psychology of Sexual Orientation and Gender Diversity, 8*(4), 440–450. https://doi.org/10.1037/sgd0000438

Koch, J., & Knutson, D. (2016). Transgender clients in rural areas and small towns. *Journal of Rural Mental Health, 40(3–4)*, 154–163. https://doi.org/10.1037/rmh0000056

Kozan, S., & Blustein, D. L. (2018). Implementing social change: A qualitative analysis of counseling psychologists' engagement in advocacy. *The Counseling Psychologist, 46*(2), 154–189. https://doi.org/10.1177/0011000018756882

Mallinckrodt, B., Miles, J. R., & Levy, J. J. (2014). The scientist-practitioner-advocate model: Addressing contemporary training needs for social justice advocacy. *Training and Education in Professional Psychology, 8*(4), 303–311. https://doi.org/10.1037/tep0000045

Nobiling, B. D., & Maykrantz, S. A. (2017). Exploring perceptions about and behaviors related to mental illness and mental health service utilization among college students using the health belief model (HBM). *American Journal of Health Education, 48*(5), 306–319. https://doi.org/10.1080/19325037.2017.1335628

Ratts, M. J., & Hutchins, A. M. (2009). ACA advocacy competencies: Social justice advocacy at the client/student level. *Journal of Counseling & Development, 87*(3), 269–275. https://doi.org/10.1002/j.1556-6678.2009.tb00106.x

Reinert, M., Fritze, D., & Nguyen, T. (2024). *The state of mental health in America 2024*. Mental Health America. https://mhanational.org/wp-content/uploads/2024/12/2024-State-of-Mental-Health-in-America-Report.pdf

Ronzio, C. R., Guagliardo, M. F., & Persaud, N. (2006). Disparity in location of urban mental service providers. *American Journal of Orthopsychiatry, 76*(1), 37–43. https://doi.org/10.1037/0002-9432.76.1.37

Rosenstock, I. M. (1966). Why people use health services. *Milbank Memorial Fund Quarterly, 44*(1), 94–127.

Safran, M. A., Mays, R. A., Huang, L. N., McCuan, R., Pham, P. K., Fisher, S. K., McDuffie, K. Y., & Trachtenberg, A. (2009). Mental health disparities. *American Journal of Public Health, 99*(11), 1962–1999. https://doi.org/10.2105/AJPH.2009.167346

Shin, R. Q., Smith, L. C., Welch, J. C., & Ezeofor, I. (2016). Is Allison more likely than Lakisha to receive a callback from counseling professionals? A racism audit study. *The Counseling Psychologist, 44*(8), 1187–1211. https://doi.org/10.1177/0011000016668814

Vera, E. M., & Speight, S. L. (2003). Multicultural competence, social justice, and counseling psychology: Expanding our roles. *The Counseling Psychologist, 31*(3), 253–272. https://doi.org/10.1177/0011000003031003001

Chapter 14

Counseling Psychology Applied to Special Settings

Where Do Counseling Psychologists Work?

Where do you think counseling psychologists work? Actually, a better question might be, before you started reading this book, and learning about the counseling psychologists in the spotlight, where did you think counseling psychologists work? Did you ever imagine that a counseling psychologist might work with Cirque du Soleil performers, for example? Or with astronauts? Did you picture psychotherapy ever happening outdoors in a woodsy area? Or under an overpass where unhoused people live?

In this chapter, we hope to introduce you to a wide range of settings in which counseling psychologists work. You may not have even known that counseling psychologists could do so many things! We hope that through the Counseling Psychologist Spotlights in each chapter, and through this chapter, you'll get a great sense of the wide variety of work that counseling psychologists can do. Ultimately, we want you to dream big and imagine what you could do as a counseling psychologist. In this chapter, we highlight hospitals and integrated care settings, university and college counseling centers, military settings, Veterans Affairs Hospitals, corporations and consultation, corrections facilities and law enforcement, Indian Health Service, private practice, community agencies such as domestic/interpersonal violence and homeless shelters, sport psychology, and other settings.

Hospitals and Integrated Care

As we mentioned in Chapter 13, counseling psychologists make valuable additions to hospitals and integrated care teams. Also, check out the Counseling Psychologist Spotlight of Dr. Gunn, who works in a healthcare setting, in Chapter 9. But did you know that counseling psychologists often work in hospitals on all kinds of different specialty teams? They may work with patients with chronic illness, diabetes patients, cardiology patients, neurology patients, cancer care patients, and pediatric patients. They can do psychological assessment and diagnosis, individual and group therapy, treatment planning, consultation, education, and prevention, all with the goal of improving patients' lives (Wahass, 2005). So, imagine that a family brings in Lindsay, who is 13, for her appointment at the diabetes clinic. The parents report that Lindsay is having a hard time managing her own care. They want to encourage her to be responsible for her own care but find themselves constantly nagging. A counseling psychologist/health psychologist can have a conversation with Lindsay and the family to determine what the barriers are to Lindsay's *compliance*, or ability to adhere to treatment. They can work with Lindsay to develop a plan that works for them.

Often, counseling psychologists who work in these settings also identify as *health psychologists* (APA, 2025a). The Society for Health Psychology (APA, Division 38) defines health psychology

DOI: 10.4324/9781003439899-14

as the exploration of "how psychological factors influence health and well-being, focusing on understanding behaviors, emotions, and beliefs that impact physical health outcomes" (Society for Health Psychology, 2023, para. 1). This sounds very familiar to the work that counseling psychologists do in general. In fact, you might not know that the body that accredits doctoral counseling psychology programs (and clinical and school psychology programs) considers all of these programs to be *health service psychology* programs. They define health service psychology as:

> the integration of psychological science and practice in order to facilitate human development and functioning. Health service psychology includes … a wide range of professional activities relevant to health promotion, prevention, consultation, assessment, and treatment for psychological and other health-related disorders.
>
> (APA, 2015, p. 2)

University and College Counseling Centers

Many counseling psychologists enjoy working in university or college counseling centers, often called *UCCs*, as the work is usually quite varied (outreach, supervision, group therapy, consultation) and there are a wide range of opportunities (community colleges, medical schools, liberal arts colleges, large universities). You might want to revisit the Counseling Psychology Spotlight of Dr. Pickett in Chapter 12. UCCs often serve a traditional emerging adult population. That means college counselors often hold broader skills and a developmental focus that help clients understand themselves and explore future careers. UCCs often have a variety of services that they offer to students. In addition to individual, one-on-one therapy (which may include video, in-person, or a mix of both), they may offer group therapy, couples therapy, testing and assessment, brief walk-in interventions, and crisis counseling. Counseling psychologists at UCCs may engage in prevention through outreach and psychoeducation; for example, they might train incoming students about study skills, coping mechanisms, and signs of depression. Counseling psychologists in UCCs often work closely with other campus offices such as student disability services, financial aid, housing, and campus police. Another unique aspect is the notion of *embedded* therapists, where, in addition to a central UCC office, therapists are also physically located across campus. For example, universities may have therapists located in the buildings or departments that house veterinary medicine, dentistry, medical colleges, business, and in residential halls (Schreier et al., 2021). UCCs often focus on the training and supervision of future counseling psychologists, so graduate students may see clients under supervision of more advanced therapists. The most frequently presenting concerns of student clients are anxiety, stress, and depression. However, there are several emerging trends that have impacted the use of college counseling services that you should be aware of:

- Although the percentage of students with concerns about anxiety has generally risen over the past ten years, this rate has actually decreased since 2021 (Center for Collegiate Mental Health [CCMH], 2024).
- Stress has gradually increased over the past ten years, with a spike in 2020–2021 that has decreased over the past four years.
- Depression has seen a decline over the past seven years.

Students also present with concerns related to academic performance, relationship problems, trauma, suicidality, alcohol use, family issues, and others. There has been a marked increase in concerns related to trauma (from about 10% to about 20% over the last ten years) (CCMH, 2024).

Despite some of these trends (depression decreasing, anxiety decreasing), we frequently hear from the media about the *mental health crisis* that college campuses are facing. This can be problematic because it may perpetuate stereotypes about mental health and may sensationalize and catastrophize normal developmental issues rather than focus on students' resilience and the fact that college counseling centers offer all kinds of services (Kafka, 2024). What do you think? Are college students all experiencing mental health crises? What is the climate like at your campus? We encourage you to look into the kinds of services your campus offers related to wellness and mental health; they may even offer some kind of report or statistics about the use of these services and their utility. If you want to learn more, you can visit the Society of Counseling Psychology's Section on University Counseling Centers website (Society of Counseling Psychology, 2025).

Military

In 2023, there were almost 2 million people serving in the US military globally, including active-duty and reserve (U.S. Department of Defense, 2023). It is likely that you know someone, or have a family member, who currently serves or has served in the US military. APA has a division specifically for people interested in military psychology, Division 19: Society for Military Psychology. Their mission is to "serve as the premier organization for the advancement of the psychological study of military, national defense, and national security organizations" (Society for Military Psychology, 2025, para. 1). The work of counseling psychologists in this specialty area is specifically geared toward military populations. Counseling psychologists who work for the military may be commissioned officers, or they may be civilian contractors. They may teach, consult, do research, and provide psychological services. They may also work with Congressional committees or advise military commands and leadership.

Most of the training to be a military psychologist is similar to that of other counseling psychologists, but there may be specialized training through a predoctoral internship or postdoctoral fellowship. The work is also similar: military psychologists offer individual and group therapy, they may work in integrated health with physicians, they conduct assessments and make diagnostic decisions, and they may do research and train other psychologists. However, their work is also uniquely specialized. For example, they may do crisis response and intervention, evaluating people's fitness for placement in different roles or opportunities, stress management and resilience training, and providing on-site therapy to service members who are actively deployed. For example, a counseling psychologist stationed at an Air Force base provides psychological support to the family members of deployed soldiers. As part of her work, she might help prepare children for their parents to be gone for long periods of time and have group therapy sessions with spouses.

Veterans Affairs Hospitals

You might imagine a counseling psychologist working in a Veteran's Affairs (VA) Hospital to basically be a combination of a military psychologist and a hospital-based psychologist. However, there is a difference that may seem small on the surface, but is actually pretty significant. Rather than working with enlisted service members, VA psychologists work with military veterans, or people who previously served and were discharged. Because the setting is a hospital, they specifically focus on health psychology, but presenting concerns among veterans can be different than those treated in a general hospital setting.

In Chapter 8, our Counseling Psychologist Spotlight features Dr. Alvarez, who works in a VA hospital. Typical issues a psychologist might see in a VA could include adjustment to an injury, especially a life-changing injury, traumatic brain injury, and intervention for suicidal ideation. Of course, veterans get treated at VA hospitals for normal health-related issues too, such as diabetes treatment, heart conditions, dementia, or needing an appendix removed. The great thing about VA is that they provide care in ways that are tailored to meet the needs and recognize the uniqueness of veterans.

In this setting, a counseling psychologist could be working with a 20-year-old veteran who was medically discharged because of an injury attained while deployed, a 45-year-old veteran who served in Operation Iraqi Freedom/Operation Enduring Freedom, or with an 80-year-old veteran who served in the Vietnam War. You may be noticing that, just like psychologists in college counseling centers, psychologists in VA get to work with diverse populations and address a wide range of presenting concerns. Whereas psychologists in college counseling centers most often work with clients on reducing depression, anxiety, and stress, psychologists in VA encounter the following dynamics:

- Approximately 40% of veterans need mental health care, and although the need is greatest within three months of being separated from the military, the need for suicide risk prevention and intervention can continue for years (Mission Roll Call, 2024).
- The most common mental health diagnoses for veterans are post-traumatic stress disorder (PTSD), traumatic brain injurty, depression, anxiety, and substance abuse (Mission Roll Call, 2024).
- Veterans have a higher completed suicide rate than the general population (U.S. Department of Veterans Affairs, 2023).

We asked earlier if you knew of anyone serving in the military. Do you know any veterans? What do you know about their health? Are they able to access health care through a VA hospital? What are some barriers to mental healthcare access for veterans (See also Chapter 13)? Also, what similarities and differences do you notice between the work done by psychologists in college counseling, military, and VA settings? So far, which of these settings do you feel most drawn toward? Do you find yourself still wanting to know more about the direction your career could take as a counseling psychologist? If so, you are in luck, because we are just getting started.

Corporations and Consultation

Counseling psychologists sometimes work in corporate and consultation settings (see the Counseling Psychologist Spotlight of Dr. Milo Dodson in Chapter 2, for example). Remember how we mentioned other types of psychology training earlier in this chapter? We mentioned social and industrial/organizational (I/O) psychologists and we pointed out that, unlike I/O psychologists, counseling psychologists receive applied training that qualifies them for licensure as a health service psychologist. That difference in training shapes how counseling psychologists versus I/O psychologists approach work in corporate and consultation settings. In other words, although the setting may be the same, the work they do can look different.

I/O psychologists are generally concerned with the functioning of the company as a whole system or as the "client" of interest. They might work to improve productivity, develop systems and policies, promote teamwork and management skills, and assess workers' satisfaction. Counseling psychologists who work in corporate settings, on the other hand, are likely to focus on individual and group mental health and psychological well-being. They might engage in conflict resolution, teach stress management techniques, offer individual therapy or support groups, or provide career counseling as discussed in Chapter 5. Their "clients" are the individual humans or teams who work in that company or organization and their role is to promote flourishing and job satisfaction. Do you see the difference it makes to focus on the company as the client instead of the people within the company? How might that impact the way a psychologist approaches this sort of work? Are you surprised to know that counseling psychologists actually work with large companies?

At this point, we have been focusing on interventions with companies and you may be wondering where the idea of consultation factors into all of this. To be fair, the term is usually thrown around like everyone should know what consultation or consulting means, but it is actually a bit nebulous. This is probably because what consultation looks like depends on the setting or company, the needs of people within the setting or company, and the counseling psychologist (Cooper et al., 2012). Consider the following unique attributes that differentiate consultant psychologists from psychologists in other settings:

- Consultation usually occurs in a work setting rather than a personal setting like individual therapy (Cooper et al., 2012).
- Counseling psychologists who work as consultants may engage in activities like problem-solving, goal-setting, or strategic planning (Fuqua & Newman, 2009) for a team, company, or organization. Counseling psychologists may work for a corporation specifically as an internal consultant, or they may be called upon as an external consultant by a system different than where they work. Or, they could have their own business specifically geared to offer consultation services.
- Consultants may offer expert work or process work. As an expert, they are called upon because of their specific area of expertise and focus. As a process consultant, they would partner with the company to collaboratively figure out how to solve a problem and prevent it in the future (Cooper et al., 2012).

For example, a counseling psychologist, Debra, might have a consultation business focused on improving the work climate and experience for women in traditionally male-dominated work environments. If she were hired by a company to improve their work climate for women workers, she would be an external expert consultant. Scholars have designed and argued the positive qualities of a lot of different consultation models and we do not have space in this chapter to review them all, but some are more consistent with the values of counseling psychology (see Chapters 2 and 3) than others.

For our example, we will use the model put forward by Fuqua and Newman (2009). Using this model, Debra, our consultant for women in business, would:

- Build a relationship using her strong counseling and interpersonal skills, and her understanding of multicultural issues and human development. This might be with the leaders in the company, the workers, and specifically with any women who work there. She would then try to figure out where the problem lies – perhaps for this company, they have learned that many women quit their jobs within six months of being hired.
- Using her understanding of work psychology and career issues, she would help them set realistic goals, such as maintaining any women workers for at least two years after being hired. She would work with leadership to consider any alternatives and possible interventions, such as a new mentorship model, training for leaders, and flexible work-from-home time for all workers.
- She would work with the company to implement the changes and to see if they are successful using assessment and research skills and then determine if her work was complete.

We hope this helps you have a better sense of what corporate work or consultation might look like. Is this kind of work something you might be interested in? Why or why not? What would it be like for you to work in a corporate setting? How might the cultural norms and expectations differ from those in other settings?

Criminal Justice and Corrections

Counseling psychologists may work with incarcerated persons or ex-offenders who are adjusting to life outside the criminal justice system. With the counseling psychology emphasis on unconditional positive regard (Chapter 2) and training in multicultural issues and social justice advocacy (Chapter 3), counseling psychologists may be highly effective in providing services to this population. To be clear – in this section – we are not discussing the work of psychologists who specifically focus on understanding and predicting criminal behavior, like you may have seen on popular television shows like Criminal Minds (Davis & Messer, 2005). Here, we are referring to the counseling work that counseling psychologists do with incarcerated people in corrections settings. You can read more about someone who does this work, Dr. Ashlee Jayne, in Chapter 7, Counseling Psychologist Spotlight.

Settings for corrections work can include local jails as well as state and federal prisons. Working in corrections might include individual and group therapy, psychological assessments, crisis intervention, collaboration with integrated healthcare teams, and psychoeducation. Incarcerated persons have a disproportionate rate of mental health disorders, with twice the rate of mental illness compared to the general population (National Alliance on Mental Illness, 2025). There are many reasons for this that are beyond the scope of this chapter, but these high rates can be attributed to: (a) the fact that many services and resources for people with serious mental illnesses were defunded in the 1970s–1980s and (b) there are harsh consequences for people who use illicit substances (Shivy & Guion, 2012).

One specific concern that arises for this population is suicide prevention. Between 2001 and 2019, suicide rates rose significantly and accounted for 5–8% of deaths in state and federal facilities and 24–35% in local jails (Carson, 2021). In local jails, more than half of suicides occur within the first 30 days of incarceration; in state and federal facilities, most occur after the first year of incarceration (Carson, 2021). Although the mental health issues that incarcerated people present with can be complex and challenging, counseling psychologists who work in corrections often find the work gratifying (Stringer, 2020). Sometimes, because clients have never received mental health services previously, they make quick progress and improvement. Other times, psychologists are able to use their expertise to reduce anxiety and stress (Stringer, 2020) or improve policies and the systems in which incarcerated people live.

Some psychologists in training can find working with people in correctional facilities to be particularly difficult or daunting. Let's do a quick check-in: As a mental health professional, do you think you could ever work with people who are incarcerated? Why or why not? What biases might you hold about this population? Are there certain groups that might be easier or harder for you to work with (for example, incarcerated youth, pregnant women who are incarcerated, or people who have committed assault)?

Indian/Tribal Health Care

One group that experiences serious mental health disparities is North American Indian, Alaska Native, and Indigenous peoples. You will probably notice that people use a lot of different terms to refer to this population such as First Nations, American Indian, and so on. As we pointed out in Chapter 3, words matter and we encourage readers to consult the (APA) Inclusive Language Guide (2023). Wherever possible, such as in clinical notes and research, it is best to refer to a client or person's specific tribal affiliation or heritage because customs, experiences, stories, and cultures can vary widely between tribes or Nations. Lumping all tribes or Nations together can obscure those key differences.

North American Indian and Alaskan Native (AI/AN) populations report the highest rates of suicide among all racial groups in the United States (Centers for Disease Control, 2022). Considering the smaller number of AI/AN people in the United States comparatively, this statistic is particularly disturbing. Other mental health issues include PTSD, violence, and substance abuse (Indian Health Service, 2023). Counseling psychologists may work with Native American clients in any of the settings we mention here, as well as through tribal mental health facilities. For example, the Indian Health Services (IHS) has mental health services representing the wide range of counseling services, including assessment, individual and family therapy, crisis intervention, prevention, and outreach (IHS, 2023).

There are also local tribal facilities, such as Citizen Potawatomi Nation Behavioral Health Services in Shawnee, Oklahoma, or the Stillaguamish Tribe of Indians Behavioral Health Programs in Arlington, Washington. Services might include individual, couples/family, and group counseling; psychological assessments; substance abuse treatment; smoking cessation classes and support groups; prevention, outreach, and education programs; psychiatric care; and culturally focused groups. Work in Indian or Tribal Health systems requires specialized training in culturally appropriate and competent practices and care. Almost all of the models and theories typically used by counseling psychologists are based on Western, individualist perspectives rather than Indigenous ones that might be more collectivist (Stringer, 2023).

A message frequently seen in Indigenous health is the notion that "culture is medicine," or that strong cultural ties promote better mental health and physical health, so counseling psychologists who work with AI/AN peoples should be open to learning how to integrate cultural beliefs and traditions into their work (Morse & Lomay, 2021; Stringer, 2023). They must also recognize the historical harm that psychologists and other healthcare providers have done to Indigenous populations (Stringer, 2023). Depending on where you live, you may or may not be near an established tribal nation. In the United States, there are 574 federally recognized Indian tribes, many of which are concentrated in Alaska, California, and Oklahoma (Schwartz, 2024). Use your favorite search engine to locate any tribal health services near you – how far would you need to travel? How familiar are you with American Indian/Alaska Native history, rights, sovereignty, and current issues? How can you learn more? We encourage you to learn more and consider ways you might advocate for greater awareness of AI/NA mental health issues.

Private Practice

There are many psychologists who enjoy working in private practice. Private practice might automatically make you think "alone" or "just one psychologist in their own office," but some private practice psychologists work in groups at group practices. In fact, more psychologists work in private practice (59%) than in any other setting (APA, 2022). Check out the Counseling Psychologist Spotlight in Chapter 12 that highlights two people in private practice, Dr. Sandra Eng and Dr. Michelle Trotter-Mathison.

Counseling psychologists who want to work in private practice usually have to acquire experience before jumping into independent practice because private practice work not only requires counseling skills but also business skills such as marketing, finances/accounting, and business law (DeAngelis, 2011). As you might guess, most business and accounting skills are not a focus of graduate psychology programs. Given this gap in training, the APA has some great resources for people in private practice on its website, including continuing education resources, tips for business management, and new trends in technology (APA, 2025b).

There is also an APA Division, 42, for Psychologists in Independent Practice, which offers benefits like one-on-one mentoring services, networking and social gatherings, webinars, and special interest online forums (Psychologists in Independent Practice, 2025). Counseling psychologists who work in private practice generally enjoy the flexibility and autonomy it offers:

- They can specialize in certain areas such as anxiety disorders, nutrition and exercise, or neurodivergence
- They can utilize a wide range of treatments such as Acceptance and Commitment Therapy or Dialectical Behavioral Therapy and other therapies we discussed in Chapter 6
- They determine their own work hours, such as working only four days a week or only in the afternoon, and develop their own schedules such as which vacation days they take each year

As you can see, there is a lot of freedom and autonomy involved in private practice, but that flexibility also comes with some limitations. Rather than being paid sick days or a salary by a business, in an independent practice, your income is tied to your work hours/days. If you become ill and need to cancel clients one day, or if you want to take a vacation, that means loss of income, so it takes careful planning. Independent practitioners also have to cover their own work benefits such as health insurance coverage fees, liability insurance coverage, continuing education, and so on. In addition to financial demands, working independently can sometimes have emotional costs such as a sense of isolation. Working in a joint/group private practice and participating in a regular peer consultation group can sometimes improve these issues.

Community Agencies

Community-based agencies offer counseling psychologists the opportunity to work with a wide range of vulnerable populations, including survivors of interpersonal violence or domestic violence, victims of sexual assault, youth, LGBTQ+ people, refugees and asylees, and homeless persons. Similar to counseling psychologists in other settings, they may provide individual, couples, family, or group therapy. There are also some unique services that they may offer in these settings, such as:

- Community-based outreach, psychoeducation, and prevention;
- Crisis intervention, especially for people experiencing acute stress after a traumatic event;
- Trauma-informed care;
- Suicide prevention, intervention;
- And advocacy and policy work.

In community-based work, counseling psychologists may also engage in some case management, or helping clients find resources to help with housing, food, or financial assistance with paying bills.

Counseling psychologists may work closely with social workers, master's-level therapists, nurses, sexual assault nurse examiners, victim advocates, law enforcement, and Court Appointed Special

Advocates (volunteers) assigned to children. These agencies are almost always local, nonprofit organizations, so counseling psychologists may assist with needs assessments, program evaluation, community-based participatory research, or writing grants or development work (fundraising). It is especially important for counseling psychologists in these settings to have a strong understanding of the role of sociocultural factors on mental health and well-being; clients who utilize community-based services often have lower incomes than those who might utilize private services (Shin et al., 2013). Counseling psychologists may also need specialized training in substance abuse treatment and trauma-informed care. In this kind of setting, counseling psychologists must also attend closely to their own experiences: working with people who have severe trauma and higher clinical complexity can contribute to vicarious stress and burnout (Katsounari, 2015; Killian, 2008).

Sport Psychology

In this chapter, our Counseling Psychologist Spotlight introduces Dr. Jesse Steinfeldt, a Sport Psychologist, and talks about the kind of work he does. Sport and performance psychologists work with athletes in a wide range of sports and settings – from amateur athletes, to four-year colleges, to professional sports, to the Olympics – and from race-car driving to equestrian sports to softball. They generally focus on clinical work with athletes. For example, a sport psychologist at a university might offer student athletes individual therapy or crisis intervention. They may offer training or psychoeducation about conflict resolution, coping strategies, relaxation techniques, and stress management. They may use tools like biofeedback to teach athletes how to recognize signals in their bodies indicating stress or anxiety.

Some of the most common mental health concerns for athletes are eating disorders/disordered eating, depression and suicide, anxiety and stress, overtraining, sleep disorders, and attention-deficit/hyperactivity disorder (Chang et al., 2020). One of the biggest issues that sport psychologists might encounter is mental health stigma, so they might also work with coaches to destigmatize therapy and to educate them about ways they can promote psychological well-being in their athletes. Another challenge might be maintaining athlete confidentiality while coaches press the sport psychologist to tell them about what is going on for the athlete. The National Collegiate Athletic Association (NCAA) developed guidelines on best practices to support student athlete mental health (NCAA, 2024). These include:

- Create healthy environments that support mental health and well-being. A plan should be created in collaboration with a licensed mental health provider and should incorporate diversity, equity, and inclusion aspects.
- There should be procedures in place for identification of student-athletes with mental health symptoms and disorders, including mental health screening tools. Screening tools should be high-quality and used in collaboration with the licensed health and/or mental health provider. Students should be screened for psychological distress at least annually.
- There should be mental health action plans that outline referral pathways of student-athletes to qualified providers. These plans should be in place for routine and emergency mental healthcare needs.
- Mental health providers who oversee and manage mental health care for student-athletes must be appropriately licensed (NCAA, 2024).

These guidelines assist counseling psychologists who work with athletes in colleges or universities to provide high-quality services.

Summary

At the beginning of this chapter, we asked you to think about where you think counseling psychologists work. We then introduced you to a wide range of settings where counseling psychologists work, and a lot of different populations that they serve. We hope we brought to life the diverse types of activities that counseling psychologists do on a daily basis. Now that you are more familiar with the kinds of settings in which counseling psychologists can work, consider these questions. Again, even if you are not a helping professional in the future, perhaps you want to engage in some kind of volunteer work and service to people in your community. What kind of environment might you be interested in? Are there settings or groups that you think would not be a good fit for you? Why? What kind of special population or group are you interested in working with or learning more about? What skills and strengths do you have that would serve you well in that work? What are some growth edges or areas you'd need more training in? Next, we move on to the final chapter, which is really written for people who are considering a career as a counseling psychologist or other helping professional.

What Would You Do?

You are a college student interning at a local youth agency. As part of the internship, you work in a high school setting with the school counselor several hours a week. Often, this falls over the lunch hour. You notice a student who frequently sits alone in the cafeteria. You ask a teacher who you know about this student, and he says that actually he's been thinking about referring this student to the youth agency for counseling services because he's been worried about how isolated the student seems to be. He tells you the student lives with his father, who works two jobs. The student is not involved in any extracurricular activities. The school counselor encourages you to visit with the student. Over time, you sit down and chat with the student once or twice a week and the student starts to open up to you. He shares that he has been feeling low and has not had much energy. Based on your bystander intervention training, you ask the student if he is thinking about suicide. He responds, "well doesn't everyone?" He goes on to share with you that he has slowly, over the past year or so, been sneaking sleeping pills from his father's prescriptions. He said he "thinks he has enough now" but is "not really sure" if or when he would take them. You consult with the school counselor and your supervisor at the youth agency, and they ask you to reach out to the father. When you call the father, he says his son is just "looking for attention" and that he is too busy to come in to talk with you; he is not able to take time off of his job in the middle of the day.

- What steps do you think you can take to support this student at this point?
- What special settings/services do you think this student could benefit from?
- What evidence contradicts the student's father's perception that the student is attention-seeking?
- What additional information might you need to know in order to connect this student with effective resources and treatment options?

Counseling Psychologist Spotlight: Sport Psychologist

Dr. Jesse Steinfeldt

Dr. Jesse Steinfeldt is a Professor of Counseling Psychology at Indiana University. Sport has had a huge influence on his life, and he appreciates that he can incorporate that into his clinical and professional life. He has been a college athlete, a professional athlete, and has sons who played

Dr. Jesse Steinfeldt at the Indiana University football stadium. Photograph by author.

college football – all these personal experiences with sport have allowed him to continue to be "that little boy chasing a ball, while still maintaining the sophistication of a doctor helping others chase that proverbial ball." Jesse says he gets to have "professional duality" because he is both a Professor and a Psychologist. In his professor role, he gets to teach, conduct research, coordinate clinical training, provide clinical supervision, consult with athletic administrators, create classes and practicum opportunities, and do a host of "professorly" things. But he also loves seeing clients in his private practice, which includes Olympic athletes, college athletes, and high school and middle-school athletes. They work with Jesse on a host of presenting issues, from grief to anxiety and mood disorders, as well as a range of performance issues from emotional regulation to visualization and focus and everything in between. He said:

> I love working with athletes to address mental health and performance enhancement. I love touching excellence and helping clients maximize their potential. I love working with teams. I love to be an empowering force in the shadows behind the athletes who do great things on the court. I love that my job allows me to do ALL of these things, and no two days look alike. I love that I have plurality of roles and responsibilities, which bring me in the company of amazing people.

He said that a colleague has a mantra, "Doing cool stuff with cool folks" which aligns with Jesse's outlook on his work.

As a professor, Jesse said that one of his favorite experiences is hooding doctoral students at graduation, helping them achieve their dreams. He also enjoys the moment when he gets to extend an offer to an applying graduate student, knowing that it will take a lot of hard work but, ultimately, he and the student will get to that stage in their doctoral robes, and he played a part in them achieving their professional and personal goals. He loves working with students and the energy they bring. He describes himself as an accommodating and student-centered professor...but one of the things that is challenging for him is students who are unmotivated. He said it's particularly hard when a student doesn't participate in class or do many of the assignments, then reaches out to him in the last week of class to ask what they can do to get an A. Unfortunately, the student missed their chance by that point. So, his message for undergrads is: Faculty are aware that college is hard. Professors know that you have lots of distractions that might feel like a better use of your time. And he encourages you to explore lots of alternative ways to learn about yourself. But soak up the learning opportunities. Do your work. Be responsible, be accountable, and embrace the great learning opportunities in front of you – the reward is in the process, not the outcome or grade.

When we asked Jesse about his background and training in counseling psychology, he said he loves the multiple ways that counseling psychology allows him to help people. He loves training doctoral students and teaching undergraduates. He gets to conduct research that is both empirically sound and clinically relevant. He loves that the field of counseling psychology embraces a strengths-based perspective which aligns directly with Sport and Performance Psychology, allowing him to have a positive impact on the lives of the clients he works with and the students he trains to work with their own clients.

Jesse stays very active in his community. In addition to being Dr. Steinfeldt, he is also Coach Jesse. He has coached youth baseball, middle-school basketball, and high school football. His teams have won multiple state championships, but he says the greatest rewards are in the ways he is able to positively impact the developmental trajectory of so many young people in his community. Jesse also stays involved in professional organizations. He is a Fellow of the American Psychological Association, an honor acknowledging his achieved expertise among his professional peers. He is a member of APA Divisions 51 (Society for the Psychology of Men and Masculinities), 17 (Society of Counseling Psychology), and 47 (Society for Sport, Exercise, and Performance Psychology). He is also a member of CCSPA (Clinical/Counseling Sport Psychology Association) and AASP (Association for Applied Sport Psychology), reflecting his commitment to these fun areas of the field.

Outside of work, Jesse is an avid noon-hour hoops player. He describes his game as "much more horizontal than vertical these days," but he loves to play. He also joins a regular faculty/staff game, in addition to "Old Man Basketball" on Sunday nights. He enjoys the camaraderie, the competitiveness, and the ability to exercise and stay healthy in his advancing years (his words, not ours). He also likes riding his bike around town with his wife, going to Indiana University sporting events, and stopping at a local pub on summer weekday nights, watching sports, and enjoying the company of his wife. Jesse graduated from the counseling psychology program at the University of Wisconsin-Milwaukee. He holds a master's in Sport Psychology from the University of Iowa. He is a Certified Mental Performance Consultant, which you can learn more about on the AASP website.

References

American Psychological Association. (2015). *Standards of accreditation for health service psychology and accreditation operating procedures*. American Psychological Association. https://www.apa.org/ed/accreditation/standards-of-accreditation.pdf

American Psychological Association. (2022). *2021 survey of health service psychologists: Technical report*. https://www.apa.org/workforce/publications/health-service-psychologists-survey/full-technical-report.pdf

American Psychological Association. (2023). *Inclusive language guide* (2nd ed.). https://www.apa.org/about/apa/equity-diversity-inclusion/language-guidelines.pdf

American Psychological Association. (2025a). *Health psychology promotes wellness*. American Psychological Association. https://www.apa.org/education-career/guide/subfields/health

American Psychological Association. (2025b). *Practice management*. American Psychological Association. https://www.apa.org/research-practice/practice-management

Carson, E. A. (2021). *Suicide in local jails and state and federal prisons, 2000–2019 – Statistical tables*. U.S. Department of Justice. https://bjs.ojp.gov/sites/g/files/xyckuh236/files/media/document/sljsfp0019st.pdf

Center for Collegiate Mental Health (CCMH). (2024). *2024 annual report*. https://ccmh.psu.edu/assets/docs/CCMH%202024%20Annual%20Report.pdf

Chang, C. J., Putukian, M., Aerni, G., Diamond, A. B., Hong, E. S., Ingram, Y. M., Reardon, C. L., & Wolanin, A. T. (2020). Mental health issues and psychological factors in athletes: Detection, management, effect on performance, and prevention: American Medical Society for Sports Medicine position statement. *Clinical Journal of Sport Medicine, 30*(2), 61–87. https://doi.org/10.1097/JSM.0000000000000817

Cooper, S. E., Newman, J. L., & Fuqua, D. R. (2012). Counseling psychologists as consultants. In N. A. Fouad, J. A. Carter & L. M. Subich (Eds.), *APA handbook of counseling psychology: Vol. 2. Practice, interventions, and applications* (pp. 515–539). American Psychological Association. https://doi.org/10.1037/13755-000

Davis, J., & Messer, E. (2005–present). *Criminal minds* [TV series]. Lionsgate Television; Erica Messer Productions; 20th Television; CBS Studios.

DeAngelis, T. (2011, November). Are you really ready for private practice? *GradPSYCH Magazine*. https://www.apa.org/gradpsych/2011/11/private-practice

Fuqua, D. R., & Newman, J. L. (2009). Consultation as a moral process. *Consulting Psychology Journal: Practice and Research, 61*(2), 136–146. https://doi.org/10.1037/a0015496

Indian Health Service. (2023). *Behavioral health fact sheet*. https://www.ihs.gov/newsroom/factsheets/behavioralhealth/

Kafka, A. C. (2024, August 23). Fighting the mental-health crisis narrative. *The Chronicle of Higher Education*. https://www.chronicle.com/article/fighting-the-mental-health-crisis-narrative?sra=true

Katsounari, I. (2015). The road less traveled and beyond: Working with severe trauma and preventing burnout. *Burnout Research, 2*(4), 115–117. https://doi.org/10.1016/j.burn.2015.10.002

Killian, K. D. (2008). Helping till it hurts? A multimethod study of compassion fatigue, burnout, and self-care in clinicians working with trauma survivors. *Traumatology, 14*(2), 32–44. https://doi.org/10.1177/1534765608319083

Mission Roll Call. (2024). *The state of veterans' mental health (2024)*. https://missionrollcall.org/veteran-voices/articles/the-state-of-veterans-mental-health/

Morse, G. S., & Lomay, V. T. (2021). *Understanding Indigenous perspectives*. Cognella.

National Alliance on Mental Illness. (2025). *Mental health treatment while incarcerated: NAMI public policy position*. https://www.nami.org/wp-content/uploads/2023/07/Mental-Health-Treatment-While-Incarcerated_final.pdf

National Collegiate Athletic Association. (2024). *Mental health best practices: Understanding and supporting student-athlete mental health*. https://ncaaorg.s3.amazonaws.com/ssi/mental/SSI_MentalHealthBestPractices.pdf

Psychologists in Independent Practice. (2025). *The community for psychologists in independent practice*. https://division42.org/

Schreier, B. A., Anderson, C. L., Galligan, P. K., Greenbaum, B., Corkery, J., Schnelle, T., Gates, C., Hong, J. E., & Kivlighan, D. M. (2021). Embedded therapists: Who do they serve? How are they funded? And where are they housed? A foundational survey of emerging models. *Journal of College Student Psychotherapy, 37*(2), 144–154. https://doi.org/10.1080/87568225.2021.1913686

Schwartz, M. A. (2024). *The 574 federally recognized Indian tribes in the United States*. Library of Congress. https://www.congress.gov/crs-product/R47414

Shin, P., Sharac, J., & Mauery, D. R. (2013). The role of community health centers in providing behavioral health care. *Journal of Behavioral Health Services & Research, 40*(4), 488–496. https://doi.org/10.1007/s11414-013-9353-z

Shivy, V. A., & Guion, D. B. (2012). Forensics and the legal system. In N. A. Fouad, J. A. Carter & L. M. Subich (Eds.), *APA handbook of counseling psychology: Vol. 2. Practice, interventions, and applications* (pp. 393–415). American Psychological Association. https://doi.org/10.1037/13755-000

Society of Counseling Psychology. (2025). *College & university counseling centers*. https://www.div17.org/college---university-counseling-centers

Society for Health Psychology. (2023). *What is health psychology?* https://societyforhealthpsychology.org/about/what-is-health-psychology/

Society for Military Psychology. (2025). *Society for Military Psychology, Division 19*. https://www.militarypsych.org/

Stringer, H. (2020). Careers in corrections. *Monitor on Psychology, 51*(2), 62–66. https://www.apa.org/monitor/2020/03/careers-corrections

Stringer, H. (2023). The healing power of Native American culture is inspiring psychologists to embrace cultural humility. *Monitor on Psychology, 54*(7), 39–43. https://www.apa.org/monitor/2023/10/healing-tribal-communities-native-americans

U.S. Department of Defense. (2023). *2023 demographics profile: Total defense department military community*. U.S. Department of Defense. https://download.militaryonesource.mil/12038/MOS/Infographic/2023-demographics-total-dod-military-community.pdf

U.S. Department of Veterans Affairs, Office of Mental Health and Suicide Prevention. (2023). *National veteran suicide prevention annual report*. https://www.mentalhealth.va.gov/docs/data-sheets/2023/2023-National-Veteran-Suicide-Prevention-Annual-Report-FINAL-508.pdf

Wahass, S. H. (2005). The role of psychologists in health care delivery. *Journal of Family & Community Medicine, 12*(2), 63–70.

Chapter 15

So, You Want to Be a Counseling Psychologist?

It's the Last Chapter! But Just the Beginning...

Wow! You made it to the last chapter of this book! Good for you for hanging in there with us. We hope you are even more excited about the possibility of pursuing a career in the mental health field. And if not, we still hope this chapter has some useful information for you. Before we jump in, please take a moment to jot down some questions you still have about counseling psychology: the training, the work itself, the potential pay, and benefits, anything!

This is the chapter you have all been waiting for! In the sections that follow, we offer advice for students who plan to pursue a career in counseling psychology such as undergraduate classes that are helpful to prepare for graduate school and experiences that will boost an application. Counseling psychology programs may look for different qualities and experiences than other psychology graduate programs do, based on the core values described earlier in this book (importance of cultural context, human development, positive psychology, and inclusion of career issues). You will also learn about how to find a program that is a good fit for you. We outline typical program requirements such as coursework, practicum, research or dissertation expectations, comprehensive exams, work with an advisor, service, advocacy or community engagement, and predoctoral internship. We introduce the concept of supervision and the role it plays in training and describe the role of the American Psychological Association's (APA's) Commission on Accreditation and competencies. We also introduce post-graduation experiences, such as postdoctoral fellowships, exams for licensure, and other requirements for licensure.

Hopefully, now that you are wrapping up reading this text, you have some sense of whether a career in counseling psychology or another mental health/helping field is right for you. Perhaps you engaged in some self-reflection and realized that although you love interacting with children, you don't want to specialize in work with children. Or perhaps you think you have what it takes to work with people in crisis and want to make that a specialty. If you are considering furthering your career and applying to graduate programs, we hope this chapter will be helpful for you. And if you are not one of those folks, perhaps you are an engineering or pre-med or business major, we still hope you will find some useful information in this chapter.

What Kind of Program?

If you are thinking about pursuing a degree after your bachelor's, the first and most important step you need to take is to determine what kind of field you feel drawn to and whether you want to pursue a master's degree or a doctorate. For example, you can work with children as a child life specialist, clinical child psychologist, school counselor, clinical mental health counselor, school

DOI: 10.4324/9781003439899-15

social worker, diagnostician, or school psychologist. All of these require different kinds of training programs and different degrees, and although some of the work might look similar, the settings and underlying philosophies are different. It is important for you to do some research on the different fields, training programs, and licensure requirements in your state. Likewise, if you plan to apply for a doctoral program, you should do some research beyond what this text offers on the differences between school psychology, clinical psychology, counseling psychology, or other types of programs. A helpful resource could be the website for the APA. Many of these fields are represented by their own APA divisions and you can find more information about a specialization area on the associated division webpage (see APA, 2025).

Something students do not always know is that every graduate program has its own unique focus or culture, which is really important to understand as you consider your educational goals and as you write your personal statement. Program websites have a wealth of information if you look closely. Usually on a program website, there will be a paragraph describing the focus of the program, unique aspects or concentrations, and other informative descriptions about the program. We recommend you pay close attention to these descriptions because the faculty in these programs spend a lot of time crafting the exact wording they want to convey the culture of the program.

Although they may seem similar at first, if one program mentions that they focus on "underserved populations, trauma, and resilience," then you need to consider whether that is what you want to focus on in your training and future career. You might ask yourself, "Is that focus a good fit for me?" If you decide to move forward with applying to the program, it will be extremely important in your personal statement for you to say something about your interest in building resilience and addressing trauma in underserved populations. If a program says that they "provide close supervision to help students build intervention skills," consider if that is a good fit for you. Do you enjoy close supervision and mentorship? If so, it will be important for you to say something about your interest in receiving supervision and mentoring to improve your counseling intervention skills. Programs work hard to build a unique focus and culture, and sometimes faculty recognize right away that an applicant is not familiar with the program or that an applicant has written a generic statement that they have sent out to multiple programs. Even if you are just tweaking a couple of sentences, the program wants to know that you are familiar with their particular program.

There are two kinds of counseling psychology doctorates: A PhD and a PsyD. The main difference is that with a PhD, programs usually focus on a balance between the scientist and practitioner – in other words, you will be expected to do research as well as practice. With a PsyD program, you may do a little research but the main focus will be on practice. This will shape how you spend your time in your program: the courses you might be required to take, expectations for research publications or presentations outside of coursework, and so on. If you are applying to programs that require a research component such as master's programs with a thesis or PhD (and some PsyD) programs, you should think about whether research is something that appeals to you or if you just want to practice. If you do want to learn about research, it might also be important for you to mention what your research interests are and what faculty member (or members, depending on the culture of the program) you are interested in working with.

Note that in some traditional doctoral programs, faculty "take" students into their "labs," and individual faculty may make decisions about whether or not a student is admitted to a program. In this model, the student will work very closely with the individual faculty member on their research. This model is what most clinical psychology programs and some counseling psychology programs use. But counseling psychology programs also sometimes use a different model: the faculty work together as a group to admit students to the program based on overall goodness of fit. In those programs, students may be assigned a temporary advisor and may make advising decisions later or they may be assigned an advisor upon admission. Research is still a requirement, but there may be more flexibility and collaboration among faculty and students. For example, two faculty members might co-lead a research team with students from multiple different advisors. So before you email individual faculty asking if they are "taking" students for the following year, you might check to make sure what kind of model the program has.

Accreditation

There are a lot of different accrediting bodies in the helping professions, at the master's and doctoral levels that regulate and require high-quality curriculum. Because accreditation requires the same specific standards across states, programs that are accredited may also be a good idea if you plan to move to another state in the future. We refer to this as *portability*. For example, let's say you attended an accredited program in Missouri, got licensed there, and practiced for a few years. Then, you decided you should move home to Illinois to be closer to your aging parents. It will be much easier later for you to secure licensure in Illinois than if you attended a non-accredited program. Not all states require accreditation for you to become a licensed professional, but some do, and attending an accredited program helps ease this process. It also ensures that you will be attending a program with rigorous standards and training, because accrediting bodies pay close attention to things like the faculty-student ratio, the kinds of practicum experiences that are available, the quality of courses, the training of faculty, and their competence to teach certain classes, and so on.

Depending on the field you are interested in, the accrediting body will be different. Here are some of the common accreditation agencies in the helping fields. Their websites usually offer a

Table 15.1 Selected accreditors of mental health training programs

Accrediting Body	*Website*	*Programs They Accredit*
American Psychological Association Commission on Accreditation	https://accreditation.apa.org/accredited-programs	Masters-level Health Service Psychology* PhD-level Counseling Psychology, Clinical Psychology, School Psychology
Council for Accreditation of Counseling and Related Educational Programs	https://www.cacrep.org/directory/	Masters-level Clinical Mental Health Counseling, Rehabilitation Counseling, School Counseling PhD-level Counselor Education
Council on Social Work Education	https://www.cswe.org/accreditation/about/directory/	Social Work
Masters in Psychology and Counseling Accreditation Council	https://mpcacaccreditation.org/	Masters-level Counseling and Psychological Services
National Association of School Psychologists	https://apps.nasponline.org/standards-and-certification/graduate-program-approval-and-accreditation/approved-accredited.aspx	School Psychology

* This accreditation by APA of master's programs is very new so there are only a couple of accredited programs currently.

directory where you can filter searches, such as a search for clinical mental health programs that have been accredited at least 12 years in the state of Massachusetts (Table 15.1).

Application Materials

You might be wondering what you have to pull together for an application to a graduate program. Traditionally, an application consists of a GRE score (which many programs are not requiring anymore so you should check their websites for their specific requirements), transcripts from undergraduate or graduate programs, a resume or CV, a personal statement, and letters of recommendation. We will discuss the resume/CV, personal statement, and letters of recommendation below. Across all of your materials, we encourage you to be as detail-oriented as possible. When a program receives 80–100 applications for perhaps an incoming class of 10–20, things like typos, misspellings, and inconsistencies can be more problematic because the environment is so competitive. For example, if you talk about how much you love a faculty member's work, you've read articles by them, and want to work with them, but you misspell a faculty member's name, this could cause a disconnect and cause the review committee to wonder if you are really familiar with the faculty member's work. If you tend to be someone who has a hard time with small details, you might consider having a friend who is detail-oriented to take a look at your materials before you submit them. (We do not currently recommend running these through Artificial Intelligence programs, as they could actually introduce more errors or stiff, odd language).

CV versus Resume

Applying to a graduate program may be the first time you have heard that there is a difference between a *curriculum vitae* (also referred to as a *vita*, or CV) and a resume. You are probably familiar with a resume, which is usually about one page and lists the most important or relevant experiences you've had when applying for a job. A CV is something that is usually used in academic settings. One difference is that a CV is a *list* of all of your experiences, so there is no expected page limit. A faculty member might have a CV that is 50 pages, for example! There is no expectation that your CV will be long, but it is important to note that you do not have to limit it to one page, regardless of what advice you are given about formatting a resume (a CV is different).

Also, generally, people use some creative formatting with a resume, whereas a CV is pretty direct and perhaps slightly boring in that sense. It would be strange to see any kind of creative formatting (lines, bars, color font, interesting designs, and so on) on a CV. We are pointing this out because we often see students choosing not to include important experiences because they are trying to fit into a one-page limit. Look closely at your program's requirements: It likely says a CV or resume and likely does not have a page limit. Reviewing the CVs of other graduate students can be helpful, especially since faculty CVs tend to be much longer and may not align well with applicants' experiences. If you have a friend or know someone who has already been accepted into a graduate program, it could be useful to ask if they're willing to share their CV as a reference. You may also look for online resources such as blogs and YouTube channels that could be helpful. For example, Dr. Joseph Hammer (n.d.) at the University of Kentucky has a great blog with some information about graduate programs.

There are things you should include, things you should not include, and things you should avoid on a CV. This helpful table breaks down some key elements for you to consider as you create or update your CV (Table 15.2).

When we review students' CVs, we frequently see them omitting important experiences. For example, Julie recently asked a student, "Wait, I don't see your work at the coffee shop here. Why

Table 15.2 Elements of a CV

Include		**Do Not Include**	
Section/Heading	*Content*	*Section/Heading*	*Content*
Contact Information	Name, email address	Personal Information	Personal address, phone number*, photo**
Education	Major, minor, certificates, GPA, special coursework	High School Experiences	Anything from high school
Research	Publications, presentations, lab experiences	Abbreviations	Acronyms, slang, or informal phrases (LOL, BTW, WFH)
Work History	Office work, management experiences, work as a teaching assistant	Large Blocks of Text	Long paragraphs (use bulleted lists instead)
Volunteer Experiences	Shadowing a mental health provider, leadership positions	Inconsistent Formatting	Dates in different places, random use of italics
Skills and Awards	Language spoken, statistical software and programs used, awards received	Inconsistent Wording	Switching between present and past tense (just pick one and stick to it)

Note. *Programs may ask for personal information like your address or phone number in your application, but later in your career, you may post your CV online and including personal information on your CV will make it publicly available. ** In the United States, it is not typical or ideal to include a headshot on a CV.

aren't you listing it?" The student felt like because it wasn't in the helping professions, it wasn't relevant enough to include. You absolutely should include any experience like this. If we see an applicant who has worked in a coffee shop for three years, for example, we can surmise the following: the applicant is responsible and dependable; has strong interpersonal skills (likely with difficult customers and with co-workers); is not afraid to do hard work (they probably have had to do dishes, clean a bathroom, deal with old milk, etc.).

If we see an applicant who has worked at a summer camp for the past couple of summers, we can surmise that they work well with children as well as parents and likely have had to complete some trainings such as CPR/First Aid, mandatory reporter trainings, or crisis response. Keeping in mind that helping professions and counseling psychology programs focus on human interactions and interpersonal skills, it is good for admissions committees to see that you have at least some experience working with humans, either in a job or through volunteer work. Examples might be volunteering for a crisis phone line; working at a day care center; tutoring English Language Learners at your local public library or a job as a receptionist at a healthcare center.

The Personal Statement

Most graduate programs pay special attention to the personal statement and resume/CV. As we mentioned earlier, it is important for you to know yourself and know the program that you are applying to. It will make no sense if your statement says you want to focus on trauma, recovery, and addiction if the program you are applying to does not offer this emphasis. Try to match some of the language that the program presents in its materials with what you say in your statement.

You may also wonder what to include in the "personal statement." Usually, the instructions for this are very broad or vague: "Write a statement of interest in the program." So how are you supposed to even approach that? It is important that your personal statement allows the folks overseeing admissions to get to know you, for example, through telling a story or sharing illustrations of how you experienced something. However, we caution you against rambling – your statement should be concise and well-organized. It should have a logical flow to it that the faculty readers can follow. For example, if your personal statement is two pages, you could organize it this way:

- Paragraph 1: Begin with a fun fact about you that explains why you are interested in a graduate education in counseling psychology.
- Paragraph 2: Relate that fun fact to your specific interests in the counseling psychology field (and make sure those interests make sense with the program you are applying to).
- Paragraph 3: Further expand on your interests in counseling psychology and what you hope to accomplish as a future counseling psychologist.
- Paragraph 4: Relate those interests and goals to the program to which you plan to submit the essay (and name specific faculty you would like to work with if possible).
- Paragraph 5: Revisit your fun fact and tie it all together.

It is important to give readers of your personal essay a sense of who you are and what you would be like to work with, but we caution you against sharing information that might be highly personal or flag concerns about your ability to complete the program. Admissions committees are looking for how you might handle the rigor of a strenuous academic program, how you might get along with peers, staff, and instructors, whether you will be able to follow through on commitments, what your approach to work at a practicum site might be like, and so on. We are not saying you cannot disclose any mental health issues if you think those are important to share regarding your development; however, more recently, we sometimes see students sharing personal traumas in ways that raise faculty concerns about their stress levels, especially given the already stressful environment of graduate school. Additionally, statements made in an unprofessional manner may raise concerns about a student's ability to communicate and collaborate effectively with colleagues. The faculty may wonder what you will carry with you into the program and how this could affect your work with clients, ability to get along with others, and persistence in the program. Think about what you might like future instructors and supervisors to know about you, as opposed to what you would want your therapist to know about you.

Letters of Recommendation

Applicants often worry about their letters of recommendation. Questions whirl through their heads like: Who should I ask? What if my professors don't remember me? If you are fairly early in your academic career (first year, sophomore, junior), we encourage you to be proactive about building working relationships with professors right away. Go to a professor's office hours if you can. Even

Table 15.3 Information to include in a letter request

Type of Program	*Program*	*Specialty*	*Deadline*	*Any Other Notes*
Master of Social Work	University #1	Veterans, military families	Jan 1	
MS Mental Health Counseling	University #1	Veterans	Feb 1	
MS Mental Health Counseling	University #2	Veterans	Feb 1	They have a trauma focus and do pet therapy training with veterans!

things like sitting toward the front of a lecture hall, asking questions, making eye contact throughout class, and being engaged will allow a professor to get to know you and remember you better. If you are a senior or have already graduated and feel like it is too late to build a relationship with a professor, it still does not hurt to ask.

Some professors have a very specific method that they want students/applicants to use to request a letter, so it is important to ask about that. The more information you can provide the professor with, the better. You can even attach your CV to your request if you have it ready and on hand. You might remind them – when you took the class, name of the class, where you sat, any interactions you had (formal or informal), what your major was, what you are doing now or have been doing since the class. If they agree, again it is helpful to provide them with a table, spreadsheet, or document with the type of degree(s) you're applying for, the programs, anything special you want them to highlight, and deadlines (see Table 15.3).

It is helpful for you to send a reminder about seven days prior to the deadline for any program if they have not submitted the letter yet.

When you ask for a recommendation, it can help to offer your prospective recommender some prompts:

> Dear Professor MacIntosh, I took your Intro to Counseling class in fall 2024. You may remember that I am into the local music scene, and you commented on my band t-shirts. We sometimes talked about music and bands that we both like. For one of my reflection papers, I wrote about how much it meant to me to hear from a guest speaker who works with veterans. My brother, mother, and father are veterans and I am hoping to work with that population as a mental health counselor in the future. Since graduation, I have been working for the police department on community outreach to our local homeless shelter and homeless population, many of whom are veterans. I am about to start applying to master's in counseling programs. I know I haven't been in touch for a while, but I am wondering if you might write a letter of recommendation for me? I can share my resume and a draft of my personal statement if that will help. Thank you so much for considering this request.

Other than former professors, you may wonder who else you can ask to write a letter of recommendation. We encourage you to consider asking a former teaching assistant to write a letter. Sometimes teaching assistants (TAs) know you better than the professor does. We have also seen TAs write a joint letter with the professor. We do *not* encourage you to ask a co-worker, boss, or friend of the family to write a letter. In our experience, these are the weakest letters. They tend to be extremely short and vague. Applicants sometimes think if they have a friend of the family who has a high-status position (such as senator, local politician, or celebrity), a letter from them will look good. We would much rather you ask for letters from people who know you well and know your potential for academic work.

If you must ask a supervisor/boss, we encourage you to emphasize with them that it should be at least a page long, should emphasize your program of study and skills you have to complete it, and perhaps offer good examples (for example, how you handled a difficult situation at summer camp with a family who forgot to pick their child up at the end of the day; how you took initiative to coordinate a fund-raiser in your office after a natural disaster). No matter who you ask, give your letter writers lots of time to complete the letter, and enter their information in the application portal with ample time – often, in addition to a letter, there are items the recommender has to respond to which take time. One of the biggest problems with applications is letter writers not getting them done in time, not completing the information the portal asks for, etc. Please be sure you give clear information to your letter writers and make sure they are folks who are conscientious and will get them completed in a timely manner. Otherwise, your application could be considered incomplete.

For Those Applying to Doctoral Programs

Now that we have reviewed the specific documents you will need to submit, you may have lingering, general questions about application logistics. We get a lot of questions about the application process in our roles as directors of training of counseling psychology doctoral programs. Here are inquiries we receive all the time. Please note that, although we offer some general answers, you may want to reach out to programs with questions if you want to know how they handle specific elements of the admissions process. Due to high volumes of applications, they may be slow to respond, so these frequently asked questions serve as a helpful guide when you are unable to get answers to pressing questions.

Question 1: Do I Have to Have a Master's before I Apply to Doctoral Programs?

It depends on the program. Some programs do require a master's degree; some require a bachelor's degree; and some accept applicants with either. It is important to note that it will likely take you longer to complete the degree if you enter with a bachelor's degree.

Question 2: Do I Have to Have a Ton of Research Experience to Get into a Doctoral Program or Competitive Research-Focused Master's Program?

Again, it depends on the program. PsyD programs may like to see that you have a little research experience but may not require professional publications or presentations, whereas more traditional PhD programs will like to see that you have some research under your belt and understand research processes.

Question 3: What Are Special Considerations if I'm an International Applicant?

There are a lot more hurdles for international applicants to jump through, and that is even more true if you are admitted and come to the United States or Canada. You must be familiar with testing requirements such as TOEFL as well as visa requirements. Most universities will have an office to support international students, and we recommend that you spend time perusing their websites.

Once admitted, international students in the United States have special requirements like Curricular Practical Training, and rules about where you can or cannot be employed. Also, some grants that faculty might have to fund students through graduate assistantships may be limited to US citizens, and some training sites (practicum/internship sites) require citizenship to practice there. All that being said, we are huge fans of international students and the beautiful diversity they bring to counseling psychology programs! There is an APA division on International Psychology, Division 52, and the Society for Counseling Psychology, Division 17, has a very active International Section – we encourage you to check out their websites.

Question 4: There Are So Many Programs Out There! Eek! How Do I Find One That Is Good for Me?

We recommend that you look for programs that are accredited by the APA; this information is on the APA Commission on Accreditation website and should be stated clearly on programs' websites. A good starting point is to think about what you are interested in researching or doing clinically. For example, if you are specifically interested in working with racial/ethnic minoritized children on career development and counseling, you could look for faculty who specialize in that area. Beyond that, however, you are also applying to a program, not just a single faculty member. Although lots of programs have a model where a single faculty member admits students into their lab, keep in mind that if that faculty member were to leave (because life happens), you might not be able to follow (it is extremely difficult to transfer to a new program as a doctoral student), so the program itself needs to be an overall fit. You should pay close attention to the culture of the program through its web materials; you can also reach out to faculty members or training directors (TDs) (keep in mind that these people are extremely busy and may not have time to look at your CV, read a long email, respond to emails from potential applicants, or meet with applicants); you could ask to be connected to one to two current doctoral students. In general, if you do reach out to faculty or current students, it is not helpful to ask questions if the information is readily available on the program's website already, so we recommend you do a little sleuthing before reaching out. It might be helpful to create a spreadsheet with tabs like "funding," "practicum opportunities," "length to completion," "specialty/focus areas," "deadline," and so on to keep you organized.

Question 5: What Is the Application Process Like?

Generally, you will submit your materials by the deadline. Depending on when the deadline is, you may hear back quickly, within a couple of weeks, or it could be much longer, for example, if the deadline falls right before winter break. Programs may or may not conduct interviews which may be in-person or may be via zoom. After this point, you may be offered admission outright, you may be rejected from the program outright, or you may be placed on a waitlist. There are some norms for doctoral programs in counseling psychology, such as they should notify you of your acceptance in writing by April 1, and you should make a decision by April 15. Further, you should not "hold" more than two offers for more than a week – this causes problems for other applicants and limits their offers. You can find the policy on admissions for counseling psychology programs through the Council of Counseling Psychology Training Programs.

Typical Doctoral Program Requirements

So you've applied and you are waiting to find out if you got into a graduate program. Let's imagine you get good news and accept an offer from a program. What's next? Every doctoral program differs so it is important to familiarize yourself with requirements as outlined through the university's catalog and the student handbook. In general, though, you can expect the following requirements.

Coursework

You will be required to take courses that fulfill the counseling psychology core area as well as what the APA Commission on Accreditation calls "Discipline Specific Knowledge" (DSK). DSKs are things that are important for professional psychologists to know and may include research, psychometrics, history of psychology, and courses that cover biological, emotional, and cognitive aspects of psychology. Your core counseling psychology courses may include things like ethics, counseling skills and theories, and practicum. Typically, counseling psychology doctoral programs have more coursework requirements than other doctoral programs (for example, in German Language Studies) because of the applied nature of our work as health providers and because of the rigorous requirements from the APA Commission on Accreditation.

Practicum

A practicum is like a field placement in some kind of agency where you work with clients under close supervision. It is a good idea to familiarize yourself with practicum sequences as you make decisions about where you want to apply and what program is ultimately the best fit for you. If you have a master's degree in an applied helping field (so, for example, mental health counseling, but not experimental psychology) and have already completed master's level training in work with clients (such as a supervised internship/practicum), your program may allow you to begin practicum and seeing clients your first semester. Others may want to assess your skills and interests for a year before allowing you to see clients. Most programs will require at least a year of coursework before starting students with a bachelor's degree in practicum. Your practicum experiences will lead to your predoctoral internship experience, which will ultimately lead you to your postdoctoral career, but we encourage you to explore and learn as much as possible through practicum experiences. These experiences usually are sequential and advance as you gain more knowledge. In other words, as a first-year student, you will likely not start off doing advanced psychological assessments in a VA Medical Setting. Rather, you might have one year of experience at a community mental health center, then a year at a university counseling center, then a year doing crisis and intake assessments at the university counseling center. What is important to know is that to apply for internship, students must have completed 450 direct contact hours (hours where you are directly working with a human being, not hours writing notes or learning a new software system). However, some internship sites have more stringent requirements; for example, it is not unusual for a site that specializes in assessment to require a student to have 1,000 hours prior to application. So it is important to balance being focused and thinking about what you want your internship site to look like, with also being open to learning and having a wide range of experiences.

Practicum Class

In your actual practicum, you can expect to provide perhaps 10–20 hours per week of service at some kind of mental health agency or site. You will likely also enroll in a practicum course, where you will present and discuss your clinical work in a group setting with your peers and a faculty member. Some of the course meeting time may be "didactic," meaning you are learning content, and other time may be "group supervision," meaning you are receiving supervision in a group format for your practicum work. You will also receive individual supervision at your practicum site. This means you have a supervisor who is licensed or a more advanced practitioner who is responsible for overseeing your work. For example, you are usually required to tape your sessions, and then you might review a portion of a session with your supervisor to see where your areas of strength or growth are. Supervision is a great way to improve your counseling skills and interventions. Many students are not aware of the role of supervision, but this is a huge component of counseling psychology doctoral training. In fact, one of the Division 17 sections is entirely focused on supervision and training. There are a variety of models and theories on supervision and best practices. Hopefully, you will be able to enroll in a supervision course yourself, where you will learn how to supervise trainees, and you may receive supervision of supervision (what we like to call "sup of sup"). For example, if you are a doctoral student supervising master's student trainees, you might receive supervision from a faculty member about how your supervision is going!

Research

If you are enrolled in a PhD program, you will likely have expectations for research beginning your first semester, even if that is just digging into the literature related to your interests. It is good for you to understand what the research and dissertation expectations are at your program. For example, do students complete a traditional dissertation? Is the dissertation in an "article format?" At our institution, we expect students to write two separate articles, one of which is the formal "dissertation" for the purposes of our graduate college requirements. When you first start as a student, you may be assigned to a faculty member's lab, or you may be in an environment where you direct and guide your own research agenda. In this situation, it can be easy to get overwhelmed by all the options. We encourage you to ask to sit in on a research team meeting, observe, or learn more about any given team and expectations before committing to something that you aren't familiar with. We also encourage you to speak to students in the program to learn what their experiences are with research. If your career plans involve future academic teaching, you may want to emphasize research more than if your career plans largely focus on practice. Prior to applying for internship, you may be expected to submit a manuscript for publication or to have presented at professional conferences.

Comprehensive Exams

Most programs have some kind of comprehensive exam that allows you to "advance to doctoral candidacy." This basically just signals that you are mostly (or fully) done with coursework and are ready to completely focus on practice and research as you complete the degree. In our experience, comprehensive exams vary so much by program that we cannot offer a good summary here. Some programs have students take a practice EPPP (Examination for the Professional Practice of Psychology, an exam required for licensure); some give students a take-home written essay question or two; some have students respond to questions on-site in a computer lab; and so on.

Work with Advisors

There is a lot that has been written about work with advisors. As we mentioned earlier, it is a good idea to look for a research mentor with similar interests to yours, keeping in mind that things change, programs change, people move, and students and advisors have human qualities and personalities that sometimes are not a great fit. As you apply to, and enter a program, there is much that is unknown, but you can get a feel for someone's advising style by talking to their current advisees. Most programs also have a TD, also sometimes referred to as Director of Clinical Training, someone who is responsible for the oversight of the overall program. Other programs have a shared responsibility model, where different faculty take on different roles (such as one person responsible for admissions, another for practicum oversight, another for prepping students for internship).

Professional Engagement in Advocacy or Service

As we discussed in Chapter 13, leadership, service, and advocacy are important components of the work of counseling psychologists. As part of your program, you may be expected to participate in professional service or advocacy. This can also help prepare you for internship and job applications. For example, you may be interested in serving in a leadership role in your state's psychological association, or you might apply to be on a special interest group or section of Division 17 (Society for Counseling Psychology) or another APA-affiliated group. Or perhaps you are interested in local work such as volunteering to tutor English Language Learners at a local house of worship. Whatever your interests, we do encourage you to participate in some activities outside of your program, as they enrich your professional experience and perspective. Some doctoral training programs have a specific focus on social justice advocacy where this work is built into the structure of the training.

Predoctoral Internship

No matter your program, you will have to complete a predoctoral internship experience to graduate. Most of the time, this is a one-year (12 calendar months), full-time experience, and interns are generally paid a stipend. If you attend an APA-accredited doctoral program, it is likely that they will require or encourage you to secure an APA-accredited internship experience. Accreditation is important because this means your internship experience will meet certain standards that will help with attaining skills and experience you need to become an independent licensed psychologist. There are also some internship programs that are members of the Association of Professional Psychology Internship Centers (APPIC) but perhaps are not yet accredited – or may not ever be able to achieve full accreditation because of funding or other reasons. This membership also indicates that internship sites are taking training responsibilities seriously and that they work to offer high-quality training for interns. Internship sites are typically at university/college counseling centers, Veterans Affairs Medical Centers, Bureau of Prisons, US military branches, hospitals, or community mental health agencies. Another interesting option is a consortium, in which several agencies join together to offer internship experiences (perhaps because individually they might not have the required resources to provide the training requirements outlined by APA Commission on Accreditation). Each internship site has its own "personality" or culture, with unique aspects that define the experience for interns. There are a number of resources for students applying to internship and often doctoral programs offer support to students in their application process, so it is just important to know that this is a required piece before you graduate. One last thing to note is that the internship application process is quite competitive, and often it is not possible for students to stay in the same geographical location – in other words, you may attend a doctoral program in one city/state but there may not be any internship sites in that location, or nearby, so you should anticipate that you will likely relocate for one year of internship.

Post-Graduation

Upon earning your doctorate in counseling psychology, there is still more work to be done before you can practice independently in most states. As with most things in the United States, these requirements vary by state. Every state has its own post-graduate requirements for licensure as a psychologist. These requirements might include passing the EPPP (we refer to this as "E-Triple P"), a jurisprudence exam (an exam about ethics and laws), an oral practice exam (where a panel of psychologists might ask you to work through a case in front of them), and additional practice hours. The practice hours really vary – At the time that we are writing this textbook, in Oklahoma, for example, if your main role is a professor, you have to be employed for two years before you can become licensed as a psychologist. In the State of Washington, there are no extra hour requirements beyond graduation. In Texas, you can be employed full time as an instructor, researcher, or practitioner but have to do that for one full year before you can become licensed.

Resources

We have done our best to help prepare you to apply to graduate programs and plan for the path ahead if you are interested in pursuing a career in counseling. We hope this chapter answered many of the questions you wrote down as you started reading this chapter, but now that you have an overview of the process, you may be curious about even more things that we did not cover. The good news is that there are a number of excellent books and resources that can give you an idea of what it might be like to actually be a counseling psychologist. Some examples are The Gift of Therapy (Yalom, 2017), Letters to a Young Therapist (Pipher, 2016), and Voices from the Field (Trotter-Mathison et al., 2010). There are also video resources showing therapists utilizing different theories and approaches in action; your public library or college/university library likely is a good place to find these.

Summary

We hope that you found this chapter helpful and relevant for you – whether you plan to pursue a career in the helping professions or something totally different. We tried to help you think through what kind of potential future career you are looking for, and what kind of programs might be a good fit for you. We reviewed the important role of accreditation in selecting a program. We described the different kinds of materials you might expect to submit as part of a graduate program application. We also specifically tried to address some questions people might have about applying to doctoral programs, as well as what students in doctoral programs can expect as they progress toward psychologist licensure. Thank you for hanging in with us to the end of this book – we wish you all the best in your future endeavors!

What Would You Do?

You are applying for a doctoral program in counseling psychology and so is your friend, Daniel. Daniel asks you to read a draft of his personal statement and you notice that it contains a lot of personal details about Daniel's history, including a lot of stuff you didn't know and didn't want to know about. In the essay, Daniel shares information about people who mistreated him, the intense emotions he felt throughout his childhood, and even some desperate thoughts that crossed his mind before he started going to counseling. The statement also mentions his college experiences and what he is hoping to focus on in a doctoral program, but the main focus of Daniel's letter seems to revolve around his experience of trauma.

- What advice might you give Daniel about edits he could make to his letter?
- How would you explain the reactions that the admissions committee might have or concerns they might express about admitting Daniel?
- How could you help Daniel reframe his experiences in a way that would strengthen his application?

Counseling Psychologist Spotlight: LGBTQIA+ Individuals

Dr. Chloë Goldbach

Dr. Chloë Goldbach is a psychologist with the LGBT+ Counseling Collaborative, a group practice in Arlington, Virginia. She said that most of her work involves individual therapy. She specializes in work with transgender and asexual individuals and sees 20–25 clients per week. She also leads or co-leads therapy and support groups, one for transgender women and one for asexual and aromantic individuals. She provides autism and attention-deficit/hyperactivity disorder (ADHD) evaluations regularly. Chloë is passionate about working with queer and trans people and communities. She said she "loves and has a deep gratitude for the opportunity to support and help trans and asexual people on their journeys of self-acceptance, identity exploration, and moving toward living lives that feel more fulfilling and truer to their authentic selves." Chloë really enjoys working in her group practice among a community of LGBTQIA+ therapists. She said it is really fulfilling to be in a space with other queer people who are also passionate about the work they do and supporting queer and trans communities. As many other counseling psychologists who we have spotlighted have mentioned, doing therapy is not an easy job. Chloë said that it is fulfilling and rewarding but also sometimes emotionally draining due to the nature of the work. She said that she finds it important and helpful to be intentional about creating time and space for relaxing and fulfilling activities outside of work. She takes time to decompress and take care of herself so she can recharge and continue to do work that brings her joy. She noted that she has her own therapist who she sees and thinks it is important to find her own support and not just provide support to others.

Chloë is engaged in outreach to the community – she said that is a big part of the work she does. She is involved in various local support and social spaces for trans people, largely for trans women. She collaborates with other providers in the community to provide holistic care to her clients and communities. She has created a lot of online content and presentations that are focused on providing information, resources, and other forms of support for trans people. She engages in research and activism to contribute to advocacy for trans and gender expansive people. For example, she is involved in several writing and research projects specifically targeted to provide awareness on issues important to transgender individuals and gender-affirming care. Her work results in recommendations and tools aimed toward continuing to improve trans-inclusive research, therapy, and other environments such as education and healthcare.

Outside of work, Chloë loves video games! She collects retro video games and likes to play horror and puzzle games. She also loves spending time with her cat, Tipsy. She also enjoys horror movies, building Legos, and hiking, as well as "going on adventures" with her partner. Chloë graduated with her PhD from the counseling psychology program at Southern Illinois University Carbondale and is a licensed psychologist. She holds an MA in counseling psychology, a MS in biomedical engineering, and a BS in mechanical engineering.

Dr. Chloë Goldbach. Photograph by author.

References

American Psychological Association. (2025). *Divisions of APA*. https://www.apa.org/about/division

Hammer, J. H. (n.d.). *Applying to clinical psychology doctoral programs: Advice for undergraduates and post-baccalaureates*. Dr. Joseph Hammer. Retrieved June 24, 2025, from https://drjosephhammer.com/psych-grad-school/

Pipher, M. (2016). *Letters to a young therapist: Stories of hope and healing*. Basic Books.

Trotter-Mathison, M., Koch, J. M., Sanger, S., & Skovholt, T. M. (2010). *Voices from the field: Defining moments in counselor and therapist development*. Routledge.

Yalom, I. D. (2017). *The gift of therapy: An open letter to a new generation of therapists and their patients*. HarperCollins.

Acknowledgments

Julie and Douglas would like to acknowledge some of the wonderful people without whose support and assistance this book would not have been possible!

First, we want to thank Martin Kivlighan, for his support and encouragement of Julie in her teaching at Iowa, for his initial help with developing this book (especially the section on mental health access), for his endorsement of this book, and for always being ready with a laugh.

Thank you to John Westefeld, for taking the initiative to introduce undergraduate students to counseling psychology so many years ago – how this class has grown and blossomed! We are grateful that you captured this history in the foreword of this book.

We want to recognize Ais Jahnke and Gihun Im, for their help with literature, citations, and other research assistance.

Thank you so much to Barry Chung and Lisa Flores for your endorsements of this book – your support means a lot to us.

We are so appreciative of all the counseling psychologists who were willing to share a little about themselves with us in the Counseling Psychology Spotlights! You really helped make this book come "alive" as students can see real people in the real world doing real counseling psychology work. Amazing!

A huge thank you to Margaret McDonald, who provided invaluable editing assistance and feedback. Your suggestions made this book so much easier to read and relate to. Thank you also to Mr. Pimento Cheese Biscuit who supervised your work attentively.

Julie wants to send a special shout-out to the University of Iowa, Obermann Center for Advanced Studies, and her Wednesday Writing Group friends. The Obermann Center writing retreat gave her amazing space and co-writing colleagues that helped get this book toward the finish line.

Julie also thanks the University of Iowa, College of Education, Department of Psychological and Quantitative Foundations for supporting her work on this book. She is especially grateful to amazing counseling psychology faculty colleagues who make meetings something to look forward to!

Douglas wants to recognize Oklahoma State University (OSU), College of Education and Human Sciences, School of Community Health Sciences, Counseling and Counseling Psychology, and the Myron Ledbetter/Bob Lemon Counseling Psychology Diversity Endowed Professorship for supporting his work on this book. He is also grateful to work with such brilliant, wise, and dedicated students in his lab and across the counseling psychology program at OSU.

And finally, a note for our families and loved ones.

From a young age, Julie felt supported by her family in her creative pursuits. She knows her dear Uncle Clay would have loved to read this book with his dog Vince on his lap. He would have asked a lot of questions and had Opinions. Julie thanks her parents, family, and extended family. She sends special love to her children, Katherine, Pecos, and Margaret for their patience and encouragement. Thanks also to Max, Hippo, Billie, Minnow, Bubbles, and Ollie. And finally, a big thank you to my academic brother, Uncle Doug, who makes writing, working, and laughing so much fun! Thank you for dragging the washing machine over the scary cellar door – truly an act from the heart that I will always cherish.

As a gay man, it was hard for Douglas to find his place in the academy until he stumbled across counseling psychology. In that moment, he felt like he had finally found his academic home. He hopes this book helps others find a place in the academy as well. Douglas is grateful to Julie for including him in this project and for the unwavering support of his partner, and Gemma, their fur baby.

And for our amazing students – thank you for being fantastic. We adore you!

Index

Note: **Bold** page numbers refer to tables.

For Product Safety Concerns and Information please contact our EU representative GPSR@taylorandfrancis.com Taylor & Francis Verlag GmbH, Kaufingerstraße 24, 80331 München, Germany